Mikhail Suslov (ed.)

DIGITAL ORTHODOXY IN THE POST-SOVIET WORLD

The Russian Orthodox Church and Web 2.0

With a foreword by Father Cyril Hovorun

ibidem-Verlag
Stuttgart

Bibliografische Information der Deutschen Nationalbibliothek
Die Deutsche Nationalbibliothek verzeichnet diese Publikation in der Deutschen Nationalbibliografie; detaillierte bibliografische Daten sind im Internet über http://dnb.d-nb.de abrufbar.

Bibliographic information published by the Deutsche Nationalbibliothek
Die Deutsche Nationalbibliothek lists this publication in the Deutsche Nationalbibliografie; detailed bibliographic data are available in the Internet at http://dnb.d-nb.de.

Cover picture: "Digital Orthodoxy". © copyright 2015 by Anton Semakin

Parts of the Introduction and Chapters 1, 3-6, 10-11, and chapter 7 (in Russian) of this book were first published in the special issue of the journal *Digital Icons* (DI), no. 14 (2015), available at http://www.digitalicons.org/issue14/.
The special issue is available for free download; DI receives no financial gain from the publication of the aforementioned parts of this issue in their current form.

∞

Gedruckt auf alterungsbeständigem, säurefreien Papier
Printed on acid-free paper

ISSN: 1614-3515

ISBN-13: 978-3-8382-0871-8

© *ibidem*-Verlag
Stuttgart 2016

Alle Rechte vorbehalten

Das Werk einschließlich aller seiner Teile ist urheberrechtlich geschützt. Jede Verwertung außerhalb der engen Grenzen des Urheberrechtsgesetzes ist ohne Zustimmung des Verlages unzulässig und strafbar. Dies gilt insbesondere für Vervielfältigungen, Übersetzungen, Mikroverfilmungen und elektronische Speicherformen sowie die Einspeicherung und Verarbeitung in elektronischen Systemen.

All rights part of this publication may be reproduced, stored in or introduced into a retrieval system, or transmitted, in any form, or by any means (electronical, mechanical, photocopying, recording or otherwise) without the prior written permission of the publisher. Any person who does any unauthorized act in relation to this publication may be liable to criminal prosecution and civil claims for damages.

Printed in the EU

Soviet and Post-Soviet Politics and Society (SPPS)   Vol. 155
ISSN 1614-3515

General Editor: Andreas Umland,
Institute for Euro-Atlantic Cooperation, Kyiv, umland@stanfordalumni.org

Commissioning Editor: Max Jakob Horstmann,
London, mjh@ibidem.eu

EDITORIAL COMMITTEE*

DOMESTIC & COMPARATIVE POLITICS
Prof. **Ellen Bos**, *Andrássy University of Budapest*
Dr. **Ingmar Bredies**, *FH Bund, Brühl*
Dr. **Andrey Kazantsev**, *MGIMO (U) MID RF, Moscow*
Prof. **Heiko Pleines**, *University of Bremen*
Prof. **Richard Sakwa**, *University of Kent at Canterbury*
Dr. **Sarah Whitmore**, *Oxford Brookes University*
Dr. **Harald Wydra**, *University of Cambridge*

SOCIETY, CLASS & ETHNICITY
Col. **David Glantz**, *"Journal of Slavic Military Studies"*
Dr. **Marlène Laruelle**, *George Washington University*
Dr. **Stephen Shulman**, *Southern Illinois University*
Prof. **Stefan Troebst**, *University of Leipzig*

POLITICAL ECONOMY & PUBLIC POLICY
Prof. em. **Marshall Goldman**, *Wellesley College, Mass.*
Dr. **Andreas Goldthau**, *Central European University*
Dr. **Robert Kravchuk**, *University of North Carolina*
Dr. **David Lane**, *University of Cambridge*
Dr. **Carol Leonard**, *Higher School of Economics, Moscow*
Dr. **Maria Popova**, *McGill University, Montreal*

FOREIGN POLICY & INTERNATIONAL AFFAIRS
Dr. **Peter Duncan**, *University College London*
Prof. **Andreas Heinemann-Grüder**, *University of Bonn*
Dr. **Taras Kuzio**, *Johns Hopkins University*
Prof. **Gerhard Mangott**, *University of Innsbruck*
Dr. **Diana Schmidt-Pfister**, *University of Konstanz*
Dr. **Lisbeth Tarlow**, *Harvard University, Cambridge*
Dr. **Christian Wipperfürth**, *N-Ost Network, Berlin*
Dr. **William Zimmerman**, *University of Michigan*

HISTORY, CULTURE & THOUGHT
Dr. **Catherine Andreyev**, *University of Oxford*
Prof. **Mark Bassin**, *Södertörn University*
Prof. **Karsten Brüggemann**, *Tallinn University*
Dr. **Alexander Etkind**, *University of Cambridge*
Dr. **Gasan Gusejnov**, *Moscow State University*
Prof. em. **Walter Laqueur**, *Georgetown University*
Prof. **Leonid Luks**, *Catholic University of Eichstaett*
Dr. **Olga Malinova**, *Russian Academy of Sciences*
Prof. **Andrei Rogatchevski**, *University of Tromsø*
Dr. **Mark Tauger**, *West Virginia University*

ADVISORY BOARD*

Prof. **Dominique Arel**, *University of Ottawa*
Prof. **Jörg Baberowski**, *Humboldt University of Berlin*
Prof. **Margarita Balmaceda**, *Seton Hall University*
Dr. **John Barber**, *University of Cambridge*
Prof. **Timm Beichelt**, *European University Viadrina*
Dr. **Katrin Boeckh**, *University of Munich*
Prof. em. **Archie Brown**, *University of Oxford*
Dr. **Vyacheslav Bryukhovetsky**, *Kyiv-Mohyla Academy*
Prof. **Timothy Colton**, *Harvard University, Cambridge*
Prof. **Paul D'Anieri**, *University of Florida*
Dr. **Heike Dörrenbächer**, *Friedrich Naumann Foundation*
Dr. **John Dunlop**, *Hoover Institution, Stanford, California*
Dr. **Sabine Fischer**, *SWP, Berlin*
Dr. **Geir Flikke**, *NUPI, Oslo*
Prof. **David Galbreath**, *University of Aberdeen*
Prof. **Alexander Galkin**, *Russian Academy of Sciences*
Prof. **Frank Golczewski**, *University of Hamburg*
Dr. **Nikolas Gvosdev**, *Naval War College, Newport, RI*
Prof. **Mark von Hagen**, *Arizona State University*
Dr. **Guido Hausmann**, *University of Munich*
Prof. **Dale Herspring**, *Kansas State University*
Dr. **Stefani Hoffman**, *Hebrew University of Jerusalem*
Prof. **Mikhail Ilyin**, *MGIMO (U) MID RF, Moscow*
Prof. **Vladimir Kantor**, *Higher School of Economics*
Dr. **Ivan Katchanovski**, *University of Ottawa*
Prof. em. **Andrzej Korbonski**, *University of California*
Dr. **Iris Kempe**, *"Caucasus Analytical Digest"*
Prof. **Herbert Küpper**, *Institut für Ostrecht Regensburg*
Dr. **Rainer Lindner**, *CEEER, Berlin*
Dr. **Vladimir Malakhov**, *Russian Academy of Sciences*

Dr. **Luke March**, *University of Edinburgh*
Prof. **Michael McFaul**, *Stanford University, Palo Alto*
Prof. **Birgit Menzel**, *University of Mainz-Germersheim*
Prof. **Valery Mikhailenko**, *The Urals State University*
Prof. **Emil Pain**, *Higher School of Economics, Moscow*
Dr. **Oleg Podvintsev**, *Russian Academy of Sciences*
Prof. **Olga Popova**, *St. Petersburg State University*
Dr. **Alex Pravda**, *University of Oxford*
Dr. **Erik van Ree**, *University of Amsterdam*
Dr. **Joachim Rogall**, *Robert Bosch Foundation Stuttgart*
Prof. **Peter Rutland**, *Wesleyan University, Middletown*
Prof. **Marat Salikov**, *The Urals State Law Academy*
Dr. **Gwendolyn Sasse**, *University of Oxford*
Prof. **Jutta Scherrer**, *EHESS, Paris*
Prof. **Robert Service**, *University of Oxford*
Mr. **James Sherr**, *RIIA Chatham House London*
Dr. **Oxana Shevel**, *Tufts University, Medford*
Prof. **Eberhard Schneider**, *University of Siegen*
Prof. **Olexander Shnyrkov**, *Shevchenko University, Kyiv*
Prof. **Hans-Henning Schröder**, *SWP, Berlin*
Prof. **Yuri Shapoval**, *Ukrainian Academy of Sciences*
Prof. **Viktor Shnirelman**, *Russian Academy of Sciences*
Dr. **Lisa Sundstrom**, *University of British Columbia*
Dr. **Philip Walters**, *"Religion, State and Society"*, Oxford
Prof. **Zenon Wasyliw**, *Ithaca College, New York State*
Dr. **Lucan Way**, *University of Toronto*
Dr. **Markus Wehner**, *"Frankfurter Allgemeine Zeitung"*
Dr. **Andrew Wilson**, *University College London*
Prof. **Jan Zielonka**, *University of Oxford*
Prof. **Andrei Zorin**, *University of Oxford*

* While the Editorial Committee and Advisory Board support the General Editor in the choice and improvement of manuscripts for publication, responsibility for remaining errors and misinterpretations in the series' volumes lies with the books' authors.

Soviet and Post-Soviet Politics and Society (SPPS)
ISSN 1614-3515

Founded in 2004 and refereed since 2007, SPPS makes available affordable English-, German-, and Russian-language studies on the history of the countries of the former Soviet bloc from the late Tsarist period to today. It publishes between 5 and 20 volumes per year and focuses on issues in transitions to and from democracy such as economic crisis, identity formation, civil society development, and constitutional reform in CEE and the NIS. SPPS also aims to highlight so far understudied themes in East European studies such as right-wing radicalism, religious life, higher education, or human rights protection. The authors and titles of all previously published volumes are listed at the end of this book. For a full description of the series and reviews of its books, see
www.ibidem-verlag.de/red/spps.

Editorial correspondence & manuscripts should be sent to: Dr. Andreas Umland, c/o DAAD, German Embassy, vul. Bohdana Khmelnitskoho 25, UA-01901 Kyiv, Ukraine. e-mail: umland@stanfordalumni.org

Business correspondence & review copy requests should be sent to: *ibidem* Press, Leuschnerstr. 40, 30457 Hannover, Germany; tel.: +49 511 2622200; fax: +49 511 2622201; spps@ibidem.eu.

Authors, reviewers, referees, and editors for (as well as all other persons sympathetic to) SPPS are invited to join its networks at
www.facebook.com/group.php?gid=52638198614
www.linkedin.com/groups?about=&gid=103012
www.xing.com/net/spps-ibidem-verlag/

Recent Volumes

147 Alexander Sergunin
Explaining Russian Foreign Policy Behavior
Theory and Practice
ISBN 978-3-8382-0752-0

148 Darya Malyutina
Migrant Friendships in
a Super-Diverse City
Russian-Speakers and their Social Relationships in London in the 21st Century
With a foreword by Claire Dwyer
ISBN 978-3-8382-0652-3

149 Alexander Sergunin, Valery Konyshev
Russia in the Arctic
Hard or Soft Power?
ISBN 978-3-8382-0753-7

150 John J. Maresca
Helsinki Revisited
A Key U.S. Negotiator's Memoirs
on the Development of the CSCE into the OSCE
With a foreword by Hafiz Pashayev
ISBN 978-3-8382-0852-7

151 Jardar Østbø
The New Third Rome
Readings of a Russian Nationalist Myth
With a foreword by Pål Kolstø
ISBN 978-3-8382-0870-1

152 Simon Kordonsky
Socio-Economic Foundations of the Russian Post-Soviet Regime
The Resource-Based Economy and Estate-Based Social Structure of Contemporary Russia
With a foreword by Svetlana Barsukova
ISBN 978-3-8382-0775-9

153 Duncan Leitch
Assisting Reform in Post-Communist Ukraine 2000–2012
The Illusions of Donors and the Disillusion of Beneficiaries
With a foreword by Kataryna Wolczuk
ISBN 978-3-8382-0844-2154

154 Abel Polese
Limits of a Post-Soviet State
How Informality Replaces, Renegotiates, and Reshapes Governance in Contemporary Ukraine
With a foreword by Colin Williams
ISBN 978-3-8382-0845-9

Acknowledgement

Parts of the Introduction and Chapters 1, 3-6, 10-11, and chapter 7 (in Russian) were first published in the special issue of the journal *Digital Icons,* no. 14 (2015), available at http://www.digitalicons.org/issue14/. I thank the journal editors Andrew Chapman (lead editor), Pedro Hernandez, Gernot Howanitz, Natalia Konradova, Maria Sidorkina, Henrike Schmidt, and Vlad Strukov for their work on these papers and their many valuable suggestions. I also acknowledge the enormous efforts of the guest sub-editors of the aforementioned issue, Maria Engström and Greg Simons. Our continuous and almost daily collaboration has turned the idea into a concrete publication, and a call for papers into a network of scholars. I am sincerely thankful to my current employer, the Uppsala Center for Russian and Eurasian Studies, for the generous financial support of this venture.

Mikhail Suslov, 30 May 2016

Table of Content

Foreword by father Cyril Hovorun IX

Introduction by Mikhail Suslov 1

Part 1. Discourses

Chapter 1.
The Medium for Demonic Energies: 'Digital Anxiety' in the
Russian Orthodox Church by Mikhail Suslov 19

Chapter 2.
Russia's Immoral Other: Moral Panics and the Antichrist on
Russian Orthodox Websites by Magda Dolińska-Rydzek 53

Chapter 3.
Wi-Fi in Plato's Cave: The Digital Icon and the Phenomenology
of Surveillance by Fabian Heffermehl 83

Chapter 4.
The Body of Christ Online: The Russian Orthodox Church and
(Non-) Liturgical Interactivity on the Internet by Alexander Ponomariov ... 111

Part 2. Divergences

Chapter 5.
Heretical Virtual Movement in Russian *LiveJournal* Blogs:
Between Religion and Politics by Ekaterina Grishaeva 141

Chapter 6.
Between Homophobia and Gay Lobby: the Russian Orthodox
Church and its Relationship to Homosexuality in
Online Discussions by Hanna Stähle 161

Chapter 7.
Post-Secularity and Digital Anticlericalism on Runet
by Maria Engström 195

Part 3. Practices

Chapter 8.
Ortho-Media for Ortho-Women: In Search of Patterns of Piety
by Anastasia Mitrofanova 239

Chapter 9.
Holy Pixels: The Transformation of Eastern Orthodox Icons
Through Digital Technology by Sarah A. Riccardi-Swartz 261

Chapter 10.
"Ortho-Blogging" from Inside: A Virtual Roundtable
by Irina Kotkina and Mikhail Suslov 285

Chapter 11.
The Religious Identity of Russian Internet Users: Attitudes
Towards God and Russian Orthodox Church by Viktor Khroul 299

List of contributors 315

Index 321

Foreword

Cyril Hovorun
Stockholm School of Theology/Sankt Ignatios Academy

This edited collection deals mostly with the Russian localization of the eastern Christianity. Most of the papers first appeared in the journal *Digital Icons* and focus on the attitude of the Russian Orthodox sub-culture to the global web-culture. The conflation of two topics: icons and the internet, has produced an intriguing story about encounter of tradition with modernity. There are many such stories. This one, however, has become particularly topical in the light of the recent developments around Ukraine and of the relations of Russia with the rest of the western world. These developments can be interpreted as a conflict between progress and inertia, or between looking forward and looking backward. It does not necessarily mean that looking backward is bad. In the case of modern Russia, however, it is myopic. This means that when Russia and its church look deep into the centuries of the history, they do not see much further than the Soviet past. The Soviet past alienates the deeper past from the present of the church. Or, better to say, it alienates the present of the church from its pre-Soviet past. It makes the very concept of tradition abusive. Although the past was not digital, it conditions the digital present. This present would have been different if the non-digital past, on which it relies most, were not so much Soviet, but pre-Soviet.

The iconic part of the story in this volume is easy. This is because eastern Christianity is iconic. Particularly its Russian edition always preferred to express itself in icons—more than in concepts. In this sense, the today's digital culture is more resonant with the iconic Russian psyché. At the same time, to identify yourself with icons is not as easy in our times as it seems to be, because the modern idea of icon/image has dramatically changed since the Middle Ages, when image was equal to icon. Modern culture rides on the antagonism between image and text, something that the iconodulic era did not know. Of course, there were iconoclasms in the past, when those who were for the text fought against those who were also for the images. Nowadays, the texts and images cannot annihilate each other—they have to compete. In this competition, the text and the image imitate one another. The texts tend to be narratives, which is an iconic genre, and the images try to animate all kinds of text: novels, poems, manifestos, chronicles, and news. One can read the images, argue with them, or accept some of their standpoints. In the past, the images edified. In our time, they mainly entertain, deceive, or tell nothing. Some varieties of the modern icons of this sort have been presented in the current volume.

The volume speaks not only of icons per se, but also of their environment. The place of a traditional icon is the inside of the church. The milieu of the icons described in this volume is digital. This is the difficult part of the story. In the church, people come to talk to God. Icons there visualize the divine reality. To use the famous phrase of Fr Pavel Florensky, 'Icon is a window to *that* world.' In the digital world, however, there is no *that*: people are not supposed to connect with the transcendental—they login to meet each other, or to meet what the other choose to be. The innate immanence of the digital world obliterates the attempts of the transcendental exodus through the icon. Apart of being iconic, the Orthodox tradition is also liturgical. It means it needs matter to purify, bless, and consecrate. This constitutes another difficulty for the Orthodox to rush to the matter-less domains of the internet. How the church can deliver its message and function in the unblessable universe of the intangible? Does it make any sense to attend virtual chapels and deliver online confessions? Is there digital evil, in the Manichaean sense of the word? If so, what the church should do about it? If not, is the internet morally neutral? The book tries to answer not these questions, but the question how the Russian church answers them.

The church has made a long journey in understanding and appreciating the digital. I remember the discussions in the church in the 1990s about whether to go or not to go to the internet. Attitude to this leap to the unknown was measured by openness of those who made their choice. I remember how proud were the progressives to launch the first website of a parish or of a whole church. And how they were criticized by the conservatives for compromising their faith. They continue their quarrels, now online. All sorts of 'culture wars' among the Orthodox Christians are waged now in the blogs and forums. These battles are thoroughly and comprehensively analyzed in the present volume as well.

The book presents in an iconic way the actual developments in the Russian church and society. It has succeeded to stretch over the gap between deontology and actuality of the church. That is why its arguments are critical and sometimes even provocative, but never boring.

Introduction[1]

Mikhail Suslov
Uppsala Center for Russian and Eurasian Studies, Uppsala University

The church, the state, and Russian society

In October 2015 Runet heatedly discussed the leak of information about the (failed) attempt of the Russian Ministry of Communications to cut the country off the internet.[2] The crackdown on the freedom of the internet is the marked tendency of President Putin's third term in power, which resulted in closing down thousands of webpages,[3] including oppositional news agencies. One of the most important sources of motivation for this prohibitive activity is religious ethics. For example, the League for Safe Internet, blessed by Patriarch Kirill, has been hunting for pedophiles in the social networks since 2011, as well as reporting online pornography, propaganda of extremism, LGBT, methods of committing suicide, and similar information, sinful from the Orthodox viewpoint. In spite of the very high level of the internet penetration in the Russian society (70.5% in 2015)[4], the idea of the state control over the digital environment has found a receptive soil among the broader public[5] and its ardent advocates in the political elite (e.g. Potupchik and Fedorova 2014).

This posits the question, how the Russian Orthodox Church (ROC) is impacting society and the state in their framing and making sense of the new media? Statistics says that only 2 to 4% of Russians keep the fast during the Lent, or take communion ('Rossiiane o

---

[1] I would like to acknowledge important intellectual contributions of Maria Engström and Greg Simons to the earlier versions of this text.
[2] E.g. here: http://www.dailymail.co.uk/news/article-3276333/Russia-tries-cut-World-Wide-Web-Kremlin-attempts-clamp-internet-freedoms.html. Accessed 1 November 2015.
[3] Today, the informal list of banned websites includes 48045 items ('Reestr' 2015).
[4] http://www.internetworldstats.com/stats7.htm. Accessed 1 November 2015.
[5] In October 2014 54% of respondents supported the idea of state censorship in the internet ('Internet-tsenzura' 2014).

religii' 2013); the Ministry of the Interior (which since the Soviet times traditionally monitors churches' attendance on the most important dates) reported 2,3 million participants of the Christmas service in 2008 (i.e. 3,3% of the population, 'Dannye' 2008). So the number of regular church-goers is not very significant, and the ROC does not play an important role in the lives of the majority of Russians. At the same time, circa 70% ('Rossiiane o religii' 2013) name themselves 'Orthodox believers'. The phenomenon of 'vicarious' religion[6] is common in all Western societies, and it is present on a remarkably great scale in Russia due to the fact that Orthodox religion serves as a synonym for the Russian national self-identification. There are signs of weariness of the ROC's assertiveness among the Russian population; WTsIOM's press release displays that in 1990 61% of people approved of spreading of religion, whereas in 2015 it is only 36% ('Religiia: Za i protiv' 2015). Still, the ROC remains one of the most highly trusted social institutions on a par with the army and slightly behind the President. Moreover, during the period 2013–2015 the ROC has slightly gained in trust (48 and 54% respectively, 'Rossiiane' 2015), so the anti-ROC's campaign and a number of scandals, connected with the 'Pussy Riot' affair and the lifestyle of Patriarch Kirill, have not significantly decreased the popularity of the ROC and its leader. This could be explained in the context of the recent turn towards conservatism in the Russian society, which entertains age-old images of Russia as a besieged fortress, morally superior to its geopolitical adversaries.

Speaking about 'vicarious Orthodoxy' it is important to keep in mind that the ROC was historically a national church of Russia, and as any national church it has tight connections with the political and historical self-description of this community. A common trope for self-positioning of the Church is that the ROC is a 'state-shaping' religion (*gosudarstvoobrazuiushchaia tserkov'*), and as such it weaves its own historical narrative with the narrative of the Russian state. Thus,

---

6   The concept of 'vicarious religion' implies that the majority, although not actively participating in religious life, approves of the small group of regular church-goers, who perform religion 'on behalf' of the rest (Davie 2006).

the Orthodox religion in Russia has an ineliminable political and geopolitical component (Engström 2014; Kostjuk 2005; Mitrofanova 2005; Papkova 2011; Simons & Westerlund 2015; Suslov 2014), although, to be sure, it cannot be reduced to it. In the ROC's intellectual history, the concept of 'symphony' is a very important one; it says that the church and the state should maintain harmonious relations of mutual support and mutual non-interference. As Patriarch Kirill argued once, it is not in the history, but here and now, in Putin's Russia, the principle of 'symphony' has being implemented in its most complete form (Kirill 2010: 251). Indeed, the state's support of the ROC's initiatives has recently been very substantial, ranging from adopting the legislation according to which all ROC's property nationalized after the revolution of 1917 should be given back to the Church, to the incorporation of the course 'Bases of the Orthodox Culture' in secondary school, to the introduction of the state-paid chaplains to the Russian army,—all these novelties would have been unthinkable without the state's benevolent backing. In return, the ROC supplies the Kremlin with a number of rhetorical devices and ideological frames, which help the political elite to consolidate Putin's predominantly conservative constituency. However, the coalescence of the Church and the state should not be exaggerated; the ROC has its own sense of mission, ideological agenda and doctrinal grounds (especially *Bases of the Social Concept,* adopted in 2000), which provide for a possibility (mostly dormant up to day) to raise an independent and oppositional voice.

Digital religions worldwide

The study of religion and digital technologies has recently become a point of growth in social sciences and humanities, reflecting on the dynamic 'colonization' of the digital terrains by different religions. Theological traditions and cultural backgrounds have variegated impact on the religion's ability to 'domesticate' digital technologies. The worldwide turn from 'religion towards spirituality' (Heelas & Woodhead 2005) rendered the actual religious experience less bounded by the tradition and ritual, and pushed it in the direction of religious syncretism and individualism. This 'spiritual turn' provides more opportunities for accommodation of the new media. Especially the representatives of the New Age religions met the early advances of the digital technologies into our everyday life with enthusiasm. Some traditional religious denominations managed to grasp and make sense of the computer-mediated technologies remarkably easy as well. For example, Hinduism relatively successfully embraced the digital technologies (Helland 2010), among other reasons, because of the idea of purity of the environment in which ritual takes place. According to this tradition, if the image of a god or a goddess is located in cyberspace, not in the physical space, this could be regarded positively by the believers who perform the ritual of *purja* (Scheifinger 2013: 125). Similarly, meditating rituals of Zen Buddhism, or their parts could be easily transferred online.

By contrast, those religions which emphasis the mystical, and corporeal, sensorial experience, rather than symbolic aspects of rituals (e.g. Eucharist) resist to transferring services into the virtual world. Another 'trench' in a position war with modern technology could be the traditionally patriarchal and hierarchical structure of the church. The Roman Catholic Church, for instance, is way more comfortable with the internet than the ROC, finding it a useful tool for the dialogue with religious and secular 'others', but at the same time, the Vatican disabled the possibility to comment on its *YouTube* channel, fearing to lose the control over the discussion (Campbell 2012). Likewise, in ultra-Orthodox Judaism the resistance of the religious authorities to destabilizing their cultural and political hegemony in the digital environment could be fierce (Rashi 2013).

The relation of fundamentalist religions to computer-mediated communication (CMC) is, however, never reduced to a straightforward rejection. Whereas Messianic religions concentrated on the idea of a covenant with a deity would tend towards isolationism and unacceptance of the new media, religions striving to expand their Messianic message would find digital technologies to be a useful tool for church mission. But even religions trying to reconstruct the basis of their faith and to return to their roots in the distant past, which usually find it difficult to accommodate any modern technology, eagerly adopt methods of 'religion online' for the purposes of propaganda, self-presentation, or search for information (Howard 2011). Likewise, CMC does not unequivocally undermine the 'epistemic power' and the authority of the religious hierarchy (Barzilai-Nahon & Barzilai 2005; Campbell 2010a; Livio & Tenenboim Weinblatt 2007). For example, in spite of the prohibition to use the internet by rank-and-file believers, leaders of Taliban could be quite active online in both recruiting new members and fighting with ideological adversaries (Bunt 2009). Modern paganism can also be seen as a 'back-to-the-roots' religious movement, and yet it is developing quite dynamically in the internet, seen as a platform to spread information, connect with fellow believers and perform some, e.g. Wicca rituals (Cowan 2005; Krüger 2005).

The Orthodox Church only recently began to pay serious attention to the possibilities of cyberspace and the Orthodox theological dimension of his mission on the internet. In 1997 Patriarch Aleksii II blessed the world-wide web information technology as a new means for Orthodox missionary work. Today believers have Orthodox search services,[7] social networks, web-based dating services, and information agencies. One can follow Patriarch Kirill on Facebook, exchange tweets with the popular priest and actor Ivan Okhlobystin, or leave comments on the blog of the controversial Deacon Andrei Kuraev. The Orthodox religious tradition, conservative disposition of the ROC's leadership and constituency, as well as the Church's participation in shaping today's state political agenda is not very accommodating to the new media, and yet its highest clerics and intellectuals understand that it is better to master the new technology than to fight with it.

The Orthodox segment of Runet, sometimes called as 'Ortho-net' is shaped by half-hearted attempts undertaken by the ROC to

---

[7] On 1 March 2015, when this research project was on its finish line, the Orthodox search engine rublev.com was launched under the auspices of the Information Department of the Moscow Patriarchate.

instrumentalize digital technologies in order to exercise a greater ascendance over society. On the one hand, 'Ortho-net' has arguably become the main source of informing people about religion, boasting extensive connections with Orthodoxy worldwide, which now numbers some 300 million believers. On the other, Russian-language 'Ortho-net' occupies a relatively modest and isolated niche in Runet. It is notoriously difficult to calculate its share, but one can have an adequate grasp of the 'big picture' by looking up into the service top100.rambler.ru, which allocates the most popular Orthodox webpage (pravoslavie.ru) only the 101st place in the list of Russian-language web-resources.[8] Another example is the number of received comments on the blogs in *LiveJournal;* the most popular Orthodox blog by deacon Andrei Kuraev (aka diak_kuraev) with its 1.1 million comments lags far behind Artemii Lebedev (aka tema) with 4,2 million (as of November 2015). It is safe to say that the share of Orthodox content in Runet roughly corresponds to (or somewhat less—due to the fact that older people tend to be more religious and less conversant with the internet) the proportion of regular church-goers in the Russian society.

State-of-the-art

This book is grounded on the vast literature, devoted to studying the interrelationship between different aspects of religious experience and new media.[9] The research of digital religion has passed through several stages (Campbell 2013), having made an important contribution to the understanding of the problem of (post)secularism. Early, 'romantic' conceptualizations of the cyber-world as a place of disembodied spirituality and sacredness, spurred this process, and affected the way how religious traditions consider the internet and utilize its affordances to practice faith and obtain religious experience (O'Leary 1996; Rheingold 1994; Turkle 1995). At the turn of the millennium, the proliferation of digital technologies in everyday life

---

8 http://top100.rambler.ru/navi/?page=4. Accessed 1 November 2015.
9 Most comprehensive books are here (Ahlbäck & Dahla 2013; Campbell 2010b; Campbell 2013; Cheong, Fischer-Nielsen, Gelfgren, & Ess 2012).

prompted scholars to contemplate the conceptual distinction between two modes of existence of religion on the web: 'religion-online', and 'online-religion'. This distinction illustrates the limits of the secularization hypothesis, because it shows how churches manage not only to colonize the internet ('religion-online') but also to develop new religious practices and sensibilities, specific to digital culture—'online-religion' (Helland 2000; 2002; 2005).

Penetration of the internet into all spheres of human culture rendered the divide between 'online' and 'offline' obsolete. Simultaneously the distinction between 'religion online' and 'online religion' is becoming less and less relevant; on the one hand, websites initially designed to inform believers ('religion online') provide increasingly more possibilities for participation and interaction, such as commenting and discussing or performing rituals (i.e. 'online religion'). On the other, social networks enabling believers to collectively obtain religious experience have become the main source of information about the life of the churches as well as the field of the churches' missionary work (Wagner 2012; Young 2004). Social networks have been usefully conceptualized as the 'third place' of non-instrumental communication (Baab 2012; Soukup 2006). In this vein, blogging believers not necessarily strive for the spread of their doctrines, but rather for self-cultivation and obtaining religious experience (Bakardjieva & Gaden 2012; Lee 2009), which more often than not reinforces their religious community (Cheong, Kwon, & Halavais 2008).

Later on, Heidi Campbell, drawing on the 'social shaping of technology' approach, argued that success or failure in mastering the digital technology depends not on 'the innate qualities of the technology but on the ability of the users to socially construct the technology' (Campbell 2012: 84), which in turn depends on traditions, values, and discursive practices of a given religious community. Such an approach helps researchers to revisit the secularism thesis. Even if the internet may be (or may not—depending on how this technology is being socially shaped) detrimental to the traditional religious authorities (Bruce 2002), it gives innumerable affordances for mediating the experience of the sacred and ritual practices beyond the churches' fences (Casas, Poon, Cheong, & Huang 2009; Hackett 2006), which has also been explored in the literature on the religious dimension of the digital popular culture (Deacy & Arweck 2009; Geraci 2014; Wagner 2012). The paradox of the social 'domestication' of the internet approach consists in the fact that the internet serves as the most important platform to 'domesticate' it; that is the internet is both the object of discursive construction and the instrument of so doing. Thus, 'domestication' of the internet is essentially different from the social shaping of other technologies. Consequently, researchers can speak of 'cybertheology' (Baab 2012; Horsfield 2012; Spadaro & Way 2014), whereas 'theology of internal combustion engines', or 'theology of electricity' is hardly conceivable without a great stretch.

An outline of the book

The chapters of the book are divided into three parts: *Discourses, Divergences,* and *Practices.* The first part deals with representations of CMC in the ROC's public discourses. It chronicles and analyzes factors conditioning the ROC's mastery of the internet. One of them is growing skepticism of the Church leaders about the new media, suspected of breaching Russia's cultural authenticity and implanting values and ideas alien to the Russian culture. Another factor is weak commensurability of the social ethos of the internet users, fostering individualism and social activism, and the ROC's traditional propensity for communitarian ethics and loyalty to the authority. At the same time, the relationship between the ROC and the internet should not be reduced to the clash of antagonistic logics, ethics, ideologies and practices. The problems of communication and mediation of the religious message, the dialectics of the 'real' and 'virtual' have always been in the heart of the Orthodox theology. For example, disputes over theology of image as a visual 'doubling' of the world date back to the iconoclastic era (8–9 centuries AD). The Russian Orthodoxy rejected the theatre and musical instruments, accepting only the chorus of voices as a proxy of the angelic singing, whereas masks and histrionics were seen as the domain of the devil. Echoing iconoclastic disputes, there were tough debate about 'new iconography', i.e. Baroque religious painting of the Catholic style in 17th-century Russia.[10] This controversy resulted in the still open sore of splitting into the Niconian church (now—the ROC) and the Old Believers.

Chapter 1 by Mikhail Suslov is centered on how both the highest clerics and rank-and-file priests continuously express disquietude or overtly negative attitudes toward the internet. Even those actively involved in blogging have paradoxically developed this 'digital anxiety', expressing it through a slew of negative metaphors around the internet ranging from drug addiction, to meaningless chattering, to a swamp in which they are drowning to a vanity fair. In their views, the internet has become associated with moral corruption, and a threat to the society and its core values, to such an extent that it is legitimate to speak about the 'moral panic' around the internet in the Orthodox discourses. The discrepancy between the officially accepted 'instrumentalization' interpretation of the internet, and widespread 'digital anxiety', however, signals that the internet *is* the issue for the ROC, in spite of its claim that it is not.

Chapter 2 by Magda Dolińska-Rydzek continues the exploration of the bunch of the demonic metaphors in the ROC's online debates, associated with the internet. It scrutinizes how Church discourses employ the notion of the Antichrist to raise ethical questions as well as to create moral panics. In this context the Antichrist serves not only as a designatum of an antagonistic system, but also as the immoral Other who threatens Russian moral, social, and political order.

Chapter 3 by Fabian Heffermehl takes the negative attitude of the Orthodox Church to the internet as a phenomenon, which derives from a complex development of theories of the icon-medium. It argues that the internet can be interpreted within the patterns of a false icon—or idol. That means a medium, which is diametrically different from an icon in substance, but appears with the icon's phenomenological attributes, i.e. an imagined gaze, watching the human being.

---

10 The author acknowledges the contribution of Maria Engström to the development of this argument.

It continues with a discussion of the meaning of the notion of *virtual reality* in relation to patristic and modern versions of icon theology.

Chapter 4 by Alexander Ponomariov rounds up this discussion, focusing on today's policy of the ROC towards the internet. This chapter pays special attention to how digital technology challenges the ROC's teaching about the Church (ecclesiology). It argues that the application of computer-mediated communication allows the ROC officials to experience a new dimension of connectivity with the flock, as well as arrange an efficient top-down and bottom-up mode of sharing, turning the offline conciliarity into what functions as a digital manifestation of the unity of all in the Body of Christ: as a kind of digital *sobornost'* (conciliarity). This is the term developed by the 19th century religious thinker and Slavophile Aleksei Khomiakov to designate a utopia of religiously motivated communitarian ideal and at the same time to reenact the Church model of the first centuries of Christianity. Bringing clerics and laypeople together, the internet revitalizes this idea.

The second part of the book gathers together chapters devoted to how new media technologies facilitate and promote intellectual differences, heresies and resistance to the hegemonic religious discourses. It considers a discrepancy between cultivation of all kinds of hybridizations and mixtures of different confessional practices and ideas, including monotheistic religions, pagan cults, esoteric doctrines and so on, which is characteristic for the new media, and the ROC's heightened sensitivity and aversion to heterodoxy and schisms. Large sectors of the Runet voice anti-Orthodox criticism, because digital technologies provide powerful levers for anti-clerical activists who effectively parody Orthodox tweeters, creating disincentives and disseminating memes that ridicule the Orthodox Church, whereas traditional media, such as the press and TV have been purged from anti-religious tendencies during the last decade and a half. All in all, the internet is not seen as a comfortable environment for the ROC, but rather as a battlefield, on which the Church is compelled to wage 'web wars' in order to remain in the public space and to maintain control over its flock.

Chapter 5 by Ekaterina Grishaeva explores how the heresy of the post-denominational community is presented in Russian *LiveJournal* by the example of Vladimir Golyshev, who creates high quality 'heretical content' which is spread by other users within the *LiveJournal* community. It shows that Golyshev's heterodoxy is highly politicized; his desire to undermine the social and political authority of the ROC leads to the non-institutionalized spiritual interpretation of Christianity which is free from any external dogmas. Golyshev's heresy is typical of post-secular society, where the line between politics and religion is blurred, and various religious ideas are mixed into a whimsical kaleidoscope of notions. The chapter shows that dissenting religious bloggers consider *LiveJournal* a unique opportunity to discuss hot political issues and serious problems related to the ROC, and to express their religious views and identity as outcasts.

Chapter 6 by Hanna Stähle addresses the Church-critical discourse on the relationship between Russian Orthodoxy and homosexuality that pervaded social media discussions after the Church hierarchy was publicly accused of engaging in homosexual relations and promoting same-sex behavior in its innermost circles. One of the most prominent critics of the so-called gay lobby within the Church is theologian and Protodeacon Andrei Kuraev whose *LiveJournal* blog entries on homosexual scandals gained significant resonance and sparked heated online debates. Combining quantitative and qualitative methods, this paper demonstrates how the discourse on the gay lobby controversy takes shape online, examines argumentation strategies and communication patterns and reveals high levels of intolerance and hostility among the internet users toward non-straight sexual desire. In broadcast media, as the subsequent analysis demonstrates, the discourse on homosexuality in relation to Orthodoxy has been significantly suppressed and remained largely invisible.

Chapter 7 by Maria Engström deals with the phenomenon of 'digital anti-clericalism' in the Russian-speaking sphere of the internet. In the context of post-secularism the claims of Russian clerical and bureaucratic elites to the ideological monopoly in the political and social life face a strong resistance from the champions of religious pluralism and preservation of a secular state. Presented here is a detailed analysis of the topics and the stylistic features of different types of anti-clerical internet communication—a variety of political folklore (memes, demotivators, photoshopped pictures). The chapter also traces the connection between the modern anti-clericalism on Runet and the late Soviet counter-culture.

The third part of the book discusses religious practices of engaging with the digital technologies rather than discourses about them. It considers how Orthodox believers express themselves in and through digital media.

Chapter 8 by Anastasia Mitrofanova analyzes how Orthodox women in contemporary Russia collectively invent, test and evaluate new patterns of pious behavior with the help of digital media. Three popular topics: culinary, clothing and relations with men are in the focus of interest. It is shown that both forums and digital magazines seem unable to indicate patterns of female Orthodox piety in real life. In the absence of 'style icons' and a living tradition female parishioners need some external authority to lean upon. They refer either to the traditions of contemporary Orthodox (and even Muslim) peoples, or to the Russian folk customs of the past. However, this works well only with regard to external manifestations of piety, such as clothing and food. Working out exemplary life styles would require more theological resources than the existing digital community has at its disposal.

Chapter 9 by Sarah A. Riccardi-Swartz addresses the dynamic vernacular understandings of iconography in Eastern Orthodox devotional practices in North America, calling attention to how practitioners employ digital technologies to purchase icons via the internet marketplace, and to (re)create photographic (re)presentations of the material holy, (re)producing images of miraculous icons and incorruptible bodies of saints, thereby displacing the homogeneity of institutional iconography and producing constructive intersensory artifacts that often function concomitantly as both icon and relic. Utilizing three years of ethnographic research in the rural Missouri Ozarks, the author emphasizes the role new technologies play in the creation and maintenance of Orthodox piety. Through interviews with interlocutors, she highlightes how the purchasing and production of icons via the digital world contributes to ongoing discourses on the thingness of objects and the sacralization of digital imagery. This study stresses how digital technology is important element in the reimagining of the mystical through material means.

Chapter 10 by Irina Kotkina and Mikhail Suslov presents a 'virtual roundtable', compiled from the written interviews with blogging Orthodox priests and religious activists. They relate their experiences and reflections on digitalization of the Orthodox religion, challenges and promises which the Church encounters in the internet. Their direct speech is framed by the introduction, in which strategies of self-presentations in 'Ortho-blogs' are surveyed.

Chapter 11 by Viktor Khroul examines the religious identity of Russian internet users analyzing attitudes towards God and Russian Orthodox Church in the internet based 'mass self-communication'. Since the religious identity debate is mostly located not in mainstream media but in the internet, the author focuses the research on the self-expressions and discussions on lovehate.ru website. Content analysis proves that young Russians in matters of belief/disbelief rely mainly on their own experience and the experience of other people (family, friends, acquaintances), and not on faith, authority or tradition, as would be expected initially. In the minds of the Russian internet users religion is located in the inner circle of communication (family, relatives, friends) and the religious identity for them is still much less significant in comparison to ethnic identity.

References

'Dannye (2008) o posetivshikh rozhdestvenskie bogosluzheniia'. Accessed: http://www.sova-center.ru/religion/discussions/how-many/2008/01/d1235 3/.

'Internet-tsenzura' (2014). Accessed 1 November 2015: http://www.leva da.ru/2014/10/14/internet-tsenzura/.

'Reestr (2015) zapreshchennykh saitov'. Accessed 1 November 2015: https://antizapret.info.

'Religiia: Za i protiv' (2015). Accessed 1 November 2015: http://wciom.ru/index.php?id=236&uid=115329.

'Rossiiane (2015) stali bol'she doveriat' armii'. Accessed 1 November 2015: http://www.levada.ru/2015/10/07/rossiyane-stali-bolshe-doveryat-armii/.

'Rossiiane o religii' (2013). Accessed 1 November 2015: http://www.levada.ru/2013/12/24/rossiyane-o-religii/.

Ahlbäck, Tore and B. Dahla (2013). *Digital Religion: Based on Papers Read at the Symposium on Digital Religion Held at Åbo/Turku, Finland, on 13-15 June 2012*. Åbo: Donner Institute for Research in Religious and Cultural History.

Baab, Lynne (2012). 'Toward a Theology of the Internet: Place, Relationship, and Sin.' In Digital Religion, Social Media and Culture: Perspectives, Practices and Futures, edited by P. H. Cheong, P. Fischer-Nielsen, S. Gelfgren, and C. Ess. New York: Peter Lang.

Bakardjieva, Maria and G. Gaden (2012). 'Web 2.0 Technologies of the Self.' *Philosophy & Technology, 25*(3), 399–413.

Barzilai-Nahon, Karine and G. Barzilai (2005). 'Cultured Technology: The Internet and Religious Fundamentalism.' *Information Society, 21*(1), 25–40.

Bruce, Steve (2002). *God Is Dead: Secularization in the West*. Oxford, UK: Blackwell.

Bunt, Gary (2009). *iMuslims: Rewiring the House of Islam*. London: Hurst.

Campbell, Heidi (2010a). 'Religious Authority and the Blogosphere.' *Journal of Computer-Mediated Communication, 15*(2), 251–276.

Campbell, Heidi (2010b). *When Religion Meets New Media*. London: Routledge.

Campbell, Heidi (2012). 'How Religious Communities Negotiate New Media Religiously.' In *Digital Religion, Social Media and Culture: Perspectives, Practices and Futures*, edited by P. H. Cheong, P. Fischer-Nielsen, S. Gelfgren, & C. Ess. New York: Peter Lang.

Campbell, Heidi (2013). *Digital Religion: Understanding Religious Practice in New Media Worlds*. London: Routledge.

Cheong, Pauline, I. Casas, J. Poon, and S. Huang (2009). 'The Internet Highway and Religious Communities: Mapping and Contesting Spaces in Religion-Online.' *The Information Society, 25*(5), 291–302.

Cheong, Pauline, K. Kwon, and A. Halavais (2008). 'The Chronicles of Me: Understanding Blogging as a Religious Practice.' *Journal of Media and Religion,* 7(3), 107–131.

Cheong, Pauline, P. Fischer-Nielsen, S. Gelfgren, and C. Ess (2012). *Digital Religion, Social Media and Culture: Perspectives, Practices and Futures.* New York: Peter Lang.

Cowan, Douglas (2005). *Cyberhenge: Modern Pagans on the Internet.* New York: Routledge.

Davie, Grace (2006). 'Vicarious Religion: A Methodological Challenge.' *Everyday Religion: Observing Modern Religious Lives,* edited by Nancy Ammerman. Oxford: Oxford University Press: 21–37.

Deacy, Christopher and E. Arweck (2009). *Exploring Religion and the Sacred in a Media Age.* Burlington, VT; Farnham, England: Ashgate.

Engström, Maria (2014). 'Contemporary Russian Messianism and New Russian Foreign Policy.' *Contemporary Security Policy,* 35(3), 356–379.

Geraci, Robert (2014). *Virtually Sacred: Myth and Meaning in World of Warcraft and Second Life.* New York: Oxford University Press.

Hackett, Rosalind (2006). 'Religion and the Internet.' *Diogenes,* 53(211).

Heelas, Paul and L. Woodhead (2005). *The Spiritual Revolution: Why Religion Is Giving Way to Spirituality.* Malden, Mass.: Blackwell.

Helland, Chrisopher (2010). '(Virtually) Been There, (Virtually) Done That: Examining the Online Religious Practices of the Hindu Tradition: Introduction.' *Online-Heidelberg Journal of Religions on the Internet,* 4(1).

Helland, Christopher (2000). 'Online-Religion/Religion-Online and Virtual Communities.' In *Religion on the Internet: Research Prospects and Promises,* edited by J. K. Hadden and D. E. Cowan. Amsterdam, London, New York: JAI Press.

Helland, Christopher (2002). 'Surfing for Salvation.' *Religion,* 32(4), 293–302.

Helland, Christopher (2005). 'Online Religion as Lived Religion: Methodological Issues in the Study of Religious Participation on the Internet.' *Online–Heidelberg Journal of Religions on the Internet,* 1(1), 1–16.

Horsfield, Peter (2012). '"A Moderate Diversity of Books?" The Challenge of New Media to the Practice of Christian Theology.' In *Digital Religion, Social Media and Culture : Perspectives, Practices and Futures,* edited by P. H. Cheong, P. Fischer-Nielsen, S. Gelfgren, and C. Ess. New York: Peter Lang.

Howard, Robert (2011). *Digital Jesus: The Making of a New Christian Fundamentalist Community on the Internet.* New York: New York University Press.

Kirill (Gundiaev), Patriarch (2010). *Byt' vernym Bogu: Kniga besed so Sviateishim Patriarkhom Kirillom.* Minsk: Belarusskii ekzarkhat.

Kostjuk, Konstantin (2005). *Der Begriff des Politischen in der russisch-orthodoxen Tradition: zum Verhältnis von Kirche, Staat und Gesellschaft in Russland.* Paderborn: F. Schöningh.

Krüger, Oliver. (2005). 'Discovering the Invisible Internet: Methodological Aspects of Searching Religion on the Internet.' *Online–Heidelberg Journal of Religions on the Internet: Volume 01.1 Special Issue on Theory and Methodology.*

Lee, Joonseong (2009). 'Cultivating the Self in Cyberspace: The Use of Personal Blogs among Buddhist Priests.' *Journal of Media and Religion,* 8(2), 97–114.

Livio, Oren and K. Tenenboim Weinblatt (2007). 'Discursive Legitimation of a Controversial Technology: Ultra-Orthodox Jewish Women in Israel and the Internet.' *The Communication Review,* 10(1), 29–56.

Mitrofanova, Anastasia (2005). *The Politicization of Russian Orthodoxy: Actors and Ideas.* Stuttgart: Ibidem.

O'Leary, Stephen (1996). 'Cyberspace as Sacred Space: Communicating Religion on Computer Networks.' *Journal of the American Academy of Religion,* 64(4), 781–808.

Papkova, Irina (2011). *The Orthodox Church and Russian Politics.* Washington, DC: Woodrow Wilson Center Press.

Potupchik, Kristina, and A. Fedorova (2014). *Vlast' nad set'iu: Kak gosudarstvo deistvuet v internete.* Moscow: Algoritm.

Rashi, Tsuriel (2013). 'The Kosher Cell Phone in Ultra-Orthodox Society: A Technological Ghetto within the Global Village?' In *Understanding Religious Practice in New Media Worlds,* edited by Heidi Campbell. London and New York: Routledge.

Rheingold, Howard (1994). *The Virtual Community: Homesteading on the Electronic Frontier.* New York, NY: HarperPerennial.

Scheifinger, Heinz (2013). 'Hindu Worship Online and Offline.' In *Understanding Religious Practice in New Media Worlds,* edited by Heidi Campbell. London and New York: Routledge.

Simons, Gregory and D. Westerlund (2015). *Religion, Politics and Nation-building in Post-communist Countries.* Farnham: Ashgate Publishing.

Soukup, Charles (2006). 'Computer-mediated Communication as a Virtual Third Place: Building Oldenburg's Great Good Places on the World Wide Web.' *New Media & Society, 8*(3), 421–440.

Spadaro, Antonio and M. Way (2014). *Cybertheology: Thinking Christianity in the Era of the Internet.* New York: Fordham University Press.

Suslov, Mikhail (2014). '"Holy Rus": The Geopolitical Imagination in the Contemporary Russian Orthodox Church.' *Russian Politics & Law, 52*(3), 67–86.

Turkle, Sherry (1995). *Life on the Screen: Identity in the Age of the Internet.* New York: Simon & Schuster.

Wagner, Rachel (2012). Godwired: Religion, Ritual, and Virtual Reality. London: Routledge.

Young, Glenn (2004). *Reading and Praying Online: The Continuity of Religion Online and Online Religion in Internet Christianity.* In L. Dawson & D. Cowan (Eds.), *Religion Online: Finding Faith on the Internet* New York.

Chapter 1.
The Medium for Demonic Energies: 'Digital Anxiety' in the Russian Orthodox Church

Mikhail Suslov
Uppsala Center for Russian and Eurasian Studies, Uppsala University

Introduction

In the last two decades religions around the globe successfully expanded into the internet, thereby questioning basic tenets of the secularism theory.[1] New ways have been uncovered in which digital technology could be and is being integrated with religious tradition. Digital technology has been increasingly seen as a new platform for the Church's mission, as well as a new communicative environment, in which people can build up religious communality, establish their religious identities, obtain religious experience (Campbell 2010b; Stout 2012) and develop 'cybertheology' (e.g. Spadaro 2014). In some religions, including Eastern Orthodox Christianity, communication lies in the center of their theological reasoning. For example, Orthodox Trinitarian theology conceives of God as a communion of three hypostases. Metropolitan of Pergamon Ioannis Zizioulas, one of the most influential Orthodox theologians of our time, argues that the mystery of the Trinity 'points to a way of being which precludes individualism and separation... The "one" not only does not precede—logically or otherwise—the "many", but, on the contrary, requires the "many" from the very start in order to exist' (Zizioulas 2006: 159). Communication from this perspective is fundamental for the development of religious identity (see also: Zizioulas 1985: 110; cf. Baab 2012: 277–291). This theological insight exhibits one of the

---

[1] I would like to acknowledge valuable comments from my colleagues Greg Simons, Maria Engström and Fabian Heffermehl, as well as suggestions of anonymous reviewers of the journal *Digital Icons*, where this paper was first published (issue 14).

possible ways for the Church to make sense of new media as a game-changer in human communication. One scholar has expressed this idea, that different media in religious life are like different translations of the Bible (Hipps 2009: 24). They are essentially about one and the same thing, but small differences can result in tectonic shifts, similarly to how the revision of liturgical books in the mid-17th century led to the schism in the Russian Church. More than this, religion itself is a kind of medium, and its manifestations are always mediated: by the written word, oral speech, icons or liturgy as a synthesis of many media (Engelke 2010: 371–379; Khroul 2012: 8–9; Vries 2001). So media are by no means irrelevant to the ROC and its doctrine, nor are they unimportant for shaping one's religious identity, and for struggling for its recognition.

Possibilities, which computer-mediated communication (thereafter CMC) has created for the Russian Orthodoxy, are gigantic and historically unique; CMC gives voice to a subculture, which was almost voiceless during the Soviet period, and provides an instrument for limitless missionary activity. Keeping the debates on (post-) secularism in due consideration, this paper argues that Russian Orthodoxy's uneasy co-existence with the internet is anchored in the incongruity between the regime of post-secularism, in which today's 'digital religion' exists, and the ROC's striving to restore pre-secular conditions. Following Habermas' line of thinking about prerequisites for post-secularism (quoted in Ziebertz and Riegel 2009: 300): acceptance of plurality, rational reasoning as a communicative strategy and acknowledgement of human rights as the fundamental value, we can suggest that the ROC is trying to instrumentalize the internet as a medium for exactly the opposite messages: the monopoly on moral judgment, the privileging of faith over reason and the relativisation of the human rights' doctrine.

New media, however, have their own communicative logic and political agenda, which may or may not facilitate democratization of the public sphere (e.g. Gorham 2014; Paulsen and Zvereva 2014; Roesen and Zvereva 2014; Schmidt and Teubiner 2009; Uffelmann 2014). They do definitely spur grassroots activism as well as 'cynical reason' (Sloterdijk 1987) and 'liquid' forms of social sensibility (Bau- (Bauman 2000). The deepest irony here is that providing unlimited access to the discourse, the internet seems to undermine something dear to the hearts of the Orthodox Christians, namely the hierarchy of knowledge, and the underlying hierarchy of power. To just have access to the discourse is not important for them, because they believe that they *already* have an exclusive access to the 'real' and the only important knowledge—about God. This means that the internet devalues their treasure and refashions their authority (cf. Hjarvard 2008). Russian Orthodoxy shares these premonitions with some fundamentalist religions, fearing that digital technologies could profane sacral truths and belittle the religious authority of the Church hierarchy (Barzilai-Nahon and Barzilai 2005: 25–40; Howard 2011).

At this juncture we can see the mechanism of the 'digital anxiety', powered by the fear of losing control over the identity of the self and the (collective and individual) other, on the one hand, and the attempt to 'securitize' the religious identity, many of whose aspects are being perceived as endangered in the age of new media. The logic of securitization produces a series of moral panics about CMC in order to reinforce the grid of values of this seemingly vulnerable religious 'self'.

The supporting primary sources for this research come mostly from qualitative analysis of the blogs of Orthodox priests and activists, official documents of ROC and statements of the Church highest clerics as well as several open-ended questionnaires.[2] The ROC has no official policy document on the internet, so opinions may vary greatly among the Orthodox clergy. This article tries not to focus too much on the extremes of positive or negative (prevailing) attitudes towards the internet, but rather—through the close reading of the blogs—it uncovers discursive structures which made those opinions possible.

---

2   In August and September 2014 questionnaires about Orthodoxy and digital technologies were sent to 28 blogging priests and Church activists; 11 of them responded, 7 of them finally submitted their answers. Chapter 10 '"Ortho-Blogging' from Inside": A Virtual Roundtable' by Irina Kotkina and Mikhail Suslov is based on those answers.

Methodology

This research is based on reflections, obtained from the internet users, mostly bloggers, who are either priests or religious activists. These reflections are contextualized in official statements about the internet from highest clerics of the Moscow Patriarchate. This means that this research is not an ethnographic study of what Orthodox believers *do* in digital environment. It is rather an examination of the Church's recent intellectual history, which revolves around questions such as: Which notions and metaphors do they employ in order to make sense of the digital world? From which intellectual layers and legacies do they borrow them? How do they recombine those ideas in order to adjust to today's reality?

In order to approach these questions, I draw on the 'social construction of technology' theory (e.g. Bijker 1987; Klein and Kleinman 2002), as it has been adapted to the studies of media and religion by Heidi Campbell (e.g. Campbell 2005). According to this conceptualization, technical innovations become meaningful for users only when they are framed mentally and emotionally. In other words, success or failure in mastering technologies depends not on their innate qualities but on the way in which people construct them, leaning on their previous experience, cultural traditions, basic values and other discursive practices (Campbell 2012: 84). However, our interpretation of technology should be fine-tuned in order to take into account hegemonic articulation of meanings (Laclau and Mouffe 1985), because the digital environment is thoroughly intersected by lines of political force. The ROC, which in defiance of the post-secularism paradigm, reclaims the role of the sole gatekeeper of culture and spirituality in Russian society, struggles to arrest the flow of many possible interpretations of CMC and thereby to (partially) fixate the religious identity of users. In this sense, moral panics (e.g. Molloy 2013: 194-201; Smith and Cole 2013: 207–223) around and about the ROC's engagement with CMC, function as dress-rehearsals of performing ROC's cultural hegemony in Russia.

The analysis of religious discourses online always faces the problem of motive, intention and the discrepancy between what is said and what is thought. To be sure, the ROC is a hierarchical au-authoritarian institution, which always tries to monitor and censor presbyters' writings online. For example, rabid anti-Ukrainian posts of deacon Pavel Shul'zhenko on his vk.com page caused him to be banned from service on account of discrediting the Church (Shul'zhenko 2015), whereas hieromonk Nikolai Savchenko, who, by contrast, reproached Russia for its involvement in the war in Donbass and its annexation of Crimea, was punitively reassigned from St. Petersburg to a monastery in Strel'na (Vol'tskaia 2015). However, censorship and auto-censorship online should not be exaggerated because the Church simply has no means to follow every single blog or page on social networks, and barely reacts to the most virally spread scandals.

So for the majority of blogging priests, this activity is not an exercise in Aesopian language, but rather a missionary outreach, or more often than not, a struggle for recognition (e.g. Honneth 1995), and particularly a self-cultivation technique (Lee 2009: 97–114; Bakardjieva and Gaden 2012: 399–413). CMC, thus, became the single most important platform on which recognition, status and identity are being debated, nurtured and negotiated, and in so doing, compensates for disfunctionalities in many other social spheres in Russia, from legislation to family life, and from the press to grassroots' organizations.

The paradox of cyber-skepticism

Patriarch Kirill ironically remarks that his attitude towards the internet is similar to his relation to electricity, or to an automobile. One can use the internet for good or for evil, because as a tool, the internet is ethically neutral (Kirill 2009: 113; Kirill 2010; Krug 2007). And yet—contrary to this 'official' instrumentalization thesis—in the eyes of Orthodox intellectuals, the internet designates a space of insecurity and discomfort, incongruent with the ROC's 'socio-religious construction' of other technologies. Patriarch Kirill employs the 'geopolitical' metaphor to express the Orthodox 'digital anxiety': the internet is the battleground, where forces of good and evil fight for human souls. Elsewhere he mentions: 'The theme of the mediasphere... is what I am thinking about now most of all, and what I am praying for, because here is the place where the devil struggles with God' (Kirill 2012a; Kirill 2008: 119). Archpriest Sergii Lepin extended the 'geopolitical' metaphor by Patriarch Kirill, stating 'we are "fighting" not against the internet, but for the internet' (Lepin 2014; cf. Kirill 2012c; Legoida 2012). Thus, contrary to the opinion that blogging is an unimportant activity for relaxation, and contrary to the 'instrumentalization thesis', Patriarch Kirill suggests here the dramatic significance of the internet is for personal salvation and the world's destiny.

Speaking about 'Ortho-blogging' in Russia bridges the offline gap between the subculture of the 'churchized' [*votserkovlennyi*], i.e. of regular Church-goers, and the rest of Russian society. The widespread justification among Orthodox priests of their online presence focuses on the fact that the non-'churchized' population, which nevertheless feels its attachment to religion and builds its identity on the Russian Church, experiences difficulties with church customs. People often do not know how to behave themselves in church, or how to approach a priest and ask him a question. Blogs of the priests effectively solve this problem, providing them with a medium, in which they feel more 'at home' and do not hesitate to speak about their religious needs. In this sense, 'Ortho-blogs' provide a new social infrastructure for practicing religion and recruiting co-believers (e.g. Lövheim 2013: 52).

All these advantages notwithstanding, for rank-and-file blogging priests the internet is paradoxically acquiring menacing contours. 'Ortho-bloggers' often mention reluctance with which they started their blogs. For example, archpriest Dimitrii Struev begins his first entry with the last words of Christ on the cross: 'It is finished', and then explains his reasons to begin blogging: 'My friends have finally persuaded me to start this blog [...] I was hesitant not only because all this virtual stuff [*virtual'shchina*, derogative for 'the virtual'] is going to suck out even more *real* time [from my life], but also because I appreciate traditional human communication too much, and there is a sort of the retrograde fear to substitute it by virtual [communication]' (presviter-ds@lj 2.01.2007). Following this line of thought, Metropolitan Ignatii (Pologrudov) of Khabarovsk and Trans-Amur, who was arguably the first bishop of the ROC to start a personal blog, recollects that it was the head of his Information department, who convinced him to launch an online diary: 'I resisted as much as I could but he displayed the prodigy of endurance and persistence... So [finally] my blog was brought to life' (Ignatii 2014). Archpriest Gennadii Belovolov (aka otets-gennadiy) sounds the same note when confessing the following: 'I have always been skeptical about all sorts of web logging, and could not think of myself doing these things...' (otets-gennadiy@lj 15.07.2010). Self-critical and derogative characteristics of web logging and the internet in general are ubiquitous: 'this virtual stuff [*virtual'shchina*]', 'this slush swallows me up' (here, there is a play on words; LiveJournal is ZhZh, *zhivoi zhurnal*, which sounds to a Russian ear like *zhizha*, slush); 'I keep on buzzing' ('to buzz' in Russian is 'zhuzhzhat''); 'cesspool of the internet' (o-paulos@lj 23.04.2007). WWW is referred to as a 'global spider's web', and experience in the internet—as being 'contaminated with the internet' (presviter-ds 11.08.2007; Iakovleva 2012[3]: 130; Osborne 2004). It is necessary to note, that this 'virtual arachnophobia' exists well beyond the Orthodox blogosphere (Schmidt and Teubener 2006: 52-53).

With the tinge of the paradox of a liar, 'Ortho-bloggers' claim that the blogosphere does not represent or express the interests and opinions of the Russian people. As inokv (hegumen Vitalii Utkin) angrily pens, it is time to limit the dependence of state and society from 'a handful of people in the internet', who in fact 'are nothing but [who] feel their importance'. Otherwise, screams of a dozen of bloggers would muffle the voice of the 'absolute majority of our people' (inokv@lj 21.07.2013). This position suggests a counter to

---

3   Olga Iakovleva is the chair of the Union of Orthodox Lawyers, who made her fame by advocating interests of Orthodox believers, refusing to accept digital documents (e.g. passports). Cf. chapter 2 in this volume.

the idea that the internet democratizes politics, and echoes the Slavophile teaching of the mid-19th century, juxtaposing 'the people', which is natural, original and authentic, and the 'public', which is unnatural, unoriginal and unauthentic. The repercussions of this division are observable in Solzhenitsyn's aversion towards '*obrazovanshchina*', i.e. superficially educated intelligentsia, which assumes the right of moral judgment on behalf of the whole people. Pretre_philippe (priest Filip Parfenov) compares bloggers with such '*obrazovanshchina*' , criticizing them for combining opinionated ignorance with aggressive imposing of their views on the rest of the population. Hence, alignment of the internet with a 'false' public sphere is common: digital technologies are believed to be used by some 'external' forces in order to create 'an illusion of public opinion' (pretre-philippe@lj 5.07.2010; Dobrosotskikh 2013: 7).

However, the majority of 'Ortho-bloggers' do not reject CMC out of hand. The most common strategy to 'normalize' the internet and to make sense of the digital environment is to represent it along the line of Patriarch Kirill's reasoning as purely instrumental to purposes of salvation and personal spiritual perfection (e.g. iereymasim@lj 15.04.2011; Kuz'micheva 2014). As father Iakov Krotov, one of the 'fathers-founders' of the Orthodox 'Runet', explains, 'the internet in general and blogs and *LiveJournal* in particular are technical tools, like paper and ink. Tools do not determine the rules of communication...' (Krotov, n.d.) Hieromonk Makarii Markish categorically professes that to believe that any technological invention including the internet could have an impact on faith or theology is 'sheer nonsense' (Markish 2014).

Annette Markham distinguishes three ways, or levels of engaging with the internet: as a tool, as a place and as a state of being (Markham 1998). For 'Ortho-users' the most common way to think about the internet is 'instrumental'. This precludes Orthodox intellectuals and grassroots users from any deep understanding of the phenomenon. The internet is not a problem for them intellectually, but it is anyway a huge problem for them emotionally and intuitively. The discrepancy between the perceived threat of the internet and reluctance to theorize it exposes the structure of the discourse, because even anxiety, vigor and irritation with which 'Ortho-bloggers' insist on instrumentality of the internet suggests that CMC is something more.

The doubling of the world: theological tradition and new media

In the ideal world of Orthodox priests, the digital environment is a means, enhancing physical connectivity among humans, not a virtual double of 'real' society. This disquietude about the 'virtual world' resonates with some deeply seated religious sensibilities, such as the fear of the 'monstrous double' in archaic cultures (Girard 1972: 213–248) or—on a more historical plane of interpretation—with iconoclastic debates of the 8th century. In a nutshell, the key iconoclastic argument against pictures of God and saints was that they violate one of the Ten Commandments (Exodus 20:4): 'You shall not make for yourself an image in the form of anything in heaven above or on the earth beneath or in the waters below', because creating the double of the world implies a kind of blasphemous encroachment on God's prerogative.

This understanding is weaved into the ROC's concept of the difference between information and knowledge. Information, from this viewpoint, is something unnecessary or even delusive, taking people away from *knowing* really important things. Sergei Chapnin, the ex-editor of two mouthpieces of the Moscow Patriarchate, wrote a programmatic article on the ROC's presence in media, in which he philosophized on the difference between the internet and icons as a traditional Orthodox 'medium'. He pointed at the Orthodox tradition to consider an icon as an invisible 'proto-image' (of God), residing behind the visible iconic image,[4] whereas information in today's media has no 'real content' because it has become a purpose in itself, a mere play of simulacra. Information, he concludes in his train of thoughts, 'has rebelled against knowledge', and first of all against

---

4   On functioning of icons in the digital environment see Chapter 3 in this volume.

'knowledge of Truth, Word and Image, united in Christ' (Chapnin 2006: 225–226). In a way, this interpretation recycles the main iconoclastic argument forbidding the 'doubling' of the world.

In tune with this conceptualization, Metropolitan Kliment (Kapalin) opines that the internet trains us to live in dependence on ready-made ideas, pleasures and values. The internet sells us a bill of goods, so that people are gradually losing the capacity for independent and critical judgment. He further argues that in the Garden of Eden Adam and Eve received all information solely from God, and therefore could not even conceive of an idea to violate the divine will. The Fall happened when people received (false) information from the devil. Likewise in our life, information about sinful deeds has power to cause these deeds, when, for example, teenagers start to smoke or drink spirits, they first learn that this is 'cool' from their peers, and then try doing it themselves (Kapalin 2012).

This line of reasoning was extended by Bishop Longin (Korchagin) of Saratov and Vol'sk; he is concerned with the stream of 'uprooted' information in the internet, which can overwhelm a young person, providing him or her with a wealth of facts about everything in the world. This information, however, has not been 'processed' and structured by an institution, representing cultural tradition and external moral authority (Korchagin 2006). As a result, a youth will be exposed to substantially homogenous and morally neutral information about Orthodoxy and, say, Jehovah's Witnesses, which, understandably, is disagreeable for an Orthodox bishop.

The image of the internet as a place of unboundedly floating of information, torn from its traditions and cultural roots, is threatening for Orthodox intellectuals, because it aligns digital technologies with the danger of losing Russia's national and cultural identity. This anxiety sometimes borders with blaming the internet for being a geopolitical weapon, which Russia's enemies use in order to undermine its sovereignty and cultural originality (Markish 2013b: 91). In a more general sense, Runet as a whole has been a locus of anti-globalist manifestations (Bowles 2006: 32; Agadjanian and Rousselet 2005: 29–57).

Another meaningful input to the debate about the internet was provided by the tradition of 'name-worshipping', an intellectual movement developed in Russian Orthodoxy in the early 20th century, and quickly spread among the Russian residents of Mount Athos and religiously minded intelligentsia in imperial capitals. From their viewpoint, 'the name of a thing is the thing, but the thing is not its name' (e.g. Nishnikov 2012: 56–65). As Aleksandr Etkind interprets 'name-worshipping', it was a kind of protest against the Enlightenment and its semiotic project to see signifiers as but loosely connected with the signified. By contrast, 'name-worshippers', as if reenacting pre-historical animism on a new level, collapsed the name and its object in one, thereby heading towards the end of discourse, when only the 'Jesus prayer' interrupts silence (Etkind 1998: 259–261).

Considering this inseverable tie between the signifier and the signified in the context of 'name-worshipping', virtual reality should be represented as the world of empty signifiers ('simulacra' in Chapnin's wording), or as the world of wretched shadows of real things. Priest Iakov Krotov reminds us that shadows, as we may know from Hans Christian Andersen's fairy tale, can try to take the place of a real person. Father Iakov opines that the internet as a communicative space seduces people to change roles with their shadows, while 'the communion of two shadows would never beget either a person or even the third shadow' (Krotov 2013); it is in this sense fruitless.

The image of the internet as the 'realm of shadows' is haunting in Orthodox blogs (kolokolchik-lby@lj 17.02.2014). The most common trope juxtaposes 'live' (offline) and online (i.e. presumably 'dead') communication. Priest Sergii Kruglov, a popular blogger himself, composed a poem 'A Priest [Logging] in a Blog', in which he reflected his sentiments about online activity:

Night is everywhere. But not in *LiveJournal*:
These are not [just] hard disks [which] spin and rub [themselves]:

> Now here it is someone who is *scratching away [his] life*,
> Now there someone squeakily writes comments.
> Oh, you have to respond to this *deadly squeak*! You have to call
> This person and that one by their *natural names*.
> And you have to bless hundreds of *ghostly friends* [...] (kruglov-s-g@lj 16.04.2008).[5]

Reading the poem, the image of internet communication appears before our eyes, which is akin to Dante's inferno: this is the nocturnal place ('night is everywhere'), inhabited by 'ghostly friends', who ceaselessly perform the treadmill ('spinning hard disks') of self-destroying ('scratching away his life'), accompanied by 'deadly squeaks'. By mentioning that the priest's mission in this place should be to recall 'ghostly' bloggers' real names, father Sergii attacks the 'evil doubling' of the world in the internet from the viewpoint of 'name-worshipping'.

Echoing this 'other-worldly' metaphor of the internet, archpriest Gennadii Belovolov refers to the short fantastic story by Dostoevsky 'Bobok' (1873). This story tells us about a writer who starts to hear strange muted voices. After a while he realizes that these are conversations of dead men and women in the graveyard; for a couple of months after death, when their flesh is gradually decomposing, corpses can still talk to each other and to relate their histories and give the final appraisal of their lives. They talk for months and months until carrion could squelch nothing else but *'bobok'*. Father Gennadii compares this story to internet communication: similarly to Dostoevsky's sick fantasy, online interlocutors 'are in complete darkness, they neither see, nor know each other, and can talk about anything they want' (Belovolov 2010).

---

5 Italics added for emphasis. All translations are mine.—M.S. In original:
Povsiudu noch'. I lish' v ZhZh ne noch':
Ne diski zhestkie, se, trutsia i vertiatsia:
To kto-to zhizn' tam vytsarapyvaet proch',
To skriplo kommenty skriniatsia.
O otzovis' na etot smertnyi skrip! O pozovi
Togo i etogo po imenam ikh krovnym,
I sotni prizrachnykh druzei blagoslovi
Perstoslozheniem imenoslovnym.

Another aspect of the 'virtual reality' was pinpointed by Patri-Patriarch Aleksii II (Rediger) who combined two images of the internet: as a theatrical play, and as 'faking for fun', and expressed his concern that the internet promotes a 'not... serious, playful approach to life' (Aleksii II 2006). Following this logic, archpriest Vladimir Vigilianskii expresses anxiety that internet discussions foster 'twaddle, mockery... It is a sign of good manners here to run down bishops, to laugh at the Church officials, and to sneer at Church events' (Vigilianskii 2008). Archpriest Aleksii Uminskii, known as a popular TV presenter and who has recently committed a 'virtual suicide'[6] by closing all his accounts on social media, argues that on the social networking sites everything can be easily turned into a fake, and even a person can change into a fake, and a fake is 'something horrendous, this is a joke which looks so much as a truth. This is a really devilish contrivance to make fun of words, to make fun of thoughts and to make fun of a human being...' (Uminskii 2013). Thus, in Orthodox criticism, the internet represents the metonymy of 'cynical reason' (Sloterdijk 1987), ubiquitous in the profit-oriented de-Christianized world.

De-sacralization of the sacraments

Put together, all these representations of the internet mark the dramatic association of CMC with the devil's agency, so that the internet is associated with the 'father of lies', whose purpose is to pervert and to mock God's creation: humans and the world around us. As archpriest Dimitrii Savel'ev answered in the popular project 'Fathers Online', 'it is not possible to improve the virtual world. It seems to me that this is a kind of an enemy's trick, devised in order to suck out people's energy, thoughts and feelings and [transform them into] words on the internet' (Savel'ev 2014a).[7] Association of the internet with the devil is even stronger, and—although much less

---

6   In another example, archpriest Maksim Kozlov, vice chair of the Educational department of Moscow Patriarchate, cancelled his *Facebook* account (Tiurenkov 2013).
7   To be noted: the 'enemy' is a common Orthodox euphemism for the devil.

sophisticated,—very explicit among some Orthodox laymen and laywomen. As one of the Orthodox radio listeners straightforwardly puts it: 'the internet is devilry' (Chinkova 2011). Likewise, Egor Kholmogorov—himself an active internet user,—calls virtual reality 'pure devilry' (holmogor@lj 22.10.2007). Hieromonk Anatolii Berestov argues that virtual reality creates a 'false universe', but this is 'in fact, the choice of demons, the choice of non-being' (Berestov 2007: 79). He further says that virtual reality is the devilish reality par excellence; when the devil seduces people, he acts through the sphere of fantasy and imagination, i.e. by creating virtual reality as a 'medium for devilish energy' (Berestov 2007: 80).

A certain level of techno-phobia has always been widespread on the conservative flank of the Russian Orthodoxy; as hieromonk Makarii Markish puts it, any technological novelty starts to serve to the enemy of humankind even earlier than it becomes useful for people (Markish 2013a: 20). Some 'Ortho-bloggers' consider the virtual world as a kind of inhumane technological utopia, capable of subordinating humans to a non-human entity of dark provenience. Building on the image of the internet as a fake reality, Orthodox bloggers tend to negate the authenticity of religious experience, obtained online, with a case in point here being the 'virtual chapel'.

In 2010, IT-specialist Denis Kapralov created a virtual chapel in the name of Nicholas the Miracle-worker (**figure 1.1**), designed, as he explained it, first and foremost for disabled people who cannot go to a 'real' church. On the webpage one can light a candle, choose an icon, or read a prayer, while listening to meditative music. 'It is not possible to substitute the spiritual experience in the [real] church by this project,—he stipulates,—'But to a certain extent it helps people to absterge, and it gives them force'.[8] This initiative, however, was met with suspicion by clerics and lay Church goers alike (e.g. Svechnikov 2012), who argue that this is not just a 'substitute', but a 'surrogate' [*podmena*] of the true religious experience (e.g. iereys@lj

---

8 http://vk.com/club15248597. Accessed 1 April 2015.

10.04.2008).[9] Some priests view it as 'de-sacralization of sacra-sacraments' (Odarenko 2012), 'de-sacralization of the prayer' (chudo_iva@lj 4.07.2013), or 'turning... prayer into a kind of the computer game' (Savel'ev 2014b). On the same note, democratization of communication online caused irritation among some Orthodox intellectuals, who claim that people lose reverence for the holy rank of a priest or a bishop, so that they can speak with them disrespectfully (Morozov 2013: 38–39).[10]

Figure 1.1. 'Virtual Chapel.'
Source: http://chasovnya.msk.ru. Accessed 1 April 2015.

The short story by archpriest Dimitrii Struev sums up Orthodox disquietudes about authenticity of the faith online. It tells us about near future when technologies would substantially transform the traditional church routine (e.g. a battery-powered censer, a touchpad

---

9   Ethnographic field research tends to show that in fact, religious experience online may be 'authentic' in the sense that it causes similar bodily effects and emotional states as 'offline' religious practice (see, inter alia Radde-Antweiler 2013: 88–103).
10 On the general concern about religious authority online see Cheong 2013: 72–87.

in place of a lectern, neon candles lit via the internet, and so on). The protagonist named Nastia listens to the prayers through earphones and confesses by choosing options from dropdown menus on the screen. Having sent the file to her confessor, she suddenly wonders if the priest opens her files at all? Perhaps, there is a special program which automatically forwards replies, but what does it mean, then? What does such an absolution would look like: 'I, IBM, absolve you from your sins in the name of...' In the name of whom? (presviter-ds@lj 30.03.2008). At this point the story abruptly ends, leaving the reader to surmise that in the spirit of Orthodox religious sensibility, if this is not done in the name of God, then it is done in the name of the devil.

Anthropological threat

According to 'Bases of the ROC's Doctrine on Human Dignity, Freedom and Human Rights' (I.2–I.5), human nature is originally sinful, so human dignity is not something which humans possess by default, but something which is to be gained by a virtuous life. Freedom is considered as one of the manifestations of God's presence in human life, but freedom 'should not be absolutized', because if a person freely chooses to live a virtuous life, this person would acquire dignity and his or her choice should be respected. If, by contrast, a person chooses to live a life of a sinner, he or she loses dignity and this person's free choice should not be respected (Osnovy 2008: II.1–II.2).

This argument has a deep and lasting impact on the official line of the ROC regarding the internet, which is being perceived as the locus of the emancipation of human passions. The alternative vision of the internet as promoting self-realization is profoundly alien to Orthodox religious sensibility, which tends to confront self-realization as releasing of person's sins with self-restriction in the spirit of Christ's teaching about *kenosis* (self-belittling). Thus, Metropolitan Hilarion (Alfeev) rebuked the internet as the place where people can freely lump together all of their dirt and negative attitudes without being censored or punished (Alfeev 2012). With a similar eloquence, Patriarch Kirill indicated that the internet was the zone of high risk of 'moral degeneration' (Kirill 2012a). Specifying his position, the patriarch has recently called social networks a 'vanity fair', detrimental to our soul's salvation (Kirill 2015). Orthodox priests and activists closely follow this argument, professing that the internet unleashes human nature, thereby inevitably allowing evil to vent (Markish 2013b: 90). In particular, they disapprovingly speak of those who post online for the sake of becoming 'seemingly important' (Uminskii 2013), or lose 'internal barriers' and stop controlling their emotions in the online debates (Chinkova 2011; Legoida 2011; Legoida 2014; saag@lj 13.10.2009). The internet from this viewpoint is not a space for self-cultivation but the opposite, a place for self-destruction in a paroxysm of carnavalesque gaiety. This vision of the internet manifests the feeling of the loss of control and agency (Schmidt and Teubener 2006: 57), characteristic for post-Soviet society in general, and for the sensibility of religious traditionalists in particular.

Armed with such an understanding of the internet as potentially impeding person's salvation, the Orthodox religious sensibility situates information in the rubric of 'sinful', or more specifically—'ferial' as an opposite to Lenten fare. In the Orthodox concept of fasting, people should shun sin and all unnecessary and excessive things in their lives. Mounting the comparison between the internet and the ferial food, some blogging priests reported that they would stop blogging or searching the internet during Lent (fater-go@lj 21.02.2004; griger@lj 14.12.2005). In 2013 archpriest Vsevolod Chaplin used the phrase 'information fasting' and called to keep it during Lent, which implicates refraining from using the internet altogether for this period (Chaplin 2013; Uminskii 2013).

The case in point here is the Orthodox interpretation of the 'internet-addiction' as a manifestation of the human corrupt nature, and a barrier on the way to spiritual perfection. From this viewpoint, 'addiction' to the internet and internet as a 'drug' of sorts are important topics in Orthodox web logs (e.g. kolokolchik-lby@lj

17.02.2014; pfarrer-tom@lj 30.10.2014). Very often they make astute and self-critical observation about their own 'dependence' on the internet, using the characteristic jargon from the sub-culture of drug addicts. Priest Vitalii Timoshenko, for example, with tongue in cheek confesses that he was 'addicted' [*podsazhen*] to *LiveJournal* by a friend of his (priest-vit@lj 4.01.2022); similarly anonymous prostopop@lj was 'addicted' to the internet by father Mikhail Shpolianskii (prostopop@lj 26.04.2014).

These playful accounts reveal a lot about perception of the internet in Orthodoxy, but some religious activists are seriously concerned with 'internet-addiction' and this concern is only growing. In 2013 the popular website 'Orthodoxy and the World' (pravmir.ru) started an anti-internet campaign; it published an opinion of bishop Iona (Cherepanov) of Obukhov, who voiced his position on people 'stuck in the internet': 'it is tempting to give up on them: well, what could you do? They are vegetables. They can only click on the keyboard and stare at the blinking screen. And nevertheless they are also God's creatures' (Sen'chukova 2013). Soon thereafter two more articles appeared on this website promoting 'digital detox': one of them was sportively entitled 'The Easy Way to Stop [Using] the Internet', parodying an announcement about harm of smoking (Solov'ev 2014; Solov'ev 2013).

'Addiction' to the internet has been substantially explored by hieromonk Anatolii Berestov, M.D., who once was the head pediatric narcologist of Moscow. He considers 'net-mania' [*setemaniia*] as a specific case of compulsive gambling, manifested in pointless rambling in virtual space. In his view, a 'net-holic' or 'info-holic' [*setegolik, infogolik*] is characterized by physiological as well as psychological deviancies such as red eyes, neural and physical exhaustion, lachrymation and yawning. 'Net-mania' has a spiritual dimension as well because 'net-holics', trained to endlessly gratify their Ego and disregard interests and feelings of their fellow creatures, gradually transform their personalities towards demonism (Berestov 2007: 25; Berestov 2013: 54–71). Demonization of humans in the internet is demonstrated by a picture published by pravmir.ru, which illustrates an article about internet-'addiction' (**figure 1.2**). A child with crooked fingers and a face, distorted in frenzy, is playing a computer game, so that the image of Darth Vader, the prince of the dark side of the Force in the *Star Wars* universe, is gleaming on the child's forehead (note that according to Revelation 14:9 the mark of the beast is on the forehead or in the hand).

Figure 1.2. 'Internet-dependency: Reasons, Characteristics, Risks.'
Source: http://www.pravmir.ru/internet-zavisimost-prichiny-priznaki-riski/.
Accessed 1 April 2015.

These views fall within the tradition of securitization of human biology in post-Soviet Russia. Accusations of pedophilia on the internet are all too frequent in 'Ortho-net', reaching the scale of a moral panic. Social networks are called, for example, the 'paradise for pedophiles', where 60% of children supposedly have been confronted with obscene advances (Dobrosotskikh 2013: 112, 116). The care for minors justifies the most radical proposals about curbing the internet (Dobrosotskikh 2013: 7). The most spectacular success in this direction has been achieved by the League for the Safe Internet (*Liga Bezopasnogo Interneta*), established in January 2011 by the Orthodox tycoon Konstantin Malofeev, and with the support from the Ministry of Communication of the Russian Federation. The League has also been seconded on the highest level in the Moscow Patriarchate, and personally by Patriarch Kirill (Legoida 2013). This organization set itself the task of fighting pedophilia and extremism on the internet, mostly by hands of the so called 'cyber-warriors' [*kiberdruzhinniki*], who provoke and expose pedophiles, and report about contentious websites to the law-enforcement bodies.

Anonymity and pseudonymity

From the time of its first advances into our everyday life in the 1980s, digital technologies captivated people's imagination by the possibility to create and nurture multiple identities. Unlike many other religious users (e.g. neo-Pagans—see Cowan 2005), blogging Orthodox priests consider anonymity as the single most important dissatisfaction with the internet when they reflect upon their online experience. In Orthodox understanding, the name is integral, perhaps even the central part of the personality, so anonymity is sinning against God's creation. Thus, according to Georgii Kovalenko, the former head of the Information department of Ukrainian Orthodox Church of Moscow Patriarchate, the internet harbors the threat of splitting personality, so that a human is being alienated from herself. Father Georgii symbolically links doubling of personalities in virtual reality with crucifying Christ the second time (Kovalenko 2012).

Here we approach the core of the Orthodox theological reflection on digital culture: personalities in the online environment become masks and the internet in general, a theater (i.e. the digital double), is absolutely unacceptable for Orthodox religious sensibility. Patriarch Kirill says that a human has not been created to live with two faces, so when we don a mask, it is so unnatural, that it will have ruinous repercussions on the integrity of our personalities.[11] The anonymity in the internet, as hegumen Spiridon Balandin argues, allows us to create multiple masks and identities and thereby transforms our online presence into a 'solo performance' theater, which is nothing else but 'evil and senseless actorism (*akterstvo*), unworthy of a Christian' (Balandin 2009). Sergei Bulgakov's *Philosophy of Name* gives us a glimpse into Orthodox understanding of pseudonymity as 'acting with names' [*akterstvo v imeni*], and 'acting can never pass unpunished: the mask eats away the heart, the 'role' [eats away] the soul, which comes loose on its axis and loses its integrity and solidity' (Bulgakov 1953: 173–174). Sergei Bulgakov points out the mystical aspects of re-naming in, for example, the practices of monastic life, when a monk takes vows, he or she changes names *and* personalities, because the whole of his or her life and its purpose will change too (Bulgakov 1953: 172). Renaming in any other contexts is, therefore, a mere mocking of the monastic feat, that is something absolutely deprecatory.

In online discussions the word 'onanim' has been coined (e.g. p-m-makarios@lj 22.06.2012), a blend of 'onanist' and 'anonym', expressing irritation and contempt towards anonymity. For an Orthodox believer anonymity is associated with evil will and the unbridling of human sinful nature. In the words of Makarii Markish, 'anonymity... becomes a universal cover for all evil' (Markish 2013a; kolokolchik-lby@lj 26.01.2010). For Orthodox bloggers anonymity is first and foremost a token of irresponsibility and a lack of trust. For example, archimandrite Alipii (Svetlichnyi) remarks that he has never befriended anybody without a realistically looking picture of their avatar: 'it is hard for me to speak to a person who does not show their face. It is absurd to communicate with a kitten or a flower' (Svetlichnyi 2014). Sometimes priests-bloggers explicitly warn their readers to enter into discussion with them only under their real names, not nicknames: 'it is too uncomfortable to converse with anonyms,' as archpriest Aleksandr Kosach says in the opening of his online diary (kosach@lj n.d.)

---

11 'A human can be spiritually healthy and [maintain] integrity when [s]he has only one face, that is [s]he should be as [s]he is.' (Kirill 2012d: 304).

In the same vein, deacon Andrei Kuraev, the super-star of the Orthodox blogging, avers that he does not see anonymous internet users as humans because for him they are being reduced from 'personalities' to their 'bare' textual expressions (diak-kuraev@lj 13.09.2010; Kuraev 2006). Similarly father Dimitrii Karpenko juxtaposes a 'real human' to 'lines of the text' on the screen: 'the real human is something, for the sake of which God has come to this world'—not for the sake of 'flickering pixels', so de-virtualization should be viewed as the ultimate objective for any computer mediated communication (otez-dimitriy@lj 23.08.2008). Following this line of argumentation, father Dimitrii commended 'de-virtualization' as a process in which a human substitutes someone who 'has previously been only a user for me' (otez-dimitriy@lj 01.07.2017). Laying a particular emphasis on the necessity to start virtual communication from de-virtualization (presviter-ds@lj 11.08.2007; 1.03.2008), Orthodox bloggers try to overcome distrust towards disembodied online interlocutors by means of physically embodying them.

The tangle of metaphors, associated with the Orthodox imagery about evil sides of the internet, is illustrated by **figure 1.3**, which shows a man in a Guy Fawkes ('Anonymous') mask, sitting in front of two computers in a menacing pose in gusts of smoke and with a bottle of beer. The picture, decorating the article by archpriest Igor Prekup on pravmir.ru, was intended to convey the message about a threat of anonymous online interlocutors and their malevolent scheming against people's security, moral integrity, and cultural authenticity (Prekup 2014).

Figure 1.3. 'Anonymous Online.'
Source: http://www.pravmir.ru/proshhenie-v-internete-virtualnoe-proshhenie/.
Accessed 1 April 2015.

The Orthodox imagery about anonymity and pseudonymity is reflected in the decision of the Council of the Russian Orthodox Church of Old-Believers, which forbade its priests to use pseudonyms in the internet in 2007 (Krug 2008: 4). The ROC did not follow these steps, but many of its clerics, such as archpriest Dimitrii Karpenko, the member of Synodic Department of Mission, benevolently commented on the decision of their more conservative brethren (Karpenko 2008). Egor Kholmogorov, the arch-conservative popular journalist, hurried to call this decision as the 'main rule of [an Orthodox believer's behavior in] the internet' (holmogor@lj 22.10.2007). Soon afterwards, father Vladimir Vigilianskii, the head of the Press Service Department of Moscow Patriarchate, reproached Orthodox priests who conceal their real names and ranks in blogs (Vigilianskii 2008). On July 22, 2010 Patriarch Kirill made an appearance in front of the believers of Odessa, where he explicitly shared his view on anonymity: 'I categorically disapprove of priests who anonymously participate in online discussions' (Kirill 2010). Soon thereafter Patriarch Kirill elaborated on the ethics of anonymity in the way that it gave a false impression of impunity and lack of responsibility (Kirill 2012b).

In 2011 the Holy Synod of the Orthodox Church in America adopted 'Guidelines for Clergy Use of Online Social Networking'. This document does not develop an explicit policy on anonymity, but it strongly encourages priests to keep online 'friendship' only with those whom they 'have met before in person' (Guidelines 2011). On this basis archpriest Aleksandr Avdiugin worked out his own recommendations for priests, who are active online. These recommendations pronounce more clearly on the unacceptability of anonymity, admonishing clergy that they must write in their profile page their real name, rank and place of service (Avdiugin 2011). The former head of the Public Relations Department of Moscow Patriarchate, archpriest Vsevolod Chaplin voiced an idea to divide the internet into two zones: the zone of 'security', where users can enter only after verification of their identity and under their real names, and the 'danger zone', where anonymity is tolerated (Dobrosotskikh 2013: 25, 110). In 2011 he vocally stated that anonymity in the internet represents a threat to society and 'a moral crime', because it destroys cultural norms of communication (Chaplin 2011). The campaign against anonymity of priests in the internet has yielded good results; our sample of blogs shows that most of them are easily attributable to real men either by explicit statements or by linking them to other social accounts where the names of the owners are displayed.[12]

Conclusions

It should be noted that 'digital anxiety' is by no means unique for the ROC. 'Digital risks' have been spotted in many public debates, rang-

---

12 A few blogs of priests do not have a clear statement on personality of the owners, but they refer to other accounts in social networks, from which it is easy to figure out who is the author (e.g. http://priest-vit.LiveJournal.com/profile#/profile._Accessed 1 April 2015.). Only two blogs in the sample are anonymous (http://peregrin.LiveJournal.com/profile#/profile, and http://prostopop.LiveJournal.com. Accessed 1 April 2015.).

ing from post-Marxist critics of the decentralized and pervasive power of the 'Empire' (Hardt and Negri 2001; Zizek 1997: 127–159) to religious fundamentalists worldwide (Barzilai-Nahon and Barzilai 2005). Following the 'social construction of technology' theory, this paper demonstrates how the ROC's intellectuals stitched the arguments of 'digital skeptics' with Orthodox traditional imagery and theology. 'Domesticating' of the internet by the Russian Church is problematic because new media sensitize the Orthodox believers to the rooted ideas of the sinful—even demonic—'doubling of the world', playing with names and de-sacralization of the religious truths.

To be sure, these concerns are not outlandish, because they resonate with the widespread sensation that if the internet 'is the message' (cf. McLuhan 1964), then this message is not neutral to our identity and quest for a meaningful life. More than that, the internet may well contribute to people's disempowerment and losing their 'true selves' in the communicative environment, which is all too often addicting, sometimes mediating an external manipulative power (Morozov 2011), and commonly facilitating dysfunctional 'brutalized' struggle for recognition instead of a meaningful deliberation (Honneth 2012).

The way, how the ROC views the 'digital anxiety', however, differs from the mainstream interpretation of a threat to human freedom and subjectivity. What accounts for this difference is the specific relation of the ROC to (post) secularism. As a national Church which reclaims cultural hegemony in the Russian society, it frames the 'digital anxiety' as a moral panic resulting from the fear of losing control over the spheres which have recently been re-appropriated by the ROC as its exclusive domain: namely, the sphere of the Russian culture and society's basic values. The 'instrumentalization' interpretation of the internet as merely a means for the Church mission collides with the vague feeling that the ROC's engagement with new media is like opening a Pandora's box, whose insidious forces could be much more destructive for the ROC's hegemony than even decades of the overt suppression of religiosity in the Soviet Union.

References

Agadjanian, Alexander and Kathy Rousselet (2005). 'Globalization and Identity Discourse in Russian Orthodoxy.' In *Eastern Orthodoxy in a Global Age: Tradition Faces the Twenty-First Century*, edited by Viktor Roudometof, Alexander Agadjanian, and Jerry Pankhurst. Walnut Creek: AltaMira Press.

Aleksii II (Ridiger), Patriarch (2006). 'Obrashchenie Sviateishego Patriarkha... Aleksiia II... na eparkhial'nom sobranii 2006 goda'. Accessed 1 April 2015: http://www.patriarchia.ru/db/text/173887.html.

Alfeev (Mitropolit Ilarion) (2012). 'Chem bol'she pozitiva budet v sredstvakh massovoi informatsii, tem men'she budet agressii'. Accessed 1 April 2015: http://www.patriarchia.ru/db/text/2486832.html.

Avdiugin, Aleksandr (2011). 'Sviashchenniki v internete: Bud' chelovekom'. Accessed 1 April 2015: http://www.pravmir.ru/svyashhenniki-v-internete-bud-chelovekom/.

Baab, Lynne (2012). 'Toward a Theology of the Internet: Place, Relationship, and Sin.' In *Digital Religion, Social Media and Culture: Perspectives, Practices and Futures*, edited by Pauline H. Cheong, Peter Fiescher-Nielsen, Stefan Gelfgren, and Charles Ess. New York: Peter Lang: 277-291.

Bakardjieva, Maria and Georgia Gaden (2012). 'Web 2.0 Technologies of the Self.' *Philos. Technol.*, 25: 399–413.

Balandin, Spiridon (2009). 'Anonimnost' v internete: Vzgliad sviashchennika'. Accessed 1 April 2015: http://www.pravmir.ru/anonimnost-v-internete-vzglyad-svyashhennika/.

Barzilai-Nahon, Karine and Gad Barzilai (2005). 'Cultured Technology: The Internet and Religious Fundamentalism.' *The Information Society: An International Journal* 21, no. 1: 25–40.

Bauman, Zygmunt (2000). *Liquid Modernity.* Cambridge: Polity.

Belovolov, Gennadii (2010). '100 dnei v internete'. Accessed 1 April 2015: http://leushino.ru/lj/30536_2010-07-15.html.

Berestov, Anatolii (2007). *Skrytye iskusiteli, ili Snasti na potrebitelia (V plenu informatsionnykh tekhnologii.* Moscow: Tsentr Ioanna Kronshtadtskogo.

Berestov, Anatolii [Hegumen N] (2013). 'Korni kiberzavisimosti'. In Dobrosotskikh 2013.

Bijker, Wiebe (1987). *The Social Construction of Technological Systems: New Directions in the Sociology and History of Technology*, edited by W. Bijker, Thomas Hughes and Trevor Pinch. Boston: MIT Press.

Bowles, Anna (2006). 'The Changing Face of the Runet.' In *Control + Shift: Public and Private Usages of the Russian Internet*, edited by Henrike Schmidt, Katy Teubener and Natalja Konradova. Norderstedt: Books on Demand Gmbh.

Bulgakov, Sergei (1953). *Filosofiia imeni*. Paris: YMCA-Press.

Campbell, Heidi (2005). 'Spiritualizing the Internet: Uncovering Discourses and Narratives of Religious Internet Usage.' *Online–Heidelberg Journal of Religions on the Internet* 1, no. 1: 1–26.

Campbell, Heidi (2010a). 'Religious Authority and the Blogosphere.' *Journal of Computer-Mediated Communication*, no. 15: 251–276.

Campbell, Heidi (2010b). *When Religion Meets New Media*. New York: Routledge.

Campbell, Heidi (2012). 'How Religious Communities Negotiate New Media Religiously.' In *Digital Religion, Social Media and Culture: Perspectives, Practices and Futures*, edited by Pauline H. Cheong, Peter Fiescher-Nielsen, Stefan Gelfgren, and Charles Ess. New York: Peter Lang: 81–96.

Chaplin, Vsevolod (2011). 'Protoierei Chaplin nedovolen tsariashchei anonimnost'iu v Internete'. Accessed 1 April 2015: http://www.interfax.ru/russia/207059.

Chaplin, Vsevolod (2013). 'Protoierei Chaplin prizval k informatsionnomu postu'. Accessed 1 April 2015: http://lenta.ru/news/2013/03/14/lent.

Chapnin, Sergei (2006). 'Blagaia vest'' i 'plokhie novosti': Khristianskie tsennosti v mass-media'. *Tserkov' i vremia* 35, no. 2: 225–226.

Cheong, Pauline (2013). 'Authority.' In *Digital Religion: Understanding Religious Practice in New Media Worlds*, edited by Heidi Campbell. London: Routledge.

Chinkova, Elena (2011). 'Sviashchennye voiny' v Internete: Mozhet li Tserkov' ochistit' Set' ot skverny?' *Komsomol'skaia Pravda v Vologde*, 22 June.

chudo_iva (2013, 4 July). 'Dorogaia Irina'. LiveJournal. http://chudo-iva.LiveJournal.com/598678.html?thread=7746966 (accessed 1 April 2015).

Cowan, Douglas (2005). *Cyberhenge: Modern Pagans on the Internet*. New York and London: Routledge.

diak-kuraev (2010, 13 September). 'Ia – sushchestvo mnogosloinoe'. *LiveJournal*. http://diak-kuraev.LiveJournal.com/2010/09/13/ (accessed 1 April 2015).

Dobrosotskikh, Alla (2013). *Etot plokhoi khoroshii internet*. Moscow: Danilovskii blagovestnik.

Engelke, Matthew (2010). 'Religion and the Media Turn.' *American Ethnologist* 37, no. 2: 371–379.

Etkind, Aleksandr (1998). *Khlyst: Sekty, literatura i revolutsiia.* Moscow, Helsinki: NLO.

fater-go (2004, 21 February). 'Spasibo vsem'. *LiveJournal.* http://fater-go.livejournal.com/2004/02/21/ (accessed 1 April 2015).

Girard, René (1972). *La violence et le sacré.* Paris: Grasset.

Gorham, Michael. 2014. 'Politicians Online: Prospects and Perils of "Direct Internet Democracy"'. In *Digital Russia: The Language, Culture and Politics of New Media Communication*, edited by M. Gorham, I. Lunde, and M. Paulsen. London: Routledge: 233–250.

griger (2005, 14 December). 'Vsio-taki zhzh...' *LiveJournal.* http://griger.Livejournal.com/2005/12/14/ (accessed 1 April 2015).

Guidelines (2011) for Clergy Use of Online Social Networking. Accessed 1 April 2015: http://oca.org/PDF/official/2011-guidelines-for-clergy-use-of-online-social-networking.pdf.

Hardt, Michael and Antonio Negri (2001). *Empire.* Cambridge, Mass: Harvard University Press.

Hipps, Shane (2009). *Flickering Pixels: How Technology Shapes Your Faith.* Grand Rapids, Mich.: Zondervan.

Hjarvard, Stig (2008). 'the Mediatization of Religion: A Theory of the Media as Agents of Religious Change.' *Northern Lights,* 6(1): 9–26.

holmogor (2007, 22 October). 'Razgovory o samoopredelenii russkogo naroda'. LiveJournal. http://holmogor.LiveJournal.com/2166717.html (accessed 1 April 2015).

Honneth, Axel (1995). *Struggle for Recognition: The Moral Grammar of Social Conflicts.* Cambridge: Polity Press.

Honneth, Axel (2012). 'Brutalization of the Social Conflict: Struggles for Recognition in the Early 21st Century.' *Distinktion: Scandinavian Journal of Social Theory,* 13(1): 5–19.

Howard, Robert (2011). *Digital Jesus: The Making of A New Christian Fundamentalist Community on the Internet.* New York: New York University Press.

Iakovleva, Olga (2012). *Novye tekhnologii i prava cheloveka.* Riazan': Zierna.

ierey-masim (2011, 15 April). 'Internet kak pole dlia propovedi blagoi vesti'. *LiveJournal.* http://ierey-masim.LiveJournal.com/2011/04/15/ (accessed 1 April 2015).

iereys (2008, 10 April). 'Antivirtualotopiia'. LiveJournal. http://iereys.liveJour nal.com/2008/04/10/ (accessed 1 April 2015).

Ignatii (Pologrudov), Metropolitan (2014). 'Ia khotel byt' prosto monakhom'. Accessed 1 April 2015: http://www.pravoslavie.ru/smi/69868.htm.

Kapalin, Kliment (2012). 'Vystuplenie na vstreche so studentami Moskovskogo universiteta pechati'. Accessed 1 April 2015: http://www.patriarchia.ru/db/text/2062578.html.

Karpenko, Dimitrii (2008). 'Idite i propoveduite... v Zhivom Zhurnale?' *Tserkovnyi vestnik* 19, no. 392.

Khroul, Viktor (2012). *Religion and Media in Russia: Functional and Ethical Perspectives.* Saarbruecken: Lambert Academic Publishing.

Kirill (Gundiaev), Patriarch (2008). 'Pravoslavnoe edinstvo i pravoslavnoe svidetel'stvo v sovremennom mire'. *Tserkov' i vremia* 44, no. 3.

Kirill (Gundiaev), Patriarch (2009). 'Doklad... na Eparkhial'nom sobranii g. Moskvy'. Accessed 1 April 2015: http://www.patriarchia.ru/db/text/1346 828.html.

Kirill (Gundiaev), Patriarch (2010). 'Otvety ...Patriarkha Kirilla na voprosy v khode vstrechi s obshchestvennost'iu Odessy'. Accessed 1 April 2015: http://www.patriarchia.ru/db/text/1227718.html.

Kirill (Gundiaev), Patriarch (2012a). 'Sviateishii Patriarkh Kirill obsudil...' Accessed 1 April 2015: http://www.patriarchia.ru/db/text/1996244.html.

Kirill (Gundiaev), Patriarch (2012b). 'Sovremennyi chelovek legko poddaetsia illiuzii anonimnosti v Internete'. Accessed 1 April 2015: http://www.pravmir.ru/patriarx-kirill-sovremennyj-chelovek-legko-poddaet sya-illyuzii-anonimnosti-v-internete/.

Kirill (Gundiaev), Patriarch (2012c). 'Vystuplenie... na zakrytii V mezhdunarodnogo festivalia pravoslavnykh SMI' (http://www.patriarch ia.ru/db/text/2560589.html).

Kirill (Gundiaev), Patriarch (2012d). *Taina pokaianiia: Velikopostnye propovedi (2001–2011).* Moscow: Izd-vo Moskovskoi Patriarkhii.

Kirill (Gundiaev), Patriarch (2015). 'Propoved' Sviatei'shego Patriarkha Kirilla posle velikogo povecheriia'. Accessed 1 April 2015: http://www.patriar chia.ru/db/text/4002375.html.

Klein, Hans K. and Daniel L. Kleinman (2002). 'The Social Construction of Technology: Structural Considerations.' *Science, Technology, and Human Values* 27, no. 1: 28–52.

kolokolchik-lby (2010, 26 January 2010). 'Instruktsiia dlia Ivana'. *LiveJournal.* http://kolokolchik-lby.LiveJournal.com/2010/01/26/ (accessed 1 April 2015).

kolokolchik-lby (2014, 17 February). 'Internet-zavisimost'. LiveJournal. http://kolokolchik-lby.LiveJournal.com/2014/02/17/ (accessed 1 April 2015).

Korchagin, Longin (2006). 'Internet daet nam bezgranichnye vozmozhnosti dlia propovedi'. Accessed 1 April 2015: http://www.patriarchia.ru/db/text/153300.html.

kosach (n.d.) 'Bio'. *LiveJournal.* http://kosach.LiveJournal.com/profile (accessed 1 April 2015).

Kovalenko, Georgii (2012). 'Pokaius', postavliu na saite svechu – v Seti bystro ia za grekhi zaplachu'. Accessed 1 April 2015: http://kp.ua/life/352048-pokauis-postavlui-na-saite-svechu-v-sety-bystro-ya-za-hrekhy-za plachu.

Krotov, Iakov (2013). 'Protiv chitatelei'. Accessed 1 April 2015: http://blog.krotov.info/2013/11/05/против-читатетелей/.

Krotov, Iakov (n.d.) 'Dlia pishushchikh v moi blog'. Accessed 1 April 2015: http://krotov.info/yakov/varia/auto/mail_blog.htm#2.

Krug, Pavel (2007). 'Chto takoe 'Pravoslavnyi Internet'. *NG-Religii* 197, no. 3. Accessed 1 April 2015: http://ruskline.ru/monitoring_smi/2007/02/21/chto_takoe_pravoslavnyj_internet/.

Krug, Pavel (2008). 'Primirenie ili kapituliatsiia'. *NG-Religii,* 29 October.

kruglov-s-g (2008, 16 April). 'Sviashchennik v bloge'. *LiveJournal.* http://kruglov-s-g.LiveJournal.com/2008/04/16/ (accessed 1 April 2015).

Kuraev, Andrei (2006). 'Pravoslavie: Elektronnaia versiia'. *NG-Religii* 14, no. 186.

Kuz'micheva, Aleksandra (2014). 'Internet otbiraet veru? Opros ekspertov.'. Accessed 1 April 2015: http://www.pravmir.ru/internet-otbiraet-veru-opros-ekspertov/.

Laclau, Ernesto and Chantal Mouffe (1985). *Hegemony and Socialist Strategy.* London: Verso.

Lee, Joonseong (2009). 'Cultivating the Self in Cyberspace: The Use of Personal Blogs among Buddhist Priests.' *Journal of Media and Religion* 8, no. 2: 97–114.

Legoida, Vladimir (2011). 'Predsedatel' Sinodal'nogo informatsionnogo otdela privetstvuet ideiu otvetstvennosti internet-SMI'. Accessed 1 April 2015: http://www.patriarchia.ru/db/text/1534151.html.

Legoida, Vladimir (2012). 'Nado bol'she informirovat' i men'she kommentirovat''. Accessed 1 April 2015: http://ekklezia.ru/blogi/839-v-leg oyda-nado-bolshe-informirovat-i-menshe-kommentirovat.html.

Legoida, Vladimir (2013). 'Liga bezopasnogo interneta reshaet ochen' vazhnye zadachi'. Accessed 1 April 2015: http://www.patriarchia.ru/db/text/3280362.html.

Legoida, Vladimir (2014). 'Tserkov' – eto vse my'. Accessed 1 April 2015: http://www.patriarchia.ru/db/text/3727033.html.

Lepin, Sergii (2014). 'My 'voiuem' ne protiv internet, a za internet'. Accessed 1 April 2015: http://42.tut.by/395131.

Lövheim, Mia (2013). 'Identity.' In *Digital Religion: Understanding Religious Practice in New Media Worlds,* edited by Heidi A. Campbell. New York: Routledge.

Markham, Annette (1998). *Life Online: Researching Real Experience in Virtual Space.* Walnut Creek: AltaMira Press.

Markish, Makarii (2013a). 'Internet kak novoe izmerenie v okolotserkovnom prostranstve'. In Dobrosotskikh 2013.

Markish, Makarii (2013b). 'Internet bez durakov i umnye s internetom '. In Dobrosotskikh 2013.

Markish, Makarii (2014, 3 October). Correspondence with Makarii Markish from the archive of the author.

McLuhan, Marshall (1964). *Understanding Media: The Extensions of Man.* London: Routledge.

Molloy, Patricia (2013). 'Sexual Predators, Internet Addiction, and Other Media Myths: Moral Panic and the Disappearance of Brandon Crisp.' In *The Ashgate Research Companion to Moral Panics,* edited by Charles Krinsky. Farnham: Ashgate: 190–201.

Morozov, Evgeny (2011). *The Net Delusion: The Dark Side of Internet Freedom.* London: Allen Lane.

Morozov, Nektarii (2013). 'Luchshii moderator – khristianskaia sovest''. In Dobrosotskikh 2013.

Nishnikov, S. A. (2012). 'Filosofiia imeni v Rossii: stanovlenie i sovremennaia diskussiia. Chast' 2. Imiaslavie i platonizm v tvorchestve A. F. Loseva'. *Prostanstvo i vremia* 1, no. 7.

o-paulos (2007, 23 April). 'Khotite pozabavit'sia?' *LiveJournal.* http://o-paulos.LiveJournal.com/2007/04/23/ (accessed 1 April 2015).

Odarenko (2012), 'Evangelie ot Facebook. Ukrainskaia tserkov' aktivno perekhodit v internet'. Accessed 1 April 2015: http://focus.ua/society/245089/#society/245089/?&_suid=14124457025600700041483442056 1.

Osborne, Vasily (2004). 'Pravoslavnyi runet na preput'e.' *Tserkovnyi vestnik* 277, no. 1–2.

Osnovy (2008) ucheniia Russkoi Pravoslavnoi Tserkvi o dostoinstve, svobode i pravakh cheloveka. In *Tserkov' i vremia* 44, no. 3: 146–150.

otets-gennadiy (2010, 15 July). '100 dnei v internete'. *LiveJournal.* http://otets-gennadiy.LiveJournal.com/2010/07/15/ (accessed 1 April 2015).

otez-dimitriy (2008, 23 August). '*Russkii vzgliad* ob internete'. *LiveJournal.* http://otez-dimitriy.LiveJournal.com/2008/08/23/ (accessed 1 April 2015).

otez-dimitriy (2017, 1 July). 'F.A.Q.' *LiveJournal.* http://otez-dimitriy.LiveJournal.com/225502.html (accessed 1 April 2015).

p-m-makarios (2012, 22 June). 'Onanim'. *LiveJournal.* http://p-m-makarios.LiveJournal.com/27203.html?thread=698435#t698435 (accessed 1 April 2015).

Paulsen, Martin and Vera Zvereva. 2014. "Testing and Contesting Russian Twitter." In *Digital Russia: The Language, Culture and Politics of New Media Communication*, Vol. 53, edited by M. Gorham, I. Lunde, and M. Paulsen. London: Routledge: 88–104.

pfarrer-tom (2014, 30 October). 'Informatsiia'. *LiveJournal.* http://pfarrer-tom.LiveJournal.com/2014/10/30/ (accessed 1 April 2015).

Prekup, Igor (2014). 'Proshchenie v internete – "virtual'noe proshchenie"?' Accessed 1 April 2015: http://www.pravmir.ru/proshhenie-v-internete-virtualnoe-proshhenie/.

presviter-ds (2007, 11 August). 'O virtual'nom obshchenii'. *LiveJournal.* http://presviter-ds.LiveJournal.com/2007/08/11/ (accessed 1 April 2015).

presviter-ds (2007, 2 January). 'Nachalo'. *LiveJournal.* http://presviter-ds.LiveJournal.com/2007/01/02/ (accessed 1 April 2015).

presviter-ds (2008, 30 March). 'Devushka pela v tserkovnom khore'. *LiveJournal.* http://presviter-ds.LiveJournal.com/2008/03/30/ (accessed 1 April 2015).

pretre-philippe (2010, 5 July). 'O nekotorykh chertakh internet-diskussii'. *LiveJournal.* http://pretre-philippe.LiveJournal.com/2010/07/05/ (accessed 1 April 2015).

priest-vit (2022, 4 January). 'Nachalo...' *LiveJournal.* http://priest-vit.LiveJournal.com/2654.html (accessed 1 April 2015).

prostopop (2014, 26 April). 'Smert' est' vsio i smerti net'. *LiveJournal.* http://prostopop.LiveJournal.com/2014/04/26/ (accessed 1 April 2015).

Radde-Antweiler, Kerstin (2013). 'Authenticity.' In *Digital Religion: Understanding Religious Practice in New Media Worlds*, edited by H. Campbell.

Roesen, Tine and Vera Zvereva. 2014. "Social Network Sites on the Runet." In *Digital Russia: The Language, Culture and Politics of New Media Communication*, Vol. 53, edited by M. Gorham, I. Lunde, and M. Paulsen. London: Routledge: 72–87.

saag (2009, 13 October). 'Nekotorye metody preodoleniia krizisa v missionerstve'. *LiveJournal.* http://saag.LiveJournal.com/2009/10/13/ (accessed 1 April 2015).

Savel'ev, Dimitrii (2014a). 'Zhit' nado v real'nom mire'. Response to Viktoria's question, 24 January at 1:56 pm. Accessed 1 April 2015: http://vk.com/id236954592#/topic-25505827_24475069?post=49877.

Savel'ev, Dimitrii (2014b). 'Mne ne nravitsia etot proekt'. Response to Mikhail's question, 5 May 2014 at 1:47 pm. Accessed 1 April 2015: http://vk.com/topic-25505827_24475069?post=57035.

Schmidt, Henrike and Kathy Teubener (2006). '(Counter) Public Sphere(s) on the Russian Internet,' in *Control + Shift: Public and Private Usages of the Russian Internet*, edited by Henrike Schmidt, Katy Teubener and Natalja Konradova. Norderstedt: Books on Demand Gmbh.

Sen'chukova, Mariia (2013). 'Missionerskii pokhod protiv virtual'noi real'nosti'. Accessed 1 April 2015: http://www.pravmir.ru/missionerskij-poxod-protiv-virtualnoj-realnosti/.

Shul'zhenko, Pavel (2015). 'Pomolimsia za Novorossiiu'. Accessed 1 April, 2015: https://www.youtube.com/watch?v=whs3pU-PcFo#t=446.

Sloterdijk, Peter (1987 [1983]). *Critique of Cynical Reason.* Minneapolis: University of Minnesota Press.

Smith, Samantha and Simon Cole (2013). 'MyMoralPanic: Adolescents, Social Networking, and Child Sex Crime Panic.' In *The Ashgate Research Companion to Moral Panics,* edited by Charles Krinsky. Farnham: Ashgate: 207–223.

Solov'ev, Dmitrii (2013). 'Son razuma rozhdaet biomonstrov'. Accessed 1 April 2015: http://www.pravmir.ru/son-razuma-rozhdaet-biomonstrov.

Solov'ev, Dmitrii (2014). 'Legkii sposob brosit' Internet'. Accessed 1 April 2015: http://www.pravmir.ru/legkij-sposob-brosit-internet/.

Spadaro, Antonio (2014). *Cybertheology: Thinking Christianity in the Era of the Internet.* New York: Fordham University Press.

Stout, David (2012). *Media and Religion: Foundations of an Emerging Field.* London: Routledge.

Svechnikov, Dionisii (2012). 'Nuzhna li pravoslavnomu khristianinu virtual'naia chasovnia?' Accessed 1 April 2015: http://www.pravmir.ru/virtualnaya-chasovnya/.

Svetlichnyi, Alipii (2014). 'Zafrendit' arkhimandrita'. Accessed 1 April 2015: http://www.pravoslavie.ru/guest/73633.htm.

Tiurenkov, Mikhail (2013). 'Protoierei Maksim Kozlov: Sotsseti – eto brosanie slov v bezdonnyi kolodets'. Accessed 1 April 2015: http://portal-kultura.ru/articles/symbol-of-faith/3804-protoierey-maksim-kozlov-sotsseti-eto-brosanie-slov-v-bezdonnyy-kolodets/?print=Y&CODE=3804-protoierey-maksim-kozlov-sotsseti-eto-brosanie-slov-v-bezdonnyy-kolodets.

Uffelmann, Dirk. 2014. 'Is There a Russian Cyber Empire?' in *Digital Russia: The Language, Culture and Politics of New Media Communication*, Vol. 53, edited by M. Gorham, I. Lunde, and M. Paulsen. London: Routledge: 266–284.

Uminskii, Aleksii (2013). 'V sotsial'nykh setiakh spaseniia ne proiskhodit'. Accessed 1 April 2015: http://www.pravoslavie.ru/news/60909.htm.

Vigilianskii, Vladimir (2008). 'Konflikty v Tserkvi'. *Tserkovnyi vestnik* 388–389, no. 15–16.

Vol'tskaia, Tat'iana (2015), 'Drugoi Savchenko' / 'Another Savchenko'. http://www.svoboda.org/content/article/26860050.html (accessed 11 January 2016).

Vries, Hent de (2001). 'In Media Res: Global Religion, Public Spheres, and the Task of Contemporary Comparative Religious Studies.' In H. de Vries and S. Weber (eds.) *Religion and Media* (Stanford: Stanford U Press).

Ziebertz, Hans-Georg and U. Riegel (2009). 'Europe: A Post-Secular Society? International Report.' *International Journal of Public Theology* 13, no. 2: 293–308.

Zizek, Slavoj (1997). *The Plague of Fantasies*. London: Verso.

Zizioulas, John (1985). *Being as Communion: Studies in Personhood and the Church*. Crestwood: Darton, Longman and Todd.

Zizioulas, John (2006). *Communion and Otherness: Further Studies in Personhood and the Church*. London: T & T Clark.

Chapter 2.
Russia's Immoral Other: Moral Panics and the Antichrist on Russian Orthodox Websites[1]

Magda Dolińska-Rydzek
Justus-Liebig University in Giessen

Introduction

'We are living in times preceding the Apocalypse', 'The kingdom of the Antichrist is approaching': these and many other analogous statements can be found on various Russian Orthodox websites, with Patriarchia.ru, Pravoslavie.ru, or Pravmir.ru among them. Indeed, in recent years, the internet has become both an important source of information and a powerful channel of social and cultural communication, with the Russian Orthodox Church and its believers being no exception. By means of numerous websites, blogs, and forums, the highest Orthodox clerics and rank-and-file priests not only negotiate and disseminate religious identity, but also influence the Orthodox discourse within the Russian society. Hence, although there are no precise data, one can freely assume that online platforms with hundreds of thousands of daily visits produce a resonance much wider than an average diocesan offline newspaper with a circulation of about one hundred copies. In this context, Orthodox online discourses, which interpret contemporary events in the light of the Apocalypse, have a much greater appeal than their offline equivalents. In consequence, by reaching a vast number of receivers, various contemporary events and phenomena described as the Antichrist's work, such as globalisation, development of digital technologies, or a 'moral laxity' of present-day societies, easily become objects of moral panics.

---

[1] I would like to thank to Mikhail Suslov for his insightful comments and suggestions which enabled me to significantly improve this article, and to Marcin Trojszczak for making it more readable.

The fact that the legend of the Antichrist, which has its roots in the Apocalypse of John, is employed in Orthodox ecclesiastical discourses on the above-mentioned websites is not a coincidence. This apocalyptic figure, which belongs to the Russian 'eschatological myth' (Berdiaev 1945), plays an idiosyncratic role within the Russian cultural imaginary. It invokes, for instance, various religious and political conceptions important for forming Russian statehood. The Antichrist is an important figure for such conceptions as the Holy Rus'[2], Moscow the Third Rome[3], or the myth of holy places such as Kitezh and Belye vody, where, as it is believed, the Antichrist will finally be defeated (de Lazari et al. 1999: 58–68). In all of these conceptions Orthodox Russia plays a central, yet paradoxical role: Russia is the place where the Antichrist was born and, at the same time, the place where he will be ultimately defeated (Isupov 1995). Nevertheless, traditionally, Russia and the Russian Orthodox Church have been portrayed as the only guardians of true (Orthodox) Christianity.

There are two re-interpretations of the Antichrist figure considered to be the most important for the Russian cultural imaginary: the Grand Inquisitor from Fëdor Dostoevsky's novel *The Brothers Karamazov* (1880) and the image of the ecumenical ruler Apollo from the *Short Story about the Anti-Christ* by Vladimir Solov'ev (1900). Dostoevsky portrays the Grand Inquisitor as a false Messiah, who preaches distorted Christian values; Solov'ev, in turn, describes Apollo as a pacifist, philanthropist, and humanist, who will, paradoxically, lead Europe and its values to final collapse. Interestingly, the image of Apollo, the 'Eurasian Antichrist', not only alludes to the vision of Dos-

---

2   A conception of Holy Rus' appeared for the first time in the sixteenth century in the letters of Andrei Krubskii to Ivan the Terrible. Over the centuries, it has been understood not only as a future project of 'the divine Russia' and social ideal, but also a category of Russian self-identification (Suslov 2013).
3   The conception of Moscow the Third Rome, developed by the monk Philotheus in the sixteenth century, portrayed Moscow as the Third Rome, the Kingdom of God where the Tsar—God's icon on Earth and the guardian of Russian (Orthodox) values—was to defeat the anti-Christian forces (Przybył 1999). Further, the conception of Moscow the Third Rome is not only a specifically Russian example of a Christian vision of the Katechon (Eingström 2015), but also a foundation of many Russian geopolitical strategies (see for example Kirillov 1914; Duncan 2000; Uspenskii and Lotman 1996).

toevsky, but also situates it in a historical dimension. In this context, the Antichrist appears to be not only a religious concept or a rhetorical figure, but, above all, the real threat (Dostoevsky 1967; Solov'ev 1990 [1900]; Kornblatt 1996; Kornblatt and Rosenshield 2000; Kantor 2001; Kostalevsky 1997).

Furthermore, throughout the centuries, the figure of the Antichrist in Russia has undergone numerous historical and semantic metamorphoses and, in consequence, gradually moved from religious to political discourse. Indeed, the Antichrist in Russia was viewed as the antagonist of Christ, the false Messiah, and the Tsar-Usurper, as well as an embodiment of evil forces and an individual who incorrectly interprets true Christian values (Korolev 2004; Ewertowski 2010; Dolińska-Rydzek, 2015; Dolińska-Rydzek and van den Berg, 2015). Russian historians and thinkers have seen the Antichrist not only in individual figures such as Ivan the Terrible, Napoleon, Peter the Great, or Lenin, but also in social and political systems: Bolshevism (Nikolai Berdiaev), liberal democracy (Konstantin Leont'ev), even the Tsarist autocracy (Dmitrii Merezhkovskii). For these reasons, in Russian culture the Antichrist has become a kind of mythological image that lost its primal meaning. By being employed in philosophy, literature, politics, and 'secular ideologies', it has gradually grown apart from its original religious context (Akhmetova 2010). Finally, the figure of the Antichrist, used to define ideological and political antagonists has been viewed as the immoral Other, who symbolises moral deprivation and who intends to destroy moral order of Orthodox Russia.

In this article, I will explore discourses that attempt to spawn moral panics over various contemporary events by employing the figure of the Antichrist, which not only denotes the immoral Other, but also refers to the vast Russian cultural imaginary. To this end, a keyword search and a frequency analysis will be employed. I will discuss dominant discursive tendencies found in 660[4] records con-

---

[4] On the websites analysed, the query 'Antichrist' had the following numbers: on Patriarchia.ru, 66 hits from January 2004 to September 2015; on Pravoslavie.ru, 96 hits from January 2002 to September 2015; on Pravmir.ru, 498 hits from August 2002 to September 2015.

taining the word 'Antichrist'[5] and published on the three most popular Russian Orthodox websites—Patriarchia.ru, Pravoslavie.ru, and Pravmir.ru[6]—from January 2002 to September 2015. The analysed materials include various examples of Orthodox online discourses, namely articles, interviews, parables, as well as re-interpretations of ancient prophecies written both by the Russian Orthodox hierarchs and priests, and people representing 'the Orthodox outlook', such as a professor of theology, Aleksei Osipov, or an artist, Andrei Yakhnin.

In my analysis, I will draw on discourse theory put forth by Laclau and Mouffe, as well as the notion of moral panics, taken in this context as a metaphor and a useful analytical tool and not a consistent methodology. For this reason, I will first explain the main premises of the chosen theories and discuss how, in the Orthodox online discourses, the notion of the Antichrist not only serves as the immoral Other, but also becomes a floating and even an empty signifier. Further, I will provide an overview of exemplary materials in which I will demonstrate how Orthodox online discourses, by referring to the notion of the Antichrist and happenings of the Apocalypse, attempt to create moral panics. Finally, I will present some concluding remarks on how these discursive strategies may be understood and valued.

Russian Antichrist:
the immoral other becomes an empty signifier

The present analysis is framed by discourse theory put forth by Ernesto Laclau and Chantal Mouffe (2001 [1985]), who argue that the perception of reality, as well as the character of physical objects, is constructed, mediated, and negotiated only through discourse. Moreover, whereas hegemony is analogous to discourse, they both

---

5   The records containing the word 'anti-Christian' (*antikhristianskii*) were not taken into account.
6   According to the Rambler.ru ratings in September 2015, all three websites were among the five most popular in the category of 'religion'. Although the results change over time, the most up-to-date Rambler.ru ratings may be found here: http://top100.rambler.ru/navi/?stat=0&pageCount=30&resourceId=558177&theme=554&page=1&view=short#558177

stand for a fixation of meanings in a particular moment; hegemony achieves this fixation only across antagonistic discourses. However, no discourse is capable of conquering a permanent hegemony in a field of discursivity where various knowledge regimes and ideologies compete (Laclau and Mouffe 2001: vii–xix; Jorgensen and Phillips 2002: 48).

In this context, moral panic, understood as 'an episode, often triggered by alarming media stories and reinforced by reactive laws and public policy, of exaggerated or misdirected public concern, anxiety, fear, or anger over a perceived threat to social order' (Kinsky 2013: 1), can be approached as resulting from various overlapping discourses of politics, popular culture, and media (Thompson 1998: 5).[7] When it comes to the role of the media, as Stanley Cohen (1972: 30) argues, it not only sets the agenda and selects deviant or problematic events, but also transmits images and sharpens the rhetoric of the moral threat. In consequence, emotionally-laden, unified discourse is produced. Furthermore, media narratives are in a deep resonance with cultural archetypes, collective myths, and exaggerated stereotypes. In fact, demonised 'folk devils' are constructed mostly out of familiar and recognizable elements. Thus, moral panic cannot be approached as a separate episode that occurs in a cultural vacuum. Rather, it should be interpreted in relation to systems of social regulations and representations which arise from broad socio-cultural tensions. Thereby, even new objects of moral panics are often just 'camouflaged versions of traditional well-known evils' (Cohen 1972: viii; Goode and Ben-Yehuda 2009: 27). In this context, one can argue that in analysed discourses modern moral panics around the Antichrist are, in fact, just new 'masks' of the 'ancient' moral panics stemming directly from the Book of Revelation.

In addition, through discursive operations based on hostility and rejection, 'folk devils' are not only perfect candidates for monster status, but also serve as the immoral Other, a threat to everything that is held sacred or fundamental to a given community (Thompson

---

[7] See, for instance, Cohen 1972; Thompson 1998; Goode and Ben-Yehuda 2009; Krinsky 2013 for more on the concept of moral panics.

1998: 9). In this context, moral panics are based upon a social antagonism, in which the morally superior 'We' are threatened by the immoral 'Them'. Further, since the immoral Other is perceived as negating 'our' identity, the relation between 'We' and 'Them' becomes a site of political antagonism which is a reaction to discursively constructed, yet imagined, dangers and threats (Mouffe 1993). In other words, political antagonism, as well as hostility towards the immoral Other, are legitimized by a need to protect moral values represented by a dominant group within society.

Drawing on the fact that Orthodoxy is considered to be the historical religion in Russia, the Russian Orthodox Church uses it as an argument in struggles over hegemonising Russian field of discursivity. Further, the argument of historical ties with the Russian state and culture enables the Russian Orthodox Church to stage moral panics and, at the same time, portray itself as the only guardian of morality in Russia. For this reason, the Russian Orthodox Church not only uses a great potential to mobilise and consolidate Russian society embedded in discursive strategies that create moral panics, but also aims at hegemonising the notion of the Antichrist to impose a certain meaning on it. In consequence, the 'Antichrist' not only becomes a floating signifier, which obtains different meanings in different contexts, but also, derived from the original meaning, is turns into an empty signifier—a 'signifier without a signified' (Laclau and Mouffe 2001; Laclau 1996: 35–46; Jorgensen and Phillips 2002).

According to Laclau (1996), an empty signifier[8] emerges as a result of limits within the system of signification, and, paradoxically, both enable and hamper the process of signification. In consequence, antagonistic logics of exclusion spread to both sides of the limits: what is excluded as a negativity, constitutes positive identity within the system. This identity, however, is rendered: difference expresses itself as a difference, and, at the same time, it cancels itself out. Hence, the empty signifier, which is 'a signifier of pure can-

---

8 Although Laclau gives notions of 'democracy', 'freedom', and 'free market' as examples of empty signifiers, in the analysed discourses the notion of the Antichrist works in the very same way.

cellation of all difference' (Laclau 1996: 38), emerges. Indeed, Laclau suggests that in a social context the very existence of empty signifiers, whose temporary signified are the result of political competition, is an inevitable condition of hegemony. Thus, whereas different discourses try to hegemonise it, an empty signifier is not only an expression of contingent and consensual character of this struggle, but also designates an absence, an unfulfilled reality—the other side of the system, its anti-thesis.

In this context, by employing the 'Antichrist' as an empty signifier, the community of Russian Orthodox believers is defined on the basis of social antagonism, based on the dialectical interplay between what Laclau and Mouffe (2001: xiii) call 'logics of equivalence' and 'logics of difference'. The former operates by dividing social space and accumulating meanings around two antagonistic extremes; the latter has an opposite function—it 'weakens and displaces a sharp antagonistic polarity' (Howarth et al. 2000: 11). The result of this ambiguity is the fact that the community of Russian Orthodox believers, constructed by the Orthodox online discourses in opposition to the Antichrist, becomes more cohesive. Indeed, since the 'Antichrist' becomes the limit of the system of signification, all differences within that system are ignored: the positive identity exists only in relation to the excluded negativity. Hence, the positive identity of the Orthodox believers exists only in relation to the Antichrist, the excluded immoral Other, who represents everything 'We' are not. Finally, the Antichrist figure, which throughout the centuries has been used in Russian discourses to define ideological and political antagonists (de Lazari 2004), becomes the embodiment of social fantasies, fears, and anxieties, and is perceived both as a constant historical threat (Korolev 2004) and as the immoral Other, who intends to destroy the only truly Christian state—Orthodox Russia.

Moral panics and the Antichrist on Runet

In recent years, the internet has become not only a universal source of information, but also a powerful channel of social and cultural communication. In this respect, the Russian Internet is no exception: it is one of the most important and widely developed parts of the global Web. The fact that in 2015 Runet's estimated audience reached 73.8 million users proves that it has a significant impact on the dynamics of social and political communication in the Russian Federation, and beyond (RIF+KIB 2015; Etling et al. 2010).[9] Furthermore, by developing into 'a fully-fledged mass medium of a national significance', Runet has become a distinctive battlefield where various discourses and ideologies, i.e. liberal and conservative, dominant and oppositional, religious and secular, compete with each other (Kondratova and Schmidt 2014: 36). As far as the religious context is concerned, Runet serves as a unique environment where religious identity is being constructed. Numerous websites, *Youtube* channels, and *Facebook* profiles not only provide unlimited access to ecclesiastical and religious readings, but also serve as platforms of communication for fellow believers (Goroshko 2012).

Interestingly, the relation of analysed online discourses towards the new media development is highly ambiguous. Indeed, the perception of the internet and new technologies among both the clergy of the Russian Orthodox Church and the Orthodox believers is not only twofold, but also often refers to the Antichrist imagery. On the one hand the internet is perceived as a useful channel of social and cultural communication, on the other hand it is viewed as an immoral, even satanic, tool; a tool of the Antichrist. In his contribution to this volume, Mikhail Suslov argues that it is the deepest irony 'that providing unlimited access to the discourse, the Internet seems to undermine something dear to the hearts of the Orthodox Christians, namely the hierarchy of knowledge, and the underlying hierarchy of power'. For this reason, the attitude represented by analysed discourses is not only highly ambiguous, but also overloaded with emotions, prejudices and speculations.

---

9   Since Runet is a social phenomenon defined by aspects as diverse as geography (Russian Federation), language (websites in Russian), or culture and tradition (Konradova and Schmidt 2014), its status as an object of research is complicated (Etling et al. 2010).

Contrary to former Patriarch Aleksii II, Patriarch Kirill (2013) represents rather negative attitude towards the internet. In fact, he describes it as 'the great temptation', which destroys the monastery life. According to him in the modern world, which 'turns away from God' and in which the concept of sin gradually disappears, the truth becomes more and more relative. And when there is no absolute truth, when the truth is confused with lies, the arrival of the Antichrist is near. In this context, only the strict monastic traditions can save the souls of humanity. In recent years, however, the internet full of 'sinful and seductive' contents, penetrated the monastery life. In consequence it not only influences the consciousness of millions of people, but also leads to degradation of the Christian values and to the victory of the sin.

In the interview on the independent TV channel *Dozhd'*, deacon Andrei Kuraev (2013), a representative of the more liberal wing of the Russian Orthodox Church, appealed to the words of Patriarch Kirill. Although Kuraev agrees with the Patriarch that in many cases the association of the internet with sin is reasonable, he argues that this way of perceiving new media is considerably simplified. According to Andrei Kuraev, the internet has its 'dark sides' and, 'just like lives of individuals and societies, is a vast space in which there is a lot of passion, intrigues, sins, not only of a sexual nature'. Further, it plays an important role in disseminating processes of globalization which, according to many Orthodox believers, will lead to the rules of the Antichrist. On the other hand, however, Kuraev evokes the words of Patriarch Aleksii II, who insisted that every Orthodox church should have a website and that each priest should own a mobile phone. In this context the internet, serving as a platform for 'online pastoring', would enable promoting the 'Orthodox outlook' on different social, political, and economical events and issues among many more Orthodox believers.

Also, an utterance of the priest Vladimir Vigilianskii (2009) indicates the ambiguous relation of the clergy of the Russian Orthodox Church towards the internet. When asked what are the parallels between the introduction of the global information network and the apocalyptic signs of the coming of the Antichrist, he said:

> The Internet, like any other means of communication, works in two ways. It can be used to promote depravation as well as to preach the truths of the Gospels. The global network is nowadays the cheapest and the most efficient means of delivering information. In this area, until 2012, the Church has experienced certain obstacles. As I have already observed, one could even speak about the information blockade, not to mention liberal censorship. Over the past few years, however, the Orthodox portals and websites have emerged and the blockade was overpassed. Nowadays, there are hundreds of websites that should be taken into account. It is now impossible to slander the Church with impunity. The Orthodox voice on the Internet sounds like any other; it cannot be stifled (Vigilianskii 2009).

In other words, as long as the internet is used to promote truly Christian (Orthodox) values, it is perceived as a useful platform of communication which can unite people against the Antichrist and his kingdom. Nevertheless, as Vigilianskii[10] argues, to reach the believers, the Russian Orthodox Church had to overcome numerous obstacles, liberal censorship being one of them.

Yet another example of ambiguous attitude towards digital technologies is the opinion of archpriest Pavel Velikanov (2009), the chief editor of the portal Bogoslov.ru, who claims that many Orthodox hierarchs and believers do not consider communication via computer to be a real one. On the contrary, online communication is viewed as nothing more than yet 'another stage of a universal apostasy' that separates people and distorts the relations between them, which will ultimately lead to the coming of the Antichrist. This approach, as Mikhail Suslov asserts, arises from perceiving new media as sinful or even a demonic 'doubling of the world' rooted in the Orthodox tradition. In fact, reproducing such a view by referring to the Antichrist imagery may lead to escalation of moral concerns, and even panics about the new media development. Nevertheless, in spite of this, the Russian Orthodox Church still uses the internet as an instrument to disseminate its outlook.

---

10 Interestingly, later on Vigilianskii would commit a 'virtual suicide' by closing all his social network accounts.

The Apocalypse, the Antichrist and eschatological fears

In fact, on the analysed Orthodox websites, discourses about new technologies are not the only ones that refer to the legend of the Antichrist and the happenings of the Apocalypse. On the contrary, apocalyptic references are relatively popular. They not only serve as indicators of 'moral laxity' of the contemporary world, but also intensify moral panics over the events considered to be dangerous to the moral, political, and social order of Orthodox Russia. Moreover, the apocalyptic tensions are intensified around such dates as the new millennium, 06/06/2006, or 12/12/12. As an outcome, numerous analyses, parables, and re-interpretations of ancient prophecies tend to portray the present-day phenomena as symptoms of the near Apocalypse.

Throughout the centuries, in the Orthodox tradition there have been various interpretations of the Apocalypse. Aleksandr (Mileant) (2006), the bishop of the Russian Orthodox Church outside Russia, argues that they can be divided into four categories. Whereas some of them associate visions and symbols of the Apocalypse with 'the last times'—the coming of the Antichrist, the second coming of Christ, and the Last Judgement—others perceive the Book of Revelation only as a metaphor of historical events. The third group of interpretations, in turn, tries to find actual apocalyptic prophecies in contemporary events. Finally, there are explanations according to which the Apocalypse is just an allegory, a parable with a deep moral sense.

For Aleksandr (Mileant) all these interpretations are nevertheless not mutually exclusive, but, rather, they complement each other. As a result, the Apocalypse, together with the coming of the Antichrist, is perceived as a real danger that, sooner or later, will occur. Many Orthodox hierarchs claim that the closer the end of the world is, greater economical, political, and geopolitical challenges will emerge (Sysoev and Maksimov 2009; Legoida 2011). According to Patriarch Kirill, it is a symptom of the growing power of the sin in the modern world. Hence, in 2011, during the celebration of the second anniversary of the Patriarchal enthronement, he said:

> The times we live in—are difficult, even though there is no such thing as easy times. Nevertheless, the difference between these times and previous ones is their apocalyptic tension, probably the power of sin has never ruled over the human race so much as it rules now. And we know that where sin wins, the devil emerges. And we know that if the sin wins across the human race, the Antichrist will arrive (Kirill 2011).

In other words, together with the domination of sin, apocalyptic tensions grow—the arrival of the Antichrist becomes real. For this reason, the Russian Orthodox Church has to stand up against the 'multiplication of evil' and, no matter how strongly criticized, tenaciously preach the Word of God in all areas of everyday life (Kirill 2011). Interestingly, this kind of narrative shows how the Russian Orthodox Church attempts to hegemonise Russian discourse: positioning itself as the only guardian of Orthodox morality, and, thus, of the cohesion within the Russian state, it tries to maintain and enhance the dominant position.

The interpretations of the Antichrist are, in fact, as vague and ambiguous as those of the Apocalypse. As Aleksandr Moiseenkov (2012), a publicist of the Orthodox journal *Foma* argues, even though we know very little, almost nothing, about the coming of the Antichrist, we can make some predictions relying on the Book of Revelation. In keeping with Orthodox Church tradition, Moiseenkov portrays the Antichrist as 'an ordinary man, who in spite of that will be endowed with tremendous power, talents and strength. This strength will be given to him by satan'.[11] Even so, the Antichrist will be perceived as 'a very nice person, the perfect Tsar who has been dreamt about by all civilizations' (Moiseenkov 2012). Besides being a great politician, diplomat, and orator, he will easily attract mankind. Many people will not only welcome his arrival, but also joyfully accept the 'seal of the Antichrist' and renounce God. In the kingdom of the Antichrist, however, there will be no space for Christ and, in conse-

---

11 In all cases, the words 'Satan' and 'Antichrist' are written with a lower case letter in accordance to the original quotations.

quence, all Christians, and especially Orthodox Christians, will be persecuted (Moiseenkov 2012; Vinogradov 2012; Kuraev 2012). Interestingly, in portraying the Antichrist as a great politician, orator, and philanthropist, who receives his power from Satan, there are echoes of the image created by Solov'ev in his *Short Story of the Anti-Christ* and directly refers to the Russian cultural imaginary.

As archpriest Aleksandr Shargunov (2011), the head of the Moral Revival of the Fatherland Committee argues, the consequences of the rules of the Antichrist will be tragic. He asserts:

> The appearance of the Antichrist will be sudden. Life will fall apart in all spheres: financial and economic crisis as well as decline of morals will reach their limits. Within one hour the International Monetary Fund, the European Union, the World Council of Churches, the United Nations and other similar organizations will sign an agreement which will give supreme power to the new dictator, who will be honoured as the last and only hope for mankind (Shargunov 2011).

For these reasons, Patriarch Kirill (2011) defines the Antichrist as 'a personified evil' and warns of his imminent coming to the temporal world. According to Patriarch Kirill, the main symptoms that the kingdom of the Antichrist is approaching include the propagation of liberal secular ideology and the popularity of post-modernist philosophy, in which truth and falsehood, good and evil, sainthood and sin are confused. In other words, civilization will reach its end when there will be no clear division between values and anti-values (Strel'chik and Kirill 2009; Kirill 2010).

In this context, Russia is again portrayed as a guardian of the true, Orthodox faith. For instance, Lev Arshakian, a priest and a member of the Commission for Social Work in the Vicariate of new territories of Moscow, argues:

> Despite its present problems and confusions in the social, political and national life, Russia still remains the stronghold and guardian of the Orthodox faith; the holding force that prevents the rules of the antichrist; and, I am grateful to God and the Mother of God, that I am a cleric of the Russian Orthodox Church (Vinogradov 2014).

In other words, Russia is traditionally perceived as the only guard of the Orthodox faith, and the Orthodox faith itself is the only salvation from the Antichrist and his kingdom. The Russian Orthodox Church, in turn, is the only guardian of morality, capable of withstanding the anti-Christian influences 'from across the ocean' and withstanding the spirit of modern times, 'the spirit of the Antichrist' (Golovko 2014). This kind of narrative corresponds with the geopolitical concept of the Third Rome, according to which Orthodox Russia is supposed to be the 'soul of the world', the Katechon[12]—the last place on earth where, due to allegiance to true Christian values, human souls will be protected from the evil powers of the Antichrist (Przybył 1999; Broda 2011; Eingström 2015).

Globalisation, electronic documents and the number of the Beast

A fervent and continuously re-appearing discussion about the introduction of electronic documents is yet another example of how Orthodox online discourses create moral panics by referring to the Antichrist figure and happenings of the Apocalypse. Furthermore, since together with the development of digital media the division between 'offline' and 'online' has become obsolete, the discussion on electronic documents shows how these two realms tend to interpenetrate each other.

The discussion on the value-added tax identification number (VATIN) and its demonic character was first triggered by an article 'Against the VATIN: Special Edition ordered by the Orthodox Christians' by Hieromonk Rafail (Berestov) published (offline) in April 2000. In his article, the Athonite elder, as Hieromonk Rafail is often called, argued that a barcode included in the VAT identification number (INN) is, in fact, the number of the Beast from the Book of Revelation. Thus, the VATIN is a 'seal of the Antichrist' and a sign of his rules in the world. For this reason, people who will accept new elec-

---

12 From the Greek, 'the withholding'.

tronic documents will 'lose the grace of God and the energy of demons will dwell in them' (Dobrosotskikh 2001).

The categorical assertion, often perceived as theological, not only was adopted by radical circles of the Russian Orthodox Church as 'the final verdict', but also strongly influenced the 'consciousness of the Orthodox masses' (Dobrosotskikh 2001). In consequence, electronic documents, e.g. the VATIN, credit cards, and new types of passports, are interpreted as forerunners of the kingdom of the Antichrist (Schevkunov 2000; Gordeev 2001; Kaverin 2001). Furthermore, a growing number of both offline and online articles condemning the acceptance of electronic documents and equating them with the 'seal of the Antichrist' led to an outbreak of moral panics.[13] In many Russian cities, Orthodox believers came out to the streets to protest. They rejected not only electronic documents and biometrical passports, but also international organizations and agreements, e.g. the World Trade Organization and Schengen (*'Okolo 300 veruiushchikh priniali uchastie v mitinge protiv zakonoproekta o sbore personal'nykh dannykh'* 2005). Moreover, in some churches, moral panics reached an extreme level: there have been 'underground groups' persuading people to abandon everything and flee 'to the forest' (Moiseenkov 2012).

More liberal circles of the Russian Orthodox Church have unequivocally criticized such views and incitements (Dobrosotskikh 2001; Sokur 2007; Reidman 2010; Sysoev and Maksimov 2009 and many others). According to Orthodox hierarchs, to conquer a human soul the Antichrist does not need barcodes or electronic documents. In fact, only by turning away from Christ and an excessive attachment to the material world can lead to the Antichrist's triumph. Hence, instead of worrying about worldly goods, people should turn to the Christian (Orthodox) faith. Only then the Antichrist will not be able to enslave or harass them (Sysoev and Maksimov 2009; Postolov 2013).

---

13 The discussion about electronic documents within the Russian Orthodox Church has been extensively discussed within academia. See for example Verkhovskii (2001).

Furthermore, according to the more liberal Orthodox hierarchs, spreading moral panics over such issues as electronic documents and barcodes can have dangerous consequences for the unity of the Russian Orthodox Church. In fact, as an elder and a seer, Archimandrite Zosima (Sokur) (2007) asserts, it may lead to a split and, in fact, allow the Antichrist to establish his kingdom. Interestingly, many critics argue that the core of such moral panics is actually a move away from Christian values or a decay within the Russian Orthodox Church. In consequence, although their subject has been changed, moral panics are still being created.

In 2012, in order to alleviate the conflict over electronic documents, the Orthodox Church hierarchy published a document, 'On the position of the Orthodox Church in relation to the appearance and prospects of development of new technologies of identification' (*Proekt dokumenta "O pozitsii Tserkvi v sviazi s poiavleniem i perspektivami razvitiia novykh tekhnologii identifikatsii lichnosti"* 2012). The main aim of the statement was to 'comprehensively respond to numerous questions about potential dangers posed by new technologies' (Maler and Sen'chukova 2012). Nevertheless, moral panic was barely tempered. Although the official position of the Russian Orthodox Church has been recognized, there are still concerns about digital identification that involves gathering and using personal information, and, in consequence, may result in influencing and manipulating people (Gordeev 2001; Chaplin 2011).

Moreover, introducing the electronic system of identification has been perceived as a symptom of globalisation, and considered to be an anti-Christian process that leads to the establishment of an Antichrist kingdom. For instance, Aleksei Osipov, a professor at the Moscow Theological Academy, claims:

> Because it is the process of preparing the Kingdom of the Antichrist, human life will soon be controlled and then dealt with. This is slavery and Christians have always been against social slavery. But globalisation is the process from which we will never flee. It is one of the most powerful harbingers of the approaching end of the world (Osipov 2015).

In other words, the unavoidable processes of globalisation aim at not only enslaving mankind, but also at establishing the kingdom of the Antichrist on earth. As a result of an anti-Christian ideology, globalisation will lead to a 'New World Order', governed by a supranational centre. According to Archimandrite Alipii (2001), the dominant religion in the global empire will be the New Age, which is 'deeply hostile towards Christianity'. In consequence, Christianity—and above all, Orthodoxy—will be persecuted. Patriarch Kirill (2010) also pairs globalisation with chasing Orthodox Christianity. For him, it is, however, a result of secular neutrality, which, in fact, is anti-Christian, and, thus, leads to 'Christianophobia'.

Interestingly, moral panic has also escalated over ecumenism, which is believed to entail similar dangers as globalisation. For instance, for archpriest Aleksandr Il'iashenko (2004), a director of the portal Pravmir.ru, the 'successes' of ecumenism are in fact 'another step towards the Apocalypse'. He argues:

> The ecumenical movement is one of the symptoms of the Antichrist with his main objective: to bring all religions together and to unite humanity in this way. People will then be deprived of their individual, national and religious qualities. After all, if you want to control the 'herd' with ease, it is necessary to paint everyone with the same brush (Il'iashenko 2004).

In order to have authority over mankind, the Antichrist will deprive people of their individual characteristics. Furthermore, since the Greek word 'anti' means not only 'against', but also 'instead', the Antichrist will act against Christianity and call himself 'Christ', even though he is no such person. As an outcome, people will bow to the false Messiah, as it is already allegedly done in the West (Il'iashenko 2004).

Pussy Riot, modern culture, and other moral dangers

On February 21, 2012, Pussy Riot's performance, 'Punk Prayer—Mother of God, Chase Putin Away!', staged in Moscow's Cathedral of Christ the Saviour was yet another subject to moral panic in the Russian Federation. Indeed, the music video, in which members of the group perform a 'punk prayer' asking the Virgin Mary to get rid of Putin, quickly went viral and triggered a fierce discussion not only in the ecclesiastical, but also in political circles. Interestingly, at the beginning the reactions of the Russian Orthodox hierarchs were rather moderate. Despite initial leniency, members of Pussy Riot were soon turned into enemies of the Russian Orthodox Church, and even the Russian state (Borkowicz 2012).[14] In fact, the most radical Orthodox discourses portrayed them as servants of the Antichrist, intending to destroy the moral, social, and political order in the Russian Federation (Iurevich 2012).

The Russian Orthodox Church discussed both the performance and the question of support to members of Pussy Riot. According to archpriest Dmitrii Smirnov (2012), a chairman of the Patriarchal Commission on Family and Maternity Protection, 'when it comes to those who defend the group Pussy Riot, there is blood of two women whose murderer wrote a slogan in defence of participants of the 'punk prayer' on the wall, and the sawn crosses, and all other anti-Church actions which exist and will exist'.

Furthermore, according to the head of the Information Department of the Diocese of Kineshma, archpriest Andrei Efanov (2012), the immoral deed of 'these women' should not be minimized. He argues that by letting blasphemers dance in churches is their first triumph in the war against the Russian Orthodox Church. Therefore, as he argues, Orthodox believers have only one choice:

> Either we continue to follow the path of self-destruction, or together we start to return. Return to the world in which Russia, with its spiritual and cultural values, can oppose the destructive influences of external ideological propaganda. The final point of no return for society—the kingdom of the Antichrist. It seems that we are approaching it (Efanov 2012).

Here, Pussy Riot's performance is seen as a result of external ideological propaganda whose main intention is to jeopardise moral cohesion of the Orthodox Russia. Interestingly, this opinion is shared

---

14 On the Pussy Riot's case see more in Bernstein 2013; Willems 2013; Etkind 2014; Prozorov 2014 and many others.

by Aleksandr Dugin[15] (2012), who suggests that it was the 'totalitarian ideology of liberalism' that pushed the members of Pussy Riot to blasphemy. According to Dugin, Pussy Riot's deed is not only against the Russian Orthodox Church and the Russian authorities, but also against Russian traditions in general. Furthermore, since Pussy Riot turned against the majority of Russian citizens, people who support the group are, in fact, against the Russian Federation. In consequence, Pussy Riot and their supporters have been turned into 'folk devils'—the immoral Other who threatens the vulnerable Orthodox majority.

However, Pussy Riot's case was not the only example of creating moral panic over performances critical of the Russian authorities and the Orthodox Church, or dealing with religious issues in an artistic, and controversial, way. Over the last few years, there have been at least three art exhibitions—'Caution, religion!' (2003), 'Two-word/Dialogue' (2010) and 'Sculptures which we do not see' (2015) —that triggered a heated discussion both in Russian society and among the clergy of the Russian Orthodox Church (Ryklin 2006; *Dvoeslovie prodolzhaetsia* 2010; Saltykov 2015). Whereas 'Caution, religion!' and 'Two-word/Dialogue' displayed contemporary art, 'Sculptures we do not see' was the exhibition of sculptures by nonconformist artists persecuted during the Soviet era. All three exhibitions dealt with questions of religion and religiosity. For this reason, two of the exhibitions, 'Caution, religion!' and 'Sculptures which we do not see', were destroyed by anonymous perpetrators, called 'Orthodox activists'. Moreover, radical circles of the Russian Orthodox Church described the exhibitions as 'blasphemous actions'. They were considered not only as signs of persecution of the Orthodox Church in contemporary Russia, but also as forerunners of the imminent coming of the Antichrist. It was claimed (*Dvoeslovie prodolzhaetsia* 2010; Saltykov 2015) the main goal of the organizers

---

15 Aleksandr Dugin—a philosopher, politician, and an academic teacher—is a highly controversial figure. Often associated with the Russian Orthodox Church, he identifies himself as an Old Believer.

was to create conflict, which would lead to the 'spiritual death' of Russian society.

Andrei Yakhnin (2012), an artist, argues that it has been long since modern cultures begin to spread 'the spiritual death and decay'. In fact, many Russian Orthodox hierarchs point out a growing number of anti-Christian phenomena that indicate 'the last days' are approaching. The issues of moral panics not only involve electronic documents, globalisation, and 'anti-art', but also growing Western influences (Kirill 2010; Alfeev 2013; Chaplin 2014; Dugin 2012 and many others). Indeed, Orthodox online discourse describes the West as a space ruled by sin and anti-Christian values. Metropolitan Hilarion of Volokolamsk, for instance, refers to the words of Aleksandr Dugin, who asserts:

> Nowadays the countries of Western Europe are transforming into the Antichrist. In these countries the persecution of Christ, even if sometimes disguised, increases. How else to explain active and deliberate destruction of the institution of the family? How to explain anti-Christian and anti-religious rhetoric of political leaders, their desire to push Christianity to the ghetto, to deprive it of its right to vote (Alfeev 2013).

It is argued that Western Europe, with what is called its secular liberalism, fraudulent humanism, the acceptance of homosexual marriages, and values, which in their core are anti-Christian, gradually transforms into the kingdom of the Antichrist, where Christianity will be persecuted. In this context the image of Western Europe corresponds with Dostoevsky's vision of the Grand Inquisitor, who, in the name of God, distorts true Christian values in order to conquer the power over the world. Moreover, according to this kind of discourse, only the Russian Federation, morally superior to the West, is capable of protecting true Christianity (Sveshnikov 2009; Archbishop Feodosii 2014; Dugin 2012).

Conclusion

Is the Antichrist Russia's immoral Other? On many occasions, the clergy of the Russian Orthodox Church employs the legend of the

Antichrist to set 'moral boundaries' within the society of the Russian Federation. In this context the Orthodox hierarchs as well as file-ranked priests act as 'moral crusaders', who attempt to hegemonise the discourse and, when the opportunity occurs, influence the state legislation in order to make it consistent with their views and interests (Goode and Ben-Yehuda 2009: 122). Moreover, since online discourses reach a vast public, one can assume that they can stage moral panics and trigger hostility, at least at the discursive level, toward the excluded, 'immoral' Other viewed as a threat to moral, social and political stability of the Russian society. In consequence, moral concerns about the imminent coming of the Antichrist are raised to the level of moral panics.

What is more, the Antichrist is in the Russian culture a sign that denotes much more than just an 'immoral Other' or a 'folk devil'. In fact, depending on the context, it refers to a wide range of signifieds: it can denote the enemy, the false Messiah, the West, but also liberal democracy, globalisation, and digital passports. For this reason, the Orthodox online discourse is in deep resonance with the Russian cultural imaginary and deep-rooted archetypes that, throughout the centuries, have been shaping the image of the Other. However, the Antichrist is not only a floating signifier, which obtains its meaning depending on the context. Rather, in consequence of Orthodox online strategies, being deprived of meaning it becomes an empty signifier, just like democracy or freedom. Being the external frontier of a system of signification (the Russian Orthodoxy), the Antichrist represents the negative side of identity constructed within it. In other words, identity of the community of Russian Orthodox believers is based on social antagonism, which is a result of an interplay between 'logics of equivalence' and 'logics of difference'. Accordingly, the Antichrist embodies everything that 'We' are not, and, and at the same time, he is a guarantor of a positive identity. Thus, since 'We' cannot exist without the negative side, the community of the Russian Orthodox believers cannot exist without its immoral Other. Interestingly, this perspective corresponds with the Jungian theory of the self, in which the Antichrist is perceived not as Christ's antithesis but as his 'dark double' (Jung 1978; McGinn 1994). According to Jung, if Christ is the embodiment of the self, the Antichrist symbolises everything that has been denied. These denied 'evil powers', however, are necessary to establish the self as a whole, to make it complete.

Moreover, the legend of the Antichrist, which throughout the centuries has been used to define ideological and political enemies, has become the embodiment of social fantasies, fears, and anxieties. Interestingly, in modern online discourses it is rather a new 'camouflage' of old apprehensions. Further, since 'projecting animosities onto an outside foe' (Schöpflin 2007) helps to maintain social cohesion, the Antichrist has played a very important role in consolidating Russian society against 'imagined dangers', especially in times of crisis and unexpected transitions. Furthermore, by means of substitution, the figure of the Antichrist figure has represented various phenomena. In Orthodox online discourse, for instance, it serves as a representation of globalisation, ecumenism, new technologies, Western influence and many other contemporary events. As an outcome, they are not only situated in a context of the approaching Apocalypse and, accordingly, perceived as ultimate and final, but also become subjects of intensified moral panics. Further, creating and escalating moral panics by referring to the legend of the Antichrist is a powerful and efficient rhetorical tool: it is an easily recognizable symbol even for those who have no theological education. Thus, the figure of the Antichrist serves as a kind of bridge between religious and secular discourses, and, in consequence, has power to consolidate all segments of society.

What is more, as Goode and Ben-Yehuda (2009) maintain, rhetoric strategies that demonise the Other are very attractive to the masses because of the need for 'a cognitive and moral reinterpretation' of a discrepancy between how it is and how it should be. For this reason, in the analysed discourse, the immoral Other portrayed as the Antichrist not only renders this discrepancy meaningful, but also points to the agents responsible for destroying 'the moral coherence of Orthodox Russia'. In this context, appealing to the eschatological and apocalyptic visions aims at explaining complex reality in an easy, more comprehensible way (Akhmetova 2010).

Besides, discursive strategies employed by Orthodox clergy that situate contemporary events in an apocalyptical context are directed at maintaining and reinforcing its ideological influence on Russian society. By ascribing temporary signifieds to the empty signifier—'Antichrist'—the Russian Orthodox Church tries to hegemonise this notion in a political competition and, by means of discourse of 'the besieged fortress', consolidate the identity within the community of Orthodox believers. The Russian Orthodox Church not only preaches the revival of traditional values in order to withstand the Antichrist and his kingdom, but also portrays itself as the only guardian of morality. Finally, the Antichrist, being an empty signifier, becomes both a cause and a result of moral panics.

References

Akhmetova, Mariia (2010). *Konets sveta v odnoi otdel'no vziatoi strane*. Moscow: OGI, RGGU.

Alfeev (Mitropolit Ilarion) (2013). 'Prosvetitel'skaia deiatel'nost' Kirilla i Mefodiia kak zhivaia tserkovnaia traditsiia. Doklad Mitropolita Volokolamskogo Ilariona na iubileinykh Kirillo-Mefodievskikh Chteniiakh'. Patriarchia.ru 25 June 2013. http://www.patriarchia.ru/db/text/3065216.html (accessed 1 November 2015).

Archibishop Feodosii (2014). 'Odnopolnye "braki" govoriat o blizosti Antikhrista'. *Pravoslavie.ru* 1 February 2014. http://www.pravoslavie.ru/smi/68075.htm (accessed 1 November 2015).

Archimandrit Alipiia (2001). 'Globalizatsiia kak instrument apostasii'. *Pravoslavie.ru* 19-20 February 2001. http://www.pravoslavie.ru/sobytia/sbk-inn/alipij.htm (accessed 1 November 2015).

Berdiaev, Nikolai (1948). *The Russian Idea*. New York: Macmillan.

Bernstein, Anya (2013). 'An Inadvertent Sacrifice: Body Politics and Sovereign Power in the Pussy Riot Affair', *Critical Inquiry*, Vol. 40, No. 1, pp. 220–241.

Borkowicz, Jacek (2012). 'Między Putiem a Cyberprawosławiem'. *Nowa Europa Wschodnia* 3–4, pp. 62–68.

Broda, Marian (2011). *"Zrozumieć Rosję"? O Rosyjskiej Zagadce-tajemnicy*. Łódź: Ibidem.

Chaplin, Vsevolod (2011). 'Onlain-koferentsiia Predsedatelia sinodal'nogo otdela po vzaimootnosheniiam tserkvi i obshchestva protoiereia Vsevoloda Chaplina'. *Patriarchia.ru* 17 March 2011. http://www.patriarchia.ru/db/text/1431168.html (accessed 1 November 2015).

Chaplin, Vsevolod (2014). 'Protoierei Vsevolod Chaplin. "Tsennosti i antitsennosti"'. *Patriarchia.ru* 21 May 2014. http://www.patriarchia.ru/db/text/3652103.html (accessed 1 November 2015).

Cohen, Stanley (1972). *Folk Devils and Moral Panics: The Creation of the Mods and Rockers.* London: MacGibbon and Kee.

Dobrosotskikh, Alla (2001). 'Razduvanie isteriki vokrug INN – Put' k raskolu'. *Pravoslavie.ru* 19–20 February 2001. http://www.pravoslavie.ru/sobytia/sbk-inn/dobrosotskih.htm (accessed 1 November 2015).

Dolińska-Rydzek, Magda (2015). 'The Idea of the Antichrist in Russia' in *Apology of Culture: Religion and Culture in Russian Thought,* edited by Artur Mrówczyński-Van Allen, Teresa Obolevitsch, and Pawel Rojek. Eugene, Oregon: Pickwick Publications.

Dolińska-Rydzek, Magda, Mariecke van den Berg (2015). '"Gays as Weapon of the Antichrist": Religious Nationalism, Homosexuality and the Antichrist in the Russian Internet' in *Religious and Sexual Nationalisms in Central and Eastern Europe: Gods, Gays, and Governments,* edited by Srdan Sremac and Reinder Ruard Gazenvoort. Leiden: Brill, 134–153.

Dostoevsky, Fëdor (1967). *The Brothers Karamazov.* London: Heron Books.

Dugin, Aleksandr, Dmitrii Smirnov (2012). 'Dialog pod chasami. V studii filosof Aleksandr Dugin (TK Spas 2012-10-19)'. *Pravoslavie i mir* 15 November 2012. http://www.pravmir.ru/dialog-pod-chasami-v-studii-filosof-aleksandr-dugin-tk-spas-2012-10-19/ (accessed 1 November 2015).

Duncan, Peter (2000). *Russian Messianism: Third Rome, Holy Revolution, Communism and After.* London; New York: Routledge.

'Dvoeslovie prodolzhaetsia' (2010). *Pravoslavie i mir* 7 July 2010. http://www.pravmir.ru/dvoeslovie-prodolzhaetsya/ (accessed 1 November 2015).

Efanov, Andrei (2012). 'Tochka nevozvrata' *Pravoslavie i mir* 24 August 2012. http://www.pravmir.ru/tochka-nevozvrata-2/ (accessed 1 November 2015).

Eingström, Maria (2015). 'Contemporary Russian Messianism and New Russian Foreign Policy', *Contemporary Security Policy,* Vol. 35, No. 3, pp. 356–379.

Etkind, Alexander (2014). 'Post-Soviet Russia: The Land of the Oil Curse, Pussy Riot, and Magical Historicism', *Boundary 2,* Vol. 41, No. 1, pp. 153–170.

Etling, Bruce, Karina Alexanyan , John Kelly, Robert Faris, John Palfrey, and Urs Gasser (2010). 'Public Discourse in the Russian Blogosphere: Mapping Runet Politics and Mobilization'. *Berkman Center Research Publication*, No. 2010-11. http://dmlcentral.net/wp-content/uploads/files/ Public_Discourse_in_the_Russian_Blogosphere_2010.pdf (accessed 1 November 2015).

Ewertowski, Stefan (2010) *Idea Antychrysta w Kulturze Współczesnej: Studium Teologiczne w Wymiarze Interdyscyplinarnym*. Olsztyn: Studio Poligrafii Komputerowej "SQL".

Foucault, Michel (1972). *The Archaeology of Knowledge*. New York: Pantheon Books.

Glynos, Jason, Davit Howarth, Aletta Norval, Ewen Speed (2009). 'Discourse Analysis. Varieties and Methods'. http://eprints.ncrm.ac.uk/ 796/1/discourse_analysis_NCRM_014.pdf (accessed 1 November 2015).

Golovko, Oksana (2014). 'Piat' let sluzheniia Patriakha Kirilla glazami sviashchennikov'. *Pravoslavie i mir* 31 January 2014. http://www.prav mir.ru/pyat-let-sluzheniya-patriarxa-kirilla-glazami-svyashhennikov/ (accessed 1 November 2015)

Goode, Erich, Nachman Ben-Yehuda (2009). *Moral Panics: The Social Construction of Deviance*. Oxford; Cambridge: Blackwell.

Gordeev, Konstantin (2001). 'Lichnye kody kak vyzov antikhristianskoi globalizatsii Khristianskoi Tserkvi'. *Pravoslavie.ru* 19-20 February 2001. http://www.pravoslavie.ru/sobytia/sbk-inn/gordeev.htm (accessed 1 November 2015).

Goroshko Y.N. (2012). 'Rol' religioznoi identichnosti v sotsial'noi i kul'turnoi kommunikatsii (na materialakh veb-saitov Ukrainy i Rossii'. http://www.obta.uw.edu.pl/pliki/akt/Articles.pdf (accessed 1 November 2015).

Howarth, David R., Aletta J. Norval, Yannis Stavrakakis (2000). D*iscourse Theory and Political Analysis: Identities, Hegemonies, and Social Change*. Manchester; New York: University Press.

Il'iashenko, Aleksandr (2004). 'Ekumenizm i globalizatsiia (Chast' 3)'. *Pravoslavie i mir* 9 February 2009. http://www.pravmir.ru/ekumenizm-i-globalizaciya-chast-3/ (accessed 1 November 2015).

Isupov, Konstantin G. (1995) *Antikhrist (Iz istorii otechestvennoi dukhovnosti): Antologiia*. Moscow: "Vysshaia shkola".

Iurevich, Andrei (2012). 'Prot. Andrei Iurevich o "Pank-molebne" i ego posledstviiakh: Oblekites' vo vseoruzhie bozhie'. *Pravoslavie i mir* 6 October 2012. http://www.pravmir.ru/prot-andrej-yurevich-o-pank-moleb

ne-i-ego-posledstviyax-oblekites-vo-vseoruzhie-bozhie/ (accessed 1 November 2015).

Jørgensen, Marianne, Louise Phillips (2002). *Discourse Analysis as Theory and Method*. London; Thousand Oaks; California: Sage Publications.

Jung, Carl Gustav (1978). *Aion: Researches into the Phenomenology of the Self*. Princetown: Princetown University Press.

Kantor, Vladimir (2001). 'Antikhrist ili vrazhda k Evrope: Stanovlenie totalitarizma'. *Oktiabr*, http://magazines.russ.ru/october/2001/1/kant or.html (accessed 20 November 2015).

Kaverin, Nikolai (2001). '2000 let INN'. *Pravoslavie.ru*. http://www.pravosla vie.ru/press/inn2000blagogon.htm (accessed 1 November 2015).

Kirillov, Ivan (1914). *Tretii Rim*. Moscow: tipo-lit. Mashistova.

Konradova, Natalija, Henrike Schmidt (2014). 'From the Utopia of Autonomy to a Political Battlefield of the "Russian Internet"' in *Digital Russia. The Language, Culture and Politics of New Media Communication* edited by Michael S. Gorham, Igunn Lunde and Martin Paulsen. London; New York: Routledge, pp. 34–54.

Kornblatt, Judith Deutsch (1996). 'Soloviev on Salvation. The Story of the "Short Story of the Antichrist"' in *Russian Religious Thought* edited by Judith Deutsch Kornblatt, and Richard F. Gustafson. Madison: University of Wisconsin Press.

Kornblatt, Judith Deutsch, Gary Rosenshield (2000). 'Vladimir Solovyov: Confronting Dostoevsky on the Jewish and Christian Questions', *Journal of American Academy of Religion*, Vol. 68, No. 1, pp. 69–98.

Korolev, Vardan B. (2004) 'Obraz Antikhrista v russkoi istoriosofskoi mysli'. *Pravaia vera* 19 January 2004. http://www.pravaya.ru/faith/11/74 (accessed 1 November 2015).

Kostalevsky, Marina (1997). *Dostoevsky and Soloviev: the Art of Integral Vision*. New Haven: Yale University Press.

Krinsky, Charles (2013). *The Ashgate Research Companion to Moral Panics*. Farnham, Surrey, Burlington: Ashgate.

Kuraev, Andrei (2012). 'Kogda nastupit konets sveta?' *Pravoslavie i mir* 2 December 2012. http://www.pravmir.ru/kogda-nastupit-konec-sveta/ (accessed 1 November 2015).

Kuraev, Andrei (2013). 'Protodiakon Andrei Kuraev: Govoria o vrede interneta, Patriarkh pytaetsia presech' obrazovanie gruppirovok vnutri Tserkvi (+VIDEO)' Pravoslavie i mir 9 June 2013. http://www.pravmir.ru/ protodiakon-andrej-kuraev-govorya-o-vrede-interneta-patriarx-pytaetsyapresech-obrazovanie-gruppirovok-vnutri-cerkvi/ (accessed 15 November 2015).

Laclau, Ernesto, Chantal Mouffe (2001 [1985]). *Hegemony and Socialist Strategy: Towards a Radical Democratic Politics*. London: Verso.

Laclau, Ernesto (1996). *Emancipation(s)*. New York: Verso.

Lazari de, Andrzej; eds (1999). *Idee w Rosji*. Warszawa: Wydawnictwo Naukowe "Semper".

Legoida, Vladimir R. (2011). 'V.R. Legoida: Pravoslavnaia zhurnalistika dolzhna byt' khristotsentrichnoi' *Patriarchia.ru* 15 June 2011. http://www.patriarchia.ru/db/text/1542308.html (accessed 1 November 2015).

Maler, Arkadii, Mariia Sen'chukova (2012). 'Plenum mezhsobornogo prisutstviia. O vyborax Patriarkha, elektronnykh dokumentakh i reabilitatsii narkozavisimykh'. *Pravoslavie i mir* 26 November 2012. http://www.pravmir.ru/plenum-mezhsobornogo-prisutstviya-o-vyborax-patriarxa-elektronnyx-dokumentax-i-reabilitacii-narkozavisimyx/ (accessed 1 November 2015).

McGinn, Bernard (1994). *Antichrist: Two Thousand Years of Human Fascination with Evil*. San Francisco: HarperSanFrancisco.

Mileant, Aleksandr (2006). 'Apokalipsis, ili Otkroveniia Ioanna Bogoslova: Znachenie knigi'. *Pravoslavie i mir* 1 August 2006. http://www.pravmir.ru/apokalipsis/ (accessed 1 November 2015).

Moiseenkov, Aleksandr (2012). 'Propoved' ob Antikhriste vmesto propovedi o Khriste'. *Pravoslavie i mir* 19 December 2012. http://www.pravmir.ru/propoved-ob-antixriste-vmesto-propovedi-o-xriste/ (accessed 1 November 2015).

'Okolo 300 veruiushchikh priniali uchastie v mitinge protiv zakonoproekta o sbore personal'nykh dannykh' (2005) *Patriarchia.ru* 16 November 2005. http://www.patriarchia.ru/db/text/58246.html (accessed 1 November 2015).

Osipov, Aleksei (2015). 'Zaviduiu i zeleneiu, ili Zachem cheloveku svoboda? – Lektsiia Professora Alekseia Osipova'. *Pravoslavie i mir* 17 March 2015 http://www.pravmir.ru/o-svobode-lekcija-osipov/ (accessed 1 November 2015).

Patriarkh Kirill (2010). 'Slovo Sviateishego Patriarkha Kirilla posle vrucheniia diploma pochetnogo doktora Natsional'nogo issledovatel'skogo iadernogo universiteta «MIFI»'. *Patriarchia.ru* 4 March 2010. http://www.patriarchia.ru/db/text/1106371.html (accessed 1 November 2015).

Patriarkh Kirill (2011). 'Slovo Predstoiatelia Russkoi Tserkvi posle bozhestvennoi liturgii v den' vtoroi godovshchiny patriarshei intronizatsii' *Patriarchia.ru* 1 February 2011. http://www.patriarchia.ru/db/text/13987 99.html (accessed 1 November 2015).

Patriarkh Kirill (2013). 'Sviateishii Patriarkh Kirill: V sovremennom mire, otkazyvaiushchemsia ot Boga, ischezaet poniatie grekha' *Patriarchia.ru* 7 June 2013. http://www.patriarchia.ru/db/text/3026946.html (accessed 15 November 2015).

Postolov, Il'ya (2013). 'Elektronnyi Antikhrist' *Pravoslavie.ru* 13 December 2013. http://www.pravoslavie.ru/jurnal/66648.htm (accessed 1 November 2015).

'Proekt dokumenta «O pozitsii tserkvi v sviazi s poiavleniem i perspektivami razvitiia novykh tekhnologii identifikatsii lichnosti»' (2012). *Patriarchia.ru* 30 May 2012. http://www.patriarchia.ru/db/text/2255365.html (accessed 1 November 2015).

Prozorov, Sergei (2014). 'Pussy Riot and the Politics of Profanation: Parody, Performativity, Verdiction', *Political Studies*, Vol. 62, No. 4, pp. 766–783.

Przybył, Elżbieta (1999). *W Cieniu Antychrysta: Idee Staroobrzędowców w XVII w.*, Kraków: Zakład Wydawniczy "Nomos".

Rear, David, Alan Jones (2013). 'Discursive Struggle and Contested Signifiers in the Arenas of Education Policy and Work Skills in Japan'. *Critical Policy Studies* 7 (4), 375–394.

Reidman, Avraam (2010). 'Kak gotovit'sia k konchine mira?' *Pravoslavie i mir* 9 November 2010. http://www.pravoslavie.ru/put/2856.htm (accessed 1 November 2015).

RIF+KIB (2015). 'Podvedennye itogi RIF KIB 2015: Auditoriia Runeta sostavliaet 73,8 mln chelovek'. http://2015.russianinternetforum.ru/news/684/ (accessed 1 November 2015).

Ryklin, Mikhail (2006). *Svastika, krest, zvezda. Proizvedenie iskusstva v epokhu upravliaemoi demokratii.* Moscow: Logos.

Saltykov, Aleksandr (2015). 'Protoierei Aleksandr Saltykov: Ob antiiskusstvie i uvazhenii.' *Pravoslavie i mir,* 18 August 2015. http://www.pravmir.ru/portoierey-aleksandr-saltyikov-ob-antiiskusstve-i-uvazhenii/ (accessed 1 November 2015).

Schevkunov, Tikhon (2000). 'Shengenskaia zona' *Pravoslavie.ru.* http://www.pravoslavie.ru/shengen/shengen6.htm (accessed 1 November 2015).

Schöpflin, George (2007). 'The Functions of Myth and Taxonomy of Myths' in *Myth* edited by Robert Alan Segal. New York: Routledge, pp. 205–220.

Shargunov, Aleksandr (2011). 'Mir bez pravoslavnoi monarkhii'. *Pravoslavie.ru* 12 May 2011. http://www.pravoslavie.ru/smi/46441.htm (accessed 1 November 2015).

Smirnov, Dmitrii (2012). '"A Bastiliiu – tozhe ia?" – Opros sviashchennikov ob otvetstvennosti'. *Pravoslavie i mir* 11 September 2012. http://www.pravmir.ru/otvetstvennost-za-vsex-ili-za-sebya-opros-svyashh ennikov-2/ (accessed 1 November 2015).

Sokur, Zosima (2007). 'Propoved' v nedeliu o mytare i farisee' *Pravoslavie.ru* 26 January 2007. http://www.pravoslavie.ru/put/2856.htm (accessed 1 November 2015).

Solov'ev, Vladimir (1990 [1900]). *War, Progress, and the End of History: Three Conversations, Including a Short Story of the Anti-Christ*. Hudson, New York: Lindisfarne Press.

Strel'chik Evgenii, Patriarkh Kirill (2009). '"Antikhrist pridet, kogda..."' *Pravoslavie i mir* 6 December 2009. http://www.pravmir.ru/antixrist-pridet-kogda/ (accessed 1 November 2015).

Suslov, Mikhail (2013). '"Sviataia Rus'": Geopoliticheskoe voobrazhenie v sovremennoi Russkoi pravoslavnoi tserkvi' *Forum noveishei vostochnoevropeiskoi istorii i kul'tury* No 2, 2013: 311–327. http://www1.k u-eichstaett.de/ZIMOS/forum/inhaltruss20.html (assessed 1 November 2015).

Sveshnikov, Sergii (2009). 'Kak zhit'' v obshchestve odnopolykh brakov?' *Pravoslavie i mir* 27 October 2009. http://www.pravmir.ru/kak-zhit-v-obshhestve-odnopolyx-brakov/ (accessed 1 November 2015).

Sysoev Yurii, Daniil Maksimov (2009). '"Gospodi, ustne moi otverzeshi i usta moia vozvestiat khvalu tvoiu» (PS. 50: 17). Interv'iu ottsa Daniila Sysoeva i religioveda Iuriia Maksimova na saite «Svetosavle.org» (Serbiia)'. *Pravoslavie.ru* 2 December 2009. http://www.pravosla vie.ru/guest/32996.htm (accessed 1 November 2015).

Thompson, Kenneth (1998). *Moral Panics*. London; New York: Routledge.

'Top 100' (2015). *Rambler.ru*. http://top100.rambler.ru/navi/?stat=0&page Count=30&resourceId=558177&theme=554&page=1&view=short#55817 7 (accessed 1 October 2015).

Uspenskii, Boris, Yurii Lotman (1996). *Iz istorii russkoi kul'tury*. Moscow: Shkola "Iazyki russkoi kul'tury".

Velikanov, Pavel (2009). 'Ataka tserkovnykh klonov, ili O khristianizatsii populiarnykh internet-brendov'. *Pravoslavie i mir* 16 February 2009. http://www.pravmir.ru/ataka-cerkovnyx-klonov-ili-o-xristianizacii-populya rnyx-internet-brendov/ (accessed 1 November 2015).

Verkhovskii, Aleksandr (2001). 'Problema INN grozit raskolom no ne tserkvi, a pravoslavnym fundamentalistam'. *Polit.ru* 19 February 2001, http://polit.ru/article/2001/02/19/479315/ (accessed 20 November 2015).

Vigilianski, Vladimir (2009). 'Nuzhen li televizor v pravoslavnom dome?' *Pravoslavie i mir* 16 April 2007. http://www.pravmir.ru/nuzhen-li-televizor-v-pravoslavnom-dome/ (accessed 1 November 2015).

Vinogradov, Leonid (2012). 'Kak gotovit'sia k kontsu sveta?' *Pravoslavie i mir* 20 December 2012. http://www.pravmir.ru/kogda-i-kak-zhdat-konca-sveta-otvechayut-svyashhenniki/ (accessed 1 November 2015).

Vinogradov, Leonid (2014). 'Sviashchennik Lev Arshakian: Vdrug ia ponial, chto smerti net'. *Pravoslavie i mir* 13 November 2014. http://www.prav mir.ru/svyashhennik-lev-arshakyan-slepogluhie-lyudi-umeyut-vosprinimat -serdtsem/ (accessed 1 November 2015).

Willems, Joachim (2013). *Pussy Riots Punk-Gebet: Religion, Recht und Politik in Russland*. Berlin: Berlin University Press.

Yakhnin, Andrei (2012). 'Smert ili Pravoslavie''. *Pravoslavie i mir*, 27 August 2012. http://www.pravmir.ru/smert-ili-pravoslavie/ (accessed 1 November 2015).

Chapter 3.
Wi-Fi in Plato's Cave: The Digital Icon and the Phenomenology of Surveillance

Fabian Heffermehl
Uppsala Centre for Russian and Eurasian Studies

Introduction

The internet is usually regarded as a tremendous media revolution in human history. But with all the problems that accompany it—everything from decapitation videos to naked selfies of movie stars—our lives are at an increasing rate becoming dominated by a parallel realm of images (in Greek *eikones*). This parallel realm, or so-called virtual reality[1], gives the feeling that our time has a certain uniqueness. We can talk about pride in the technological achievements of our epoch, which at the same time turn into fear, as exemplified by the scandal around Edward Snowden's revelations of the activities of US National Security Agency (NSA). However, this virtual reality does not necessarily represent something substantially new in the perception of images. The perception of the internet is, rather, formed in a complex intermedial relationship between different iconic paradigms, which can be traced far back in our culture.

The task of this article is to map some of these paradigms within a Russian-Orthodox approach to the internet. My aim is—on basis of literary sources related to the icon tradition—to give *one* possible explanation (among many others) for the Orthodox negative attitude to internet. I will limit my research to the Orthodox *denouncement* of the internet. The value-neutral everyday use of the internet by millions of Orthodox believers (including all levels of the

---
1 I use the term 'virtual reality' in its most extended etymological sense as a possible reality, which is perceived in images, not to be confused with *cyberspace*, which Scholz understands as an extreme form of virtual reality, where the illusion of a three-dimensional space is made perfect by using a helmet with a screen inside (2010: 660).

Church clergy), or positive attitudes will not be a part of my research. I will study the negative attitude to the internet as a phenomenon and will seek to explain it within different, to some extent contradicting, attitudes to the historically and theologically main medium of the Orthodox Church—*the image* (in Greek: *eikon*. In Russian: *icona*).

My first hypothesis is that the Orthodox icon-medium provides one of the possible mental frames for perceiving and conceptualizing the internet-medium. The Orthodox 'technophobia' can therefore be regarded as a result of an internalization of both archaic and modern tendencies of image theory. I am going to research the *effects* of certain phenomena associated with images—like transparency, mirror-reflection and gaze—in four textual/visual discourses: medieval icon theology, 20th century secular image theory, 20th century icon theology, and internet surveillance. My approach will be from the 'point of view' of the media themselves, not from the 'point of view' of the thinkers (their intentions and social context). How, for instance, does the mirror-medium change, develop or pervert itself from discourse to discourse? In its variation between a patristic and modernistic position the icon will be regarded as a cultural technique for conveying a contemporary negative attitude to the internet. My second hypothesis will then be that the Orthodox fight with the internet is a fight with what is historically regarded as 'false icons', or idols, which resemble the icon without being the icon.

My second hypothesis can be demonstrated by a photograph from an article on pravmir.ru about internet-addiction[2]. We see the face of a child at an early stage of a transformation, which may perhaps end in the child's complete disappearance and replacement by the demonic mask of Darth Vader. The face is like a palimpsest where different layers symbolize different levels in his development towards either salvation or perversion. These levels correspond to a platonic distinction in Pavel Florensky's book *Iconostasis* (1996: 433 ff.) between 'litso' (=face), 'lik' (=iconic idea / ontology of the face) and 'lichina' (=mask / perversion of the face). The child's eyes are *iconic*, but the demonic mask—*lichina*—is reflected in his forehead.

---

2 See **figure 1.2**, p. 37 in this volume.

The teeth of the child resemble the grid in the mask. At the same time the teeth are the only visible part of the skull—this death's head, which every human being wears under the face, and which in its hard, material consistence is similar to Darth Vader's metallic mask. In this way the photograph demonstrates two typical features of the anti-icon or idol, which in the perspective of cultural history can be traced back to either the biblical narrative of the golden calf (Ex. 32, 4) or the shadows in Plato's cave. On the one hand, the idol is a false god, which lacks reality. Darth Vader is no more than a computer image, similar to a shadow. On the other hand, this lack of reality does not prevent the idol from influencing our behaviour. The prisoners in Plato's cave believe that the shadows are bodies, just as the Israelites in the Sinai Desert believe that the golden calf is alive. By virtue of a certain psychological force both the calf and the shadows are able to replace the reality or shape their own reality (see Bredekamp 2010: 37). In this meaning the internet—represented in this picture of a boy—can be interpreted as a false icon. Then 'internet-addiction', regardless of which form it takes, will necessarily turn into false praying.

This picture of a boy completely emptying himself into a virtual reality illustrates a technophobia, which is of course not only Orthodox. In secular contexts, too, there is a fear of internet addiction or different kinds of radicalisation arising through the internet. The internet—or more precisely a kind of *imagined internet*—is provided with agency. The most prominent example is the perception of NSA as a gaze, observing us wherever we are. The peculiarity of the Orthodox perception of the internet—and this will be my third thesis—is the anti-evolutionary view of history, where any development in society and technology is perceived within patterns from the far past. In this collapsed chronology, contemporary problems, concerning the media, are partly perceived under the consideration of medieval dogma, partly by the internalization of modern intellectual tendencies.

The article develops along two lines of research: for the first I will focus on the fear of virtual reality as a phenomenon within the conceptual *history* of the Orthodox image. For the second I will draw a few parallels to the *contemporary* Orthodox attitude to internet.[3] Because of the article-format of my investigation, the second line of research will naturally be of a more speculative character than the first one. Different from other approaches to digital Orthodoxy in the present volume this is not an empirical investigation. This is rather an attempt to discover *theoretical mechanisms*, explaining why the negative discourse about internet (like in the example with the boy's face turning into a mask) in the Russian-Orthodox Church seems to suppose proximity of internet to idol. Thus my article addresses the need for further research, which, building on the theoretical problems described here, can investigate the connection between theory and practice in the Orthodox attitude to internet.

Figure 3.1. 'A Black Mirror'.
Source: www.nsa.gov. Public domain. Accessed 5 May 2014.

---

3   This is further elaborated in Chapter 1 of this volume.

The surveillance-mirror

I will start by describing the architectonic features of a quadrangular building (**figure 3.1**), connected with the thus far most 'apocalyptic' scandal concerning the internet. We see an interaction between black and white elements. At the same time the walls function as gigantic black mirrors reflecting the entire surrounding environment. The building is the headquarters of the NSA. I interpret its appearance as a medium for the functions ascribed to NSA by international newspapers. Like a mechanical reflection of the world in a black mirror, the electronic double of the world with its billions of e-mails and websites is automatically copied into the software of the agency.

As a mirror NSA has two distinctive features. The first is its own invisibility. The mirror's transparency is its opacity. An ideal mirror veils itself in the illusion of being a continuation of our three-dimensional reality, like in Leon Battista Alberti's notion of the painting as an 'open window' (1888: 79). The eyes can grasp the 'hardware' (or building) of this American 'Kaaba'. But the NSA's 'software'—its rules, routines, aims and capacity—exceeds the (public) human mind. Analogous to an icon, the NSA emerges into visibility from invisibility. Like a mirror it remains invisible in a bodiless visibility.

The second feature of a mirror is its complete impotence. A mirror receives forms without creating them. In the case of the internet this ability can be related to the automation of all kinds of functions in today's society. At an increasing rate everything from the instruments of our daily life to artworks, prognoses etcetera are becoming *acheiropoietic*—a Greek word, which means *not made by hands* (in Russian: *nerukotvornyi*). However, this *acheiropoiesis* goes hand in hand with both a quasi-religious fear and market capitalism. This connection between apparently different fields can be illustrated by a screenshot from the *Frankfurter Allgemeine*, asking the rhetorical question 'Do the secret services claim to be God?':

Figure 3.2. 'A Screenshot.'
Source: *Frankfurter Allgemeine Zeitung*. Accessed 5 May 2014.

Already in its appearance the 'apocalyptic' message of the article is neutralized by the elements on the screen. In the left column we have the unpleasant image of video cameras forbidding the mind to go beyond their visible surface. In the right column are some apparently pleasant people offering me the attributes of success: career, power and an attractive body. The technocratic eyes of surveillance contradict the seductive eyes of market capitalism, which invite me to look at and click on them.

As in George Orwell's famous dystopia *Nineteen Eighty Four,* the NSA is presumed to possess information about our individual desires, needs, values, and psychological strength to promote those values. However, there is a profound difference between the 'omnipresent' NSA, and Orwell's both omnipresent and omnipotent state. If the condition for Orwell's dystopia was a dysfunctional Marxist economy, then the internet as a virtual 'Doppelgänger' of reality is made possible by efficient capitalism. Therefore the internet on the one hand realizes an ideal of freedom, anonymity and grassroots' activism; but on the other hand it produces unprecedented tools for exerting control. The NSA incorporates both tendencies. The shape of the NSA is a 'mirror reflection' of consumers' preferences. In this sense the agency is a product of my freedom to express myself either verbally on different websites, or with mouse-clicks on what ironically enough are called 'icons'. Through Snowden's revelations, the NSA acquires a power similar to the power of my own mirror-reflection over me—a power expressed by the influence of the mirror on my appearance, on what I show and what I hide.

In other words: the NSA achieves its imagined omnipresence by the apparent negation of its omnipotence. The question 'Do the secret services claim to be God?' is then answered negatively in the way the question is graphically presented. A mirror is merely a medium. The NSA's 'surveillance mirror' incorporates an immanent model of the omnipresent 'Eye of Providence' gazing back at the person standing in front of it. This brings the question posed by the *Frankfurter Allgemeine* from the centre of theology to its periphery, where religion confronts the society and culture in which it exists. I will in the following argue that the idea of the icon contains two contradicting aspects of the phenomenology of internet surveillance: on the one hand the mirror's feature of passive reflection; on the other hand the NSA's alleged omnipresent gaze.

The acheiropoietos-icon as an imaginary image

From pre-Christian times the principle of *acheiropoiesis* has been embedded in the idea of what an image is. We find it in Pliny's description of how the first painting was produced: The shadow of a Corinthian soldier—i.e. an acheiropoietic image—was projected on a wall. Around the contours of this image a woman drew an outline. Later her father filled the contour with clay, and made an image, which was worshipped in the temple (Stoichita 1999: 11 ff). The story implies an age-old distinction between painted images (*technei eikones*) and images like shadows, mirror reflections and prints (*physei eikones*)[4], which are caused by natural factors (Scholz 2010: 620 ff). To the last category Karlheinz Lüdeking even considers

---

4 To avoid confusion with the aspect of the icon as a *physical* thing, I will in the following use the term *caused images* instead of *physical images*.

adding technical images like photographs, where the human being doesn't produce the image itself, only the conditions for its produc- production. The success of acheiropoietos-legends in the history of images can be explained by the fact that we would usually regard an image, caused by what it depicts, to be more reliable and *objective* than a drawing. As Lüdeking points out: 'Images are either generated from the subjects, which use them, or from the objects, which in them become visible' (2006: 13). The following **figure 3.3** documents an image 'not made by hand', but *caused* by the hands of the model and projected into both reflection and shadow:

Figure 3.3. 'Acheiropoiesis'.
Source: http://fabianheffermehl.wordpress.com. Accessed 2 July 2014.

In late antiquity legends of *acheiropoietic* images were incorporated into Christianity. According to the most common narrative, Christ's face made a print on a piece of cloth. The cloth was sent to king Abgar of Edessa to heal him from a disease.[5] Another legend tells

---

5   The alleged contact between king Abgar and Jesus Christ was mentioned for the first time by Eusebius, who does not write about the icon (Eusebius. *History of the Church.* 1.13.5–1.13.22).

how the cloth saved the city from a Persian attack. During the battle the king bricked it up inside the city wall to save it from the enemy. But the light from the icon penetrated the stones and became visible to the Persians, who fled the city (Iazykova 2012: 97). In other words the *Acheiropoietos-icon* is realized through both natural and supernatural projections. The icon is defended, not in its aspect of being a painting, and not as being a trace of the human intellect, but as a print showing the archetype in a 'mirror' reflection. The painted images are replicas of the reflection and secured in a genealogical, subordinated relationship to the archetype. This acknowledgment is demonstrated in the famous Novgorod-icon *Spas nerukotvorny* [The Saviour not made by hand—12th century]. The head is put into the, in the platonic sense *ideal*, geometrical forms of a circle and square (*Timaios* 20, 53c–55c), which demonstrate the icon's origin in an intelligible principle of nature:

Figure 3.4. 'The Saviour not made by hand.'
Source: Wikimedia Commons. Accessed 6 June 2014. Public domain.

John of Damascus (8th century) relied in his image theory on the cosmology of Pseudo-Dionysius Areopagita (5th century), who proposed both a dualistic and a hierarchic structure of the universe. The church hierarchy on Earth is a mirror reflection of the angels' hierarchy in the heavenly realm. At the same time each level of the hierarchy is compared with 'mirrors without flaws' (*esoptra dieidestata*), transferring an image from the upper to the lower level:

> The purpose, then, of Hierarchy is the assimilation and union, as far as attainable, with God, having Him Leader of all religious science and operation, by looking unflinchingly to His most Divine comeliness, and copying, as far as possible, and by perfecting its own followers as Divine images, mirrors most luminous and without flaw, receptive of the primal light and the supremely Divine ray, and devoutly filled with the entrusted radiance, and again, spreading this radiance ungrudgingly to those after it, in accordance with the supremely Divine regulations (Dionysius the Areopagite 1899: chapter III).

Pseudo-Dionysius Areopagita drafts a world-view, which to my point of view is similar to a virtual reality—i.e. a reality in images, where everything belonging to the earthly realm is only an 'image' of the 'real' reality of God. Similar, at least in its algorithmic construction, to the automatic collection of information into an electronic cosmos of the NSA, these reflections exclude the creative interference of the human being. The mirror functions as a union between mechanics and divine energy. In an icon *not made by hand* there is neither place for the icon-painter, nor for his studio, nor for the technical or aesthetic experiments which are prior to the final image. John of Damascus does not write a single sentence about how a painting comes into being. Instead he proposes a *given image*, a result without a process, like a print or mirror reflection.

In his *Logoi* against the iconoclasts, John of Damascus defines the icon as '...a likeness and pattern and impression of something, showing in itself what is depicted' (2003: 95). The emphasis on likeness or similarity (*homoioma*) means that the icon resembles Christ by appearance. But by its substance the icon is not Christ. The difference between appearance and substance can be illustrated with the icon and the Eucharist. The icon looks like Christ, but is of another substance. The Eucharist *is* Christ by the same substance, but has no similarity with Christ (see Schönborn 1984: 156). The definition of the icon as venerable in its appearance implies in my view that the *finished* icon, which has achieved similarity, and therefore shows 'in itself what is depicted', is on a higher level of reality than its materials before they are completely adapted to the image of Christ. It follows the meaning of icons in terms of *kenosis* (=emptying). In the process of the icon's creation the painter has to 'kill' both the artist in himself (Zinon 2003: 36) and the means of producing an artwork. Venerable is neither the craftsman, nor the craftwork, but the image alone.

By his emphasis on *likeness,* John of Damascus disregards the physical substance of the icon. This implies in my opinion a deeper understanding of the concept of acheiropoiesis. What is not *made* by hand is also not intended to be *touched* by hand. The image appears as an abstract idea, as an imaginary image, because in a physical, non-imaginary painting every visibility remains dependent on its haptic materials. For instance, will the golden sky in the icon look golden simply because it is made of gold; the blue looks blue because it contains lapis lazuli. Because a painter has to use certain materials, which at least in their physical pigments are similar to what they depict, a painting can never be a sole appearance independent of what it consists of. The only images, which are sole appearances by virtue of negating their materials, are mirror reflections or mental images in our memory, thoughts, dreams, imaginations or hallucinations. If you 'dissect' a painting by taking away the upper layers of colour, you will still see in the lower layers traces of the process, which are similar to the finished painting (**figures 3.5, 3.6, 3.7**). But if you dissect a brain, you will not see any images, and the same is the case if you jump into the image reflected on a surface of water, or break the mirror wall of the NSA. Between the image and its manifestation in a material substance there is no nexus. Mental and caused images have no physical body, and are not results of a process, which involves human activity.

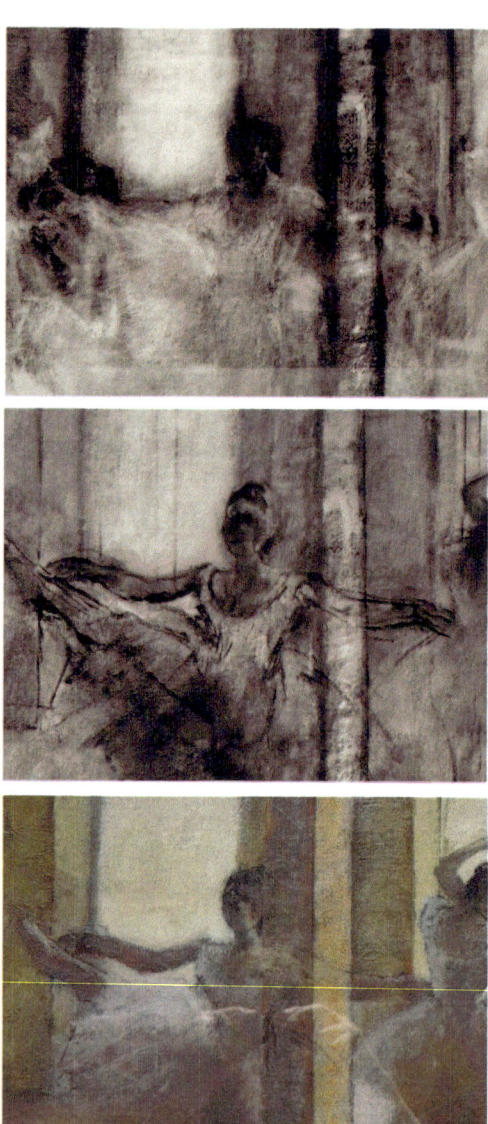

Figures 3.5, 3.6, 3.7. 'Roentgen analysis of a painting by Degas showing different steps of the painting process.'
Source: Glyptoteket, Copenhagen. Photo: Fabian Heffermehl.

Where the pictures on computer screens are concerned, they should be considered as new 'species' among images. The image on a screen is a caused immaterial picture, a projection of an image based on a code of binary numbers hidden in plastic and aluminium. We have a chain of discontinuity between the image and its material manifestation. The image is both in its essence and appearance different from the binary code. The binary code is both in its essence and appearance different from plastic and aluminium. Like a mirror reflection or shadow the electronic image is *not made by hand*, and it occurs without any direct human interference. Electronic automation can here be seen as a transformation of the icon's kenosis into a new pattern. But at the same time the electronic image avoids the icon's contradiction of being both an appearance *not made by hand* and a hand-made object. The paradox of electronic images can be formulated as a phenomenological coincidence with the icon as an imaginary image of its theological idea, but at the same time an opposition to what an icon *is* as a non-virtual, physical thing, existing in the world.

The surveillance-gaze

Pretending to reformulate the conditions for visibility, both the internet and the doctrine of the icon represent structures with universal, all-embracing pretensions. **Figure 3.2** shows that this is also how the internet is perceived. But the fear of surveillance is not so much a fear of electronic globalization or omnipresence, as of our own transparency confronted with a gaze, which is as opaque and transparent as a black mirror. This fear of being gazed at brings a problem into the discourse, which unlike the acheiropoietos-mirror is not so much connected with the phenomenology of the icon's material substance or lack of substance, but rather with the phenomenology of perception.

Articles in German newspapers accuse the NSA 'of having access to our thoughts' (Bamford 2013). More precisely, the secret services can know the *traces* of our thoughts in what we write, say or click on, but not the thoughts as such. The NSA can only know what we *look at*. Through the electronic media, which in this context are not so much media as a parallel virtual reality, we get an effect, which Jacques Lacan described in the field of psychoanalysis: *We are gazed at by what we see.*[6]

Lacan characterized the relationship between the gazed seeing subject and the world as an 'inverted use of perspective' (1981: 92). In fact the 'inverted perspective' is a term which was introduced by the Russian art historian Dmitrii Ainalov (1900: 103, 111, 219) and in 1919 adopted by Pavel Florensky in the title of his essay *Obratnaia perspektiva*.[7] At around the turn of the 20th century, linear perspective goes through both a geometrical deconstruction by Cezanne, Picasso and Braque, and a no less important ideological deconstruction with the introduction of new terms. Florensky connects the so-called 'reverse' or 'inverse' perspective to peculiarities of the Orthodox icon. In a broader sense, which includes not only Florensky, but also Lacan, the reverse perspective can be interpreted as an organic and dynamic counter conception to linear perspective.

First, a few words about what actually is being inverted: Alberti in his book *Della pittura* [The Picture—1435] introduced perspective as a rational, geometrical construction, allowing the artist to create a perfect illusion of space. In Alberti's own words the flat surface of the painting should be transformed into 'an open window'—*una fenestra aperta* (1888: 79). To see something in a painting was now made equivalent to seeing something in the three-dimensional world. The main principles of perspective are shown in **figure 3.8**:

---

[6] 'This is how one should understand those words, so strongly stressed, in the gospel, *They have eyes that they might not see*. That they might not see what? Precisely, that things are looking at them' (Lacan 1981: 109).

[7] Florensky's essay *Obratnaia perspektiva* was published for the first time in 1967, three years after Lacan gave his lecture on *Line and Light*. Florensky, Pavel (1967). 'Obratnaia perspektiva', in Lotman, Yury / Uspensky, Boris (ed.). *Trudy po znakovym sistemam / Works on Sign Systems*. Sb. 3. Tartu.

Figure 3.8. 'Leonardo da Vinci:
Perspectival study of the Adoration of the Magi.'
Source: Wikimedia Commons. Accessed 11 June 2014. Public domain.

We have a vanishing point far back in the painting, where the lines along the floor go together. This point was meant to correspond to a single eye in a fixed position in front of the painting—and only by this static position would the illusion be regarded as complete.

In Byzantine thinking the icon became part of a cosmological structure, which comprised not so much the material picture as its immanent context as a whole. With his linear perspective Alberti brings the image 'down to earth'—to the 'area' of seeing. At the same time this perspective, by regulation of the particular position of the observer, introduces a clear distinction between the subject and the object of seeing. Internet surveillance, on the contrary, transforms in its own virtual reality the objects, which we see, or the texts, which we read, into 'subjects' 'looking back' at us. In this sense the perception paradigms of surveillance are opposed to those of linear perspective.

The fear of surveillance can be regarded as a reflection of the phenomenological consequences of a struggle with linear perspective. Instead of a 'dead' object for the eye constructed by means of a geometrical mechanism, the painting should 'organize a matrix' for the materialization of a gaze (Boehm 2006: 25). The famous anamorphosis in the painting of Hans Holbein's *The Ambassadors* (1533) serves as an example. At first glance the painting is a typical albertian 'window', into which the eye projects its desire for wealth and power—a desire which is symbolized by a mystical figure similar to a phallus rising up from the floor. This is how the painting seems to an 'ideal' observer, standing in a place corresponding to the vanishing point. But what happens if we move from this fixed position, for instance down to the left—to a more 'Oriental' and 'obedient' position according to Florensky's contemporary art critic Anatolii Bakushinsky (1923: 256)—or up to the right, to a flying position, maybe corresponding to the weightlessness we feel in dreams? From both alternative points of view we will be confronted with our own 'nothingness, in the figure of the death's head' (Lacan 1981: 92). The phallus appears to be a skull, and, if we follow Lacan, a symbol of castration gazing back at the observer. In Holbein's picture there is a chiasmus (crosswise reversal) between the human eye and the gaze of the skull, which both adapts to and rejects the rules of perspective. It has a doubleness, approaching the antinomy between fertility and death, Eros and Thanatos, between the desire to click on everything tempting and to be under surveillance in our desire.

Figure 3.9. 'Hans Holbein: *The Ambassadors.*'
Source: Wikimedia Commons. Accessed 23 May 2014. Public domain.

For Lacan the gaze belongs not only to portraits, but also to every part of the material world. Another of his examples is a sardine can, 'gazing' at him while floating in the sea off the coast of Britanny (1981: 95). The gaze is not the same as a representation of the biological eye. Lacan refers to the legend of Parrhasius, who made a painting of a curtain, which was so perfect that even Zeuxis was tricked. In the belief that the curtain was real, Zeuxis asked Parrhasius to draw it aside, so he could see the picture. The gaze in Parrhasius' image is connected with what is 'behind' the curtain— with a desire to see something beyond the illusion, which through our desire to see it becomes valuable for us, and in this sense gazes back.

With his sardine can Lacan makes visible some implications of modernist painting, which in my opinion can be illustrated by a story from Wassily Kandinsky's autobiography from his time in Munich before the First World War. One evening Kandinsky entered his studio, filled with impressions after a long day's painting, and suddenly saw a picture 'too beautiful to be described, and filled with an inner glow' (1977: 20). At first he hesitated, not understanding what he saw. Then he realized that the picture was his own, but at an angle like Holbein's skull. Kandinsky was gazed at by something without any similarity to an eye—an anamorphosis in the painting, which suddenly came into his consciousness, where it hadn't been before, and therefore depended solely on the painting's own reality.

Figure 3.10. 'Wassily Kandinsky: *The first abstract aquarelle.*'
Source: www.wikiart.org. Accessed 2 July 2014. Public domain.

Instead of Alberti's image window, which served the eye, and had no meaning outside the realm of perception, Kandinsky, according to my interpretation, is a protagonist for an idea of an image, acting on its own. As a gazed-at observer I am not alone in the process of perception. Who is the observer and what is the image becomes relative. In Vologda, in connection with his ethnographic research, Kandinsky became aware of himself as a part of the image's reality: 'They taught me to move inside the image, to live in the image' (1977: 18). The logical conclusion of this chiasmus between the observing subject and the observed object is that the image is no adaptation to what I expect to see in 'an open window', but in an interaction between itself and me as an image. The image becomes a reality in itself, in its own materiality, corresponding to me as a material being.

The icon's gaze

The transformation from the classical academic perspective to the non-figurative autonomous painting is the consequence of an upgrade of the matter—or more precisely of the material picture's ability to create reality. In accordance with my hypotheses, modernistic theories of painting have been adapted by the 20th century's theories of the icon. When, in 1900, the art historian Ainalov used the anachronistic notion of *reverse perspective* for the first time it was with reference to a deconstruction of perspective:

> Cases of application of the reverse perspective are especially obvious in the depiction of books in the hands of the four evangelists. These books are represented with an unnatural extension upwards as a result of the circumstance that the carver shows the thickness of the book not from two sides, but from every side (1900: 111).

In other words, 'unnatural' deformations in Byzantine paintings are associated with a diversification of the observer's point of view. Ainalov expresses this diversification in negative terms. The reverse perspective is regarded as a failure due to the icon painter's lack of knowledge of linear perspective. Nevertheless Ainalov gives words to a phenomenon, which would soon become normative for modern art. Kandinsky's painting proposes an intuitive point of view, which is not determined by the geometry of linear perspective.

The German art historian Oscar Wulff translated in his article of 1907 Ainalov's term into 'umgekehrte Perspektive'. According to Wulff's theory there is an imagined point of view within the image. The icon painter chose the biggest figure in the painting as his imagined subject ('Einfühlung'). All other elements in the composition are seen with decreasing dimensions dependent on the distance from this subject. In fact this theory of reverse perspective remains within both a methodological and a dialectical dependence on linear perspective. Like linear perspective, reverse perspective is understood as a model of seeing, where things close to the subject look bigger than things far from the subject. The only difference is that the subject is located somewhere inside the image, while the vanishing point is placed in front of it. This can be illustrated by the left pedestal in the Trinity icon of Alberti's contemporaneous painter Andrei Rublev:

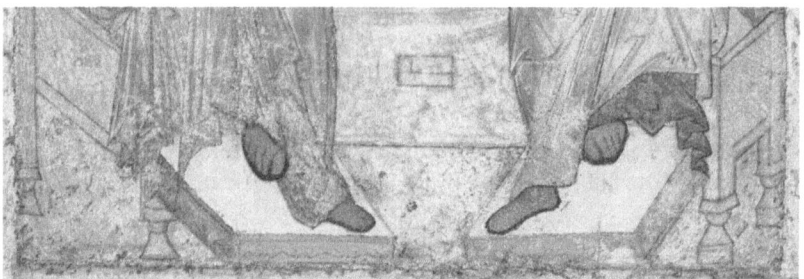

Figure 3.11. 'Andrei Rublev: *The Holy Trinity* (detail).'
Source: Wikimedia Commons. Accessed 8 June 2014. Public domain.

If we understand the left pedestal by means of perspective, the lines on each side, presumably parallel in physical reality, seem to go in a 'reverse' direction. They do not meet at a point in the depth of the picture (compare with **figure 3.8**), but somewhere in front of it. In other words, the notion of 'reverse perspective' is founded on an idea of a diametrical opposition between the icon and the renaissance painting. Leonid Uspensky claims that 'the perspective of the visible world is in [the icon] opposite to the evangelical perspective; the world lying in sin [is opposite to] the resurrected world' (2008: 361).

As a symbolist Florensky understands the gaze as something belonging to every part of the visible world: 'All things gaze at each other. They reflect each other thousands of times. All things are centres of outgoing mysterious forces' (1999b: 151). In *Iconostasis* he defends the icon as a 'window' from heaven to earth (1996: 443).[8] The window metaphor of Alberti is inherited, but at the same time transformed. Instead of a subject, which arbitrarily sets its optic perception of a three-dimensional space in place of the canvas, the icon is now understood in terms of God's gaze back on the human being. The difference from Wulff is that it is no longer the icon

---
8   See also Bakushinsky 1923: 228.

painter, who *imagines* himself to be a point of view from the icon's inside, but rather a point of view, which objectively exists. Therefore Florensky writes: 'For no matter where on earth the saint's remains are, and no matter what their physical condition, his resurrected and deified body lives in eternity, and the icon that constitutes him does not *depict* the holy witness but *is* the very witness himself' (1996: 165—translation modified, FH). Paul Evdokimov writes:

> Perspective is often reversed in icons. The lines move in a reversed direction, that is, the point of perspective is not behind the panel but in front of it. (...) The effect is startling because the perspective originates in the person who is looking at the icon. The lines thus come together in the spectator and give the impression that the people in the icon are coming out to meet those who are looking on. The world of the icon is turned *toward man* (Evdokimov 1990: 225).

In other words, the icon is a technique, which by its geometrical reversal of the vanishing point creates an interaction between the observer and the depicted saints. The icon *is* the holy. The signifier *is* the signified.[9] Therefore it gazes back toward man.

The digital icon

The different notions of gaze proposed by Lacan, Kandinsky, Ainalov, Wulff, Florensky and Evdokimov have a common root in the modernistic discourse of meta-reflection on what characterizes the painting as a medium, i.e. a discourse, which finally implies a displacement of the point of view. Nevertheless, this analysis should not keep out of mind the fact that the mentioned thinkers operate with strikingly different methodological and scientific 'languages'. Lacan constructs his gaze as an 'inverted use of perspective' (1981: 92) within psychoanalysis, which in this case is not compatible with esthetical and theological theory. Kandinsky's intuition of a gaze belongs to the area of modernistic aesthetics. Ainalov, Wulff, Florensky, Uspensky and Evdokimov are closer to a geometrical understanding of the gaze as far as they argue for a systematization

---

9   See Chapter 1 in this volume on name worshipping.

of space within the icon. Wulff approaches a psychological under-understanding of imagination ('Einfühlung'). While Florensky, Uspensky and Evdokimov's reverse perspective denies psychology. The reality of the icon's gaze is a witness of God's omnipresence, and not of a human mental construction.

However, it is the *differences* in psychological and theological methodological approaches to the gaze, which I regard as constitutive for a Manichean rejection of the internet as it is shown in **figure 1.2.** in Chapter 1 in this volume. The 'inverted use of perspective' functions as a technique for the gaze within discourses, which mutually negate each other. The alleged incorporation of a gaze in surveillance technology transforms the internet into the antipode of the Orthodox icon—into this dark world, where Darth Vader replaces the child's iconic face (*lik*) with his mask (*lichina*). The boy appears so to speak as a prisoner on the inside of the computer's virtual reality, which is a perversion of the icon's perspective. This confirms my hypothesis: the Orthodox fight with the internet is a fight with false icons—i.e. idols. And as shown by the example of the golden calf, the idol's power over the Israelites is of a psychological character. There is no objective life in the statue, as there is no body in the shadows in Plato's cave. But nevertheless life is perceived.

As shown by the example of reverse perspective, the framework for an Orthodox rejection of the internet combines both modernistic aesthetic and archaistic rhetoric. Therefore, reverse perspective can be understood as both a break with, and dictate from, the Orthodox tradition. Icon theology is no monolithic phenomenological system. Through 1,300 years it has developed partly in accordance with Orthodox self-understanding as a coryphée of the tradition, partly in response to tendencies within the secular culture.[10] A clash of iconic paradigms becomes evident in a question

---

10 For a more thorough comparison between modern and patristic icon theology see my book-chapter *Kuss eines Zyklopen – Die umgekehrte Perspektive zwischen Weltbild und Kunstbild*, forthcoming in Pape / Sederström (ed.): *Dialog – Диалог – Dialogue. Russisch-deutsche Dialoge in Wissenschaft und Kultur*. Verlag Königshausen & Neumann GmbH. Würzburg.

posed in some Russian-Orthodox online forums: *Am I allowed to pray in front of an icon on a computer screen?* In all its simplicity this question illustrates the double media context, which confronts millions of Orthodox believers. On the one hand the internet is without doubt their most *used* medium. Through the internet the human being orientates itself in the world's complexity of practical and theoretical issues. On the other hand the most authoritative medium for an Orthodox believer is the icon. But then the next question arises: which idea of the icon—the idea of John of Damascus or Florensky? In my view, patristic and modernistic icon theologies produce different effects for a contemporary Orthodox discourse about the internet. If the question above is answered negatively, then it is with reference to modern theologians like Florensky or Uspensky.[11] But when the question gets a positive answer, then it is mostly[12] with reference to the Council of Nicaea of 787 A.D. or John of Damascus.[13]

The different answers to a relatively simple question reveal a split within icon theology. On the one hand, Florensky, Evdokimov and Uspensky propose a distinction between the 'icon' (*ikona*) and the artistic picture (*kartina*) in order to underline the uniqueness of the icon, even in relation to its reproductions in other materials, e.g. paper icons or digital icons. They define the icon primarily with regard to concrete icon paintings—like the *Trinity* of Andrei Rublev— and therefore also to explicit painting techniques and materials. On the other hand, in the icon theology of the Church fathers there is no

---

11 blogs.privet.ru/community/divo/69174634, chayka.org.ru/forum/viewtopic.php?p=145278, accessed on 24 October 2014.
12 In my analysis I do not consider internet discussions where the question above is answered positively on the basis of a general assumption that praying is always desirable as long as it is conducted faithfully. Such an assumption implies a reduction of the medium of prayer, where the central question does not concern icon theology, but the believer and his / her psychological relationship to God. See: old2.taday.ru/vopros/20285/85918.html, www.bolshoyvopros.ru/questions/147023-molitva-cherez-internet-schitaetsja-nast ojaschej-molitvoj.html, accessed on 26 February 2015.
13 wap.drevlepravoslavie.forum24.ru/?1-1-150-00000937-000-0-0, accessed on 24 October 2014. In the online forum orthodox.etel.ru/2008/42/_otveti.htm the priest paraphrases John of Damascus without directly referring to him.

fundament for rejecting images occurring from a computer file. In-Instead the material world is subordinated to a reality, which in modern terms can be regarded as virtual. For John of Damascus too great an emphasis on the icon's material aspects would be accompanied by a suspicion of idolatry. For Florensky, on the contrary, the material is linked with a symbolic meaning. It is the virtual or illusive which has the attributes of the idol.

As asserted by Uspensky, every image made of 'artificial' materials, such as plastic, is witness to a denial of nature—of God's creature—and therefore of God himself: 'The border between permitted and non-permitted in the material is there, where the matter looses its originality and character, passing itself off as something other than it is, that means creating an illusion' (2008: 467). In this way Uspensky incorporates a modern auto-thematization of the image's medium-specificity, where materials like wood and tempera have to appear as nothing other than what they actually are—wood and tempera—but with a rhetoric rooted in an age-old narrative of the icon's resistance to the idol. The problem of the internet as a virtual reality can be reduced to the problem of an icon on a computer screen. A digital icon is similar to an icon painted on a piece of wood, but it lacks the wood's being. Within a Manichean paradigm this combination of an *identity in appearance* and *difference in substance* amounts to a diabolic formula: 'No wonder, for even Satan disguises himself as an angel of light' (2. Cor. 11, 14).

Conclusion

This article started with a hypothesis of the internet as a false icon, resembling the icon without being the icon. During the course of the article I have shown that, translated into modern terms, the Byzantine mirror as a medium and cosmological metaphor can be interpreted in the category of 'virtual reality'. It is on the basis of this virtual reality that the internet resembles the icon. However, the denouncement of this resemblance as a falsification derives from a modernistic framework. The 20th century's struggle with linear perspective makes clear the distinction between the image as a virtual illusion and the image as a material thing.

However, I regard the very Manichean nature of the discourse—where God-given reality is opposed to virtual reality, God's creature to Darth Vader—as an extension of the rhetoric, which can be traced at least as far back as iconoclasm—a violent struggle about icons, which in the 8th and the 9th centuries almost brought the Byzantine Empire to civil war. The medieval context was different from today, where we have a concurrence between a multitude of categories of images, like the internet, kitsch, ready-mades, advertisements, blogs, Hollywood-films, computer games, concerts, street-art, tattoos, museums etcetera. In the 8th century there was no struggle for one image in relation to other images, but for the very *existence* of the image. Because of its history as an apologia for the image as such, the Orthodox icon tends by its doctrine to proclaim itself as being representative, not of one type of image among others, but of visibility itself. Images which are outside the definition of icons are therefore not to be considered as *competitive images*,[14] but as *non-images*, for instance as 'instruments (...) like cars or electricity' ('Patriarkh i molodezh' 2009: 113), or as demonic idols.

The icon's claim to be a true 'model' for visibility itself is expressed in Florensky's polemic against linear perspective, which he blames for being an 'apparition' or 'double' of the world (1999a: 79). The illusion of space in the appearance of a Renaissance painting is for Florensky a false reality, which distracts our attention away from truth. He refers to Plato's *Politeia* [The Republic], where a seductive reality is realized deep inside a cave, in front of prisoners chained to the wall: '...now people felt the need of *illusion*. And so, presupposing that the spectator or the stage designer was chained fast, like the prisoner of Plato's cave, to a theatre bench and neither

---

14 An example of what I here characterize as 'competition' is in the Catholic Church of Santa Maria degli Angeli in Rome, where postmodern installations are exhibited together with religious paintings from the Renaissance, both as valid expressions of belief.

could nor should have a direct vital relationship to reality...' (2002: 210).

Is this narrative so different from worried newspaper articles about children neglecting their health, while spending all their time in front of electronic images of perfect bodies; or unfortunate gamblers, losing their money to websites promising wealth and power; or when a constructed reality of antagonism on the internet attracts confused outsiders to terrorism? What is image and medium replaces what is mediated. The icon replaces the archetype. Maybe Wi-Fi in Plato's cave gives the clammy, dripping stalactites a more trendy design, but it makes no substantial difference to the shadow-game, which is also a medium game if we follow Marshall McLuhan's famous assertion that the "content' of any medium is always another medium' (1964: 8).

According to the church-historian Konrad Onasch, an Orthodox church resembles a cave by its introvert architecture (1996: 11). However, if the image-world inside Plato's cave is the centre of ignorance, then the innermost part of the church—the sanctuary separated from the nave by the image-wall—corresponds to the highest level in a hierarchy of reality. An Orthodox church is in my view a platonic cave with the inside out. The secular world, physically existing outside the church, is reduced to shadows, while the interior with its cosmos of icons mirrors paradise. The dialectic between the church and the cave is also a dialectic between two acheiropoietic images—shadow and mirror—both shown in **figure 3.3**. And as far as an acheiropoietic medium denies its materials—as stated in section 3—the icon achieves its most complete realization as an icon in a state of antinomy: by its similarity to Christ together with its non-similarity to the piece of wood which carries the image. In its veneration of visibility, icon theology contains a paradoxical 'Gnostic' element in the sense of denying the icon's dependence on physical matter. At the same time this 'Gnosticism' serves an argument for the unification of images in the one and only print and mirror reflection of Christ. Not only is the matter denied, but also every alternative image – not to mention a virtuality pretending to replace the reality. A cult of images is not separable from a fear of images. By its boundless production of acheiropoietic images, and by generating surveillance-gazing back on human beings, the internet-medium intensifies the icon-medium and brings it to a new scale, pace and pattern. At the same time the internet re-invents an age-old iconoclastic conflict, which lies at the core of Orthodox Christianity.

References

Ainalov, Dmitrii (1900). *Ellinisticheskie osnovy vizantiiskogo iskusstva*. Saint Petersburg: Tipografiia Skorokhovoda.

Alberti, Leone Battista (1888). 'Della pittura', in Janitschek, Hubert (ed.). *Leone Battista Albertis kleinere kunsttheoretische Schriften*. Vienna: Wilhelm Braumüller.

Bakushinsky, Anatolii (1923). *Lineinaia perspektiva v iskusstve i zritel'nom vospriiatii real'nogo prostranstva*. Moscow: Iskusstvo.

Bamford, James (2013). 'Die NSA hat Zugang zu unseren Gedanken', in *Die Zeit*. 20. June. http://www.zeit.de/2013/26/nsa-geheimdienst-james-bamford (accessed 12 June 2014).

Boehm, Gottfried (2006). 'Die Wiederkehr der Bilder', in Boehm (ed.). *Was ist ein Bild*. Munich: Wilhelm Fink.

Bredekamp, Horst (2010). *Theorie des Bildakts*. Berlin: Suhrkamp.

Dionysius the Areopagite (1899). *The Celestial Hierarchy*. www.tertullian.org (accessed 16 June 2014).

Eusebius. 'History of the Church'. www.tlg.uci.edu (accessed 6 June 2014).

Evdokimov, Paul (1990). *The Art of the Icon: a Theology of Beauty*. California: Oakwood.

Florensky, Pavel (1996). *Iconostasis*. New York: St. Vladimir's Seminary Press.

Florensky, Pavel (1999a). 'Obratnaia perspektiva', in Andronik Trubachev (ed.). *Sochinieniia v chetyrekh tomakh*. Vol. 3 (1). Moscow: Mysl'.

Florensky, Pavel (1999b). 'Smysl idealizma', in Andronik Trubachev (ed.). *Sochinieniia v chetyrekh tomakh*. Vol. 3 (2). Moscow: Mysl'.

Florensky, Pavel (2002). *Beyond Vision. Essays on the Perception of Art*. London: Reaktion Books.

Iazykova, Irina (1995). *Bogoslovie ikony*. Moscow: Izdatel'stvo obshchedostupnogo pravoslavnogo universiteta.

John of Damascus (2003). *Three Treatises on the Divine Images*. Crestwood / New York: St. Vladimir's Seminary Press.

Kandinsky, Wassily (1977). *Rückblicke*. Bern: Benteli Verlag.

Kotter, P. Bonifatius (1975). *Die Schriften des Johannes von Damaskos*. Berlin / New York: Walter de Gruyter.

Lacan, Jacques (1981). *The Four Fundamental Concepts of Psycho-Analysis*. New York / London: Norton & Company.

Lüdeking, Karlheinz (2006). *Grenzen des Sichtbaren*. Munich: Wilhelm Fink.

McLuhan, Marshall (1964). *Understanding Media. The Extensions of Man*. New York / Toronto / London: McGraw Hill Book Company.

Onasch, Konrad (1996). *Ikone, Kirche, Gesellschaft*. Munich / Vienna / Zürich: Ferdinand Schöning.

Patriarkh i molodezh': Razgovor bez diplomatii (2009). Moscow: Danilov Muzhskoi Monastyr'.

Patriarkh Kirill prizval monakhov otkazat'sia ot interneta. http://lenta.ru/news/2013/06/08/monks/ (accessed 18 July 2014).

Rieger (2013). 'Halten sich die Geheimdienste für Gott?' in *Frankfurter Allgemeine Zeitung*. 9 September. http://www.faz.net/aktuell/feuilleton/debatten/ueberwachung/ueberwachungsaffaere-halten-sich-die-geheimdienste-fuer-gott-12564894.html (accessed 2 July 2014).

Scholz, Oliver Robert (2010). 'Bild', in Barck (ed.). *Ästhetische Grundbegriffe*. Stuttgart / Weimar: Metzler.

Schönborn, Christoph (1984). *Die Christus-Ikone – eine theologische Hinführung*. Schaffhausen: Novalis Verlag.

Stoichita, Victor (1999*). Eine kurze Geschichte des Schattens*. Munich: Wilhelm Fink Verlag.

Uspensky, Leonid (2008). *Bogoslovie ikony pravoslavnoi tserkvi*. Moscow: Dar.

Wulff, Oscar (1907): 'Die umgekehrte Perspektive und die Niedersicht – eine Raumanschauungsform der albyzantinischen Kunst und ihre Fortbildung in der Renaissance', in Wulff (ed.). *Kunstwissenschaftliche Beiträge A. Schmarsow gewidmet*. Leipzig.

Zinon, Arkhimandrit (2003). *Besedy ikonopistsa*. Pskov.

Chapter 4.
The Body of Christ Online: The Russian Orthodox Church and (Non-)Liturgical Interactivity on the Internet[1]

Alexander Ponomariov
University of Passau

Introduction
1. Digital religion and the Russian Orthodox Church

Religion, including Russian Orthodoxy, operates with various types of media, including the 'old' ones, and yet in this regard, 'digital religion' is viewed as a developing field of research. Despite many years of research, one can still come across accounts that 'it is early days for evaluating the full implications of the internet upon religious identity' (Cohen 2013: 52), or that 'theological reflection about the internet remains in its infancy' (Baab 2012: 277). Another instance, evidencing the novelty of the subject, comes from a recent collection of proceedings:

> The theme for our symposium was 'Digital religion' and in our call for papers we described it in the following way: '"Digital religion" aims to explore the complex relationship between religion and digital technologies of communication.' [...] As can be seen from the conference proceedings, we did not achieve what we aimed for. The theme was too vast. We knew as much; a new field is always difficult to handle.' (Ahlbäck 2013: 5)

Western scholarship covers a number of religions in their interaction with new media, including Hinduism (e.g., Scheifinger 2013), Buddhism (e.g., Connelly 2013; Foxeus 2013), Islam (e.g., Schlosser 2013; Sisler 2013; Becker 2011), Judaism (e.g., Cohen 2013; Golan

---

[1] This is a corrected and extended version of the article, first published in *Digital Icons*, issue 14 (2016). I want to thank Dr. Christopher Jones, who agreed to proofread my English, as well as the peer reviewers for the valuable suggestions and improvements.

2013; Rashi 2013), and Protestant and Roman-Catholic Christianity (e.g., Jonveaux 2013; Fischer-Nielsen 2012; Noomen/Aupers/Houtman 2011). Nonetheless, Russian Orthodoxy is vastly underrepresented in the Western research agenda. In this regard, Russian scholars argue that 'the religious segment of the Runet [the Russian language internet] is developing in line with the same laws as the internet in general' (Luchenko 2009a), and religious organizations use it for both external (missionary) and internal purposes (Luchenko 2009b). Until recently, one of the main ROC internet functions used to be the unidirectional communication of documents, allowing a better coordination between various Church units (Luchenko 2008). The situation has changed after 2011, when lay believers were encouraged to partake in the discussion of ROC documents through the Web 2.0 platforms.

'Digital religion' has come through three phases or waves of study, moving from the 'utopian or dystopian discourses about how the internet would save or ruin the world' (Campbell 2013: 8) to the questions of 'ritual, community, and identity' and how 'the internet in everyday life was influencing religious practice' (Campbell 2013: 9). The current fourth wave includes studying religious practices in the virtual worlds (Campbell 2013: 10; cf. Campbell/Grieve 2014 and Geraci 2014). Challenging the established Church authority is one of the most interesting points that arises at the crossroads of traditional religions and the new media, which can be defied through technical use of the internet (Lundby 2012: 36). It is argued that authority is 'a key concern for communities which have a strong hierarchal structure' (Campbell 2010: 186), and that the internet activity can both strengthen and weaken it (Cheong 2013: 82). Against this background, we can hypothesize that control and authority would be sensitive issues for ROC hierarchs.

2. Object

The object herein is the new dimension of Orthodox ecclesiology, the ROC online conciliarity, both in terms of context and conduits of communication. The three 'sacramental' case studies, chosen for this paper, include digital discussions of recent official ROC documents on the sacraments of Communion and Confession, as well as on the Church-Slavonic language. Promoted by the incumbent ROC leadership, they highlight the non-liturgical interactivity of this traditional and rather closed entity. I have chosen 'sacramental' topics because they manifest the very idea of the Church, which, according to Apostle Paul, is described as the Body of Christ. The Eucharist, being the Body of Christ per se in Orthodox theology, and the other liturgical aspects actualize the Church as a union of believers with and in Christ, and make this union visible and palpable. However, the offline Bread and Wine aspect of the ROC, as well as some other peculiarities mentioned below set certain limits for online liturgical practices. Following the theoretical premises, this paper outlines the modern internet policy of the Russian Orthodox Church, drawing upon its corporate guidelines. This is followed by the case studies presented in order to shed light upon the non-liturgical 'interplay between individuals and institutions enacted online' (Campbell/Lövheim 2011: 1088).

3. Liturgical and non-liturgical interactivity

Religion in the age of the internet can be looked at in two broad, yet intertwined, aspects: as religion online and online religion. Current scholarship argues that religion online 'presents information about religious institutions and groups via internet transmission,' whereas online religion is understood as a '*doing* of the religion through online channels' (Stewart 2011: 1205). Speaking of the Christian context, the latter represents 'online churches' that are in fact 'internet based Christian communities using a range of digital media to conduct worship' (Hutchings 2012: 207), that include 'rituals, prayers, and hymns, but also individual activities such as devotion, candle lighting, personal prayer, etc.' (Fischer-Nielsen 2012: 127). Moreover, scholars operate with two forms of the internet use, one-way information sharing and interactive dialogue: 'the first of these reflects a classic view on communication, focusing on the distribution of information from an active sender to a passive receiver. The second use acknowledges that the receiver is an active part of the communication process' (Fischer-Nielsen 2012: 123). The latter can be described as 'contact, debate, conversation, network, openness, democracy, co-influence, and interactivity' (Fischer-Nielsen 2012: 125).

The radical distinction between religion online and online religion was first proposed by Christopher Helland, whose idea marked a clear dichotomy between the two: information (the former)—interaction (the latter). For him, religion online was 'based upon traditional religious hierarchal structure, attempting to harness the internet as a tool of top-down, organized communication', presenting 'religion based upon a vertical conception of control, status and authority' (Helland 2000: 207). In contrast to this, Helland defined online religion as an 'unstructured, open, and non-hierarchal interaction' (Helland 2000: 207). Helland's approach was criticized, among others by Glenn Young, who highlighted the importance of both information and interaction: 'religion online and online religion, rather than being strictly opposed, are two types of religious expression and activity that exist in continuity with one another in internet Christianity' (Young 2004: 93). For him, filling out online prayer request forms at 'informational' church websites (Young 2004: 95) or visiting a prayer-of-the-day webpage (Young 2004: 96) is a form of online religion, blurring the clear distinction between interaction and communication of information suggested by Helland. In turn, Helland admitted the existence of a 'gray area of classification' between the poles of information and participation (Helland 2005: 8).

An example from Russian Orthodox practice may help elucidate the problem. Amongst the Russian Orthodox, there is a tradition of the so-called concerted prayer (*molitva po soglasheniiu*), which can be seen as a spatial extension of the regular congregational prayer, with or without a priest. In this practice, a number of believers, being in different geographical areas, agree to simultaneously pray about a certain problem at a certain point of time. In such a case, they transcend only temporal limitations. The prior agreement to pray is reached through some media of communication, nowadays often through the new media, yet the very act of praying takes place offline. Spatially, each participant is separated; but temporally, they are united in a simultaneous offline liturgical act. Although the details of the act can be discussed online beforehand, does this technical interaction constitute 'online religion' ipso facto? To describe it, I use the term 'non-liturgical interactivity.' Similarly, sending an e-mail to a priest asking for a prayer is certainly interactivity, yet it is non-liturgical.

Furthermore, does visiting a prayer-of-the-day website constitute an online liturgical act? In other words, is reading a prayer text on the screen liturgical? The proposal here is that, although the ROC leadership promotes interactive participation of its members and looks for their online feedback on many an issue, this interactivity does not necessarily constitute a liturgical act ipso facto. Instead, a prayer becomes an online liturgical act only if the participants number more than one person and if they simultaneously participate in a live audio/video conference service, such as Skype, which can offer a more interactional technology. This preserves the distinction between the informational and interactive approaches, especially when the latter consists of the liturgical and non-liturgical aspects.

4. Bridging time and space

Proceeding from the discussion on the concerted prayer, I see another frame for researching digital Orthodoxy—namely, viewing the internet as a bridge between time and space, that is, as an effective link in spacetime continuum. This frame joins two secluded dimensions, creating a productive crossroads on the back of a new media technology. The English language has the technical term 'space bridge' that corresponds with the Russian term 'TV bridge' (*telemost*), whose very name indicates a physical thing with a spatial dimension. This term appeared in the 1980s, when first TV bridges between two TV studios in the USA and USSR took place. The 'older' medium, television, lacked free interactivity; besides, it was a rare, costly, and complicated event in terms of time organization. The concerted prayer, on the other hand, is capable of surmounting time, while being hindered by space. These days, however, through the internet's video/audio conferencing technology, all parties to the prayer act can transcend both time and space—and yet maintain a direct connection to offline liturgical patterns. That is, despite their remote geographical locations and different time zones, the participants can see and hear each other in the real time and in one 'place.' It means that the Orthodox Church could, in principle, conduct some of its liturgical acts using the spatiotemporal bridge.

Etymologically, the word 'liturgy' implies a public work or act, which is a simultaneous collaboration of all in the same location and time. In the offline perspective, participants normally see and hear each other through the air, which is a natural physical medium. For the participants, an offline location normally means a certain building. Through conferencing on the spacetime bridge, participants can simultaneously see and hear each other via the internet and be present in one space point, thus combining time and space.

Nevertheless, the suggested frame has practical limitations. Antonio Spadaro, a Roman-Catholic theologian of the internet, wonders: 'Could you conceivably say a valid Mass by Skype? These are the kinds of (cyber) theological questions we're going to be dealing with very soon' (Spadaro 2012). The assertion made here, however, is that yes, you can 'say' it, just like you can 'say' it over the telephone, but can you *perform* it this way? In the Orthodox context, liturgy is not confined to verbal activity: its culmination is the sacrament of Communion, which is an act of actual eating Bread and Wine, received from a priest. If live prayer conferencing is fully imaginable, the process of eating is not, because the Host cannot be transmitted through the internet. The offline Communion model is unmediated in this regard (cf. Luchenko 2008; Geraci 2014: 118).[2]

---

2   It remains so, however, unless we introduce another paradigm: if those on the other side of the spacetime bridge already have the pre-sanctified Particles (*prezhdeosviashchennye dary*)—a well-known practice in Orthodoxy for cases of contingency, such as for dying persons in need of immediate spiritual help. If the pre-sanctified Particles could be safely delivered offline to the other side before

The sacrament of Confession for individuals cannot be performed online either: apart from the interactive verbal and visual confessing before the priest, the procedure further requires the priest to lay hands upon the confessed. Given that the latter is impossible online, the sacrament cannot take place. Finally, many Orthodox liturgical acts include incensing, whose smoke cannot be transmitted through the internet. However, Orthodoxy sometime practices the so-called 'common Confession' (*obshchaia ispoved'*), whereby the priest reads aloud an absolution prayer without laying his hands on the believers. This liturgical act is performable online, and it could be useful in extreme situations, such as during war.

Text messaging in the real time can also be problematic for the Orthodox practice, mainly due to verification issues: one cannot be certain, who exactly is writing the text on the screen, even if the alleged author is believed to be known. Perhaps, a combination of video and text conferencing (live video streaming along with live chatting) could serve as a solution, though this would be in the gray area of practice. Therefore, I see simultaneous live audio and video streams online as the most effective means of bridging time and space for the Orthodox Church. Regarding Christian communities with no binding offline sacramental acts involving non-verbal activity, as well as non-Christian religions meeting the same criterion, bridging time and space online has all the potential for successful application in full.

In addition to the above, further refinement of the online interactivity classification can be offered: to subdivide 'liturgical interaction' into *sacramental* and non-sacramental interaction. In this light, for example, the concerted prayer or another group prayer performed in the video/audio mode online turns out to be liturgical, yet non-sacramental, since not all the elements of the procedure are fulfilled

---

the respective online video/audio session, and then correctly administered to the participants in due time of the conferenced liturgy, the Eucharist as an interactive—yet *hybrid*—liturgical and sacramental act would be quite imaginable. The term 'hybrid Communion/Eucharist' (*gibridnoe prichastie*) suggests itself in the context. Moreover, in the hi-tech future, this hybrid interactivity can become quite standard, although without replacing the offline model.

to be called a sacrament. On the other hand, a common confession per Skype with a priest, who says an absolution prayer without laying his hands, does meet the prerequisites for the Church sacrament: for instance, this is practiced in the Russian Orthodox Church. Thus, the following structure helps better conceptualize how Orthodox religion can use the internet opportunities: 1) non-liturgical and liturgical interaction, on the first level of approximation; and 2) sacramental and non-sacramental interaction, on the second level *within* the liturgical type.

5. *Vox populi* and media theories

The central focus for the Russian Orthodox Church is its sacramental life. It is noteworthy that, after years of traditional reserve with respect to publicity, the ROC leadership came up with the initiative to organize a wide interactive discussion of some liturgical practices. For this sake, they uploaded a number of provisional texts, dedicated to Communion, Confession and the Church-Slavonic language, and called on the audience to speak up. Interestingly, the popular feedback (especially on the Church-Slavonic language) fit well in the key theoretical approaches to the problem of media and religion, considered in modern scholarship. These approaches are (see Lundby 2013): Marshall McLuhan's technological determinism: 'the medium is the message' (1964/1995); Stig Hjarvard's mediatization theory: media is an independent institution integrated by religion (2008); Stewart Hoover's mediation of meanings: reception of meanings via media (2006); and Gordon Lynch's mediation of sacred forms: communication of the sacred (2012). Apart from these, social shaping of technology (SST) defies technological determinism, arguing that 'technology is negotiable and that user groups may shape technology to their own ends' (Campbell 2010: 50). As a version of SST, Campbell suggests the religious-social shaping of technology theory, focusing on the 'specific conditions that occur within a religious user's negotiations with a technology' (see Campbell 2010: 58), which is also applicable to the ROC. Three of these frames may be described alternatively: for instance, technological determinism is also known as 'media as a mode of knowing'; mediation of meanings is also known as 'media as a conduit'; and mediatization is also known as 'media as a social institution' (Campbell 2010: 44–49). I discuss the specific reflection of the theories in the ROC online experience in the case studies.

6. The ROC's online standards

Current scholarship points out three themes 'regarding interaction between religion and computer technology and the spaces this creates' (Campbell/Lövheim 2011: 1088). One of these themes is 'how offline religious institutions organize and integrate their activities and aims in online context' (Campbell/Lövheim 2011: 1089). In this connection, the present online footprint of the Russian Orthodox community encompasses both corporate (institutionalized) and private sectors, as well as both lay and clergy personal websites and blogs, covering various issues of ecclesiastic and secular character. Institutionally, the Moscow Patriarchate has its own official portal *Patriarchia.ru* in three languages (Russian, Ukrainian, Moldovan), and more and more local dioceses and other entities, such as monasteries, arrange their own respective portals. In cooperation with *Google* (*YouTube* 2010), in 2010, the ROC also launched its official video channel on *YouTube* with sixteen playlists ('Russkaia Pravoslavnaia Tserkov"). This active media promotion was preceded by a structural shift within the ROC, when the Synod Informational Department was organized in early 2009 ('SINFO'), following the enthronement of Patriarch Kirill. Its main task is to provide a unified media and communications policy of the ROC, coordinate its subdivisions in the dioceses and cooperate with other mass media, both within and without the ROC. Overall, since 2011 the ROC leadership officially encourages online activity and computer-mediated communication, although, of course, under certain corporate standards. In general terms, the latter standards appear as follows:

120 ALEXANDER PONOMARIOV

> Self-governing churches, exarchates, metropolitan districts and metropolies may have their own internet websites publishing information on all dioceses, subdivisions and facilities of a given structural unit. At the same time, the portal should be an independent platform with its own editorial team and original content. It may contain links to diocese websites. However, the official dioceses websites should be independent and should not be organized as sub-websites of one portal of a self-governing church, exarchate, metropolitan district or metropoly. (Standard 2011b)

Corporate Church portals may have both open and closed domains, the latter reserved for internal purposes. The open, public domains should be multifunctional and rich in terms of design. At the same time, the ROC leadership warns the Church internet community not to abuse the Web 2.0 technology, as it would be incorrect to equate the official diocese websites with social networks lacking a recognized authorship. Nevertheless, links to respective Church-related blogs and other similar online resources are deemed possible, and blogs are acknowledged as often more efficient media than official websites (Standard 2011b).

The ROC requires the official diocese websites to be multi-structured. Besides, they must follow specific reference terms containing thirteen subsections: on the ruling hierarch (his CV and contact information, interviews, publications, meetings, preachings, photo album, etc.); on the diocese and its activity (its history, departments, activities, documents, and photo album); on the deaneries (their history, CVs, and churches); on the parishes (history of their churches, shrines, activities, and their contact information); on the diocese priests (their CVs, interviews, preachings, and publications); on the diocese mass media (newspapers, journals and magazines, radio and/or video channels, and online editions); on the calendar (menology, vitas of local saints, and celebrations); on the Inter-Council Office (discussions on respective documents within the diocese, feedback of the diocese, and overall diocese activities under the Inter-Council Office); on general ROC news; on the contact information of the diocese administration; on regional mass media; on the website search engines; on the editors' feedback and technical support (Standard 2011b). All in all, the corporate websites must be accessible all day every day, all year round. In so doing, each diocese may outsource technical specialists and web designers, as they can be hard to find within the Church community. It is highly interesting that the ROC leadership recommends creating mobile versions of the official corporate websites, thus acknowledging (and making use of) the ubiquity of the latest internet technologies, in general, as well as a deep involvement of the Russian Orthodox believers in contemporary internet developments and the techboom, in particular. The non-liturgical online interactivity, considered in the case studies below, fits well in and exemplifies the new internet policy of the Moscow Patriarchate.

Case Studies
1. Websites for interactive discussions

I take up some of the websites that the ROC leadership officially employs for the online conciliarity, such as an academia-oriented portal *Bogoslov.ru*, tailored to the Web 2.0 communication. The online discussions in question also intersect with the famous and popular, yet conceptually different, Orthodox web platforms *Pravoslavie.ru* and *Pravmir.ru*. These are multimedia projects, encompassing text, video, image, and sound materials on various aspects of the Church-related life. I also refer to the comments on the official website of the Inter-Council Office, *Msobor.ru*, and on the popular in the Runet blogging platform *LiveJournal.com*, used by the ROC.

Pravoslavie.ru is a 'veteran' launched in 1999 and run by the Sretenskii monastery in Moscow, headed by Bishop Tikhon (Shevkunov), who is believed to be close to the Kremlin. This authoritative portal appears to attempt to keep a certain balance between tradition and modernity. It promotes traditional forms and meanings of Russian Orthodoxy by uploading respective materials, while at the same time, for example, it also hosts the Russian Center for the Study of the Shroud of Turin, which researches this phenomenon from a scientific point of view, including molecular physics ('Rossiiskii Tsentr').

By contrast, *Bogoslov.ru*, launched in 2007, is the official theological portal of the Russian Orthodox Church, focusing on interaction among leading scholars and universities in the field of theology, Bible study, and other Church-related matters. Its distinct academic character is perhaps best described by the following statement of the portal's board: 'Neglecting the fruits of science today means, for spiritual education, to be doomed to marginalization and to the inevitable degeneration' ('O proekte').

Pravmir.ru (launched in 2004) aims at a wide Russian-speaking audience with a current monthly traffic of up to three million visitors ('O portale'). It is run by laymen with academic degrees in philology, ecclesiology, and mathematics, many of whom are women, under the auspices of Vladimir Medinskii, the sitting Minister of Culture of the Russian Federation ('O portale'). They have explored gender and religious practice in connection with Communion.

2. Online challenge to gender conventions

Until recently, there existed no uniform guidelines prescribing the ROC practices as regards Communion, and every diocese and even parish could keep their own. Whether the faithful may and should come to Communion often or seldom, whether they should confess each time before Communion or only occasionally, whether they should fast during the week in addition to Wednesday and Friday—all of those may vary in detail in terms of forms and meanings.[3] The document draft on Communion, uploaded by the ROC in September 2013, provides a useful outline of the range of established corporate approaches to the sacrament. In consists of seven inextensive parts and combines a rather liberal approach to the Eucharist with some rigorous ones. For one thing, it recognizes frequent Communion practices as normal, cutting off proponents of Orthodox 'scholasticism' and their 'over-pious' approach to the sacrament. On the other hand, unlike the Greek Orthodox practice, the ROC draft emphasizes the traditionally obligatory role of Confession for laymen before Communion. Moreover, it confirms the prohibition of receiving Com-

---

[3] Cf. Kozlov 2013: 'The practices, existing at present, are quire diverse, and they go down to various eras of the Church history.'

munion in the state of the so-called ritual female impurity, a stance attributed to ancient canon law. The latter more traditional and rigorous approach prompted resistance and indignation amongst some internet users. Some Orthodox women and even some of their clerical advocates utilized the online initiative of the ROC in order to express their disagreement and to try deconstruct the position of canon law, as well as to claim equal liturgical rights for modern women in general.

Participation in the Eucharist is closely connected with offline prescriptions and restrictions. For instance, the Church canons, referred to in the draft, forbid taking Communion during menstruation. The uploaded draft refers to the prohibition and gender discrimination, taking it for granted, without any theological explanation of why modern women should refrain one week every month from going to the Church. It is no wonder that one of the most interesting online discussions was generated by the gender issue, for instance:

> It sounds like an ostensible anachronism: 'Canons forbid taking Communion in the state of the female impurity [...].' One should not indulge in intimidating using the canons. They contain many prohibitions that have outlived themselves, and nobody applies them anymore. Why is precisely this canon so dear to us? (Priestal. 11 September 2013 // Communion 2013c)

In this online statement, the gender issue comes to the fore, making clear that ritual female impurity in the modern Orthodox community has a tendency to be seen as anachronistic. Users do not understand why the Russian Orthodox Church remains so strict regarding gender in the 21st century. Moreover, they draw from a modern biological perspective, when interpreting the ancient prohibition, and conclude that there can be nothing 'impure' in the human body per se (Mariia. 2 January 2014 // Communion 2013d).[4] These canons, therefore, seem for the internet opponents of the ritual prohibition obsolete and even inhumane. Moreover, they need not be complied

---

4 'The natural physiological processes of the organism, that are neutral in terms of the morals, cannot be 'impure,' they do not separate one from God, and accordingly, they should not separate one from the Eucharist because they do not depend on human will.'

with, since women are left outside the Church in their 'most difficult period' (Rinon. 16 September 2013 // Communion 2013c). These Orthodox female users want to be able to take Communion irrespective of whether they may be menstruating at the time or not (Mariia. 2 January 2014 // Communion 2013d).[5]

Considering this, there are attempts to explain the existence of the gender restrictions as reasonable. Usually, references are made to the Old Testament and to hygiene problems in the ancient times. This does not seem satisfactory to all discussants. Perhaps the most radical approach is that the canons on ritual impurity should be abolished. Some Orthodox users are deeply interested in solving this 'injustice,' sharing hyperlinks to interesting opinions on other online resources, including Orthodox priests who disagree with the applicable canon. One of the hyperlinks referenced a learned Orthodox nun Vassa, whose text was uploaded by *Pravmir.ru*. Vassa adduced plenty of references to various ecclesiastic sources and opinions, concluding that the idea of ritual impurity is not a Christian phenomenon (Vassa 2010).[6] Vassa's online statement appears to be one of the clearest voices raised for gender equality in modern Russian Orthodoxy. This voice is limited to the internet as a 'third place.' The tendency is however quite pronounced: a part of Orthodox women with access to the internet cannot come to terms with the existing offline practice and mediate their claim for equality through Web 2.0 communication.

---

5   'There are a lot of women, who take Communion with awe, faith and love throughout all days of the month without an exception, and they rejoice and live in Christ. Would anyone dare say that Christ rejects them in certain days? Is Christ like THAT?'

6   'An attentive consideration of the sources and the nature of the 'ritual impurity' notion discovers a quite confusing and essentially a non-Christian phenomenon under the guise of the Orthodox piety. Regardless of whether this notion infiltrated the Church practice under the direct influence of Judaism and/or paganism, it has no substantiation in Christian anthropology and soteriology.'

3. 'Cybergrace'

In Russian Orthodox practice, Communion is preceded by Confession, mandatory for laymen. This issue received broad public attention in 2006 (Prutianu 2013), and it was again highlighted by discussion of the ROC initiative. Its mandatory character caused an indignation online, directed against inequality of the clergy and laymen, since priests do not have to confess each time before the Eucharist.[7] It should be noted that, although the problem pertains to all the laymen regardless of their gender, more commonly it is female Orthodox writers online,[8] who express distaste for this offline sacramental tradition (Inna. 31 December 2013 // Communion 2013b).[9] Thus, the problem of modern offline Confession and Communion receives a radical online denial through some female users of this medium.

The conventional conservative approach to Confession[10] faces interactive materials dedicated to equality, such as an interesting view that was uploaded at *Bogoslov.ru* by a learned Orthodox hieromonk Petr (Prutianu 2013). Father Petr applies a historical and

---

7   For instance, (Protosinghel. September 11, 2013 // Communion 2013c): 'The document on Communion [promotes] a policy of double standards towards clerics and the lay. This is unacceptable for such documents. When our hierarchs and priests begin to fast and confess every time before Communion, only then let them adopt such a document.'
8   The question whether the nicknames in the respective comments correlate with the females implied (e.g., as opposed to males who might write these comments under the female nicknames) poses a problem of identification and verification on the internet. With a certain degree of certainty, we can assume that the persons behind the given nicknames are indeed women: the websites and their content are very specific, and tailored to specific audience, which fact reduces the chances of fraud.
9   'However, making up something beyond what is contained in the Rules of the Orthodox Church means hypocrisy of the clergy and the hierarchy. For they themselves do not comply with this, yet impose the burden hard to carry upon parishioners. The Rules contain nothing on mandatory Confession and fasting before Communion. These are very late and primitive fables in semi-pagan Russia.'
10 Cf. Fotii. February 5, 2014 // Communion 2013d: 'One should not come to the Cup without the Sacrament of Confession, and every Orthodox believer realizes and feels this, living a Church life. The rest is from the evil one who very subtly and cunningly promotes the renovationist ideas on cancelling the mandatory Confession.'

liturgical approach to the issue and argues that the existing 'sacred form' of Confession in the ROC is a relatively late (12th century) and 'wrong' phenomenon that twists the Christian message (Prutianu 2013). Father Petr suggests practical flexibility as a solution: according to his experience, those taking Communion a few weeks in a row and confessing only once are more responsible in their spiritual life than those who have to confess each time (Prutianu 2013). Another learned priest at *Bogoslov.ru*, Maksim Kozlov, supports this differentiated approach (Kozlov 2013). It is noteworthy that Father Maksim refers to modernity. He believes that a certain amount of control from the clergy should be preserved; still, it could be mediated in a less sacred form, as a blessing, for the experienced Orthodox parishioners. In general, both online accounts tend to disregard the necessity of different forms for the clergy and laymen.

By recognizing this, the ROC priests exemplify the idea of *sobornost'*, so strongly emphasized by Aleksei Khomiakov († 1860), a famous Russian philosopher. Khomiakov rejects the division of the Church as a medium into the clergy (those who teach) and laymen (those who are taught) as a Roman-Catholic idea and views Orthodoxy as a unity of all:

> Why were the (heretic) councils, which had no external differences from the Ecumenical Councils, rejected? It was only due to the fact that their resolutions were not recognized as the voice of the Church by all the Church people; those people and in that milieu where in the issues of faith there is no difference between a scholar and an ignoramus, a member of the clergy and a layman, a man and a woman, a sovereign and a subject, a slave-owner and a slave, [...]. This is the dogma lying in the core of the idea of a council. (Khomiakov 1907b: 70 [first published in 1853])

In this context, it could be expected that the digital environment would make for a wider, faster, and easier participation by the Orthodox grassroots with access to the internet, as well as a much more active role of individual judgment in the Church-related agenda. The Web 2.0 initiative appears to be moving towards interactive conciliarity, transfiguring the ideas of Khomiakov and acknowledging that 'the unity of God's grace' (Basis 2000: 1.1) stretches over to the internet as well.

4. Language as a medium

One of the burning issues of the modern Russian Orthodox Church is the use of the Church-Slavonic language as a sacred medium in Orthodox liturgy. A poll conducted in 2011 shows a sizable split in opinions on that score amongst Orthodox believers in Russia (Opros 2011): 37% of the polled would welcome a Russian-language liturgy, whereas 36% support the traditional Church-Slavonic service.

4.a. Sacred forms and meanings

The problem of the insufficient understandability of Church-Slavonic, as well as questions of the Church-Slavonic culture in Russian Orthodoxy are targeted in the special ROC's document *The Church-Slavonic Language in the Life of the Russian Orthodox Church of the 21st Century*, uploaded for discussion (Church-Slavonic 2011a). The document contains both history and resolution parts, aimed at presenting a comprehensive outline of the language's origin and development, as well as the actual approach to the language put forward by the ROC. The draft suggests a way of convergence to solve the language conundrum. On one end of the spectrum, it implies a mediation of meanings (further redacting liturgical books), and on the other end, it mediates the sacred forms via increasing the level of acquaintance with and performance of Church-Slavonic in practice. By wanting to keep Church-Slavonic as the sacred medium, while at the same time admitting that in some cases national spoken languages should be permissible (provided these are able to mediate original meanings and retain the elevated forms of the Orthodox service), the ROC document testifies that it does not view Church-Slavonic either as a value of its own (as a mode of knowing) or as a social institution. As for formal corrections and alterations, they should pertain only to the textual forms that indeed mediate obscure meanings. In some cases, it is permissible to simplify the underlying Greek forms. As can be seen, here the ROC authors attempt to achieve a relatively balanced approach, trying to avoid radical ruptures with either the medium or its meanings.

4.b. Mediation of meanings

Bogoslov.ru gave voice to a range of interesting responses to the initiative. Kirill Mozgov, a lay Orthodox professor, uploaded an article whose title suggests that the liturgical language can and even should be replaced by a 'better' medium (Mozgov 2011). His online article confronts an aspect that is widespread among the Russian Orthodox community: namely, Church-Slavonic not only mediates sacred forms and flavor—it is a 'God-given' tongue, that is, Church-Slavonic is an independent social institution, which can only be integrated as part of the given religion (cf. Lundby 2013: 229). For Mozgov, there are neither profane nor sacral forms; any language is just a mediation of meanings (Mozgov 2011).[11] He deconstructs the 'sacred form' of Church-Slavonic, arguing that the language is an implication of its poor meaning mediation for contemporary believers. This tendency can be explained by his rejection of the polar extreme, represented by medium determinism and by its more sophisticated 'ramification,' discussed below.

4.c. Mediatization

The mediation-of-meanings article of Mozgov received many interactive comments and also generated some articles as a reaction. For example, archimandrite Rafail (Karelin), a famous Russian monk, responded from an institutional language perspective, drawing on the special independent character thereof. His online text was published at *Pravoslavie.ru*. In particular, he argued:

> In order to translate liturgical texts [i.e., to mediate meanings], it does not suffice to be a poet, it requires acquiring a spiritual vision [i.e., an institutional quality]: ancient hymnographers used to be devotees and, if it be possible to express it this way, even co-authors of grace. Contemporary poets can hardly repeat the feat of the Saint Fathers—they will tinge their translation with passions and imagination. (Karelin 2011)

---

11 'Freedom in choosing the language of the liturgy implies a certain active position in the Church life and a respective responsibility for the choice. This approach allows one not to wallow in the established—even if sanctified by centuries— forms, that to date have often lost or are losing their true contents'.

'Co-authorship of grace' is a vivid metaphor, reflecting a traditional concept of synergy of man and God on earth. It raises the question, however, of why Rafail deprives modern generations of a possibility of this co-authorship. In this regard, he especially stresses the 'established' ancient character of Church-Slavonic and attaches special spiritual qualities to ancient languages in general, opposing them to modern ones (Karelin 2011).[12] It is clear that Mozgov's and Rafail's approaches are mutually exclusive. Mozgov is 'user friendly,' and, in a language, he looks for an optimal tool in a given context. Rafail, however, refers to the exclusive 'sacral' qualities of Church-Slavonic. Moreover, he applies a traditional philosophy of historical and spiritual decline of mankind, whereby the sacred medium has no competitors:

> The spiritual level of mankind is constantly decreasing, albeit this decrease is undulatory. In this regard, parallel to it, the spiritual orderliness of a language, that is, a possibility of expressing spiritual actualities via a contemporary language, is decreasing too. Therefore, even a perfect translation of liturgical texts from Church-Slavonic into Russian will be a damage and a loss. (Karelin 2011)

Rafail uses the internet to promote the idea of Church-Slavonic as of a standalone living substance or institution, and that humans are not free in their spiritual relations with God, as they need special media institutions to bridge those relations.

4.d. The ROC's shaping of technology

Referring to such extant language difficulties, however, neither the ROC leadership nor the interactive discussions mention a critical edition of the Church-Slavonic Bible. Strange as it may seem, Slavic

---

12 'Mozgov does not consider the difference between ancient and modern languages, and their figurative capabilities. In the meantime, the language is directly connected with human thinking and emotions. The language is a reflection of the soul, and the life of the previous generations was more theocentric than that of ours. Ancient languages to a certain extent help preserve and transmit this spirituality trough the word. Modern languages are more anthropocentric, they are more capable of transmitting the psychological life of the man.'

Orthodoxy has no critical Slavic edition of the Holy Scripture, similar to such media as *Biblia Hebraica Stuttgartensia* and *Novum Testamentum Graece*. Further, the ROC has no official digital text of the Slavic Bible, used for the offline Church service, although the new media and online activity may require the introduction of new technologies, such as Church-Slavonic fonts and other software for online texts. Neither the official website of the ROC nor the official website of the Synod Informational Department contain options that would enable users to download fonts. The Russian Orthodox and Orthodox-affiliated community demonstrates, nevertheless, that they can successfully adapt to typical technological challenges around fonts. Starting in 2000, a group of enthusiasts organized the Community of Slavic Typographics to develop and promote Church-Slavonic software tools and standards ('Tipografika'). Regarding specifically the fonts, its subdivision is a website *Irmologion.ru* that provides a collection of Church-Slavonic fonts for the free download. In addition, they took further strides technologically toward making the fonts available:

> In March 2008, the international Unicode Consortium considered the proposition filed by the Community, underpinned by the Publishing Council of the Russian Orthodox Church, the Institute of the Russian Language of the Russian Academy of Sciences and other organizations, and included extended Church-Slavonic fonts into the Unicode standard of the world alphabets that will enhance the Church-Slavonic language in the new versions of operational systems and software products. ('Kathisma')

Moreover, *The Journal of the Moscow Patriarchy* recently came up with a mobile application of the *Journal* for iPads. The editor-in-chief substantiated the event as follows:

> Today, it does not suffice for a printed edition to have only an internet version. It requires separate versions for tablet devices, too [...]. It is quite possible that, in the future, the print edition and its tablet version will have a different content. We have an opportunity to publish fuller articles and considerably more illustrative material in the tablet version. I also hope to see a multi-media content. ('iPad')

One of the most interesting projects is the official ROC's website dedicated to swift sharing of new liturgical texts, corporate journals, calendars, etc., with the subordinated subdivisions of the ROC ('Teksty'). For instance, the liturgical texts are accessible for downloading in different formats (printer friendly, Word, and PDF) and in two types of fonts (in Church-Slavonic in the PDF version and in Modern Russian transliteration in the remaining two versions). Because it is becoming common practice for Russian Orthodox priests to use mobile devices during the service instead of or along with the traditionally bulky print media in the 'sacred form,' this website can be especially useful for parishes with a visiting priest who has all the required liturgical texts either already downloaded and stored, or accessible online. In practice, these electronic texts are used akin to the offline print ones—they are read aloud or sung, by the priest himself and/or the choir. The difference is the medium used: digital texts on mobile gadgets. Such developments show how the Russian Orthodox media community can actually shape the required technology and domesticate it. This is a compelling field of research and fertile area for further academic attention and development.

Conclusion

I considered the ROC online activities from the perspective of non-liturgical interactivity. Most likely, the ROC leaders will keep focusing on 'how the internet can be used to support their religious identity and theology in their social and spiritual outreach' (Campbell 2010: 39). Today, ROC officials are actively promoting the use of the internet among the clerics and the flock, paying attention to the latest technical achievements such as mobile devices and at the same time trying to control the online activity. The ROC does not turn into a cyberchurch, but rather, it is an established offline entity with significant online extensions, complying with the 'the researches [that] have concluded that "faith-related activity online is a *supplement* to, rather than a *substitute* for offline religious life"' (Lundby 2012: 34). As an example of how a technological innovation has become woven into the fabric of Church life, an 'older' medium, television, has become a regular tool that is used to broadcast Orthodox liturgies on major holidays in Russia, yet it has changed nothing in terms of the priority of gathering in the offline Church.

The case studies considered in this paper show that the Russian Orthodox grassroots has gotten an opportunity to partake in the contemporary Church agenda en masse and influence it by contributing their comments (albeit, for the time being, it remains to be seen, given the recent character of the ROC initiative, whether the comments can significantly influence the content of the document drafts posted for the public consideration). In particular, the discussion of the ritual impurity problem gives voice to Orthodox internet users with a potential to challenge 'the conventions of gendered speech in offline ritual genres' (Campbell/Lövheim 2011: 1092). The online discussion of the Confession problem, contrary to the established offline practice, tends to view the lay and the clergy as one 'medium,' converging the former and the latter in line with the Khomiakovian ecclesiology of *sobornost'* as a unity of all in the Body of Christ. The language issue demonstrates a range of media approaches. The conventional approach institutionalizes ancient languages in general and Church-Slavonic in particular, in compliance with the mediatization theory. It is noteworthy that the chief proponent of this view, Rafail, uses a personal website as a new medium in order to disprove the opposite position on the language as a mere conduit. Besides, the ROC engages in domestication and shaping of technology.

The desire of the ROC leadership to involve Orthodox internet users in the Web 2.0 era points to a search for a new dimension of 'unity in multitude' (Khomiakov 1907a: 313 [first published in 1860]). The ROC under Patriarch Kirill attempts to act, at least formally, 'according to the understanding of all' (Khomiakov 1907a: 313 [first published in 1860]), aiming at the idea of 'the Church of a free and complete unanimity' (Khomiakov 1907a: 313 [first published in 1860]), which includes the digital aspect. By instrumentalizing the new media, the ROC initiative transfigures the conventional offline conciliarity, turning it into an online conciliarity: *sobornost'* 2.0. The synonyms can be internet-*sobornost'* (iSobornost'), interactive *sobornost'*, or online-*sobornost'*, respectively.

References

Ahlbäck, Tore (2013). 'Editorial Note' in *Digital Religion*, ed. by Tore Ahlbäck. Abo/Turku: Donner Institute for Research in Religious and Cultural History. P. 5.

'Tserkovnoslavianskii iazyk v zhizni Russkoi Pravoslavnoi Tserkvi. Diskussiia.' *Pravoslavie.ru.* http://www.pravoslavie.ru/polemika/4863 6.htm (accessed May 1, 2014).

Baab, Lynne (2012). 'Toward a Theology of the Internet: Place, Relationship, and Sin' in *Digital Religion, Social Media and Culture. Perspectives, Practices and Futures*, ed. by Pauline Hope Cheong, Peter Fischer-Nielsen, Stefan Gelfgren, Charles Ess. New York: Peter Lang. pp. 277-292.

Basis (2000) – The Basis of the Social Concept of the Russian Orthodox Church. *The Russian Orthodox Church. The Official Web Site of the Department for External Church Relations.* https://mospat.ru/en/documents/social-concepts/ (accessed April 17, 2014).

Becker, Carmen (2011). 'Muslims on the Path of the *Salaf Al-salih*: Ritual Dynamics in Chat Rooms and Internet Discussion Forums' in *Information, Communication & Society. Special Issue: Religion and the Internet. Considering the Online-Offline Connection*, ed. by Heidi A. Campbell and Mia Lövheim. Vol. 14. No 8. December 2011. pp. 1181–1203.

Campbell, Heidi (2010). *When Religion Meets New Media (Media, Religion and Culture).* New York: Routledge.

Campbell, Heidi and Lövheim, Mia (2011). 'Rethinking the Online-Offline Connection in the Study of Religion Online' in *Information, Communication & Society. Special Issue: Religion and the Internet. Considering the Online-Offline Connection*, ed. by Heidi A. Campbell and Mia Lövheim. Vol. 14. No 8. December 2011. pp. 1083–1096.

Campbell, Heidi (2012). 'How Religious Communities Negotiate New Media Religiously' in *Digital Religion, Social Media and Culture. Perspectives, Practices and Futures*, ed. by Pauline Hope Cheong, Peter Fischer-Nielsen, Stefan Gelfgren, Charles Ess. New York: Peter Lang. pp. 81–96.

Campbell, Heidi (2013). 'The Rise of the Study of Digital Religion' in *Digital Religion. Understanding Religious Practice in New Media Worlds*, ed. by Heidi A. Campbell. New York: Routledge. pp. 1–22.

Campbell, Heidi and Grieve, Gregory (ed., 2014). *Playing with Religion in Digital Games*. Bloomington: Indiana University Press.

Church-Slavonic (2011a) – 'Proekt dokumenta *Tserkovnoslavianskii iazyk v zhizni Russkoi Pravoslavnoi Tserkvi XXI veka.*' *Ofitsial'nyi sait Moskovskogo Patriarkhata.* http://www.patriarchia.ru/db/text/1542 499.html (accessed May 1, 2014).

Church-Slavonic (2011b) – 'Proekt dokumenta *Tserkovnoslavianskii iazyk v zhizni Russkoi Pravoslavnoi Tserkvi XXI veka.*' *Pravoslavie.ru.* http://www.pravoslavie.ru/polemika/47105.htm (accessed May 1, 2014).

Church-Slavonic (2011c) – 'Proekt dokumenta *Tserkovnoslavianskii iazyk v zhizni Russkoi Pravoslavnoi Tserkvi XXI veka.*' *Bogoslov.ru.* http://www.bogoslov.ru/text/1762795.html (accessed May 1, 2014).

Cohen, Yoel (2013). 'Awkward Encounters: Orthodox Jewry and the Internet' in *Digital Religion*, ed. by Tore Ahlbäck. Abo/Turku: Donner Institute for Research in Religious and Cultural History. pp. 42–54.

Communion (2013a) – 'Proekt dokumenta *O podgotovke ko Sviatomu Prichashcheniiu.*' *Patriarchia.ru.* http://www.patriarchia.ru/db/text/32256 77.html (accessed April 17, 2014).

Communion (2013b) – 'Proekt dokumenta *O podgotovke ko Sviatomu Prichashcheniiu.*' *Bogoslov.ru.* http://www.bogoslov.ru/text/3480916.html (accessed April 17, 2014).

Communion (2013c) – 'Proekt dokumenta *O podgotovke ko Sviatomu Prichashcheniiu.*' *LiveJournal.* http://mpr.livejournal.com/20467.html (accessed April 17, 2014).

Communion (2013d) – 'Proekt dokumenta *O podgotovke ko Sviatomu Prichashcheniiu.*' *The Inter-Council Office of the Russian Orthodox Church.* http://www.msobor.ru/discussion.php?id=74 (accessed April 17, 2014).

Connelly, Louise (2013). 'Virtual Buddhism: Buddhist Ritual in Second Life' in *Digital Religion. Understanding Religious Practice in New Media Worlds*, ed. by Heidi A. Campbell. New York: Routledge. pp. 128–135.

Fischer-Nielsen, Peter (2012). 'Pastors on the Internet: Online Responses to Secularization' in *Digital Religion, Social Media and Culture. Perspectives, Practices and Futures*, ed. by Pauline Hope Cheong, Peter Fischer-Nielsen, Stefan Gelfgren, Charles Ess. New York: Peter Lang. pp. 115–130.

Foxeus, Niklas (2013). 'Esoteric Theravada Buddhism in Burma/Myanmar' in *Digital Religion*, ed. by Tore Ahlbäck. Abo/Turku: Donner Institute for Research in Religious and Cultural History. pp. 55–79.

Garner, Stephen (2013). 'Theology and the New Media' in *Digital Religion. Understanding Religious Practice in New Media Worlds*, ed. by Heidi A. Campbell. New York: Routledge. pp. 251–265.

Geraci, Robert (2014). *Virtually Sacred: Myth and Meaning in World of Warcraft and Second Life*. New York: Oxford University Press.

Golan, Oren (2013). 'Charting Frontiers of Online Religious Communities: The Case of Chabad Jews' in *Digital Religion. Understanding Religious Practice in New Media Worlds*, ed. by Heidi A. Campbell. New York: Routledge. pp. 155–163.

Helland, Christopher (2000). 'Online Religion / Religion Online and Virtual Communities' in *Religion on the Internet: Research Prospects and Promises*, ed. by Jeffery K. Hadden and Douglas E. Cowan. Amsterdam: JAI Press/Elsevier Science. pp. 205–223.

Helland, Christopher (2005). 'Online Religion as Lived Religion. Methodological Issues in the Study of Religious Participation on the Internet' in *Online – Heidelberg Journal of Religions on the Internet*. Volume 01.1. Special Issue on Theory and Methodology. pp. 1–16. http://archiv.ub.uni-heidelberg.de/volltextserver/5823/1/Helland3a.pdf (accessed September 12, 2014).

Hjarvard, Stig (2008). 'The Mediatization of Religion: A Theory of the Media as Agents of Religious Change' in *Northern Lights: Film and Media Studies Yearbook*, 6. Bristol: Intellect Press. pp. 9-26.

Hoover, Stewart (2006). *Religion in the Media Age*. Oxon: Routledge.

Hoover, Stewart (2013). 'Imagining the Religious in and through the Digital' in *Digital Religion. Understanding Religious Practice in New Media Worlds*, ed. by Heidi A. Campbell. New York: Routledge. pp. 266–268.

Hutchings, Tim (2011). 'Contemporary Religious Community and the Online Church' in *Information, Communication & Society. Special Issue: Religion and the Internet. Considering the Online-Offline Connection*, ed. by Heidi A. Campbell and Mia Lövheim. Vol. 14. No 8. December 2011. pp. 1118–1136.

Hutchings, Tim (2012). 'Creating Church Online: Networks and Collectives in Contemporary Christianity' in *Digital Religion, Social Media and Culture. Perspectives, Practices and Futures*, ed. by Pauline Hope Cheong, Peter Fischer-Nielsen, Stefan Gelfgren, Charles Ess. New York: Peter Lang. pp. 207–226.

Hutchings, Tim (2013). 'Considering Religious Community through Online Churches' in *Digital Religion. Understanding Religious Practice in New Media Worlds*, ed. by Heidi A. Campbell. New York: Routledge. pp. 164–172.

iPad – '"Zhurnal Moskovskoi Patriarkhii" predstavil versiiu dlia iPad.' *Patriarchia.ru.* http://www.patriarchia.ru/db/text/3004257.html (accessed July 30, 2014).

Jones, Mark (2012). 'Voting "Present": Religious Organizational Groups on Facebook' in *Digital Religion, Social Media and Culture. Perspectives, Practices and Futures*, ed. by Pauline Hope Cheong, Peter Fischer-Nielsen, Stefan Gelfgren, Charles Ess. New York: Peter Lang. pp. 151–168.

Jonveaux, Isabelle (2013). 'Facebook as a Monastic Place? The New Use of the Internet by Catholic Monks' in *Digital Religion*, ed. by Tore Ahlbäck. Abo/Turku: Donner Institute for Research in Religious and Cultural History. pp. 99–109.

Karelin, Rafail (2011). 'Zametki k stat'e Kirilla Mozgova o perevode tserkovnoslavianskikh tekstov na russkii iazyk.' *Pravoslavie.ru.* http://www.pravoslavie.ru/smi/48754.htm (accessed May 3, 2014).

Kathisma – 'Vypushchen novyi tserkovnoslavianskii shrift Kathisma.' *Patriarchia.ru.* http://www.patriarchia.ru/db/text/452495.html (accessed July 30, 2014).

Khomiakov, Aleksei (1907a). 'O znachenii slov "kafolicheskii" i "sobornyi" (s frants.)' in *Polnoe sobranie sochinenii Alekseia Stepanovicha Khomiakova.* Sochineniia bogoslovskiia. Izdanie piatoe. S portretom. T. II. Moskva: Tipo-litogr. T-va I.N. Kushnerev i K°. pp. 305–314.

Khomiakov, Aleksei (1907b). 'Po povodu broshiury g-na Loransi (s frants.)' in *Polnoe sobranie sochinenii Alekseia Stepanovicha Khomiakova.* Sochineniia bogoslovskiia. Izdanie piatoe. S portretom. T. II. Moskva: Tipo-litogr. T-va I.N. Kushnerev i K°. pp. 27–90.

Kozlov, Maksim (2013). 'Vazhno ukazat' predely, dal'she kotorykh trebovat' ot mirian nevozmozhno.' *Bogoslov.ru.* http://www.bogoslov.ru/text/3508575.html (accessed May 3, 2014).

Lomborg, Stine and Ess, Charles (2012). '"Keeping the Line Open and Warm"': An Activist Danish Church and Its Presence on Facebook' in *Digital Religion, Social Media and Culture. Perspectives, Practices and Futures*, ed. by Pauline Hope Cheong, Peter Fischer-Nielsen, Stefan Gelfgren, Charles Ess. New York: Peter Lang. pp. 169–190.

Luchenko, Kseniia (2008). 'Internet i religioznye kommunikatsii v Rossii.' *Relga.ru.* http://www.relga.ru/Environ/WebObjects/tgu-www.woa/wa/Main?textid=2228&level1= main&level2=articles (accessed July 18, 2014).

Luchenko, Kseniia (2009a). 'Internet v informatsionno-kommunikatsionnoi deiatel'nosti religioznykh organizatsii Rossii.' Avtoreferat. *DisserCat.* http://www.dissercat.com/content/internet-v-informatsionno-kommunikats ionnoi-deyatelnosti-religioznykh-organizatsii-rossii (accessed July 18, 2014).

Luchenko, Kseniia (2009b). 'Internet v informatsionno-kommunikatsionnoi deiatel'nosti religioznykh organizatsii Rossii.' Avtoreferat dissertatsii na soiskanie uchenoi stepeni kandidata filologicheskikh nauk. *Mediascope.* http://mediascope.ru/node/269 (accessed July 18, 2014).

Lundby, Knut (2011). 'Patterns of Belonging in Online/Offline Interfaces of Religion' in *Information, Communication & Society. Special Issue: Religion and the Internet. Considering the Online-Offline Connection*, ed. by Heidi A. Campbell and Mia Lövheim. Vol. 14. No 8. December 2011. pp. 1219–1235.

Lundby, Knut (2012). 'Dreams of Church in Cyberspace' in *Digital Religion, Social Media and Culture. Perspectives, Practices and Futures*, ed. by Pauline Hope Cheong, Peter Fischer-Nielsen, Stefan Gelfgren, Charles Ess. New York: Peter Lang. pp. 25–42.

Lundby, Knut (2013). 'Theoretical Frameworks for Approaching Religion and New Media' in *Digital Religion. Understanding Religious Practice in New Media Worlds,* ed. by Heidi A. Campbell. New York: Routledge. pp. 225–237.

Lynch, Gordon (2012). *The Sacred in the Modern World: A Cultural Sociological Approach.* Oxford: Oxford University Press.

McLuhan, Marshall (1995). *Understanding Media. The Extensions of Man.* Cambridge, Massachusettes: The MIT Press.

Miczek, Nadja (2013). '"Go Online! Said My Guardian Angel": The Internet as a Platform for Religious Negotiation' in *Digital Religion. Understanding Religious Practice in New Media Worlds,* ed. by Heidi A. Campbell. New York: Routledge. pp. 215–222.

Mozgov, Kirill (2011). 'Voz'mem li my na sebia otvetstvennost' za bezdeistvie, otkazavshis' ot perevoda bogosluzheniia, ili pochemu v Rossii rasprostraneno mnenie, budto obrashchat'sia k Bogu mozhno tol'ko na tserkovnoslavianskom?' *Bogoslov.ru.* http://www.bogoslov.ru/text/1929089.html (accessed May 1, 2014).

Noomen, Ineke; Aupers, Stef; Houtman, Dick (2011). 'In Their Own Image? Catholic, Protestant and Holistic Spiritual Appropriations of the Internet' in *Information, Communication & Society. Special Issue: Religion and the Internet. Considering the Online-Offline Connection*, ed. by Heidi A. Campbell and Mia Lövheim. Vol. 14. No 8. December 2011. pp. 1097–1117.

O portale. *Pravmir.ru.* http://www.pravmir.ru/redakciya/ (accessed August 26, 2015).

O proekte. *Bogoslov.ru.* http://www.bogoslov.ru/about.html (accessed August 26, 2015).

Opros 2011 – 'Iazyk bogosluzhenii: tserkovnoslavianskii ili russkii? Rezul'taty Vserossiiskogo reprezentativnogo oprosa, provedennogo Sluzhboi SREDA (polevye raboty: FOM-Penta, vyborka 1500 chelovek),' *Pravoslavie.ru.* http://www.pravoslavie.ru/press/48856.htm (accessed May 1, 2014).

Prutianu, Petr (2013). 'Snova o glavnom, ili piatomu punktu posviashchaetsia.' *Bogoslov.ru.* http://www.bogoslov.ru/text/3494522.html (accessed May 3, 2014).

Rashi, Tsuriel (2013). 'The Kosher Cell Phone in Ultra-Orthodox Society: A Technological Ghetto within the Global Village?' in *Digital Religion. Understanding Religious Practice in New Media Worlds*, ed. by Heidi A. Campbell. New York: Routledge. pp. 173–181.

Rossiiskii Tsentr. Rossiiskii Tsentr Turinskoi Plashchanitsy. *Pravoslavie.ru.* http://www.pravoslavie.ru/sm/page_1110.htm (accessed August 26, 2015).

Russkaia Pravoslavnaia Tserkov'. *YouTube.* https://www.youtube.com/user/russianchurch (accessed May 17, 2014).

Scheifinger, Heinz (2013). 'Hindu Worship Online and Offline' in *Digital Religion. Understanding Religious Practice in New Media Worlds*, ed. by Heidi A. Campbell. Abingdon. pp. 121–127.

Schlosser, Dominik (2013). 'Digital Hajj: The Pilgrimage to Mecca in Muslim Cyberspace and the Issue of Religious Online Authority' in *Digital Religion*, ed. by Tore Ahlbäck. Abo/Turku: Donner Institute for Research in Religious and Cultural History. pp. 189–203.

SINFO – Sinodal'nyi informatsionnyi otdel. *Patriarchia.ru.* http://www.patriarchia.ru/db/text/602595.html (accessed August 26, 2015).

Sisler, Vit (2013). 'Playing Muslim Hero: Construction of Identity in Video Games' in *Digital Religion. Understanding Religious Practice in New Media Worlds*, ed. by Heidi A. Campbell. New York: Routledge. pp. 136–146.

'Sostoialas' prezentatsiia ofitsial'nogo kanala Russkoi Pravoslavnoi Tserkvi na YouTube' (2010). *Patriarchia.ru*. http://www.patriarchia.ru/db/text/1295600.html (accessed April 2, 2014).

Spadaro 2012 – *A Conversation with Antonio Spadaro, SJ, Journalist at Civiltà Cattolica Review, Rome*. Berkley Center for Religion Peace & World Affairs. July 21, 2012. http://berkleycenter.georgetown.edu/interviews/a-conversation-with-antonio-spadaro-sj-journalist-at-civilta-cattolica-review-rome (accessed February 11, 2015).

Standard 2011a – 'Sozdan *Standart prisutstviia eparkhii Russkoi Pravoslavnoi Tserkvi v Internete*.' *Patriarchia.ru*. http://www.patriarchia.ru/db/text/1794546.html (accessed April 2, 2014).

Standard 2011b – 'Standart prisutstviia eparkhii Russkoi Pravoslavnoi Tserkvi v Internete.' *Zhivaia voda* [Aqua Viva]. http://aquaviva.ru/standart_prisutstviya_eparkhiy_russkoy_pravoslavnoy_tserkvi_v_internete_standart_prisutstviya_eparkh.php?clear_cache=Y (accessed April 2, 2014).

Stewart, Anna (2011). 'Text and Response in the Relationship between Online and Offline Religion' in *Information, Communication & Society. Special Issue: Religion and the Internet. Considering the Online-Offline Connection*, ed. by Heidi A. Campbell and Mia Lövheim. Vol. 14. No 8. December 2011. pp. 1204–1218.

Taira, Teemu (2013). 'Does the "Old" Media's Coverage of Religion Matter in Times of "Digital Religion"?' in *Digital Religion*, ed. by Tore Ahlbäck. Abo/Turku: Donner Institute for Research in Religious and Cultural History. pp. 204–221.

Teksty – Novye bogosluzhebnye teksty. Ofitsial'naia publikatsiia bogosluzhebnykh tekstov, utverzhdennykh Sviateishim Patriarkhom i Sviashchennym Sinodom Russkoi Pravoslavnoi Tserkvi. http://nbt.rop.ru/ (accessed August 26, 2015).

Tipografika – 'Soobshchestvo slavianskoi tupografiki'. http://cslav.org/ (accessed August 26, 2015).

Vassa 2010 – 'O ritual'noi ne/chistote: Chto eto i zachem?' *Pravmir.ru*. http://www.pravmir.ru/o-ritualnoj-nechistote-chto-eto-i-zachem/ (accessed April 22, 2014).

Young, Glenn (2004). 'Reading and Praying Online: The Continuity of Religion Online and Online Religion in Internet Christianity' in *Religion Online: Finding Faith on the Internet*, ed. by Lorne Dawson and Douglas Cowan. New York: Routledge. pp. 93–105.

Chapter 5.
Heretical Virtual Movement in Russian Live Journal Blogs: Between Religion and Politics

Ekaterina Grishaeva
Ural Federal University

Introduction

Since the religious renaissance of the early 1990s, the Russian Orthodox Church (ROC) has become an important social institution which has a significant influence on Russian society. The growing political and social influence of the ROC is not openly discussed in the press but instead has become a subject of constant debate in cyberspace. The Russian blogosphere is full of discussions about the ROC as a political actor, in particular in Patriarch Kirill's work. In 2012, just before and after the presidential election, these debates were especially intensive, fuelled by Pussy Riot's performance in the Cathedral of Christ the Saviour (February 2012) and the notorious photographs showing Patriarch Kirill's luxurious apartment in the centre of Moscow and his luxury watch (March/April 2012).

In 2012 Russian *LiveJournal* (thereafter LJ) became the most suitable platform to discuss problems associated with the ROC. Evgenii Gornyi points out that Russian LJ is well structured and provides a highly intellectual level of discussion (Gornyi 2009). LJ is used as a place for discussion and cooperation, as a source of information and the latest news (Kurchakova 2006). For that reason, LJ is also a good source of empirical information about intellectual and socio-political movements in Russian society. In 2012 the post-denominational bloggers were particularly active in LJ. This group is a kind of heretical community criticizing Orthodox clergy. They also use heretical ideas to express their own religiosity.

Post-denominational bloggers define their views as heretical and consider their heterodoxy as a tool for discerning true Christianity from false doctrine. The Christian doctrine of the post-denominational bloggers is very close to the ideas of post-denominational believers, especially in their understanding of the nature of the Church. The understanding of the Church as a non-institutionalized group of believers is at the heart of both doctrines; the true Church is always Christ-centred and does not aim to have any significant social and political influence. The post-denominational bloggers seek to introduce liberal changes and innovations to the traditional Christian theology; their 'do-it-yourself' theology contravenes the ROC's conservative line of theological thinking.

On the basis of the same heretical ideas, the bloggers create a branching network of users with varying degrees of involvement in the discussion and creation of heretical content. The most influential post-denominational blogger, the so-called 'opinion leader' or heresiarch, is Vladimir Golyshev (golishev.livejournal.com[1]). He creates high quality 'heretical content', and other users spread his ideas within the LJ community through reposts and comments, sometimes making minor additions. This article concentrates on an analysis of the ideas put forward by the heretical post-denominational community, more specifically on the ways in which this heterodoxy is presented in cyberspace. This analysis will address three main research questions:

> What is the difference between the definition of heresy in the theological discourse and that presented in the post-denominational heretical discourse of Golyshev's blog?
> How are traditional Christian concepts such as God, the Church, and sin, transformed in Golyshev's heterodoxy?
> How does cyberspace influence the way in which heterodoxy is presented?

---

1   Vladimir Golyshev is a popular blogger and publicist who discusses political and religious issues in Post-Soviet space. When this research was conducted, in 2014, Golyshev was on 402 place of 500, according to the *Yandex* ranking of the most popular Russian LJ bloggers; by autumn 2015 he made 10 069 post, sent 84 360 comments and received 236 079 comments via his LJ account. Since 2014 his activity is mainly concentrated on *Facebook*, where he has over 4200 followers.

The activity of the post-denominational Orthodox bloggers does not go beyond cyberspace: bloggers do not assemble offline, have no specific rituals, and for many of them discussion of their personal heretical views is possible only on the internet. Therefore, it can be concluded that this new heretical movement exists only online and has a relatively minor impact on social reality.

Methodology

By means of discourse analysis (Foucault 2000; Fairclough 1989; T. van Dijk 1998) the author discusses bloggers' subject positions that are shaped by religious and political discourses. Discourse is a social practice which systematizes and regulates social interactions through power relations, relationships of communication and objective capacities. Within the discourse, the language is controlled by power institutions: people cannot say everything they think to whomsoever they wish (Foucault 2000). The traditional religious discourse is highly regulated: power relations are institutionalized by the ROC and expressed, for example, through the inequality between the priesthood and the laity; the content of the discourse is based on the requirements set in the Scriptures and Tradition. Golyshev, who created a heretical doctrine, constructs an alternative religious discourse, free from the ROC as a subject power, transforming the meaning of existing terms.

The language of the blogs reflects any changes in the discourse and beliefs of the participants in power relations as well as any of their knowledge transformations. An analysis of the blogs allows us to describe the conceptual content of Golyshev's heretical discourse and his political criticism of the ROC. All entries (from golishev@lj, elijah-morozoff@lj, vasia-tapkin@lj,) in the period from February to May 2012 and posted key papers were studied and sorted according to their titles and content. The text fragments were analyzed to identify the religious views of the users, and then copied to separate files. The selection of relevant blog posts has depended on the texts and this researcher's underlying values and perspectives, as a consequence of which the research has become a co-production between the researcher and the individuals studied (Burr 2003: 152). To systematize the disparate ideas expressed by the bloggers on religious topics and to present their heretical beliefs as a unity, the research applied the elements of grounded theory (Strauss 1997), which were used as an auxiliary tool to organize different ideological meanings in clusters. The method of an online survey was used to cast light on the way cyberspace influences the presentation of heterodoxy.

Vladimir's Gospel, or why one should not believe in God

Vladimir Golyshev is the mastermind of this heretical movement. By analyzing the basic facts of Vladimir Golyshev's biography, we can reveal the background for the evolvement of this heresy. According to Golyshev's 'User Info' page, he lives in Rostov-na-Donu and Moscow; for several years he was involved in journalistic and public activity. He worked on the newspapers 'Zavtra', 'Effective Policy Foundation (FEP)', 'Russian Journal', 'National Information Group'; he was the editor-in-chief of the website *Nazlobu.Ru*; supported Vladimir Putin and had anti-opposition views in 2002–2005 but then turned to liberal ideas. In 2006–2008 he was a regular contributor to the website kasparov.ru. In 2009 Golyshev deliberately refused to continue his career as a journalist and political consultant and began to write plays: '*Barnaul'skii natariz*', 'Prebiotics', '*Lyzhneg*' (a satirical play with the protagonists being Patriarch Kirill and Metropolitan Hilarion Alfeev).

Vladimir Golyshev has a higher theological education, which allows him to construct his own heterodoxy (he graduated from St. Tikhon's Orthodox University). In the 1990s, he, like many others, came to accept the Orthodox Church and became a very active parishioner; many people saw in him a future priest. His active church-going (*votserkovlenie*) was the reason for his entering St. Tikhon Orthodox University. In one of his posts, he writes:

> When in 1990 I came to the Church, I was captured by the idea of following the wonderful man of faith who was honoured to 'see God as He is' I was reading the 'Philokalia', Abba Dorotheus, 'The Ladder', 'The Unseen Warfare', and similar works, saw myself exclusively in monastic clothes, once a week (invariably!) went to the Holy Trinity-St. Sergius Lavra to make a confession to a red-bearded monk who I identified as my spiritual father (golishev@lj, 30.01.2015).

Golyshev left the parish after five years of active church-going. He does not regret his decision to 'turn his back on the ROC', because he sees it as a secular structure that has no relation to true Christianity and personal salvation. Golyshev evaluates modern Christianity through the opposition of true/false, personal/social. The personal spiritual experience of fr. Seraphim as filled with grace is opposed to the ROC, which is presented as a corrupt social mechanism stifling people's freedom. Thus, Golyshev perceived his decision positively, as a rejection of untrue Christianity, and became fiercely critical of the ROC, denouncing it as corrupt.

Golyshev's heterodoxy: a shift from theological to political definition

In Orthodox theology, heresy is defined through its opposition to the concept of dogma. Dogma is a divinely revealed doctrine about God and His economy (from the Greek word εκονομια) in the world which is adopted by the Church and has a binding character. Heresy is a false opinion which distorts the essence of dogma and is shared by a group of people who deny their affiliation to the official Church (Davidenkov 2013). The word 'heresy' comes from the ancient Greek 'αἵρεσις', which means selection, direction, doctrine and from the verb 'αἱρέω': to take, seize, choose, elect. Andrei Kuraev (Kuraev 1994) clarifies that heresy is always a rational interpretation, a simplification of the content of dogma. Various kinds of heresies focus on only one part of the doctrine and try to make it more comprehensible to the human mind. It is necessary to distinguish between heresy and theologumen, a private theological opinion, which does not contradict and does not affect the essence of dogma.

The post-denominational bloggers do not turn to the classical theological definition of heresy but use another one, proposed by Patriarch Kirill in his sermon on the Sunday of Orthodoxy in 2008. This definition inadvertently equates to heresy and schism and in some aspects contradicts the definitions of Orthodox theology. The concept of heresy is used to protect the Church from internal schisms and to criticize Orthodox fundamentalists. It is closely linked to the political situation and has an ideological significance. The post-denominational bloggers have applied Patriarch Kirill's definition of heresy to construct their own concept of heterodoxy. They use the notion of heresy mostly in political contexts to struggle against detractors by simplifying its theological meanings; they repeat phrasings from Patriarch Kirill's sermon such as 'the dangerous fire of anger appears in his eyes', 'a wolf in sheep's clothing' etc.

> Every heresy produces schisms, but where there is schism there is no love [...] Where there is no love, there are no honest relations and no unity [...] If we meet a man who claims to struggle for the purity of Orthodoxy but there is a dangerous fire of anger in his eyes .... he is ready to fight for the schism of the Church [...] when we do not find love but find only anger in the man who is the leader of heterodoxy, this is the first sign that he is a wolf in sheep's clothing (Patriarch Kirill 2008).

Theologians point out that the wrong interpretation of the Christian doctrine as well as the lifestyle and spiritual mistakes of the theologizing individual could provoke heresies. Patriarch Kirill uses a less complicated method by pointing out that the main problem of heresy is the lack of love and the anger at one's neighbour; he absolutizes the role of the psychological preconditions for a heretical movement against the theological. The post-denominational bloggers mentioned the same qualities: anger, the lack of love, dissimulation, pride, but they invert the definition of heresy given by Patriarch Kirill and attribute the heretics' characteristics to the Orthodox hierarchy itself, and see heretics as true Christians.

On the contrary, in the works of theologians there is no idealization of heretics; they are characterized as followers of the antichrist, as liars and thieves, which should emphasize their negative effect on the Church and the need for their anathematization. Patriarch Kirill, like the post-denominational bloggers, idealized heretics when he wrote that they had always attracted people by their high moral and spiritual qualities. Golyshev understands heresy in a positive way as a tool that can improve modern Christianity. In this sense a heretic is a true Christian who, following Christian precepts, denounces the ROC clergy, whose way of life contravenes Christian principles, and denies his / her affiliation with the ROC. As Golyshev puts it, 'I even want to call my heresy KHRISTOSLOVIE [theology of Christ]' (golishev@lj, 30.01.2015).

The definition of heresy put forward by the post-denominational bloggers resembles that of Patriarch Kirill: it is not deeply rooted in the theological tradition. The bloggers invert Patriarch Kirill's definition and criticize the ROC hierarchy, comparing it to false Christians who have forgotten Christ. They use the concept of heresy as a marker of their marginal position in the ROC, of their deep spiritual and political confrontation with the traditional religious institutions. They also tend to liberalize the main concepts of the Orthodox doctrine to construct their personal Christian theology, appropriate to their lifestyle and political views. Golyshev's heterodoxy is used as a tool to criticize the ROC, which sometimes makes it difficult to determine whether or not these religious ideas are used as political attention-getters.

Concepts of Church, sin and the role of the Scriptures in Golyshev's heterodoxy

As part of his politically charged criticism of the ROC, Golyshev points out that the Church as a social institution is not a prerequisite for salvation because of its bureaucratization and the drive to accumulate profits. The Orthodox clergy are identified with the hieratic priesthood; thereby Golyshev emphasizes how far they are from true Christianity. Golyshev identifies institutional Christianity with paganism by drawing an analogy with primitive societies and the Byzantine Empire, where state power was closely associated with religion.

In demonstrating the pagan and heretical character of the Orthodox clergy, Golyshev named Patriarch Kirill the antichrist, and mentioned the following signs of the advent:

> Try to make a 'composite sketch' of the antichrist:
> he Is distanced from Christians,
> but active in missionary work;
> he speaks a lot about sins and the Church,
> about heavenly bliss and the torments of hell,
> about the virtue of maidens, of sheep's wool;
> about anything except Christ,
> who came in the flesh,
> was crucified and was raised from the dead (golishev@lj, 22.12.2010).

According to Golyshev, Patriarch Kirill as the antichrist serves the Church but does not serve God: his activities are formal, hypocritical, and pharisaical; they are primarily concentrated on the retention of power and the preservation of the Church's material well-being. Moreover, such activity contradicts the voice of conscience and thus deprives the person of the grace of the Holy Spirit.

In naming the ROC a heretical organization, Golyshev contradistinguishes faith in Christ and faith in the 'United Holy Apostolic Church'. He writes that bureaucratic games and acquisitiveness are more important than the imitation of Christ for the modern Orthodox clergy who have betrayed Christian ideals. The Church has ceased to be a marginal social institution as it was at the time of the Roman persecutions of the early Christians or in the Soviet period. Nowadays it is no longer open to marginalized people (such as beggars, homosexuals etc.), and non-acquisitiveness has been replaced by the pursuit of luxury. The Church today is a social institution which tries to solve the economic and demographic problems of Russian society, and protect its traditional values, but it does not perform its basic function: to provide its parishioners with spiritual guidance on their way to Christ. Recognizing the importance of fasting, prayers and worship established by the Church, Golyshev believes that in modern society these practices are useless because the Church itself no longer abides by Christian ideals.

To be free from the corrupt institution of the Church, Golyshev develops his own understanding of the nature of religion which is different from that of Orthodox theology. A true believer should leave the ROC in order to remain a true Christian and to save his/her soul; personal salvation does not depend on affiliation with the ROC. Faith in God is no longer a value in itself; the direct, personal encounter with Christ is much more important and is associated with spiritual knowledge, not faith. Abstract inenarrable Christian faith emerges as a result of formal observance of the Christian commandments, while spiritual knowledge is something different, being based on continuing spiritual practice: 'internal doing' (*vnutrennee delanie*). Golyshev's 'internal doing' is not described exclusively within the framework of the Hesychastic tradition but can also be compared to Zen Buddhist practice; for example, the apostles and saints are called '*sensei*'. The narrative of Orthodox theology and the ideas of Zen Buddhism are mixed in many of Golyshev's posts on religion:

> Sensei taught us not only faith but something else:
> To hope for the Father,
> To be Christlike,
> Inhale the Holy Spirit (golishev@lj, 21.12.2010).

Golyshev emphasizes the importance of the right attitude, 'the correct posture' in 'internal doing'; he uses metaphors borrowed from Zen Buddhism to explain the way of Christ and how to follow it. The ideas of Zen Buddhism are clearer and more understandable to the reader than Orthodoxy; consequently, they are more suitable to explain Golyshev's ideas to his followers.

> What exactly should I do?
> 1. Hope for the loving and forgiving Heavenly Father and wait for a meeting with him;
> 2. To imitate Jesus Christ, who was crucified and rose from the dead;
> 3. Become a tabernacle for the Holy Spirit, who will eliminate all misunderstandings;
> So, here we are dealing not with an abstraction or the Code but the Path ('dao'),
> modus vivendi and modus operandi rolled into one.
> To accept the apostolic teaching means practice, it means following Christ (golishev@lj, 30.03.2014).

Golishev wants to overcome the formal rituals and rules of institutionalized religion because the Church as a social institution is corrupt; this connects Golyshev's heresy with Protestant theology. Another common feature is that Golyshev uses the concept of predestination but has not developed it in detail in his posts. As some Protestant leaders, Golyshev spiritualizes Christianity, but he claims that external religiosity and formal reading of the Scriptures is not helpful. For him the voice of conscience and the internal spiritual experience of a believer is more important than the Scriptures. Protestantism, on the contrary, admitted the importance of the texts of the Old and New Testament for Christians. In the words of Bengt Hegguld, 'we must hold on to certain commandments and apostolic writings to prevent the Church from being destroyed' (Hegguld 1989).

Golyshev initially creates his heterodoxy within the framework of his political criticism of the ROC and his own political activity; that is why his heretical ideas are mainly concentrated on criticizing the Church as a social institution and tend to be shallowly theological and profane. He is interested in non-institutionalized Christianity free from formal theological dogma, which will allow believers to realize personal spirituality. At the same time it means contradictions or even the absence of any theological background in his heterodoxy.

To present Christianity as an internal personal practice, Golyshev narrows the concept of sin adopted in Orthodox theology. In order to have the Holy Spirit inside one, one need not succeed in fulfilling the commandments formally (it is equivalent to being hypocritical), but instead succeed in following the 'voice of conscience'. Conscience should prompt a person in how to act, so his actions will be endorsed by Christ.

> Sin is commonly called a bad thing
> or not a good tendency (passion) but
> what is sin, generally speaking?
> I think it's the wilful destruction of conscience
> and silencing the voice of the heart, that is, Dukhoborchestvo.
> A man tries to expel the Holy Spirit from his soul,
> It leaves him,

> But there remains an 'alarm button', a flashing heart forever'
> 'The fact is that for Christians there is ultimately only one sin:
> To think I have no sin
> or: I am not as sinful as that tax gatherer (or harlot)
> (golishev@lj, 22.12.2010).

Sin has nothing to do with the external observance of commandments; it just depends on the extent to which a person is internally close to Christ. Conversely, external God-likeness is often associated with a self-righteous attitude toward Christianity; a person who has violated the commandments and is aware of his or her sin is closer to God than the righteous one who formally follows all Christian commandments but does not see his or her sins. On the one hand, this approach certainly emphasizes personal freedom and the importance of human freedom for God but, on the other hand, it makes moral choice vague and shaky.

By contrast, in Orthodox theology the person's consciousness and his/her actions are closely interrelated. Sin is damage to human nature in general, to its physical and spiritual components. Having the willingness to commit a sin actually means committing a sinful act. Sin manifests itself in non-observance of the commandments, which are the preconditions for physical and moral health. Golyshev emphasizes only the inner aspect of sin; for him a person's conduct is secondary.

The redogmatization of the concept of sin leads to the liberalization of Christianity in Golyshev's posts. In the series of posts entitled 'Sex with Christ', Golyshev formulates his attitude toward the possibility of premarital sex for Christians. Initially, he describes three hypostases of human nature: angelic, human, and animal. In sexual relations in a family a person can appear in the animal hypostasis despite following the commandments; externally virtuous behaviour does not mean a change in the inner man. Golyshev does not justify but nor does he prohibit premarital sex; he emphasizes that the eternal taboo is less important than the person's internal attitude to what is happening. For Golyshev it is unacceptable to perceive another human being only as a sexual object: if a person seeks to be Christ-like, this behaviour is unacceptable for him.

Golyshev emphasizes that the clergy who require everybody to obey the commandment 'thou shalt not commit adultery' actually do not obey this commandment themselves. This devalues their external pharisaical righteousness even more.

The idea of personal salvation and the denial of the significance of the institutional Church, the concept of predestination, and the criticism of the ROC as a social institution and political actor—all this at some point brings together Protestantism theology and the doctrine of Golyshev. Golyshev makes a sincere attempt to reform the existing Church, to return to the true Christianity of the first centuries, but Golyshev's heterodoxy is highly politicized. The desire to undermine the social and political authority of the ROC leads to a personal interpretation of Christianity, which is liberal and spiritual, free from any external dogma. Golyshev's doctrine is a simplified version of Christian theology; he has also mixed Christianity and Zen Buddhism, presenting his heresy as a light version of religion which does not imply any deep religious search.

Golyshev's online heterodoxy and offline mixed religiosity

The non-institutionalized post-denominational version of Christianity appeared as a result of political criticism of the ROC. Golyshev's heterodoxy is not deeply rooted in Orthodox theology; it is focused on individual needs and personal spiritual experience with rituals and commandments being perceived as formal and unnecessary. The combination of various religious ideas and the simple, understandable model of Christianity are not the preeminent features of Golyshev's online heterodoxy, they correspond to the mixed postsecular religiosity in offline society.

Mixed religiosity is a combination of different elements of traditional religious concepts, spiritual ideas, and practices. In some cases, mixed religiosity is conjoined with traditional religion, while in other cases it is a 'religion in my own way'.

In modern Russia, on the one hand, the role of the Russian Orthodox Church has become extremely important, but on the other hand, the number of actively practicing believers is decreasing (Lebedev, Sukhorukov 2013; Pronina 2014; Sinelina 2013) because of religious pluralism, pragmatic values, and a utilitarian approach to life, an interrupted tradition of religious socialization, and the lack of basic religious education (Grishaeva, Cherkasova 2013). For all the above-mentioned reasons, mixed religiosity prevails in Russian society. Thus, the representation of mixed religious ideas in Golyshev's blog reflects the level and the forms of religiosity in offline society. This conclusion is confirmed by the results of other research which has demonstrated that online religion is an integral part of the transformations undergone by offline religion (Lövheim 2012; Lövheim, Linderman 2005; Campell 2010).

The salience of cyberspace particularly influences the way in which Golyshev's mixed religiosity and heterodoxy are presented. Such high-ranking bloggers as Golyshev are engaged in a struggle for rating supremacy: they know that their posts should be clear, interesting, and original in order to win readers' recognition. The fragmentary perception characteristic of internet users and the high speed of information transmission also require the texts to be more simplified. Most texts are written in order to convince the reader, which makes original but simple ideas more suitable for this purpose.

Golyshev, like other top bloggers, often refers to the mass media: he discusses hot news to attract readers to his blog and to express his political and religious views. This makes the content of Golyshev's heterodoxy even more politicized. Golyshev covers current news about the ROC by writing several posts a day, which enables him to repeat his basic heretical ideas; his posts tend to be monotonous and contain little new information. The specificity of the news format affects the stylistic patterns of Golyshev's posts on religion. Information should meet the criteria of novelty and edginess to become popular and sell well: therefore, preference is usually given to conflicts, scandals, and breaches of norms (Luman 2000). Most of

Golyshev's heretical posts have a polemical, provocative, even shocking character.

Golyshev has found a good way to express his religious ideas in an original literary form, which allows him to attract many followers. He is not a religious prophet with a deep personal religious experience; first and foremost he is a public activist, so his clearly expressed heterodoxy is capable of affecting the thoughts of his numerous followers. Golyshev often refers to the Scriptures and quotes from the writings of the saints; some posts resemble a prophet's sermon, some mimic biblical poetics in a caricatured way. It is important to note that, while offering his own understanding of Orthodox theology and asceticism, Golyshev is self-critical and understands his lack of theological knowledge. In most cases, his statements are emotion-driven; sometimes he makes logical mistakes in his arguments or substitutes notions. Despite his ironic, pathetic and provocative texts, in some posts Golyshev emphasizes the intimate significance of the content, the seriousness of his attitude to what he is writing about:

> What is VERY, very important to me (I wrote it the whole night and in the morning)
> is the case when I humbly ask my respected friends TO TAKE NOTICE
> and click this link: http://golishev.livejournal.com/1503063.html
> and have a taste of this text
> and then 'it's in your power...to punish me with your derision'
> (golishev@lj, 20.11.2010).

To sum up, the mixed religiosity inherent in Golyshev's heterodoxy is widespread in offline society and it is not determined by the salience of cyberspace. In its turn, the internet environment affects the presentation of Golyshev's heterodoxy: his heretical posts are clear, understandable, monotonous, even provocative. Although Golyshev's religious views represent a holistic system, they are superficial and profane, targeted at attracting the audience's attention.

The LJ heretical community as an online religious minority

A heretical community is a unity of religious bloggers who have no formal affiliation with the ROC; in some sense they are outcasts and the only way they can share and discuss their 'do-it-yourself' Christianity is online. Such religious ideas are unlikely to be supported by the majority of Orthodox believers offline. Some of the post-denominational bloggers use Golyshev's blog as a platform to systematize their political and religious views; they often make reposts or leave positive comments but in that case they do not provide their own interpretation of the situation. For many LJ bloggers the amount of reposted content significantly exceeds the content they produce themselves.

Other LJ users actively support Golyshev by reposts, call themselves heretics and supply his heterodoxy with new ideas. For example, vasia-tapkin@lj mixes heretical views with philosophical criticism of consumer society; elijah-morozoff@lj makes libertarianism part of his heretical identity. Both are in opposition to the existing social order and play marginal social roles. LJ user groups are not isolated from each other. In LJ the discussion of various problems within one group is often determined by the opponent: for instance, Golyshev's posts are usually read not only by the post-denominational bloggers but also Orthodox users, who get involved in heated disputes and argue against heretical ideas. Thus, different online behavioural strategies can be identified: simple reposting, rethinking of Golyshev heterodoxy, and argument.

The heretical community does not exist outside cyberspace. So, perhaps, religious beliefs which are described in the posts of Vladimir Golyshev and are shared by his followers are only a part of an alternative virtual identity which does not coincide with any online identities. The question of whether the discussion of heretical views is connected with the bloggers' need to find like-minded people in cyberspace or whether it is just a game, a performance, an attempt to attract attention, is still unclear. In one online survey LJ bloggers were asked to describe their online behaviour. Most found it difficult to answer this question because they do not give much thought to their own virtual behaviour: one blogger reflected on his/her offline behaviour quite often but online behavioural strategies tend to be produced unconsciously.

As expected, users evaluate the degree of openness in LJ differently: some claim that there is no difference between their online and offline behaviour, some point out that they create an alternative identity which can be used, for example, when they engage in trolling. Bloggers of the first group mentioned the private character of their posts, they perceive LJ as a personal diary; therefore, the reader is seen as their listener or interlocutor.

'If my presence in LJ was just a game, then any discussion would not be serious. And now I am completely sincere about what I write in LJ and in my comments, so I say what I think and I am ready to repeat the same offline. Sometimes I say even more than I would say offline because it is always easier to write than to speak directly to a person'.

The second group identifies the construction of a virtual identity with the creation of a persona in literature. In this case the difference between the virtual and real identity can be compared to the difference between a written text and speech; it occurs by itself, the same way as a persona does in poetry, regardless of the author's intentions, when he/she begins to create a text. For this category of user, the questions about sincerity online are completely irrelevant. Any text is an independent reality where the author tends to construct a kind of ideal personality.

'We communicate here in writing, so we can change and edit what we write and analyze the words of our interlocutor as long as we want, and we are always aware of the fact that anybody else can read our posts and comments. On LJ I have used foul language only twice (and both times quickly removed those words). In offline communication it is impossible, that is why the word "sincere" can be applied only to personal, real-life conversation'.

Many LJ users emphasize that in LJ posts they talk only about the things they are willing to discuss with others. A conscious choice of topic and a manner of speaking is also a way of constructing a virtual identity. Participation in the survey was voluntary and, hypothetically, it is also possible to single out a third group of bloggers who identify blogging with trolling and who did not want to participate in the survey for obvious reasons.

Most LJ bloggers think that virtual identity mostly manifests itself in debates, while the greatest seriousness and sincerity is mostly found in posts. Online religious discussions are characterized by competitiveness and the desire to win and to prove one's point. Bloggers emphasize that debates about religion often turn into trolling; deeply religious people as well as non-religious users can trick the reader and 'play with their head', so to speak. As a rule, discussions on religious themes in Golyshev's blog have an intellectual character; bloggers have a good level of theological education, are able to provide arguments to support their points of view, and quote from the Bible and from the texts of the Holy Fathers. At the same time a large number of comments cannot be called well-reasoned; they appeal to everyday experiences and emotions. Such comments are not approved of by the readers, who immediately ask the blogger to cite a passage or provide additional arguments. Some of these comments were removed by the users themselves or by Golyshev.

Some of the post-denominational bloggers (elijah-morozoff@lj, vasia-tapkin@lj) who actively participate in discussions make reposts, and produce their own heretical content, and view participation in the life of the online heretical community as a kind of serious experience which enables them to share and construct their own outcast religious identity. The internet provides a relatively safe space where they feel comfortable and protected. On the other hand, the line between bloggers' religious and political identities is blurred and they often use heretical ideas as a means to point out the political mistakes of the ROC and even the Russian government.

Conclusion

The post-denominational bloggers use the internet as a space where they can freely discuss religious and political problems, and construct and maintain their outcast religious identities. The post-denomination definition of heresy is not connected with the Orthodox theological background but rather with the definition of heresy given in Patriarch's Kirill sermon: in both cases heretics are idealized and the political context evidently prevails over the theological meaning. Golyshev uses heretical ideas to criticize the policy of the ROC; in his heterodoxy the boundary separating religion from politics is blurred. Political criticism of the ROC is a key reason why Golyshev presents Christianity as a non-institutionalized spiritual practice which is more focused on individual experience than on theological dogma. Golyshev's heretical ideas are profane, secular, and do not imply any deep religious search. Golyshev constructs a model of Christianity which is simple to understand and follow: to that end he has mixed different religious concepts such as Zen Buddhism, Protestantism, and mystical elements of Eastern Christianity. Mixed religiosity in Golyshev's posts is a widespread phenomenon in offline Russian society and it does not depend on the salience of the internet.

Internet space, which does not support a serious and attentive style of reading, influences the way in which Golyshev's heterodoxy is organized and presented. Complex theological ideas are presented in a simple and understandable manner, they do not require any great religious or intellectual effort on the part of the readers and they do not take too much of their time. Nevertheless, like other bloggers, Golyshev emphasizes his seriousness and personal involvement when he creates his posts. The post-denominational bloggers consider LJ as a unique opportunity to discuss serious problems connected with the ROC and hot political issues because offline discussion is impossible. Thus, bloggers organize their own heretical community to express their minority religious views and their outcast identity. Despite the large number of supporters and opponents, Golyshev's doctrine has not exercised a significant effect on the external social reality but it is likely to create the conditions for social change within the Church.

References

Burr, Vivien (2003). *Social Constructionism*. London: Routledge.

Campell, Heidi (2010). *When Religion Meets New Media: How to Negotiate New Technology Religiously*. New York: Routledge.

Dijk, Teun van (1998). *Ideology: A Multidisciplinary Approach*. London: SAGE Publications.

elijah-morozoff. Various posts, LiveJournal. http://elijah-morozoff.livejournal.com/ (accessed 31 August 2015).

Fairclough, Norman (1989). *Language and Power*. London: Longman.

Foucault, Michel (2000). 'The Subject and Power' in *Power. Vol. 3 of Essential Works of Foucault 1954–1984*, edited by James D. Faubion. New York: The New Press, 326–348.

Golyshev. Various posts, LiveJournal. http://golyshev.livejournal.com (accessed 31 August 2015).

Gornyi, Evgenii (2009). *Russkii LiveJournal: vliianie kul'tumoi identichnosti na razvitie virtual'nogo soobshchestva*. Moscow: NLO.

Grishaeva Ekaterina, Cherkasova, Anastasia (2013). 'Orthodox Christianity and New Age Beliefs among University Students of Russia: a Case of Post-Communist Mixed Religiosity'. *Religion and Society in Central and Eastern Europe*, 1:9–20.

Hegguld, Bengt (1989). Istoriia *teologii* / The history of theology, http://www.gumer.info/bogoslov_Buks/History_Church/hegglund/index.php (accessed 31 August 2015).

Kashkin, Vasilii (2007). *Osnovy teorii kommunikatsii: kratkii kurs*. Moscow: AST Vostok-Zapad.

Kuraev, Andrei (1994). 'Dogmat i eres' v khristianskom predanii'. *Voprosy filosofii*, 9:112–147.

Kurchakova, Natal'ia (2006). Formy samoprezentatsii v bloge. St Petersburg: Novaia real'nost'.

Lebedev, Sergei, Sukhorukov, Vladimir (2013). 'Tesnyi put' v netuda'. *Sociological Studies*, 1:118–126.

Lövheim, Mia (2012). 'Identity' in *Digital Religion: Understanding Religious Practice in New Media Worlds*, edited by H. Campell. New York: Routledge, 47–54.

Lövheim, Mia, Linderman, A. (2005). 'Constructed Religious Identity on the Internet' in *Religion in Cyberspace,* edited by M. Hojsgaaard and M. Warburg. London: Routledge, 121–137.

Luman, Nicolas (2000). *The Reality of the Mass Media.* Stanford: Stanford University Press.

Patriarch Kirill (2009, 8 March). 'A Sermon on the Sunday of Orthodoxy', *patriarchia.ru.* ttp://www.patriarchia.ru/db/text/577278.html (accessed 31 August 2015).

Pronina, Tat'iana (2014). 'Religioznaia identichnost' v sovremennoi Rossii'. *Religiovedenie,* 2:134–144.

Sinelina Iuliia (2013). 'Religioznost' v sovremennoi Rossii'. *Otechestvennie zapisky,* 1(52). http://www.strana-oz.ru/2013/1/religioznost-v-sovremennoy-rossii (accessed 31 August 2015).

Strauss, Anselm, Corbin, Juliet (1997). *Grounded Theory in Practice.* London: SAGE Publications.

vasia-tapkin. Various posts, LiveJournal. http://vasia-tapkin.livejournal.com/ (accessed 31 August 2015).

Chapter 6.
Between Homophobia and Gay Lobby: the Russian Orthodox Church and its Relationship to Homosexuality in Online Discussions

Hanna Stähle
University of Passau

Introduction

After years of repression and persecution under the Communist Regime, Russian Orthodoxy experienced an unprecedented spiritual revival and became central to national identity in the early 1990s (Batalden 1993: 3f.). With the dissolution of the Soviet Union, the majority of the Russian population underwent a deep existential crisis and rapid social decline. Along with radical economic and political reforms, Russian society faced profound social upheaval and a breakdown of trusted public institutions, common values and norms. In these times of traumatic and sudden changes, the Russian Orthodox Church, widely perceived as a victim of Marxist-Leninist ideology and state atheist politics, faced a tremendous religious demand among the people. In search for stability and legitimacy, Russian political leaders embraced Orthodoxy and promoted its role as a moral authority and as a symbol of Russia's national resurgence.

Strongly favoured by the state, the Russian Orthodox Church managed to overcome its marginal social status and substantially increased its influence and public presence over the course of the last two decades. With the consolidation of state power and increasing control over society under Vladimir Putin, the Church gained even more relevance as a carrier of national values and traditions and as a "foundation" of Russian statehood. When, on Christmas Eve in 2014, the Gifts of the Magi were delivered from the Agiou Pavlou monastery on Mount Athos in Greece to Moscow, tens of thousands of Orthodox believers lined up in front of the Cathedral of

Christ the Savior to worship the relics. Images of endless queues of the faithful, waiting for hours in the cold were broadcasted throughout the country and serve as evidence of Church's power and influence in people's everyday life. However, increasing criticism by public figures, scholars and activists undermines this positive perception of the Orthodox Church in post-Soviet Russia. Particularly in the era of new technologies and Web 2.0 with its unlimited networking, opinion-sharing and interacting possibilities, the Church became a constant object of intense discussions and swingeing attacks. Numerous Russian-language websites, chat forums, blogs, wikis and social media platforms address Orthodox Christianity and its role in a (post)secular society. In particular, current discussions in digital media show a contrasting picture to the state's acceptance and endorsement of the Church. Online portals abound with heated debates and severe criticism regarding the state's close cooperation with the Moscow Patriarchy, the Church's increased media presence, its visibility in public schools and the army, Church property restitution and controversial opinions expressed by Orthodox hierarchs.

The article seeks to represent and analyze this segment of the Russian Internet that has become visible to large online audiences, but that has been insufficiently studied and accessed so far. The study seeks to gain insights into the Church-critical discourse in present-day Russia and to outline its dynamics, patterns of communication, argumentation strategies, confrontations or even 'web wars' (Rutten *et al.* 2013). The following essay focuses on the gay lobby controversy that was triggered by homosexual scandals at the Kazan' Theological Seminary and widely discussed in blogs and social networks in early 2014. My research approach combines quantitative and qualitative methods.[1] In order to define the online event and to narrow the dataset, I formulated a list of key words associated with the research topic, which will be introduced and discussed in greater depth in the subsequent chapters. The data was retrieved from two databases—from *Yandex Search for Blogs* for analyzing social me-

---

1 As the following investigation is set in the Russian-Orthodox context, the article discusses first and foremost *male* homosexuality and homophobia.

dia and blogs, and *Integrum* for investigating print and online newspapers. The quantitative part of the research, visualized through various charts throughout the text, provides not only an overview of discourse dynamics and thus enables a comparison of various sources but also helps to focus the qualitative phase of the investigation and makes the dataset accessible to a close reading analysis. Further, the article explores how the Russian Orthodox Church is perceived and interpreted online: it provides insights into a multilayered, complex debate on homosexuality, and analyzes how it is affected by state-imposed homophobia and the anti-gay campaign.

Homosexuality in Russia: position of state and Church

With the enhancement of gay rights, increasing liberal legislation and greater social acceptance of same-sex relations in West-European countries, the issue of gender and sexuality became an arena for political and moral discussion in Russia. While the discourse on homosexuality in the West is largely framed in terms of civil rights, equality and societal inclusion, it follows different patterns in the Russian context. In contrast to the heterosexuality that is portrayed as normal, natural and genuinely Russian, homosexuality is referred to as abnormal love, as non-traditional and immoral behaviour and, what is more, as a product of Western cultural influence (Baer 2009: 6). As historian Dan Healey claims in his extensive study on homosexual desire and state regulation of same-sex practices in late-tsarist, revolutionary and Soviet Russia, by thinking and understanding homosexuality in geographic terms and by situating the Russian cultural realm between the perverted West and the pure East 'permitted and permits Russians to imagine their nation as universally, naturally, and purely heterosexual' (2001: 253). This is also true for post-Soviet Russia.

Although official policy toward homosexuality was different and inconsistent throughout history, ranging from tolerant and affirmative to openly homophobic and repressive, same-sex relations were documented for centuries and were part of sexual experience in Russia. First attempts to regulate and control sexuality were undertaken under Peter the Great, resulting in a legal ban on male homosexuality in the armed forces (ibid.: 22). In 1835, this regulation was extended to the civilian population and the Criminal Code that defined homosexual intercourse as illegal was introduced (ibid.). Legal measures on sodomy and a number of medical documents as well as personal diaries demonstrate the visibility of same-sex relations in the public sphere in nineteenth-century Russia. These accounts show that same-sex relations were viewed as part of patriarchal society and masculine culture before transforming to a homosexual subculture in its modern sense (ibid.). After a short period of liberal legislation on homosexuality in revolutionary Russia, sodomy law was reintroduced to the Soviet Criminal Code in 1934 and homosexual issues became socially taboo (Kondakov 2013: 158).

The silencing of homosexual discourse and its representation in arts, literature and science during the Soviet period (Baer 2009: 43) contributed to the absence of the gender language and to the denial that sexual and gender dissent ever existed in Russia:

> Soviet information controls created [...] the impression that homosexuality was a vice of Western capitalism. In the press there was no reporting of closed prosecutions for male sodomy, while sexological literature about the 'female homosexual' was supposed to be issued to specialists alone. The biographies of literary and cultural figures were distorted, heterosexualized, or suppressed. (Healey 2001: 256)

With the collapse of the Soviet Union, sexual minority issues returned in the political and public domain. In 1993, homosexual intercourse between consenting adults was decriminalized. However, the repeal of the Article 121 of the Criminal Code was not a result of public discussion but rather a necessary condition for Russia to become a member of the Council of Europe (Kondakov 2013: 161), and a consequence of growing international pressure. In 1999, homosexuality was removed from the official list of clinical pathologies and mental diseases by the Russian Psychiatric Association (Sapper, Weichsel 2013: 3; Kondakov 2013: 161). Despite these legal measures, strikingly persistent views of homosexuality as a mental condition and as a foreign import continued to dominate the understanding of gender and sexual dissent in post-Soviet Russia. Decriminalization and depathologising of homosexuality in Russia were not preceded by any scientific research and public debates, as historian and sociologist Igor' Kon rightly emphasizes in his study on the relationship between homophobia and democracy in post-Soviet Russia (2013: 51). Sudden and unprecedented visibility of same-sex issues in media and politics after the demise of communism only strengthened the impression that homosexuality was a product of Western influence.

Feared, condemned and demonized, homosexuality has been used for contesting power relations, articulating Russia's sovereignty and defining the *Self* and the *Other*. Since Vladimir Putin's accession to power, a rising tide of nationalist and traditionalist rhetoric put forward by public figures and politicians can be clearly observed in Russia. As Brian James Baer puts it persuasively, '[t]he idea of homosexuality as a symptom of the sorry state of Russian society in general and of Russian masculinity in particular is widely voiced' (2009: 10). While homosexual visibility during the Yeltsin era was conceived as a 'crisis of masculinity' (Baer 2009: 10), 'the return of the Russian male to social, economic, and political power under Putin was expressed in [...] the dispersal by the Moscow police of the gay pride parade in 2006' (ibid., see also Zogrdrader 2013: 221f.). This open suppression of gay rights activists created a symbolic rupture with the previous political agenda of perceived adaptation and mimicry of Western values, and marked an appearance of an allegedly strong, masculine state with its own ideological portfolio.

With the legal ban of homosexual propaganda among minors, introduced and enacted by the Ryazan' region in 2006 (Sapper, Weichsel 2013: 3), condemnation of homosexuality has left the symbolic realm and entered the realm of law. In the following years, similarly restrictive regulations were introduced by twelve Russian regional governments (ibid.). In response to a wave of gay marriage and same-sex relationship legislation in the West, a nationwide anti-gay campaign was initiated by the Russian government in 2012 before approving the new legislation at the federal level. The East-West-dichotomy provided important discursive parameters for this campaign. Arguing that Russian society was endangered by individualism, consumerism, secularism, and homosexuality, the Russian Orthodox Church made a significant contribution to the articulation of traditional family values and moral standards during the campaign (Mitrokhin 2013: 71; Michajlov 2013: 87). Patriarch Kirill described the legislation of homosexual relations in Western Europe as a 'dangerous apocalyptic symptom' and emphasized the necessity to 'ensure that sin is never sanctioned in Russia by state law because that would mean that the nation has embarked on a path of self-destruction' (Patriarch Kirill 2013).

Historically, the official position of the Church toward homosexuality has been unequivocal. Same-sex relation is condemned as sinful and inconsistent with the Christian teaching and the teaching of the Russian Orthodox Church. The current stand of the Moscow Patriarchy on homosexuality is described and articulated in the *Basis of the Social Concept of the Russian Orthodox Church*, passed by the Bishops' Council in 2000. This major official document reflects the Church's position on its relation with the state and a number of social issues and secular matters. Apart from numerous references to the Holy Scriptures that reject homosexuality as a 'vicious distortion of the God-created human nature' (Social Concept 2000: XII. 9), the text is also embedded in contemporary discussions on sexuality. The document fundamentally opposes the perception of homosexuality as a gender identity and a sexual orientation among others that has 'the equal right to public manifestation and respect' (ibid.). Further, the Church strongly disagrees with the statement that homosexuality 'is caused by the individual inborn predisposition' (ibid.) and argues 'that the divinely established marital union of man and woman cannot be compared to the perverted manifestations of sexuality' (ibid.). Framed in terms of family, marriage and procreation, heterosexuality is perceived as the only possible and acceptable form of sexual activity, whereas homosexuality is regarded as a deviation from the norm.

> The difference between the sexes is a special gift of the Creator to human beings He created. [...]. Man and woman are two different modes of existence in one humanity. They need communication and complementation. However, in the fallen world, relationships between the sexes can be perverted, ceasing to be an expression of God-given love and degenerating into the sinful passion of the fallen man for his ego. (ibid. X. 1)

Homosexual desire, put in line with other passions and human temptations, is believed to be healed by 'the Sacraments, prayer, fasting, repentance, reading of Holy Scriptures and patristic writings, as well as Christian fellowship with believers who are ready to give spiritual support' (ibid. XII. 9). Within the context of the *Social Concept*, homosexuality is considered as a result of a sinful social choice or societal influence. The document continues:

> [...] the Church is resolutely against the attempts to present this sinful tendency as a 'norm' and even something to be proud of and emulate. This is why the Church denounces any propaganda of homosexuality. Without denying anybody the fundamental rights to life, respect for personal dignity and participation in public affairs, the Church, however, believes that those who propagate the homosexual way of life should not be admitted to educational and other work with children and youth, nor to occupy superior posts in the army and reformatories. (ibid.)

When the State Duma passed a law banning the dissemination of propaganda for homosexual relations to minors on 30 June 2013 and imposed heavy fines for violations thereof (Michajlov 2013: 87), the Russian Orthodox Church was supportive of the new legislation and actively promoted its view of homosexuality as a phenomenon alien to the Russian cultural tradition. Commenting on the anti-gay propaganda law, archpriest Vsevolod Chaplin, then Chairman of the Synodal Department for the Cooperation of Church and Society, stated that many see Russia 'as a defender of Christian values and traditional ethics, as a country that provides a real alternative to the cult of the golden calf and to a self-destroying understanding of what freedom is' (01.07.2013).

Arguing that the main objective of the law was to protect children from sexually explicit material and information, and to advocate national traditions and public moral norms, the notion of 'propaganda' of homosexuality to children and youth, first introduced in the *Social Concept* of the Russian Orthodox Church and discussed above, was officially employed in the wording of the new legislation. The only difference is that there is not a single mention of the term homosexuality in the text of the secular law that officially prohibits this:

> Propaganda of non-traditional sexual relationships to minors, expressed in the dissemination of information aimed at forming non-traditional sexual attitudes among minors, attractiveness of non-traditional sexual relationships, distorted image of social equality of traditional and non-traditional sexual relationships, or the forced imposition of information of non-traditional sexual relationships, which can attract interest to such relationships [...]. (Federal Law No 135 2013)

Following this argumentation, homosexuality appears not only abnormal and dangerous but even worse: non-traditional. According to the law, any demonstration in favour of gay rights or visibility of homosexual relations in the public sphere might be declared illegal. Although the law does not criminalize or *explicitly* discriminate homosexuality, it further marginalizes and stigmatizes sexual minorities, as many critics and scholars have pointed out (Sapper, Weichsel 2013: 4, Mitrokhin 2013: 71f., Michajlov 2013: 87).

While the vaguely formulated anti-gay law made front-page headlines abroad and received forceful international condemnation, the overwhelming majority of Russian society approved this legal restriction against same-sex couples. According to the survey carried out by the state public opinion polling agency shortly before the anti-gay law was adopted, 88 percent of respondents indicated, they are in favour of the new law while only 7 percent did not support the legislation (VTsIOM 11.06.2013). An opinion poll conducted by the independent Levada Centre in April 2013 demonstrated that 67 percent of those who answered would support the ban on homosexual relations; 14 percent were against such legislation. Further, 35 percent of Russians characterised homosexuality as a disease and 43 percent linked same-sex desire to a lack of discipline or a bad habit (Levada Centre 2013: 114). Only 12 percent of respondents considered homosexuality normal (ibid.). When asked why the law prohibiting propaganda for homosexual relations was introduced, 60 percent of those polled answered 'concern for the morality of the population, strengthening of public ethics' (ibid.). In response to the question how homosexuals should be treated, 22 percent of respondents suggested to 'heal' them, 16 percent wanted to 'isolate them from society', 5 percent would 'eliminate' them, 27 percent answered 'provide psychological and other help' and 23 percent would 'leave them alone' (ibid.). Even though the responses might differ depending on questions, chosen survey strategies and methods, the numbers given above unequivocally demonstrate what negative attitudes toward homosexuality and massive rejection of gay people are dominant in Russia. In a climate of widespread conservative views and increasing anti-Western and anti-gay sentiments in contemporary Russian society, it appears hardly surprising that the Putin administration, allied with the Russian Orthodox Church, was perceived as a guardian of public good and succeeded in promoting itself as a supporter of the majority view.

Lifting the veil: Gay scandals at the Kazan' seminary

While supporting the anti-gay propaganda law, condemning sodomy as a grave sin and bearing down on all forms of non-traditional behaviour (Papkova 2011: 49f.), the Russian Orthodox Church has itself been accused of covering and protecting homosexuality in its innermost circles. In December 2013, there were reports in the Kazan' local media on sexual harassment incidents involving hierarchs and priests of the Kazan' Theological Seminary. According to kazanweek.ru, the Education Committee of the Russian Orthodox Church urged a special commission headed by the Archpriest Maksim Kozlov to investigate sexual abuse and assault allegations by the seminarians ('Tatarstanskuiu mitropoliiu' 2013). When asked by the delegation about cases of sexual harassment, most of the students confirmed being victims of homosexual actions, and complained about hegumen Kirill (Iliukhin) and other members of the administration of the seminary (ibid.). Based on the testimony gathered during the inspection, Kirill Iliukhin was removed from both his vice chancellor and press secretary positions, and expelled from the Kazan' diocese (ibid.).[2] The incident was neither followed by further investigation nor did the commission take administrative measures in order to reverse the policy of the seminary.

It seems clear that the Church tried to avoid publicity and to conceal the scandal, but the effect was quite the opposite. As with many other similar cases in the past, the Kazan' gay scandal was likely to remain of local relevance, if any relevance at all. However, soon after the incident it was reported that the notorious hegumen—despite serious accusations revealed by the Church inspection committee at the Kazan' Seminary—was appointed head of the department of Theology at the Tver' State University that belongs to the diocese of Tver' and Kashin ('Gomoseksualist-igumen' 2013). Andrei Kuraev (born 1963), Protodeacon, theologian, popular blogger and, until recently, prominent voice of the Russian Orthodox Church offering a Christian perspective on church-state relations and various contemporary issues, followed the gay scandals in Kazan' closely. He reposted media and social networks' reports on his *LiveJournal* blog (diak-kuraev.livejournal.com) that gained broad attention by the general public. Since its foundation in 2008, Kuraev's blog provides regular updates to a large and growing audience, including the clergy of the Russian Orthodox Church. After Kuraev published a number of anonymous letters and confessions about further homosexual incidents within the Church, the scandal increasingly expanded beyond Kazan' Theological Seminary and its spiritual leadership to encompass the whole body of the Church, thereby gaining an entirely new dimension. In one of his blog posts, Kuraev himself refers to homo-

---

[2] This information was refuted by a Kazan' diocese representative who claimed that hegumen Kirill was not dismissed but voluntarily resigned from his office at the Kazan' Theological Seminary and moved to another diocese ('Igumen Kirill' 2013).

sexuality as a common problem of the Church and claims that 'metastases of the 'gay' tumour in the church can be only removed by a miracle' (diak-kuraev 19.12.2013).

As a result of his blog posts and public statements, Kuraev was expelled from the lecturing corps of the Moscow Theological Academy—an unexpected and radical turn of events. At its regular session on 30 December 2013, the Academic Council resolved to dismiss Kuraev from the teaching staff and to exclude him as a Professor of Missiology of the Moscow Theological Academy: 'The Academic Council noted that Protodeacon Andrei Kuraev regularly makes flamboyant statements in the media and blogosphere, and that his activity in this area remains scandalous and provocative in a number of cases' ('Moskovskaia Dukhovnaia Academiia' 2013). Kuraev commented on his dismissal from office in his blog, arguing that the decision by the Academic Council was a direct response to his publications revealing homosexual scandals within the Church, and claimed that he had become a victim of a Russian Orthodox 'gay lobby' (diak-kuraev 31.12.2013).

Obviously the clash between desired and existing reality, and a sharp conflict between harsh and openly anti-homosexual rhetoric by the Moscow Patriarchy officials, as well as the emerging visibility of homosexuality or even gay networks within the Church—made accessible through testimonial assertions by seminarians and priests published on Kuraev's blog—contributed to the relevance and presence of the topic in public discourse. Yet, it was never Kuraev's intention to justify and accept homosexuality as normal or to present same-sex relations in a positive light. On the contrary, Kuraev's attitude toward homosexuality corresponds entirely to the official stance of the Russian Orthodox Church and its narratives, discussed above.

Quantifying online discourse

Kuraev's *LiveJournal* blog entry 'Torzhestvo golubogo lobbi' [Triumph of the gay lobby] published on 31 December 2013 (diak-kuraev 31.12.2013) gained unprecedented resonance and triggered heated online debates on homosexuality and the role played by the Orthodox Church in today's Russia. The number of comments to the blog entry alone demonstrates its significance. While the average number of comments that Kuraev received to each blog entry in December 2013 did not exceed 355, his post on the gay lobby in the Church generated in total 1.938 responses. Only the blog entries related to Mikhail Khodorkovskii and Pussy Riot received a comparable number of comments: 1.146 and 1.827 respectively. One might get the impression that the gay revelation scandal did not actually start with the unscheduled investigation at the Kazan' Theological Academy but with this particular blog post by Kuraev. In this respect, it is not surprising that blog posts, comments on social networking sites as well as media reports—inside and outside Russia—referred to Kuraev as the primary source of information regarding the gay revelation wave.

In order to tackle the debates and to demonstrate how the discourse on homosexuality and Orthodoxy in Russian blogs and social media developed over time, I first conducted a quantitative analysis using *Yandex Search for Blogs*.[3] The key purpose of the research was not to provide absolute numbers, but rather to trace changes and highlight differences over time within the scope of Russian social networking sites. The time frame chosen for the investigation was from 1 December 2013 until 28 February 2014. The data was collected manually, as *Yandex Pulse of the Blogosphere*, an online service that helped visualize trends in Russian blogs and social media, had been terminated in February 2013 due to low attendance. Even though *Yandex* promises to provide necessary data for research purposes upon demand, according to the information on its official website ('Pul'sa net' 2014), the request sent in Russian to info@blogs.yandex.ru on 20 March 2014 remained unanswered.

---

3   *Yandex Search for Blogs*, service founded in 2004, provides information and statistics not only for Russian-language blogs but also forums, social networks and microblogging services.

After creating a list of keywords associated with the research topic, I searched for these terms within the context of ROC[4] or church or orthodox (see Figure 6.1.) on a weekly basis. My exact query on *Yandex Search for Blogs* was ['search term' << (РПЦ && церковь && православный)]. As Figure 6.1. demonstrates, the debates in the blogosphere and social media started in December 2013 and were at their peak from 1 to 13 January 2014, gradually decreasing in the following weeks and disappearing entirely at the end of February 2014. The term 'scandal' was mentioned 1620 times, 'lobby'—1439 times. The first intensification of the discussions can be observed in the week from 9 to 16 December 2013. Here, the term 'homosexuality' appeared 362 times. This slight rise can most probably be traced back to the investigations at the Kazan' Theological Seminary on 13 December 2013. Within the selected time frame, the keywords 'scandal' and 'lobby' were most frequently used, followed by 'homosexuality' and 'gay' while the terms 'LGBT', 'paedophilia', 'homophobia' and 'sodomy' occurred less than 200 times.

---

4   Russian Orthodox Church.

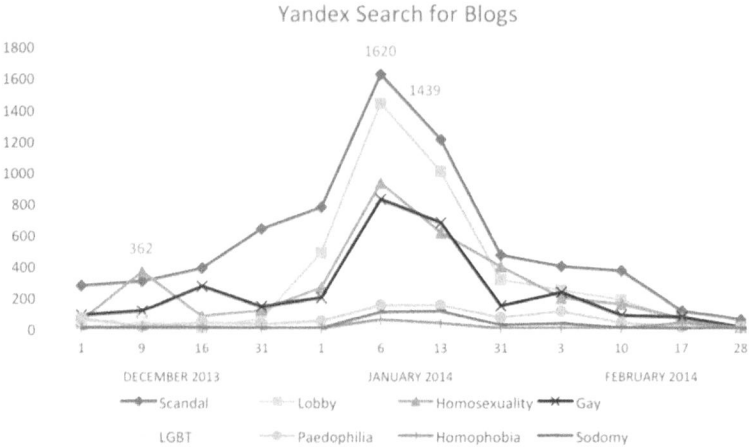

Figure 6.1. 'Frequency of keywords mentioned in the Russian blogosphere and social media within the context of 'ROC' or 'church' or 'orthodox'.
Data collected on 23 March 2014.

As demonstrated in **Figure 6.1.**, the terms 'scandal' and 'lobby' dominated social media debates within the specified time frame and context. While the term 'scandal' appears rather broad and can be related to various issues, although this is less likely within the chosen research framework, the term 'lobby' seems to be more specific and is closely associated with the research topic. In the next phase, employing again *Yandex Search for Blogs* I searched the keyword combination 'голубое лобби' [gay lobby] in any possible context from 2004 to 2014. Broken down by year, research results in Figure 6.2. provide evidence that the use of the 'gay lobby' combination has risen considerably over the last three years, reaching a new level of intensity in 2014. In 2013, 'gay lobby' was mentioned 1969 times; at the beginning of 2014 the term appeared 6448 times in Russian blogs and social media. While these particular outcomes appear rather predictable, the mere fact that there were debates over 'gay lobby' provides interesting insights and is worth noting. While corresponding with the internet usage statistics, the graph curve demonstrates that the 'gay lobby' controversy was everything but new to the online audience. Even though the most intense debates started in 2013 and continued to increase significantly in 2014, the first peaks were in 2010 with 672 mentions and in 2012 with 730 mentions. A search query for 'lobby' on the official website of the Moscow Patriarchy returns several references dating from 2005 to 2013. None of them, even the latest one published on 14 December 2013, is related to the gay scandal within the inner circles of the Church ('Vy iskali' 2014), which is, of course, not surprising.

Figure 6.2. 'Frequency of the keyword 'gay lobby' mentioned in the Russian blogosphere and social media in any possible context from 2004 to 2014.'
Data collected on 23 March 2014.

To situate the research outcomes into a broader context and provide a comparative dimension, a keyword search similar to the analysis illustrated in Figure 6.1. was conducted in Russian print and online media. The data was retrieved from the database *Integrum* that archives and provides access to the largest collection of Russian print and online newspapers.[5] The timeline examined was the period from 01 December 2013 to 28 February 2014. The exact query I used on *Integrum* was: 'search term' и (РПЦ или церковь или православный). As one can see in Figure 6.3., the way the discourse emerged in the mainstream media is different from the way debates took shape in blogs and social media. While social media responded immediately to Kuraev's blog post published on 31 December 2013, the story built up slowly in the Russian print and online media. In the week from 31 December 2013 to 05 January 2014, the time of New Year celebrations and public holidays in Russia, there were almost no reports on the issue. Rediscovery of the 'gay lobby' topic occurred much later, after significant decrease of the discourse in social media. Within the selected time frame, the term 'scandal' was most frequently used, followed by 'homosexuality'. 'Homophobia' and 'Sodomy' were mentioned less than 20 times.

---

5 According to its website, *Integrum* provides an archive of 500 million documents collected from over 7000 databases. The archive covers, among other, all national and regional print and online media ('Integrum World Wide' 2014).

BETWEEN HOMOPHOBIA AND GAY LOBBY 177

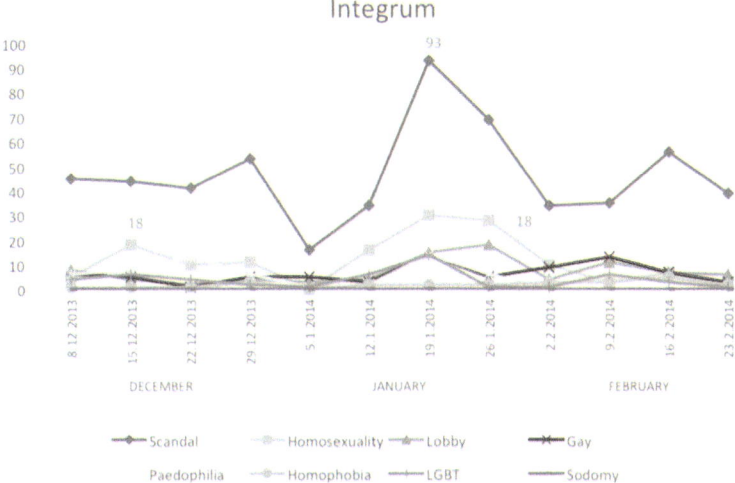

Figure 6.3. 'Frequency with which keywords were mentioned in the Russian print and online media within the context of 'ROC' or 'church' or 'orthodox'.
Data collected on 23 March 2014.

The data presented in Figure 6.1. and 6.3. and discussed above appear to demonstrate a similar discourse dynamics. In order to provide a basis for comparison, I put this data together in one single chart. For the purpose of clarity, only the two most frequent terms from Figure 6.1. and the three most frequent terms from Figure 6.3. were included. Based on this comparison, a completely different picture emerges. Against the background of intense discussions in social media and blogs, the discourse in the central press and online newspapers is of only marginal relevance. According to Figure 6.4., the "trends" discussed above are almost invisible and, thus, completely irrelevant. The online discourse on gay lobby scandals within the Church did not spill over to the mainstream media. It appears that the topic was too controversial to be covered and discussed in depth in central and regional newspapers, both print and online, and would contradict the positive image of the Russian Orthodox Church and its uncompromising stance toward homosexuality.

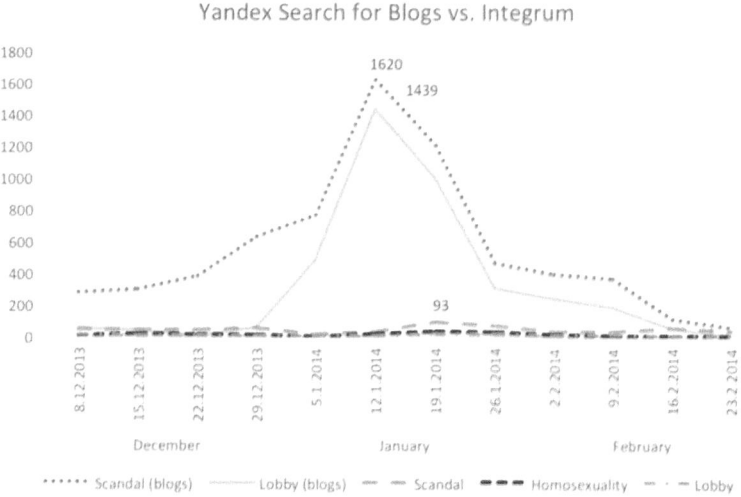

Figure 6.4. Comparison of data retrieved from *Yandex Search for Blogs* and *Integrum*, illustrated in Figure 6.1. and Figure 6.3. respectively.

What conclusions can be drawn from the quantitative research results and how can they help when conducting a close reading study? Based on the data analyzed, a clear-cut distinction between mainstream media coverage and social media debates has emerged. The difference is not only that print and online newspapers reacted almost two weeks later to the events but also the scale and intensity of discussions. Compared with the debates in blogs and social media, the discourse in the mainstream media was almost non-existent. As was illustrated in Figure 6.1., the interest of social networking sites was not generated by the offline events related to the sexual harassment cases at the Kazan' Theological Seminary but by the blog post published by Kuraev after his dismissal from office. The most intense discussions on the gay lobby scandals took place in the first weeks of January 2014—this outcome is relevant for focusing the qualitative part of the research. According to Figure 6.2., the gay lobby issue was not a tabula rasa to the online audience but the scale and intensity of discussions over the topic was unique. Through a close reading study, the following chapter provides insights into the debates surrounding gay lobby scandals.

Online discussions: close reading study

> I am not sure whether the way of publicity is for the good. But I am sure that it will at least provide an opportunity. The self-cleansing path in the Church is firmly clogged. Nothing will change without a strong external constraint to a cleansing. (diak-kuraev 01.01.2014)

With these words, Kuraev depicted the situation in the inner structures of the Russian Orthodox Church and legitimized his lonely fight against homosexual networks and intimate alliances within the Church. While remaining faithful to the official stance of the Moscow Patriarchy—at least in his own understanding and perception—Kuraev launched a campaign against the institutionalized protection of homosexuals in the Church. His blog posts about the incidence of homosexuality in the Russian Orthodox priesthood, further enhanced and dramatized through eyewitness reports and Kuraev's sudden and poorly explained dismissal from his academic position, provoked a discursive explosion and controversial debates in the Russian blogosphere and social media, as illustrated in the previous chapter.

Hundreds of blog posts, comments, tweets, memes and videos appeared within days on the Web, some of them original—analyzing, contradicting, complementing and contextualizing information on Kuraev's *LiveJournal*, others were reposts, links and shares that were massively disseminated through blogs and social networks. A multitude of online platforms has been involved in discussing gay scandals and Kuraev's role in revealing the issue: *LiveJournal* appeared as the most significant one, followed by *Vkontakte* and a number of forums. While *Vkontakte* focused on spreading the information, often retelling what exactly happened at the Kazan' Theological Seminary and explaining offline and online events that followed the revelation wave, *LiveJournal* served as a facilitator of discussion and as the main discourse site. Focusing on the time frame from 31 December 2013 to 14 January 2014, I zoom-in on the *LiveJournal* discussions that Kuraev's blog posts generated in order to outline personal reflections as well as users' main argumentation strategies and narratives, and to explore how Russian Orthodoxy and homosexuality are imagined and intertwined online.

A wide range of responses, positive, negative and, in many cases, aggressive ones, often referring to the same sources and names but articulating different views and perspectives, can be found in *LiveJournal* blog posts and comments. Among these many facets of responses, the recurrence to the Soviet heritage of the Russian Orthodox Church appears as a dominant discursive framework when reflecting on the culture of homosexuality in monastic circles. For the user 'ponomarev_a_n' the gay lobby revelation is unsurprising. By comparing the Russian Orthodox Church with the Soviet Writer's Union, he deprives it of its spiritual function and religious meaning, and puts it in a secular environment. 'ROC is an organization that calls itself religious but its genetic code makes it look like the Soviet Writer's Union that was founded by the 'genius' Iosif Vissarionovich [Stalin] in order to manipulate the people' (ponomarev_a_n 08.01.2014). It is further stated that both the Writer's Union and the Orthodox Church were founded by Stalin and had similar objectives (ibid.). Similar argumentation is employed by 'melancholy_gay' who is convinced of the existence of a powerful gay lobby within the Church and its roots in the Soviet anti-religious approach:

> There is indeed a gay lobby in the ROC and it is rather powerful. However, it is far away from the LGBT activism, gay prides and from supporting same-sex marriages. Moreover, it publicly accuses the 'perverted West' and the gays. Modern ROC—this is an institution founded by Stalin who made the priests agree to his conditions. With the help of various techniques, the church was brought under the total control of the atheist state. (melancholy_gay 04.01.2014)

What seems remarkable is that it was not called into question that homosexual practices existed and were widespread among clerics during Soviet times, not even by Kuraev's strong opponents. However, unlike the Church-critics who see a continuation of Soviet religious narratives and practices in post-Soviet Russia as being adopted or simply tolerated by the Moscow Patriarchy, they emphasize an incisive rupture with the previous atheist politics due to the demise of communism. Here, a significant role is attributed to the Patriarch Kirill who 'initiated a politics of missionary work and total cleansing of the Church, cleansing from idler-missionaryphobes and the 'gay lobby'' (kirillfrolov 08.01.2014). As a prominent Orthodox activist Kirill Frolov claims in his blog post 'Who, with what purpose and why prepares a new anti-Church campaign?' (kirillfrolov 08.01.2014). Directly responding to Kuraev's publications, he asks a rhetorical question at the end of the contribution: 'Who then cleanses the Church from traitors and perverts in priest's robes and who speculates on the topic of 'gay lobby' in the Church in order to discredit the Holy Patriarch Kirill?' (ibid.). A similar argumentation pattern emerges in the blog post by the user 'russkiy_malchik':

> Through Kuraev, perverts in priest's robes declared a war on the 'gay lobby' by trying to attribute their sins exactly to those who are extirpating it [the lobby] —what can be meaner? (russkiy_malchik 12.01.2014)

When analyzing online reactions to Kuraev's blog posts, it becomes clear that many Internet users as well as communities and groups have decisively taken sides, before the discourse even emerged and positions were articulated. The mere fact that Kuraev was the one who initiated the debates and caused a stir on the Russian Internet was enough to decide how to engage with the issue. Many bloggers and commenters even focused on discussing Kuraev himself—as a person, missionary, theologist, blogger and, first and foremost, as a prominent public figure with non-conventional and rather controversial views—, rather than dwelling on the issue of homosexuality and gay networks within the Church. Widely discussed and reverberated in the social media was Kuraev's image as a reformer. When reflecting Kuraev's criticism on homosexual cover-ups by the Church and the possible changes this revelation might bring, many users drew historical parallels with the Protestant Reformation and compared Kuraev—not without ironic connotation and a hidden agenda—to Martin Luther, as in the following example:

> ROC is pregnant with renewal and perestroika, will Kuraev become a new Luther or Yeltsin of the Orthodox faith? Kuraev has already nailed his theses to the door of his home church in Wittenberg on the Internet. However, he neither publicly burned the 'Papal Bull Exsurge Domine' in the backyard of his seminary in order to excommunicate him from the Church seminary, nor did he declare in his appeal 'To the Orthodox believers of the ROC' that the fight against 'Papal' pedophilic indulgences concerns all Orthodox believers and is the outset of the reformation of the ROC. (chudinovandrei, posted in ru-antireligion 04.01.2014)

Others question the sincerity and credibility of Kuraev's intentions and mock his attempts to challenge homosexual networks in the Orthodox clergy and to contribute to the spiritual cleansing of the Church. Recalling numerous gay scandals that involved Orthodox priests and bishops that had gained publicity in the 1990s and at the outset of the 2000s, the users emphasize that Kuraev remained silent on the issue for many years, if not decades. In an ironical reversion, they "celebrate" Kuraev as a hero of gay scandals revelation and attribute to him the alleged authorship of the list of homosexual priests that currently circulates in the internet. Set in the context of a traditional Orthodox iconography, Kuraev is depicted as a saint and martyr (see **Figure 6.5.**). Playing with the boundaries between the sacred and profane, users transfer a double meaning and, thus, ridicule Kuraev's reformist desires.

BETWEEN HOMOPHOBIA AND GAY LOBBY 183

Figure 6.5. 'Andrei Kuraev portrayed as a saint, holding the "Bible"—list of Orthodox gay priests.'
Source: http://anticlericalism.livejournal.com/1678816.html. Accessed 12.08.2014.

The notion of reformation or, rather 'schism', finds its continuation in the blog posts by Kuraev's opponents. Kuraev, who challenges traditional forms of Church authority and allegedly undermines its ability to produce sense and meaning, is often referred to as a sectarian, renovationalist or simply as a 'spiritual terrorist' whose aim is 'to plant a bomb into the base of the Russian Orthodox Church' (deltaplann 03.01.2014). In the comment by 'alekseysc' Kuraev is portrayed as a representative of a Khlyst movement: 'Kuraev himself has been long part of the Khlyst sect. And he decoys his admirers into the abyss. Kuraev discredits the Russian Orthodox Church and now openly harms it' (alekseysc 08.01.2014).

Another dominant and recurring motive in online discussions is reference to the punk band Pussy Riot and Kuraev's outspoken positive assertion of the anti-Putin punk prayer in the Moscow Cathedral of Christ the Savior. 'In the Russian Orthodox Church, the first voice on the action happened to be a positive one. A prominent figure of the ROC, Deacon Andrei Kuraev, posted his (now 'legendary') text three hours after the punk action in the Cathedral, assessing the action as 'NORMAL' [...]' (Ponomariov 2013: 190). In contrast to Kuraev, the official Church hierarchy condemned the action as blasphemy and sacrilege (ibid.). Even though the opinions on the Pussy Riot performance were rather controversial, the *majority* of the population raised criticism of the female band or openly opposed the action. It is no wonder that Kuraev is, until now, associated with this particular performance. In light of the homosexual scandals, this association gained a further relevance and meaning. For many bloggers and commenters, Kuraev's public campaign against homosexual practices in the Orthodox priesthood provides a direct comparison to the Pussy Riot protest. By publicly accusing the Church for tolerating and even promoting homosexual relations in the clergy, Kuraev himself performed a protest action, a discursive one that the internet users simply refer to as 'Kuraev Riot' (see **Figure 6.6.**).

Figure 6.6. 'Kuraev Riot'.
Source: http://vk.com/wall152784535_4461. Accessed 13.08.2014.

For many, speaking about Kuraev and his controversial statements is seen as a strategic opportunity to set a different agenda, to turn the issues he criticizes against him and to avoid what is actually being discussed, such as in the *LiveJournal* community 'Kuraynik', a mimicry of Kuraev's blog. Community's main purpose is to provide regular responses to Kuraev's statements, to contradict, mock and deconstruct the information found on the Protodeacon's platform. In the context of the gay scandals revelation, the terms attributed to Kuraev are 'homodeacon', 'professional atheist' or 'sectarian', Kuraev's publications are considered to be 'provocations' (Kuraynik 2014). However, while Kuraev reaches hundreds of online users on a daily basis who actively engage with his opinions and statements, leave comments and interact with each other, 'Kuraynik' suffers its lack of readership and is trying to combat its own insignificance.

When turning to Kuraev's blog that, without any doubt, provided the impetus for and served as the main platform for discussions, a more detailed picture emerges. Close reading of comments sent not only as direct responses to Kuraev's publications, but also to comments written by other users[6], provides further insights into the discursive field with its variety of voices, perspectives and personal reflections. In the first two weeks of January 2014, the total number of comments Kuraev received to 50 blog posts was 46.758. The analysis of the comments revealed that while the internet users voice severe criticism of the Russian Orthodox Church, they almost entirely echo the anti-gay rhetoric and homophobic statements put forward by the Church officials. The stance toward homosexuality is a highly negative one. In line with the official position of the Church, homosexuality is regarded as sinful and abnormal. This can be highlighted by the words of the user 'Aleksandr Vinnik' who associates homosexuality with sodomy and perversion: 'How can they possibly stand at the Altar in the Church, celebrate the Eucharist, receive communion? [...]. It even sounds strange: 'gay bishop', how can he be a

---

6 Comments on Kuraev's blog were contributed not only by *LiveJournal* users but also by users of different plattforms, such as *Facebook, Vkontakte, Google+, Moi Mir, Twitter* etc.

bishop if he is a sodomite and pervert?' (Vinnik 01.01.2014). A similar argumentation pattern can be found in the comment by the user 'nibudu' who considers homosexuality as a "normal" sin, comparing it to other human temptations, among them paedophilia: 'And it is not about a special sinfulness, sin is always a sin, whether envy, anger, gluttony, greed for money, power, pederasty...' (nibudu 31.12.2013). Conflation of homosexuality, paedophilia and child seduction underlies the discursive structure of a range of comments analyzed in this article.

The following discussion between an openly gay person who appeals to the Church authorities to recognize homosexuality as a sexual orientation that cannot be healed or changed and two other commenters who deconstruct this notion—for them homosexuality is beyond all doubt a sin and deviation from the norm—appears illustrative and is quoted in full length:

> I was raised in a religious family and, from childhood on, I believed in God. At the time I realized I was gay, I could not accept it because of my religious education. As a result—years of self-rejection, depression and struggles. Today I believe that the church destroys the lives of thousands of gays by trying to convince them that their orientation is a 'caprice', a 'sin' and that 'man can change with the help of God'. The church should honestly recognize that there is a homosexual orientation. In most cases, it is innate. Yes, the church has the right to consider homosexual relations sinful. However, it should be fairly admitted that [sexual] orientation cannot be changed. From the point of view of conservative Christianity, there is a way of full sexual abstinence. (melancholy_gay 05.01.2014)
> It is not a matter of whether the church has a right to or not... All this filth, bro, is in your head. You can get rid of it but you simply don't want to, you follow your temptation and are engaged in self-justification. Nothing more... No hard feelings, of course. God willing, you will return to the path of righteousness... I wish this day will come soon. Good luck! (caruss 05.01.2014)
> +1 Apart from sodomy, there is a variety of abonimations that are extremely hard to get rid of, depression and so on. The main thing is to not consider it as a norm and to not justify yourself, even though it is hard and 'life is not all sweet' because of such awareness. (aljieksey1974 05.01.2014)

Despite this open confession by 'melancholy_gay' and a personal description of his suffering and depression when he, as a religious person, discovered his sexual desire and tried to suppress and overcome it, the reactions by other commenters are motivated by the extreme heteronormativity that does not allow any other forms of sexual identity.

Another concern voiced by many users is related to the repeal of the anti-sodomy law in post-Soviet Russia. Many discuss the necessity to introduce new legislation that would prohibit not only the propaganda for homosexual relations but homosexuality itself: 'The sodomy law was repealed for nothing. Under Soviet rule, life was better' (iskop 04.01.2014, see also business_mag777). Many comments are openly homophobic and aggressive, as in the following example: 'Vile sodomites! burn in hell! Here it the nest of these disgusting creatures! Father Andrei, burn even more' (sidorov785 04.01.2014). On the one hand, according to commenters, homosexuality demonstrates a wide range of meanings and negative connotations. On the other hand, it is simply reduced to sexual intercourse; understandings and interpretations of homosexual relations to be an expression of intimacy, mutual understanding, care and spiritual union are rarely, if ever, invoked. According to this perception, user 'infin56' stresses: 'Yeah damn, I do not understand people fucking asses and crying out loud for special rights... So you might understand it, but I don't' (infin56 04.01.2014). As demonstrated above, homosexuality is associated with abnormality and deviation; it is neither socially acceptable nor does it even have the right to exist.

In the context of the gay lobby controversy, a highly contested and negative picture of the Russian Orthodox Church emerges. While adopting official argumentation and explanation lines of the Church officials toward homosexuality, the users portray the modern Church as an institution struggling for political power and societal influence: 'For me, ROC is a public organization that massively evades taxes by the state and uses any instrument to increase its power' (newtricker 08.01.2014).The Church's unequivocal condemnation of homosexuality articulated in the public domain is perceived as hypocritical and distrustful and further reinforces the user's criticism:

> Father Andrei, like it or not, you belong to the blessed ones, well to those who are 'expelled because of telling the truth', firstly, and secondly: who can give

orders to the administration of the Moscow Theological Academy? Why not call things by their proper names—the so-called 'holy' Synod that people have long called the (Metro)polit(an)buro is headed by the so-called 'holy' Patriarch who, in fact, covers up (guards, protects, supports, consoles, cherishes) pederasts in priests' robes. [...]. In words, THEY speak about the rotten West but, in actual fact, they openly despise a man who denounced pederasts within the church. (alex_skayriver 31.12.2013)

Recalling numerous political scandals and financial affairs in which the Church authorities were involved, the users describe the current stand of the Church in terms of deep institutional and spiritual crisis and disease.

Conclusion

Why assess and analyze web data for cultural research? Why count term frequencies, visualize discourse trends and generate meaning based on data provided by users whose (nick)names appear to be quite the opposite: largely unknown and insignificant? What new insights can be gained from web-based analysis and how can these complement our research on religion in general and Russian Orthodoxy in particular? While analyzing the Web, the research outcomes are not restricted to the online culture only, but are rather grounded in the offline (see Rogers 2013). A web data analysis can draw a more nuanced picture of the Russian Orthodoxy and challenges its unquestioned and hegemonic image conveyed through the state-controlled media. The quantitative part of the research provides evidence that the event evolved differently in the online media and mainstream media. While the discussions in social media and blogs were characterized by harsh criticism of the Russian Orthodox Church and its leadership, the discourse on homosexuality corresponded completely to the official narratives proclaimed by the Church hierarchs.

Not the fact itself that homosexual practices are widespread in the Orthodox priesthood, but its scandalization and the attempts by the Church officials to silence the discourse, attracted the widespread public attention. By dismissing Kuraev from his position as a

Professor for Missiology at the Moscow Theological Academy, the Church sought to deprive Kuraev of a strong voice in public religion. While this strategy proved successful for the mainstream media where only a few reports related to the homosexual scandals in the Church appeared, social media and blogs responded with a wave of controversial discussions. Contrary to the expectation that Internet users critical of the Church and its authorities are more likely to express alternative or tolerant views regarding homosexuality, a high level of hostility and homophobia toward same-sex desire was identified through a close reading study. Despite harsh criticism of the Church as an institution, many users adopted its conservative views on homosexuality and its argumentation and explanation strategies. The vast majority of comments is framed by the common perception of homosexuality as a dangerous and abnormal phenomenon. Homosexuality frequently arouses feelings of aggression, fear, various tensions, disgust but rarely leaves commenters indifferent. Reinforced by homophobic political and religious public discourse, homosexuality is frequently associated with paedophilia and child seduction. Even more: homosexuality and paedophilia become interchangeable terms. Only marginal comments demonstrate tolerance toward sexual minorities, their demands and rights. In the Russian cultural realm, homosexuality demonstrates a wide range of meanings. Same-sex desire is, however, not restricted to sexual relations only but can be attributed to everything negative and disgusting. Notions of homosexual *love*, mutual understanding and spiritual union of same-sex partners are unimaginable for the commenters. While homosexuality is beyond acceptance and is considered abnormal, hostility toward homosexuality and explicit denial of same-sex desire as a form of sexuality appears to be an accepted norm, both on the official level but more importantly in the social networks and blogs as well as in the mainstream media.

As homosexuality provides a wide range of connotations and associations, it is not surprising in this respect that online discussions were not restricted to the issues of sexuality and gender. They depicted a much broader discourse on a range of interconnected societal issues and problems. Many blog posts and comments that address the role of the Russian Orthodox Church in today's society express severe criticism of the Church authorities that is almost invisible in the mainstream media. The gay lobby scandal even intensified this emotionally charged discussion and negative perception of the Moscow Patriarchy. From the perspective of Internet users, the Patriarchy portrays itself as a carrier of national traditions and norms, and defines what is socially acceptable and normal not only for the religious community, but for the whole Russian society. This article has illustrated that the picture of the Russian Orthodox Church is much more complex and that it is not merely an ally of the Putin administration. By giving voice to those who are underrepresented in the mainstream media and by focusing and analyzing new forms of religious thinking, the web data research provides valuable insights into religious discourse in the post-Soviet Russian society and goes beyond analyzing church-state relations and Church attendance statistics.

References

alekseysc (2014, 8 January). 'Nekhoroshaia khlystovskaia „missiia' protod'iakona Andreia Kuraeva'. Available: http://alekseysc.livejournal.com/1319791.html (accessed 14.08.2014).

alex_skayriver (2013, December 31). 'Otets Andrei voleiu i nevoleiu, no vy popali v chislo blazhennykh'. Available: http://diak-kuraev.livejournal.com/571617.html?thread=154321633#t154321633 (accessed 14.08.2014).

aljieksey1974 (2014, January 05). '+1 Krome sodomii est' kucha drugich merzostei'. Available: http://diak-kuraev.livejournal.com/576445.html?page=3 (accessed 14.08.2014).

Batalden, Stephen K. (1993). *Seeking God. The Recovery of Religious Identity in Orthodox Russia, Ukraine, and Georgia*. DeKalb: Northern Illinois University Press. DeKalb.

Baer, Brian James (2009). *Homosexuality and the Crisis of Post-Soviet Identity*. New York: Palgrave Macmillan.

business_mag777 (2014, January 05). 'Odnako pora vnesti v Dumu zakonodatel'nuiu initsiativu'. Available: http://diak-kuraev.livejournal.com /576445.html?thread=158840765#t158840765 (accessed 14.08.2014).

caruss (2014, January 05). 'Tut dazhe delo ne v tom imeet tserkov' pravo ili net...'. Available: http://diak-kuraev.livejournal.com/576445.html?page=3 (accessed 14.08.2014).

Chaplin, Vsevolod (2013, July 01). 'Protoierei Vsevolod Chaplin: Rossiia dolzhna oshchutit' sebia tsentrom khristianskogo mira'. Available: http://www.patriarchia.ru/db/text/3075418.html (accessed 07.04.2014).

chudinovandrei (2014, January 01). 'Bomba pod RPTs tikaet. Stanet li Kuraev novym Liuterom ili novym El'tsinym pravoslavia'. Available: http://ru-antireligion.livejournal.com/11160169.html (accessed 13.08.2014).

diak-kuraev (2012, February 21). 'Maslenitsa v Khrame Khrista Spasitelia'. Available: http://diak-kuraev.livejournal.com/285875.html (accessed 14.08.2014).

diak-kuraev (2013, December 19). 'Po sledam kazanskogo gei-skandala'. Available: http://diak-kuraev.livejournal.com/564360.html (accessed 08.08.2014).

diak-kuraev (2013, December 31). 'Torzhestvo golubogo lobbi'. Available: http://diak-kuraev.livejournal.com/571617.html (accessed 25.02.2014).

diak-kuraev (2014, January 01). 'Novogodniaia skazka'. Available: http://diak-kuraev.livejournal.com/572426.html (accessed 14.08.2014).

deltaplann (2014, January 03). 'Diakon Kuraev – dukhovnyi terrorist'. Available: http://deltaplann.livejournal.com/147500.html (accessed 13.08.2014).

'Federal'nyi zakon Rossiiskoi Federatsii N 135-FZ' (2013, June 29). Available: http://www.rg.ru/2013/06/30/deti-site-dok.html (accessed 04.08.2014).

'Gomoseksualist-igumen' (2013). 'Gomoseksualist-igumen Kirill (Iliukhin) poluchil povyshenie?' Available: http://kazanweek.ru/article/11278/ (accessed 08.08.2014).

Healey, Dan (2001). *Homosexual Desire in Revolutionary Russia. The Regulation of Sexual and Gender Dissent*. Chicago: The University of Chicago Press.

'Igumen Kirill' (2013). 'Igumen Kirill Iliukhin po sobstvennomu zhelaniiu pereshel sluzhit' v druguiu eparkhiiu'. Available: http://www.tatar-in form.ru/news/2013/12/23/388053/ (accessed 08.08.2014).

infin56 (2014, January 04). 'Da mlia'. Available: http://diak-kuraev.live journal.com/572761.html?thread=1559716738& (accessed 12.08.2014).

'Integrum World Wide' (2014). Integrum World Wide. Available: http://www.integrumworld.com/about.html (accessed 10.08.2014).

iskop (2014, January 04). 'Teper' poniatno'. Available: http://diak-kuraev.live journal.com/576445.html?thread=158840765#t158840765 (accessed 14.08.2014).

kirillfrolov (2014, January 08). 'Kto, zachem i pochemu gotovit novuiu antitserkovnuiu kampaniiu?' Available: http://kirillfrolov.livejournal.com /2894807.html (accessed 11.08.2014).

Kon, Igor' (2013). 'Lackmustest. Homophobie und Demokratie in Russland'. *Osteuropa-Zeitschrift, Heft 10.* Berlin: Berliner Wissenschafts-Verlag, pp. 49–67.

Kondakov, Alexander (2013). 'The Silenced Citizens of Russia: Exclusion of Non-heterosexual Subjects From Rights-Based Citizenship'. *Social & Legal Studies 2014 23: 151.* Online. Available: http://sls.sage pub.com/content/23/2/151 (accessed 27.07.2014).

Kuraynik (2014). 'Kurainik / Navigator po blogu pussid'iakona Online'. Available: http://kuraynik.livejournal.com/2014/01/ (accessed 15.08.2014).

Levada Centre (2014). *Obshchestvennoe mnenie – 2013.* Moscow: Levada-Tsentr. Online. Available: http://www.levada.ru/books/obshchestvennoe-mnenie-2013 (accessed 04.08.2014).

melancholy_gay (2014, January 04). 'Kuraev protiv golubogo lobbi v RPTS?'. Available: http://melancholy-gay.livejournal.com/157186.html (accessed 12.08.2014).

melancholy_gay (2014, January 05). 'Smotria chto vy podrazumevaete pod 'polomali''. Available: http://diak-kuraev.livejournal.com/576445.html ?page=3 (accessed 14.08.2014).

Michajlov, Konstantin (2013). '"Propaganda der Sünde'. Die ROK und die Rechte der sexuellen Minderheiten'. *Osteuropa-Zeitschrift, Heft 10.* Berlin: Berliner Wissenschafts-Verlag, pp. 87–97.

Mitrokhin, Nikolay (2013). 'Gottes Wort und Priesters Tat. Die Orthodoxe Kirche und die Homosexualität'. *Osteuropa-Zeitschrift, Heft 10.* Berlin: Berliner Wissenschafts-Verlag, pp. 71–85.

'Moskovskaia Dukhovnaia Academiia' (2013, December 30). 'Sostoialos' ocherednoe zasedanie Uchenogo soveta MDA'. Available: http://www.mpda.ru/news/text/2027629.html (accessed 09.08.2014).

nibudu (2013, December 31). 'Konechno, gomoseksualisty est' vezde'. Available: http://diak-kuraev.livejournal.com/571617.html?thread=154753 505#t154753505 (accessed 14.08.2014).

newtricker (2014, January 08). 'Dla menia RPTS – obshchestvennaia organizatsiia'. Available: http://diak-kuraev.livejournal.com/579299.html?thread=163132643#t163132643 (accessed 14.08.2014).

'Osnovy sotsial'noi konceptsii Russkoi Pravoslavnoi Tserkvi' (2000). English translation: https://mospat.ru/en/documents/social-concepts/ (accessed 03.08.2014).

Papkova, Irina (2011). *The Orthodox Church and Russian Politics*. Washington, D.C., New York: Woodrow Wilson Center Press, Oxford University Press.

Patriarch Kirill (2013). 'Sviateishii Patriarkh Kirill: My dolzhny delat' vse dlia togo, chtoby na prostranstvach Sviatoi Rusi grekh nikogda ne utverzhdalsia zakonom gosudarstva'. Available: http://www.patriarchia.ru/db/text/3113641.html (accessed 04.08.2014).

Ponomariov, Alexander (2013). 'The Pussy Riot Case in Russia: Orthodox Canon Law and the Sentence of the Secular Court'. *Ab Imperio*, 4.

ponomarev_a_n (2014, January 08). 'D'iak Kuraev zabivaet poslednii gvoz'd' v RPTS'. Available: http://ponomarev-a-n.livejournal.com/232493.html (accessed 12.08.2014).

'Pul'sa net' (2014). 'Pul'sa net, a zhizn' prodolzhaetsia'. Available: http://blogs.yandex.ru/pulse (accessed 09.08.2014).

Rogers, Richard (2013). *Digital Methods*. Cambridge, Massachusetts: MIT Press.

russkiy_malchik (2014, January 01). 'Kuraev nakazan, no nedostatochno'. Available: http://russkiy-malchik.livejournal.com/405361.html (accessed 12.08.2014).

Rutten, Ellen, Fedor, Julie and Zvereva, Vera (ed.) (2013). *Memory, Conflict and New Media. Web Wars in Post-Socialist States*. London, New York: Routledge.

Sapper, Manfred and Weichsel, Volker (ed.) (2013). 'Homophobie und autoritärer Staat'. *Osteuropa-Zeitschrift, Heft 10*. Berlin: Berliner Wissenschafts-Verlag, pp. 3–4.

sidorov785 (2014, January 04). 'Merzkie sodomity!' Available: http://diak-kuraev.livejournal.com/576445.html?thread=158839485#t158839485 (accessed 14.08.2014).

'Tatarstanskuiu mitropoliiu' (2013). 'Tatarskuiu mitropoliiu zhdet novyi skandal: press-sekretar' mitropolita Anastasiia ulichen v gomoseksualizme'. Available: http://kazanweek.ru/article/11186/ (accessed 08.08.2014).

Vinnik, Aleksandr (2014, January 01). 'A kak voobshche, esli oni golubye, oni mogut stoiat' u Prestola v Khrame'. Available: http://diak-kur aev.livejournal.com/571617.html?thread=155465697#t155465697 (accessed 14.08.2014).

VTsIOM (2013, June 11). 'Zakon o propagande gomoseksualizma: za i protiv'. Available: http://infographics.wciom.ru/theme-archive/society/re ligion-lifestyle/moral-relations/article/zakon-o-propagande-gomoseksualiz ma-za-i-protiv.html (accessed 04.08.2014).

'Vy iskali' (2014). 'Vy iskali 'lobbi''. Available: http://www.patriarchia.ru/search /?text=%D0%BB%D0%BE%D0%B1%D0%B1%D0%B8&x=0&y=0 (accessed 10.08.2014).

Zorgdrager, Heleen (2013). 'Homosexuality and Hypermasculinity in the Public Discourse of the Russian Orthodox Church: An Affect Theoretical Approach'. *International Journal of Philosophy and Theology, 74:3*. Routledge: London, pp. 214–239. Online. Available: http://www.tand fonline.com/loi/rjpt20 (accessed 01.08.2014).

Chapter 7.
Post-Secularity and Digital Anticlericalism on Runet

Maria Engström
Dalarna University

Introduction

The modern times are often described by sociologists and historians of religion as a situation of 'post-secularism' and the 'New Middle Ages', the 'New Mysterious Epoch' (Berger 1999; Kyrlezhev 2004; Ionin 2004). The Orthodox expansion in the political and cultural sphere that has recently attracted scholarly attention (Knox 2009; Richters 2013; Fagan 2013) has affected the Russian segment of the internet. The rapid development of the Orthodox Runet as an important tool of the Christian mission is accompanied by a no less intense development growth of 'digital anti-clericalism'; i.e., online resistance to the clericalisation process of the Russian society and to various forms of 'political Orthodoxy' and religious extremism.[1] The main object of criticism on the part of neo-atheists and champions of secularism is the very situation of post-secularism that manifests itself in a number of relatively recent social and political developments—such as non-constitutional expansion of a religious world view on secular spheres of life; de-secularisation of political life; the newer legislative initiatives of the State Duma aimed at protecting the rights of the 'Orthodox majority'; archaisation of consciousness; the blossom of ritualism and neo-paganism/new dual faith; commercialisation of the Church and the evolvement of pseudo-Orthodox goods and services market.[2]

---

1 On the phenomenon of "political Orthodoxy"—see Mitrofanova 2005, Engström 2015.
2 By pseudo-Orthodox goods and services one could mean, for instance, holographic icons, thermos stencils for Easter eggs, VIP-pilgrimages, etc. (see Zaitsev 2014).

Simultaneously, the claims made by the post-Soviet Orthodoxy on the ideological monopoly and standard-setting role in the life of Russian society, on the part of the major figure in the new authoritative discourse,[3] come into conflict with the manner of the post-secular epoch in which no preference for one religious form over another exists. As a sociologist of religion Alexander Kyrlezhev states in his famous *Post-Secular Epoch* article (2004),

> [...] the specifics of the post-modern is such that it, having lifted religion from the bottom, simultaneously plunged it [...] into a field of an absolute cultural pluralism. Thus, it gave a powerful momentum to a variety of new forms of religious beliefs and legitimised them. Therefore, traditional religions suffer a new identity crisis in the domain of the 'European culture' (or 'post-culture'). Unlike modernism, the post-modern does not mind piousness and religious traditions as such but it rejects their right to be the dominant and constitutive ones for the 'post-culture'.

Thus, the post-secular epoch does not stipulate for restoring the sacred/secular opposition. However, the Russian Orthodox Church (ROC), by trying to implement the Byzantine ideal of 'symphony' between the Church and the State (Knox 2009: 105–131), functions within this opposition using, according to its critics, an outdated archaic language. On the other hand, Marxist atheist critique also seems old-fashioned, as the post-secular epoch does not allow for criticising Christianity as an 'outdated' and 'irrational' system of beliefs, since the very ideas of progress and rationality are then thrown into doubt.[4]

Anti-clericalism on the Net is a relatively new phenomenon dating back directly to a number of high-profile media events, scandals and court cases of the past decade, which were connected to the ROC and were widely discussed in the Russian society. The most notorious were the exhibitions 'Attention! Religion!' (2003), 'Forbidden Art' (2006), the Pussy Riot case and the exhibition 'Spiritual Invectives' (2012), which presented the images of Pussy Riot mem-

---

3   On Soviet authoritative discourse—see Yurchak 2014.
4   On the post-Soviet atheism—see Zhuravsky 2001, Kyrlezhev 2013. The phenomenon of post-Soviet neo-atheism is currently examined to a much lesser degree than the post-Soviet neo-piety.

bers in the icon-painting manner. The hey-day of anti-clerical activity on Runet was between 2011–2012; i.e., the times when protest movements in Russia were on the rise, the Pussy Riot trial took place, and there was rigorous discussion over the bill presented by the State Duma aimed at protecting the rights of the believers. After the passing of the Federal Law 136–F6 'On Amending the Criminal Code of Russian Federation and Certain Legislative Acts of Russian Federation for the Purpose of Counteracting the Abuse of Religious Beliefs and Feelings of Citizens' endorsed by President Putin on June 29, 2013, open critique of the ROC on the Net dropped off.[5] The law is described by its opponents as a serious step towards the introduction of 'Orthodox censorship' and limitation of civil rights in the Russian Federation.

Despite a large number of research works dealing with neo-piousness, the relationship between the ROC and the Russian state during the post-Soviet period (see Anderson 2007; Knox 2009; Simons 2009; Papkova 2011; Richters 2013; Fagan 2013), as well as research on the protest movement in modern Russia (see Bikbov 2012; Erpyleva and Magun 2014), anti-clericalism and neo-secularity on Runet, has never been a subject of scholarly analysis.[6] Simultaneously, the sheer volume and variety of anti-clerical and atheist resources on the Net gives evidence that anti-clericalism is becoming an important political and cultural factor in present-day Russia. This investigation is a first attempt to describe and classify verbal, visual and hybrid forms of digital anti-clericalism in the Russian-speaking sector of the web while we lay no claims on it being an all-encompassing description.

By using specific examples, we present a cultural and historical analysis of various genres of anti-clerical Internet communication; namely, of memes, demotivators, photoshopped images, comic

---

5 The abuse of religious beliefs is punished by fines up to 500.000 Roubles, or community service, or incarceration for up to three years.
6 With the exception of the articles *Genesis and Forms of Post-Soviet Atheism in Russia* by A. Zhuravsky (2001) and *Anti-clericalism in LiveJournal* by T. Chumakova (2011).

strips, mock prayers, etc. When extracting the material the universally accepted criteria of selecting Net sources was used; i.e., the country of origin, language, content, and credibility. While the authorship was established on several occasions, the vast number of examples is anonymous. As a result of endless replicating and a lack of record in the virtual chronotopos, the authorship of memes, demotivators and other forms of Internet communication is near impossible to trace.[7] The anonymity of virtual anti-clericalism places it in close quarters with folklore. Due to the superfluity of material and limits set by an article's volume, we used only those images that have become a subject of public discussion both in modern and traditional media.

Part one deals with the primary genres of anti-clericalism on the Web, demonstrating the main distinctions between this new type of anti-clerical propaganda and both the Soviet atheist tradition and the earlier anti-clerical outbursts in Russian history. Part two is devoted to analysing the activities of several noted post-Soviet atheists and anti-clerical web-based communities.[8] The twelve most visited and credible anti-clerical and atheist Russian websites were selected.[9] Both parts of the research deal with the phenomenon of anti-Orthodox Internet-mockery seen as a universal language of web-based resistance to political clericalism. It is also worth noting that the article covers the verbal and visual genres of Russian web-folklore criticising the present-day Russian Orthodox Church; primarily, the new political role played by it in the past decade. The exam-

---

7   Disclaimer: The article is illustrated with anonymous photoshopped images and demotivators which are replicated on the Net without the authorship attribution; instead, the URL of a website is cited as a source.
8   Beyond the scope of the research is the mock "Russian Pastafarian Church of Macaroni Pastariarchat" (RPC MP), since pastafarianism is not a strictly Russian phenomenon but a global strategy of resistance to de-secularisation. The activities of the Russian branch of the Church of the Flying Spaghetti Monster is no different from its counterparts in other countries. For details see the website of the Russian Pastafarian Church http://www.rpcmp.ru/#!groups/c1tfz (accessed on: 15.04.2015).
9   For list of sites, see the 'References' part at the end of the article.

ples of anti-clerical criticism towards other religions and confessions are not discussed here.[10]

Digital Anti-Clericalism: Anti-Church Internet Memes

The weapon of choice for Runet anti-clericals are memes. Memes, as a ready-made unit of meaning, transmit a maximum possible amount of information while requiring minimum time for perception. In this way, a meme is a highly effective propaganda weapon. An important characteristic of memes, as well as of many other web genres (demotivators, photoshopped images and comic strips) is anonymity,[11] which allows some scholars to reckon them among post-folklore and the 'culture of popular laugher' (Shchurina 2012; Savitskaia 2013; Schmidt 2014).

The origins of digital anti-clericalism should be traced back not to Soviet atheism but to the unofficial culture of the late-Soviet period. Runet knows a number of sites and communities that transfer, almost unaltered, Marxist and scientist criticism of Christianity into the digital environment (those are mentioned in the second part of the article), but those are not the trendsetters. The parallel between the late-Soviet anecdotes, as an unofficial culture phenomenon, and the internet memes of the 2000s, is drawn specifically by D. Golynko-Wolfson (2012):

> In 2000s, Internet memes grew to be a large enclave of web folklore. Its tongue-in-cheek scepticism towards the 'epoch of stability and prosperity' reminded of the urban folklore of 1970–80s jokes and gags. By using anecdotes, the late Soviet generation jeered and mocked the symbolic values of Brezhnev's standstill period (the significance of humour for the self-identity of that generation is thoroughly discussed by Alexei Yurchak). In the meantime, the generation of 'Putin's second term' sets itself against the current times and their conformist mythology by using Internet memes.

---

10 In the meantime, Runet is filled with demotivators and photoshopped images mocking Islam, Judaism, Buddhism, New Age and the neo-pagan practices.
11 On rare occasions, as in the case of a 'Brain Orthodoxy' meme (see below), there is information on those users who were the first to document the use of a specific meme, but such situations tend to be an exception to a rule.

When making memes one more often than not uses the language typical of the culture of late Soviet underground—namely, *'stiob'* (the gibe, caustic irony). The stylistics of *stiob* and the nonsense talk are indicative of countercultures in their resistance to the dominant culture (Dubin 2001, Yurchak 2008). Boris Dubin defines *stiob* as

> a variety of public intellectual epatage which is a provocative and aggressive, bordering on scandalous, lowering of any symbols of other groups, images of projective partners—both protagonists and addressees—by means of an emphatic use of these symbols in an unlikely, parodical and parodistic context which consists of stereotypes that lie in two (a minimum of two, to be exact) different lexical and semantic levels (Dubin 2001:163).

Stiob stipulates for a certain meta-position—an 'exterior' position (Yurchak 2008), which is free of any axiological views. It makes this device extremely effective when fighting systems based on some or other values and norms. These characteristics of *stiob* prevent the ROC from using it as a propaganda tool as this would contradict the axiological system of Christian doctrine. Let us take a closer look at some vivid examples of web anti-clericalism aimed at criticising the ROC and Russian Orthodoxy as a whole (hereafter 'anti-Church/anti-Orthodoxy memes, demotivators and photshopped images), leaving outside the scope of the article the anti-clerical folklore aimed at other religions and confessions.

Of those anti-Orthodoxy memes, the first to be mentioned is a meme 'Orthodoxy of the Human Brain' ('PGM'). It was originally documented on Runet in February 2005 in a phrase 'outbreak of acute mystical orthodoxy of the human brain' by an LJ-blogger, Robin of Locksley (roflocksley).[12] The abbreviation PGM appeared later. It was used in May 2005 by a user Denis Absentis (absentis) on the webpage of an LJ-community called AntiReligion:

---

12 The hypothesis that the term PGM appeared first on the web was debated by a famous journalist Alexandr Nevzorov in a 2011 interview given to a TV show "Minaev LIVE". Nevzorov sees Internet only as a reflection of the real world, where the meanings are copied and disseminated (Nevzorov 2011).

> A few years ago, a friend of mine caught a deadly contagious disease—a PGM syndrome (Orthodoxy of the Human Brain). Since then he cannot resolve any routine issue without first consulting with a priest.[13]

'Lurkmore', the online encyclopaedia,[14] similarly, defines Christianity as 'Christosis of the Human Brain' (HGM):

> PGM is the most common form of Christosis in Russian Federation[15].

By reflecting the claims of the ROC as playing the part of a political subject, digital anti-clericals connect 'Orthodoxy of the Human Brain' with 'Glorifying Putin'. Thus, they make a travesty out of the image of a Church-State 'symphony'. As an example of anti-Orthodox internet *stiob*, we can give an extensive definition of PGM from the GAZENVAGEN website:

> PGM—Orthodoxy of the Human Brain (known in English as BOH—Brain Orthodoxic Human). A disabling condition of a human's central nervous system. Proceeds after a long abuse of opium for the masses. Can be caused by airborne transmission or after a shared use of devotional articles with a PGM carrier. In latter case is known as SPPGM—Acquired PGM Syndrome. Normally, proceeds quite peacefully with insignificant relapses during the traditional periods (Easter in springtime, Saviour of the Apple Feast Day in autumn, various sacred processions in winter).[16]

It is emphasised that, in particular, 'Internets' are the cure from PGM[17]:

> Should be emphasised that PGM is a public health hazard and its carriers must be isolated from the society. In rare cases, self-healing is possible under the influence of the Internets.[18]

---

13 http://absentis.livejournal.com/2413.html (accessed on 15.04.2015).
14 'Lurkmore' is an online encyclopaedia, which is wholly based on the stylistics of *stiob* and trolling (see also below).
15 http://lurkmore.to/%D0%9F%D0%93%D0%9C (accessed on 15.04.2015).
16 http://maydan-news.blogspot.se/2014/03/blog-post_2009.html (accessed on 15.04.2015).
17 Cf. statement on the danger presented by the internet and the social networks made by ROC, see Chapter 1 in this volume.
18 http://maydan-news.blogspot.se/2014/03/blog-post_2009.html (accessed on 15.04.2015).

Another popular meme in the opposition/anti-clerical blogosphere are the 'spiritual bonds'. If 'PGM' is, primarily, an Internet meme, 'spiritual bonds' are widely used by the traditional media as well. This collocation turned into a meme after having been used by Vladimir Putin in his Address to the Federal Assembly in December 2012:

> You know, dear colleagues, it pains me to talk about it but I feel the obligation to. Russian society today suffers an obvious deficit of spiritual bonds—charity, empathy, compassion towards each other, mutual help. We are talking about the lack of everything of what throughout history has always made us stronger, of what we have always been proud of.[19]

Earlier that year, Patriarch Kirill called the ROC a 'spiritual bond' in a *Shepherd's Word* TV show dedicated to establishing the autocephaly of the Russian Church in 1448, when the Ryazan Saint bishop Iona was elected the metropolitan of Moscow and of Russia:

> The contemporaries of metropolitan Iona perceived Our Church as it has always been perceived throughout our country's history. Just as today, most people perceive it as something that unites our nation. It is a spiritual bond, the line of our nation's self-identity. This is the common ground we have and by destroying it, we would destroy our homeland.[20]

By drawing parallels between the Orthodox Church, the Russian state, the nation and the citizens, both President Putin and Patriarch Kirill support the ROC's claims that they have a right to an ideological monopoly; thus, immediately causing an outburst of anti-clerical slogans, to which the 'spiritual bonds' meme, naturally, belongs.[21]

In modern Russian, the noun 'bond' (*skrepa*) is considered archaic. One of the sources for this anti-clerical meme's popularity could be another meme from 2010—*sosulia* ('isuckle'). The parallel between the two memes is often played upon on Runet; for instance, in the demotivational comics 'Spiritual bonds are like isuckles. Except bonds' (see **figure 7.1**)

---

19 http://special.kremlin.ru/events/president/news/17118 (accessed on 15.04.2015).
20 http://newsland.com/news/detail/id/991611/ (accessed on 15.04.2015).
21 The very noun 'bond', however, was known before the times of the meme. It can be found in the works of several contemporary authors; namely, Dmitry Bykov, Zakhar Prilepin, Olga Slavnikova (see Turkova 2012).

Figure 7.1. Demotivational comics by anonymous 'Spiritual bonds are like isuckles. Except bonds'.
Source: http://risovach.ru/kartinka/6214253 (accessed on 15.04.2015)

The word *sosulia* ('isuckle'), instead of the regular *sosul'ka* ('icicle'), was documented in a speech by Valentina Matvienko, then Governor of Saint Petersburg (2003–11), during a press conference in 2010:

> It is the 21st century and using crowbars to knock down the isuckles is the Stone Age, if you'll excuse me [...] We need to find another way. Cut them down with lasers, use hot steam.[22]

One might presume that Valentina Matvienko used the ill-sounding *sosulia* because the icicles (the regular Russian *sosul'ki* containing the diminutive 'k') that threatened the lives of the city's residents were of massive size. The noun *sosulia* is documented in the New Russian Dictionary by T. Yefremova (2000) as a colloquialism, but

---

22 http://odnostishia.ru/xi-xi/srezaem-lazerom-sosuli.html (accessed on 15.04.2015).

before Matvienko used the word it had been virtually unknown to the public. The frozen drippings have always been called *sosul'ki* with no regard to their size. We can find *sosulja* in Vladimir Dahl's dictionary but the definition given there is 'something that can be sucked'; i.e., a candy.

It is worth noting that both memes we discussed, while being an element of critical satire towards the post-Soviet 'symphony' of clerks and clergy, make a reference not so much to the Soviet period but to the 'Saint Petersburg text' in Russian culture. The images of the celestial chancellery and of a paper clip are represented in Russian history by the holy governing synod and Gogol's Petersburg. It is not by accident that Runet reacted to the bureaucratic newspeak of Matvienko ('isuckles') and Putin ('bonds') by labelling them 'Petersburg dialect'.

Anti-clerical demotivators

A demotivator (demotivational poster, deme) is an image, compiled according to a certain format. It includes a picture in a frame (normally, black or red) and inscription that comments on it. Demotivators belong to creolized texts; it is a hybrid polycode genre, the popularity of which can be attributed to its combination of visual and verbal communication (Bugaeva 2011). Creolized texts are semiotically complicated and utilize various combinations of natural language and elements of other sign systems (visual images, animation, and music). The general process of visualisation in post-culture and the internet also promotes the substitution of verbal forms of communication for visual ones. Understanding a demotivator requires presupposition; i.e., its elements can be understood only with the help of a certain background knowledge. Like other creolized texts of present-day digital communication, demotivators are built upon a principle of cut-and-paste, a contrast between the image and the text, and on word play that creates comic effect. Originally, demotivators were a parody on political propaganda posters and corporate propaganda of 'positive thinking'. However, today we can see that they cover a much larger variety of topics (Rabkina, Kameneva 2013; Baslina, Ukhova 2014).

Undoubtedly, demotivators are one of the most well-loved genres of mass internet-art, new popular print, and visual anecdotes.[23] Thanks to its semantic concision and carnivalesque nature, anti-Orthodox demotivators have rapidly become one of the most widespread forms of digital resistance and anti-clerical humour on the Web. They function as a 'direct-action detachment' that gives an instaneous response to a news topic. Demotivators work as an effective means of anti-clerical and atheist propaganda by using satire, *stiob*, and rich visuality, and thus, draw the attention of users to aspects of post-secular Russian society such as commercialization of the Orthodox church, the vogue of Orthodoxy, and claims of the ROC as becoming a political subject. Many of the modern day anti-clerical demotivators are close, if not genetically but typologically, to posters and newspaper images of the Soviet 'godless men' from the 1920–30s. That was the epoch of mocking the 'symphony' of the Orthodox Church and the Tsarist regime, the negative influence of the church on education, gluttony, excessive drinking and other sins of the clergy.[24] However, there exists a whole group of demotivators that reflects specifically present-day issues; i.e., the subject of the church's attitude towards homosexuals, same-sex marriage, transvestites, and modern art, as well as the topic of 'Orthodox glamour'.

During the past decade, faith, religion and the relationship between the church and the state has also been a central theme for contemporary Russian art, which follows the traditions of soc-art criticism towards all forms of rule. Anti-clerical protest sentiment manifests itself in such exhibitions as 'Attention! Religion!' (2003), 'Forbidden Art' (2006), 'Soc-Art: Political Art in Russia since 1972' (2007) and others. However, it is important to note that the spheres of the contemporary anti-clerical art and of the visual anti-clericalism

---

23 For parallels between the traditional Russian popular print (*lubok*) and the flash-animation popular on Runet before the arrival of demotivators see Strukov 2007.
24 See the newspaper *Bezbozhnik* ('Godless Man') and the magazine *Bezbozhnik u stanka* ('Godless Man by the Machine-Tool"), published in the Soviet Union in 1922–1941.

on the Web exist separately. Thematically, anti-clerical demotivators on Runet largely follow the traditions of Soviet atheist propaganda, but aesthetically they lag behind the Soviet anti-clerical posters. It is worth reminding that the leading Soviet atheist periodicals, *Bezbozhnik* and *Bezbozhnik u Stanka*, employed the services of leading Russian artists of the 20th century; such as, Alexander Deineka, Nikolai Kupriianov, Dmitrii Moor (Orlov) (see **figure 7.2**). The Kukryniksy brothers, Konstantin Vialov, Mikhail Cheremnykh and many others actively participated in carrying out the 'Five-Year Plan of Militant Godless Men' that aimed at showing the incompatibility of socialism and religion.

Figure 7.2. Dmitrii Moor.
The cover of *Bezbozhnik u stanka* magazine, 1923 №7.
Source: http://www.davno.ru/posters/обложка-журнала-безбожник-у-станка-1923-7.html (accessed on 15.04.2015).

From an artistic viewpoint, post-Soviet demotivators are an unsophisticated amateur paste-up of a photograph and an inscription that contrasts the image. Anti-clerical demotivators based on an original drawing are extremely rare with the exception being the works of a designer and blogger Artemii Lebedev (see below). Demotivators as a product of a collective anonymous creative activity (the textual element may vary while the visual remains intact, or vice versa) are closer to the folk visual and verbal genre; first and foremost to the popular print, 'lubok', and artistic 'primitivism', the characteristic features of which are grotesque and parody (Yurkov 2003; Strukov 2007; Bragina 2014). As opposed to the Soviet atheist posters where the inscription clarified or emphasized the visual message, the text of a demotivator always contains elements of *stiob*.

Runet boasts tens of thousands of anti-clerical demotivators. Let us take a look at the most frequent themes and subjects of anti-Orthodox demotivators, putting aside the ones of a more general anti-Christian nature. It is worth noting that the textual component of the demotivators often employs the named memes 'spiritual bonds' and 'PGM'. For instance, the following simple demotivator plays upon the subject of the 'eternal Russian drunkenness', as the iconic logo for the *Pshenichnaya* vodka is substituted for 'Spiritual Bond' (**figure 7.3**).

Figure 7.3. Demotivator by anonymous 'A Spiritual Bond'.
Source: http://pikabu.ru/story/dukhvnaya_skrepa_3048842 (accessed on15.04.2015).

One of the most popular subjects of anti-Church demotivators is criticism towards the claims of the ROC on being part of the state ideology. A fitting example is an anonymous demotvator 'Together we will put a cross on it. The ROC as it is', which pictures Patriarch Kirill and President Putin against a map of Russia as a background (**figure 7.4**). The comic effect is achieved by playing upon the multiple meanings of the Russian expression 'to put a cross'. This idiomatic expression is frequently used with the meaning 'to give up for lost, to write off' originating from the parlance of civil clerks who used to strike out the unnecessary parts of documents with a slanting cross. At the same time, the 'cross' element refers to the religious code, Christian tradition and the symbolism of cemeterial crosses.

Figure 7.4. Demotivator by anonymous
'Together we will put a cross on it'.
Source: http://www.metapolicy.ru/2013/03/24/vmeste-my-postavim-na-nej-krest/
(accessed on 15.04.2015).

A large number of anti-clerical demotivators are devoted to the issue of the ROC's growing involvement in matters of science and education. Here, the objects of satire include, besides Patriarch Kirill, such Orthodox newsmakers as the former ROC's Head of the Synod department, Archpriest Vsevolod Chaplin, and a (former) professor of Moscow Ecclesiastical Academy senior deacon, Andrei Kuraev, who is the author of the school textbook *Foundations of Orthodox Culture*.[25] This plot has similarities with Soviet atheist propaganda, but a distinct difference must be acknowledged. While in Soviet propaganda the cartoonish image of a priest was anonymous, demotivators employ photographs of actual priests and hierarchs that have achieved 'celebrity' status in modern Russia; namely, Patriarch Kirill, and such priests as Dmitrii Smirnov, Andrei Kuraev and Vsevolod Chaplin.[26]

Another popular subject of anti-clerical demotivators, which dates back to a long Russian verbal and visual tradition, is the appearance and obesity of Orthodox priests (**figure 7.5**).

Figure 7.5. Demotivator by anonymous 'Sinners will be eaten'.
Source: http://demotivators.to/p/452579/greshniki-budut-sedenyi.htm
(accessed on15.04.2015).

---

25   http://kuraev.ru/ (accessed 15.04.2015).
26   On construction the image of 'celebrities' on the Web see Strukov 2011.

It might be worth noticing that the politically incorrect criticism of obesity is a trend among the Russian opposition. If, for Mayakovsky, obesity was the symbol of capitalism ('Since childhood have I hated fatsos'), in present-day anti-clerical discourse it has become the symbol of backwardness, stagnancy, anti-Western sentiment, and corruption in Russian state machinery, army and Church. It is in this context that one might consider a controversial Instagram post of Ksenia Sobchak, one of the most flamboyant figures of the anti-clerical opposition. In August 2015, her twit 'I hate fat people' caused quite a stir both on Runet and the traditional media.[27]

The victory of Thomas Neuwirth, known for his stage image of the 'bearded woman' Conchita Wurst at Eurovision 2014, and the vociferous condemnation of Europe's choice on the part of the Orthodox patriotic circles, Runet was filled with demotivators on the subject of 'beards and gowns'. One of the most famous ones was a tweet from Rustem Adagamov, an opposition blogger, with a demotivator 'The ROC is dead set against bearded men in evening gowns' (**figure 7.6**). Here, the satirical edge is achieved by the discord between the photograph of the bearded Church hierarchs in their traditional attire and the inscription.

---

27 https://instagram.com/p/6nz92uCCHT/ (accessed on 26.08.2015).

POST-SECULARITY AND DIGITAL ANTICLERICALISM ON RUNET 211

Figure 7.6. Rustem Adagamov 'The ROC is dead set against bearded men in evening gowns!'
Source: Rustem Adagamov's *Twitter*
https://twitter.com/adagamov/status/466484975412736001 (accessed on 15.04.2015)

Figure 7.7. Demotivator by anonymous
'Be a stylish believer—attain salvation with a swag!'
Source: http://blog.i.ua/user/1862657/302310/ (accessed on 15.04.2015)

Another popular subject of anti-Orthodox demotivators is the exposure of the modern Church's commercialization, the 'Orthodox glamour' phenomenon (**figure 7.7**), as well as the Archpriest Vsevolod Chaplin's proposal to introduce 'an all-Russian dress code'.[28] The inscriptions for these demotivators include memes, commercial slogans and famous quotations on the subject of the corporate nature of the present-day Orthodox Church; such as, for instance, Viktor Pelevin's 'Respectable Lord for respectable lords' from his *Generation 'P'* novel (1999).

Photoshopped images[29]

Photoshopped images (*fotozhaby*) are a popular web variety of visual stiob that can function as both a visual element of demotivators and a separate image without any inscriptions. Unlike demotivators, photoshopped images achieve comic effect not by contrasting the visual and the verbal, but by creating a contrast between two or more incompatible visual elements. Concurrently, video manipulation on anti-clerical subjects, which is a variety of still image manipulation, is a rarity on Runet.

One of the most notorious doctored-image contests of an anti-clerical nature was organised by Artemii Lebedev, a famous designer and blogger, and son of Tatyana Tolstaya, a prominent contemporary Russian author. Dubbed 'Doctor Patriarch's face with Moustache!', it took place in 2012. Using his *LiveJournal* page Lebedev urged users to doctor an image using a portrait of Patriarch Kirill as a template. The winner was a minimalist image on the subject of close cooperation between the ROC and the State (**figure 7.8**). The manipulation consisted of adding crab legs to the icon face on the front side of the Patriarch's cowl; thus, making a reference to one of the

---

28 In 2011, Archpriest Vsevolod Chaplin proposed introducing "an all-Russian dress-code" that would regulate the appearance of men and women in public. For details of the discussion see http://www.pravmir.ru/vazhno-vse-prot-vsevolod-chaplin-o-diskussiyax-vokrug-dress-koda-nochnyx-klubov-i-pravoslavii-v-smi/ (accessed on 15.04.2015).
29 Known on Runet as *photozhaby*—"phototoads".

most famous memes on Runet and the no-less famous photoshopped image of Vladimir Putin 'Crab on the galleys'.[30] The origins of this photo manipulation can be traced back to the tradition of intentional desecration of sacred images—icons, portraits of the tsar and his family, as well as of Soviet leaders (after 1917).

---

30 'Crab' (originally, 'crab on the galleys', later shortened to 'Putin is a crab!")—is a popular nickname of President Vladimir Putin. The meme became popular on Runet after a publication of a distorted quote from Putin's speech on February 14, 2008: "I have nothing to be ashamed of in the face of the citizens who voted me twice to be the president of Russia. Throughout these eight years I toiled like a slave on the galleys, day and night, giving my best". The Russian *kak rab na galerakh* ("like a slave on the galleys") got misprinted as *kak krab na galerah* ("like a crab...") giving life to the meme. Source: http://ria.ru/politics/2008 0214/99185527.html (accessed 15.04.2015)

Figure 7.8. Photoshopped image by anonymous, winner of the 'Doctor Patriarch's face with Moustache!' (2012).
Source: Artemii Lebedev's *LiveJournal*, 2012:
http://tema.livejournal.com/1219024.html (accessed on 15.04.2015)

Figure 7.9. Photoshopped image by anonymous
'The country's leaders listen to the Presidential Address to the Federal Assembly on December 12, 2013'.
Source: http://tjournal.ru/paper/putin-2013 (accessed on 15.04.2015).

A variation on the subject of blurring the distinction between the secular and the sacred in the political sphere is represented by the following photoshopped image. This popular picture shows the Russian dignitaries wearing white cowls of the Patriarch. The raised 'ears' of Dmitry Medvedev, Head of Government of the Russian Federation, correspond to his 'Nyan'-image cultivated on Runet (**figure 7.9**).

A popular stand-alone subject of *stiob* on the net that gave birth to a multitude of photoshopped images are two members of the Russian parliament, Elena Mizulina and Vitaly Milonov, who have lately gained notoriety thanks to their legislative initiatives. Those two assert themselves as champions and guardians of the nation's morals, and have initiated a number of bills aimed at prohibiting homosexual propaganda as well as at establishing state control over the internet, which is seen as a platform for promoting pornography and paedophilia. Due to the specifics of the subject, those photoshopped images are extremely provocative and tend to visualize those 'deviations' which, according to those parliament members, should be severely censored.

Another variety of anti-clerical visual satire are pseudo-icons, where the images of saints are substituted for heroes of American mass culture (**figure 7.10**).

Figure 7.10. Photoshopped image by anonymous.
Pseudo-icons of Batman, Spiderman and Iron Man.
Source: http://marvel.joyreactor.cc/post/632223 (accessed on 15.04.2015)

In post-secular times the pseudo-icon genre has become rather sought after, as well as profitable, both commercially and ideologically. Thus, in modern Russia one can find instances of uncanonical images of Iosif Stalin, Georgii Zhukov, Grigorii Rasputin and others, which are created by 'Orthodox Stalinists' (Bodin 2009). The hot and happening artists also strive for blurring the borders between the secular and sacred levels, for instance, Lenin, Mickey Mouse, and Christ (cf. A. Kosolapov's sculpture 'Hero. Leader. God', 2007). We can also mention the pseudo-icons of Robert Lenz, a Franciscan of Russian origin (Lentz and Gately 2003), who paints 'counter-cultural' icons depicting not Catholic or Orthodox saints, but famous 'outcasts' representing various epochs and cultures (Engström 2014).

The triptych of pseudo-icons depicting Batman, Spiderman and Iron Man, as well as similar anti-clerical images, employs the device of intentionally mixing the sacred and the secular, levelling pop culture with a millennium-old Christian tradition. This equalisation of narratives is specific to the post-secular epoch in general, but it is especially visible on the Web as the hierarchical structure of the Church collides with the horizontal ties typical of the new media. This particularity of the technical environment of the internet shuts out the possibility of both preserving the inner hierarchy (for instance, the audience of such well-known preachers as Deacon Andrei Kuraev or Dmitrii Smirnov on the net is much greater than that of Patriarch Kirill) and the monopoly of the ROC on authority. It seems that this conflict between a vertical structure and a network one is one of the main reasons for the growing scepticism on the part of both the ROC officialdom and the Orthodox bloggers towards the new media and social networks.[31]

Anti-Clerical Communities on the Web and Anti-Clerical Stiob

In this part of the article, we will take a closer look at the activities of the most prominent anti-clerical communities in *LiveJournal* and the

---

31 For details, see Chapter 1 in this volume.

social networks *VKontakte* and *Facebook*.³² The websites of those communities contain widespread criticism towards the ROC, Christianity and other traditional religions. Axiological abasement, mockery, pointing out the senselessness of the Christian tradition, and criticism of the post-secularity's side-effects are achieved mainly by means of *stiob*, assemblage, pastiche and other devices typical of literature and culture of the post-modern.

The most notorious counter-cultural Web resource on Runet is the mock encyclopaedia 'Lurkmore'.³³ It has been criticised numerous times by the ROC for its anti-clerical and anti-Orthodox entries; however, an attempt to close the site down in 2012 was made not by the ROC but by the Federal Drug Control Agency of Russia, citing propaganda for prohibited substances (for entries 'Weed' and 'Cannabis. Ways of consumption'). In the meantime, Dmitrii Khomak, the creator of 'Lurkmore', has assessed his project as a unique collection of the new folklore, which deserves scholarly investigation:

> 'Lurk(more)' nowadays is a good base of knowledge. It is hard to describe the project. There is a bit about blogs, a bit about memes, and about many other things. In the meantime, this database is both an encyclopaedia, something constant, and a very objective source of information, much more objective than the majority of the media. It is rather sad that they are trying to tear it to pieces with censorship. I do not know if the Institute of Slavistics still functions but I would be happy to pass everything to them. And I mean everything, without anything cut out. It should be interesting for them to study this folklore. I, actually, tried to enter the faculty of philology back in 1997 but did not pass. Well, maybe that was for the better (Maksutova 2015).

One other leading anti-religion website on Runet is *Assotsiatsiia torgovtsev slovom bozhiim* ('Merchants of God's Word Association').³⁴ As on other anti-clerical resources, it raises timely issues of

---

32 T. Chumakova (2013) singles out 34 *LiveJournal* communities that define themselves as anti-clerical. Among those are *Antiklerikal* ('Anti-cleric'), *Aktivnye antiklerikaly* ('Militant Anti-clerics'), *Soobshestvo nepostiashikhsia* ('Community of those who do not observe the Lent'), *Antiklerikalnoe dvizhenie v zashchitu kotiat* ('Anti-clerical Movement for Championing Kittens'), *Soobshestvo Antipatriarkhal'noi Koalitsii* ('Communitity of Anti-Patriarch Coalition') and others.
33 https://lurkmore.to/ (accessed on 15.04.2015). 'Lurkmore' has existed since 2007 but in 2015 the project was put on hold. See Maksutova 2015.
34 http://realigion.me/ (accessed on 15.04.2015)

the relationship between secular society and the ROC. *Stiob* that can be found in the texts published on this site is a carnivalesque, exaggerated reduction to the absurdity of those traits that are typical of the object of criticism; i.e., Orthodoxy and the ROC. The site boasts a remarkable collection of nonsensical texts united by a common device—excessive *stiob*, reductio ad absurdum, that characterise the style of Venedikt Erofeev, Viktor Pelevin, Vladimir Sorokin, Maksim Kononenko and a number of other authors from the late-Soviet and post-Soviet period.

In particular, users criticise the projects of the so-called 'new Oprichniks', who call for the canonisation of Iosif Stalin. As an example, we can produce an abstract from a mock letter 'On the Issue of Canonising Joseph, the son of Vissarion':

> Dear comrade Patriarch,
> We, a group of monks from the Saint Daniel monastery named after Mao Zedong, address you with a petition to hear out our argument in favour of canonising Iosif Dzhugashvili, son of Vissarion, secularly known as Stalin. When studying the historical closeness of the consecrated Saint Nicholas the Martyr (the last emperor of Russia from the House of Romanovs), we have discovered that the merits of elder Iosif greatly surpass the miracles performed by Nicholas...[35]

Besides criticising attempts at canonising 'the creators of the Russian state', this quote serves as a typical example of deconstructing the Orthodox 'newspeak', which gradually starts to resemble the bureaucratic parlance of the Soviet times. The accelerating process of the ROC turning bureaucratic is noted on other atheist and anticlerical sites. For instance, on *Rascerkovlenie* ('Leaving Church'):

> Official Orthodox sites (patriarchy.ru) as if cloning the style of the major Soviet newspapers: 'The proceedings took place, the speech of Comrade Patriarch on the visit to...' Some speeches and photographs could be easily swapped with those from five years ago, with no loss to meaning and quality.[36]

---

35 http://realigion.me/hagiography.asp?act=review&nID=1727 (accessed on 15.04.2015)
36 http://rascerkovlenie.ru/index.php/o-proekte (accessed on 15.04.2015)

Under the heading 'Prayers' on the 'Merchants of God's Word Association' site one can find a variation on a rather popular blog theme 'Crude Oil is what makes us!' In this case it is a mock prayer called 'Petroleum Noster', which is based, naturally, on the main Christian prayer 'Pater Noster'/'Lord's Prayer':

> Petroleum Noster who art in the ground,
> Thy octane number riseth and your price increaseth,
> Thy deposits spread under water as they art under ground.
> Give us this day a hard currency reserve,
> And pay our debts better than our debtors pay,
> And deliver us from national bankruptcy,
> For thine is the budget,
> The rating, and Courchevel,
> Forever and ever, until the third presidential term.
> Feed us and amen.[37]

The abovementioned prayer not only brings together in a single mocked image the oligarchy, the powers of the state, and the Church, but also constructs 'us' as a subject that is radically deprived of all three of those. 'We' will be having 'neither the budget, nor the rating, nor Courchevel' which belong to the bureaucratic, political and oligarchic Trinity. Simultaneously, the subject is estranged from those who partake of those new gifts, from the mass consumer of that stability 'based on oil'.

Such 'anti-behaviour' (Boris Uspenskii's term), 'religious burlesque', and play on the sacred texts have a long history in Russian culture. In the Soviet times such device was employed by a number of proletarian poets; for instance, by Demian Bednii in his *New Testament with No Flaws by Evangelist Demian* from 1925. One can also recall Andrei Platonov's prayer of labour *Let Your Name Live Sacred* from 1920. 'Misbehaviour' is also typical of the Russian Age of Enlightenment of which a vivid example is Mikhail Lomonosov's *Anthem to a Beard* (1756–1757).[38] We can also name Peter the

---

37 http://realigion.me/prayer.asp?act=review&nID=1685&dID=1752 (accessed on 15.04.2015)
38 For details on Russian anti-clerical poetry and folklore, see Bomstein 1958 and Vilchinsky 1961.

Great's The All-Jestering All-Drunken Most Foolish Assembly.[39] The Assembly functioned for no less than thirty years (from the early-1690s to mid-1720s) and was a blasphemous parody on the hierarchy and rites of the Russian Orthodox Church. During the sessions and various 'ceremonies' the participants used 'anti-language'; i.e., a travesty of Church Slavonic mixed with the use of taboo words and the pedlars' slang. The parallel to anti-clerical Web *stiob* can be found in 'praises' that were sung by the members of the 'All-Jestering Assembly' on yuletide, as well as other burlesque ceremonies which mocked the religious rites. Similarly, a famous series of satirical cartoons that depict Tsar Peter's associates as 'jesters' from the Assembly (the so-called 'Transfiguration Series') is typologically close to the photoshopped images that mock the representatives of both clerical and secular modern-day elites. However, there is a significant distinction between these two phenomena; namely, that Peter the Great's Assembly was strictly an institution of the elite, while present-day digital anti-clericalism is a mass culture feature.

Anti-clerical sites on Runet are bursting with criticism towards archaicism and blind faith in religious rites, which has become a typical feature of post-Secular Russian society over the past decade. It materialises in travesty texts, which mock the consecration of various industrial objects, new technologies in nuclear sphere, and the 'attribution' of the Orthodox saints as patrons to these sectors. The 2004 deacon Kuraev's proposal to celebrate the 10th anniversary of Runet by 'appointing' the saints Theophan the Recluse and John the Evangelist as patron saints of the Russian Web[40] caused a severe backlash from the atheists on the Net who proposed a much broader list of potential patrons for the Web. A *LiveJournal* entry, an abstract from which is given below, achieves the travesty effect and axiological abasement by reducing to an absurdity the search for patron saints in the spheres of science and high-tech. Another device, gen-

---

39 For the history of the Assembly, see Uspenskii 2002, Zitser 2004, Trakhtenberg 2005, Trakhtenberg 2008.
40 http://www.sova-center.ru/religion/news/amusing-incidents/2004/09/d2712/ (accessed on 15.04.2015)

erally typical for Web *stiob*, is a mixture of the Church Slavonic and formal syntax with the internet argot:

> Our Lord Jesus Christ—main patron of the Internet.
> Virgin Mary—Deputy main patron of the Internet in charge of the issues of women, family and marriage.
> [...] John the Evangelist—the patron of those who issue bans and delete comments since he used to write webmaster-like bullshit, like The Revelation, and told everyone to shut up.
> [...] Thomas—the patron saint of Wikipedia as one always doubts what it written there.
> [...] Mark—the patron saint of copy-pasters as he himself penned the most half-assed gospel writing not as a witness but at second hand.
> Luke—the patron saint of the web painters and photoshoppers since he was an artist himself.
> [...] Saint George—the patron saint of comments and flushing the opponent down the drain. Because f**k you that's why!
> [...] John Damascene—the patron saint of all web hoaxers. Just look at him; he's grown a third hand—LOL![41]

Another example typical of modern anti-clericalism is the prayer 'Consecration of the Computer'. The device employed here is related to *stiob* form 'mimetic critique', which is an 'over-identification' with the object of the criticism (Yurchak 2008). Comic effect is achieved by a consistent imitation of Church Slavonic spelling and syntax as well as archaisation of the vocabulary.[42]

This example belongs to the popular Runet genre of mock prayers and hymns in which modern political and cultural realia are described by means of (pseudo-) Church Slavonic or archaic Russian and pre-1917 spelling. This genre is closely connected to a known tradition of mocking 'Slavic antiquities' which nowadays is cultivated, primarily, in the creative works of Vladimir Sorokin.[43] As

---

41 http://otvet.mail.ru/question/29184133 (accessed on 15.04.2015)
42 The author of this mock player is a popular blogger Igor Lebedev. Its text was published on the site of the "Association" by the user known as Digger on November 1, 2006. Source: http://realigion.me/prayer.asp?act=review&nID=1639 (accessed on 15.04.2015)
43 In the late Soviet period this genre became widely popular thanks to the comedies *12 chairs* (1976, directed by M. Zakharov) which was based on a novel of the same name by I. Ilf and E. Petrov, and *Ivan Vasilievich: Back to the Future* (1973, directed by L. Gajdaj), based on Mikhail Bulgakov's play *Ivan Vasilievich*. Both movies contain phrases in Church Slavonic.

an illustration, we can produce a pseudo-prayer written in the 'suit speak' from his *Telluria* (2013):

> And if seeks Sovereign's top manager for the glory of the CPSU and other saints for the people's blessedness and by the will of God, by the rule of the world imperialism, by the volition of the enlightened Satanism, by the enthusiasm of the Orthodox patriotism [...] Amen.

The abovementioned mock prayer 'Consecration of the Computer' is not a singular example of criticism towards archaisation of Russian society. Runet boasts a character created by *Facebook* user Konstantin Petrovich Katkov-Suvorin who writes his posts using pre-Revolutionary spelling and syntax. His character, Монахъ Дестилирій ('Friar Distillerius'), keeps a chronicle of the current political events in Church Slavonic (figure 7.11).

Figure 7.11. Friar Distillerius.
Acathistos to the Moscow City Duma elections.
Source: https://www.facebook.com/katkov.suvorin (accessed on 15.04.2015).

It can be assumed that the emergence of that kind of pastiches, which attests to Runet's sensitivity towards the linguistic bureaucratisation of the Church, reflecting the more general process of the ROC's transfer from the marginalised sphere to the space of a dominating culture, is caused by the very personalities of those anti-clericals. The godfathers of internet *stiob*, which characterises the texts above, represent the late-Soviet counter-culture and literary underground who always opposed the Soviet officialdom and authoritative discourse. It is worth noting that such 'linguistic' criticism of the Church's newspeak and language games, typical, in particular, of the 'Merchants of God's Word Association', has nowadays become less common. Starting from the second half of the 2000s, anti-clerical genres with a dominant visual component (i.e., demotivators and photoshopped images) began developing rapidly, with their language component reduced to a minimum.

Scientific Atheism Sites and Ideologists of the Atheist and Anti-Clerical Runet

Besides the named communities, where the dominant forces are post-modernist *stiob* and mockery of various activities on the part of the ROC and the governmental sector, there exists only minor and not-very-active atheist communities of different sorts. These are normally those that continue following a Marxist approach and the Soviet tradition of criticising the Church as the tool of capitalist supremacy. One such atheist community is 'The Council of Runet Atheists'.[44] There is also a site called 'Scientific Atheism', which publishes the scholarly works of both Soviet and foreign atheists. One could also name 'The Russian Federation Union of Militant Godless Men' (SVB) established in 2008.[45] This organisation has declared itself the legal successor of the cognominal association that was active in the Soviet times.[46] The Union stands out from other atheist sites on Runet for its archaic Soviet rhetoric. Thus, the first article of the first chapter of the SVB RF Statute defines the Union's goals as follows:

---

44 http://sovet.ateist.ru/ (accessed on 15.04.2015)
45 http://svb.net.ru/ (accessed on 15.04.2015)
46 The Union of Militant Godless Men was established in 1925 but put its activities on hold with the start of the Great Patriotic War and was officially disbanded in 1947. Its function of waging a war on religion was transferred to the *Znanie* ("Knowledge") society.

> The Union of Militant Godless Men is a volunteer proletarian public organisation that is committed to uniting the great masses of working people in the Russian Federation for purposes of active, systematic and consistent struggle against religion in all its forms as it is a hindrance on the way to the socialist and cultural revolution.[47]

All these communities are distinct for their 'seriousness' and closeness, which are untypical for Runet as a whole. In their anti-clerical criticism, they employ mostly scientific arguments instead of *stiob*, and never the newer genres of digital atheism (memes, photoshopped images, demotivators).

Now we will take a look at the activities of some major figures among the 'Godless people' on the Web, as well as of several anti-clerical organisations who, besides functioning in the virtual world, are also involved in active atheist propaganda offline.[48] One of the most famous atheist headliners in present-day Russia is Alexander Nevzorov (born in 1958), a well-known reporter, director, publicist and a public figure who rose to prominence in the 1990s as the editor-in-chief and presenter of a cult TV show '600 seconds'. The show holds a Guinness Book of Records title as a TV project with the highest viewers' rating. Nevzorov participated in a number of military conflicts, both as a reporter and a foot soldier. He is the author of the documentary *Ad* ('Hell', 1995) and the motion picture *Chistilishche* ('The Purgatory', 1997), devoted to the Chechen war. In traditional media, Nevzorov as a 'public face' of atheism participates in various debates with representatives of the ROC and different governmental structures (Archpriest Vsevolod Chaplin, parliament member Vitalii Milonov, and others).

He is no less active on Runet. Besides having a *YouTube* channel, he runs the website nevzorov.tv,[49] where he broadcasts the popular show 'Atheism Lessons' and other materials. Every 'lesson' is a video-blog; a ten-minute long clip devoted to one or another timely topic connected to the relationship between the Church, the

---

47 http://svb.net.ru/about.php (accessed on 15.04.2015).
48 'Pussy Riot' is an example of an anti-clerical project that received wide international acclaim (Rutland 2014; Prozorov 2013).
49 http://nevzorov.tv/ (accessed on 15.04.2015).

state, and society. The clips appear irregularly with four issues per year on average. New 'lessons' are posted once a new topic connected to the Orthodox Church draws attention from the public and is actively discussed elsewhere. For instance, the last few issues were devoted to the infamous federal law protecting the feelings of the believers (issue 'Benefits of the Blasphemy Law', June 1, 2013), 'Orthodox patriotism' ('The Fishing Rod of Patriotism', November 20, 2013), paedophilia among the clergy ('Blue Horizons of the ROC', January 15, 2014), public discussion upon Conchita Wurst's win at Eurovision 2014 and the 'spiritual bonds' ('Priest's Lament', June 15, 2014).

Nevzorov controversially defines Christianity as 'Jewish mythology', 'Jewish folk-tales', 'a hobby', and exclusively uses derogatory Russian *popy* when talking about the clergy, referring to the ROC as a 'business corporation'. Nevzorov, a militant atheist, utilises scientific arguments in his criticism of the Orthodox Church, which, for the post-secular epoch, looks dated and engrained in an enlightenment project. There is a self-contradiction in Nevzorov's activities, as he tends to mix the elements of atheist propaganda both from the secular and post-secular epochs. He often appears to be a modernist, using the language and meanings of 'scientific atheism' and progress, but can lapse into the stylistic of *stiob* and post-modern discourse of prohibiting any hegemony.

Another recognized star of the atheistic Runet is the above-mentioned designer and top-blogger Artemii Lebedev (born 1975), who was behind the 2012 photoshop contest 'Doctor Patriarch's face with Moustache!'[50] The contest took place after the Pontifical convention issued a document 'The attitude of the Russian Orthodox Church towards intentional public blasphemy and slander towards the Church' (February 4, 2011), but before the ratification of the 'blasphemy law' in 2013. Lebedev himself and his contest met with a stern official response from the ROC. Patriarchy's press-secretary deacon Alexander Volkov instigated launching a complaint to the

---

50 See Lebedev's site http://www.artlebedev.ru/ and his blog http://tema.ru/ (accessed on 15.04.2015).

LiveJournal Abuse Prevention Team, but his attempts at shutting down Lebedev's blog were unsuccessful.

When on September 25, 2012 the media spread the news of a draft bill aimed at suppression of crime inciting sectarian discord on the internet, a post titled 'Feelings of the Believers' appeared on Lebedev's blog in *LiveJournal*. In his post, the designer proclaimed his contempt towards the feelings of the believers and inquired as to why there was no law to protect the feelings of those who refuse to believe. Together with Marat Gel'man, a gallery owner and a political strategist, he launched a political ad on the subject of the law (**figure 7.12**).

Figure 7.12. A project of Artemii Lebedev and Marat Gel'man to protect the feelings of the non-believers 'Nothing is Sacred'.
Source: http://suvenir.segment.ru/review/notr/nichego_svyatogo_lebedev_i_gelman _provodyat_konkurs_znachkov/ (accessed on 15.04.2015)

It is worth noting that the media darlings from among the atheists— Alexandr Nevzorov and Artemii Lebedev—stand against the no-less famous Orthodox newsmakers; namely, Dmitrii Enteo (Tsoreonov) and Kirill Frolov. In Frolov's opinion, Lebedev's actions prove the necessity to stiffen penalties for the instigation of sectarian discord on the Net:

Those brazen blasphemers and teomachists destroy the secular nature of our state by inoculating militant atheism as an ideology and quasi-religion.[51]

Dmitrii Uslaner, a religious studies scholar, describes the neo-atheism of the post-secular epoch as a variation of religious fundamentalism:

> New atheists are a structural counterpart of religious fundamentalists. Those are antireligious fundamentalists. Generally speaking, fundamentalism can be treated outside a religious context. It appears as a backlash from the society whose tranquil, comfortable and steady existence was challenged by radical social transformations. Fundamentalism is based on striving for bringing back the lost stability, restoring the crooked frame of references. This causes the uncompromising stance, love for simple decisions, the search for solid, impregnable base, etc. (Korablev 2015).

Besides Nevzorov, Lebedev and Gel'man we can name other noted anti-clericals who are active both offline and on Runet, such as Victor Bondarenko, a philanthropist and founder of the advocacy group 'Russia for all', as well as Roman Bagdasarov, a religious studies scholar and editor-in-chief of the 'Russia for all' website.[52] This civic movement advocates for preserving the 14th Article of the Russian Constitution that secures the secular nature of the state as well as the equality of all peoples and religions. Other notable sites are *Rascerkovlenie* ('Leaving Church')[53] and the *Zdravomyslie* fund ('Common sense'),[54] which both take a rather aggressive stance towards Orthodoxy and the ROC. For instance, *Rascerkovlenie* states its goals as follows:

> [...] our project aims at summarising and orchestrating the experiences of such people, those who are, in a certain way, professional traitors of the Church. By professionalism, we mean their bravery in discussing and summarising personal experiences in the publicly open digital space.[55]

---

51 http://www.securitylab.ru/news/430473.php (accessed on 15.04.2015).
52 http://russiaforall.ru/ (accessed on 15.04.2015).
53 http://rascerkovlenie.ru/ (accessed on 15.04.2015).
54 http://zdravomyslie.info/ (accessed on 15.04.2015).
55 http://rascerkovlenie.ru/index.php/o-proekte (accessed on 15.04.2015).

A softer stance is taken by the information web-portal 'Credo' (editor-in-chief Alexander Soldatov).[56] The group of atheist organisations that exist both on Runet and offline includes also 'Moscow Atheist Society ATOM', established in 2000.[57] All these organisations voice their criticism of Orthodoxy and all traditional religions while actively supporting the new wave of Orthodox dissidence; that is, the interior criticism of corruption and bureaucracy of the ROC, often articulated by the former Orthodox priests.

In that context, it might be worth examining the internet-film *Orthodox Kingpins*, the first showing of which took place online on March 14, 2014.[58] It is a documentary dedicated to the 20th anniversary of the current Constitution of the Russian Federation, made by a former Orthodox priest Mikhail Baranov with support from the abovementioned *Zdravomyslie* fund, the web-portal 'Credo', and the website *Rastserkovlenie*. The film, banned from offline screening in Russia, attacks the politicisation of Orthodoxy, the clericalisation of society and the system of the 'interior offshore', i.e., the fiscal privileges of the ROC as a state within a state. Some radical movements frequently mentioned in the media, namely, the Orthodox Brotherhood of Blessed Sergius of Radonezh and the Orthodox civic movement 'God's Will', founded by Dmitrii Enteo,[59] are described in the film in terms of 'Orthodox fascism' and 'Orthodox Taliban'.

One must note that the past few years saw a rise of interior criticism within the Church, aimed at commercialisation, bureaucratisation and 'Putinisation' of the ROC (Sokolov-Mitrich 2011, Zaicev 2014). 'Functional' Christianity, represented by Patriarch Kirill himself, as well as by Metropolitan Hilarion (Alfeev), Head of the External Church Affairs Department of Moscow Patriarchate, and Savva (Tutuov), head of the control-and-analysis service of the ROC, has become gradually less and less understood among the common clergy and has often led to dissent within the Church.

---

56 http://www.portal-credo.ru/ (accessed on 15.04.2015).
57 http://ateizm.ru/ (accessed on 15.04.2015).
58 http://orthodoxlaw.info/ (accessed on 15.04.2015).
59 http://www.zakrest.ru/ (accessed on 15.04.2015).

The Response of the Church: Orthodox Demotivators

The ROC has conflicting attitudes towards the internet and the activities of the Church and its members on the Web.[60] The Patriarch's office issues with growing frequency bans on any criticism, while discussions on Runet are growingly frowned upon and believers are being called to instead 'unite':

> We must always remember our mission of preaching the Orthodoxy, stand as one on the social networks, as our close front should demonstrate the unity of the Church of Christ. We should not bring up our internal disagreements up to a public view and discussion.[61]

With an increase of bans on criticism towards the ROC, the internet nowadays is seen as a space for clerical dissidence, as *Samizdat 2.0*.

In the meantime, there are attempts at resisting the 'anti-mission'; i.e., defamation of the Orthodox Church and its clergy on Runet. In that respect, one could notice the rise of Orthodox motivational posters, the so-called 'motivators'. Most of them appear on the site *Otsy.ru* created by the Orthodox laity.[62] The goals of this resource are named in its slogan 'For the non-believers—about Orthodox priests'.

Several communities on the most popular Runet social network *VKontakte* publish Orthodox motivational posters. Those are 'motivators' aimed at strengthening Christian morals, and hence protecting the ROC from defamation. As in the following example, 'No pot-belly, no expensive watch, no foreign car' (**figure 7.13**).[63]

---

60 See Suslov 2015.
61 http://sinod.ruschurchabroad.org/Arh%20Sobor%202014-Pravila-vedenia-diskuss iy.htm (accessed on 15.04.2015).
62 http://www.otsy.ru/ (accessed on 15.04.2015).
63 This poster makes a reference to the subjects popular in anti-clerical demotivators (obesity of the clergy, the financial wealth of the ROC) as well as to a notorious anecdote known as "Patriarch Kirill's watch". In April 2012, the ROC was heavily criticised both by the Russian media and on Runet for editing the photograph of the Patriarch on which an expensive Breguet watch was airbrushed from his wrist. However, the reflection of the expensive airbrushed watch in the varnished table surface became a symbol of the ROC corruption for many opposition and anti-clerical bloggers.

However, in terms of numbers, anti-clerical demotivators have a strong advantage over the Orthodox ones.[64]

Figure 7.13. Orthodox motivational poster by anonymous
'No pot-belly, no expensive watch, no foreign car'.
Source: http://demotivators.to/p/812986/ne-tolstyij-bez-dorogih-chasov-net-inomarki-no-tyi-vsyo-ravno-nenavidesh-ego.htm (accessed on15.04.2015).

In theory, the situation in which the visual dominates in modern culture should be to the advantage of the Orthodox Church, which has a millennium-old tradition of icon painting and image theology. An icon has always been a testimony and the most effective Christian 'motivator'. However, the biggest problem for the Orthodox mission on Runet lies in the character of the internet-language itself, with *stiob* dominating as a de-constructor of any serious utterance. In contrast to the straightforward message of the Soviet agitprop, anonymous

---

64 We do not have the exact statistics on the amount of anti-clerical demotivators. According to a certain Orthodox blogger, in 2012 the ratio of anti-clerical demotivators was 300.000 for each 1000 of the Orthodox ones (Boyko 2012).

authors of anti-clerical demotivators employ such devices as duplication, placing a serious utterance in inappropriate context, exaggeration, reductio ad absurdum, and abnegation. Since originally Internet lingo developed as a protest of the unofficial culture against all types of 'norm', to resist it effectively, the ROC should diverge from this norm and use a similar language that would allow deconstructing the opponents' claims on ideological dominance. However, as the Church is not ready to take that step, the rebuff to the 'heresies' and the 'harassers' is not produced. When browsing Runet, one can come across Orthodox 'motivators' bearing the same characteristics as anti-clerical demotivators; that is, intentional simplification, axiological abasement of the opponent's viewpoint, use of expletives, etc. (**figure 7.14**). However, the Church is out of position when arguing against digital atheists and it cannot fully employ those effective *stiob* devices that stipulate for a certain meta-position liberated from any axiological views. Such nihilistic stance of 'exteriority' comes into conflict with the Christian doctrine, and limits the facilities the Church has at its disposal when resisting digital atheism and anti-clericalism while they become more and more prominent.

Figure 7.14. Orthodox motivational poster by anonymous 'What the pagans, atheists and Satanists have in common'.
Source: http://www.otsy.ru/main/motivatori/demotivatory_pravoslavie_atheism.htm (accessed on 15.04.2015).

Conclusion

Our analysis draws the conclusion that currently two types of anti-clericalism exist on Runet: 1) 'digital anti-clericalism' proper with dominating genres that are connected to the development of new digital technologies and the new media (memes, photoshopped images, demotivators), and 2) 'anti-clericalism on the Web' which transfers the old forms of anti-clericalism and atheism (mock prayers, pastiches) into a new digital sphere without transforming them. The specifics of digital anti-clericalism lie in an active use of anonymous hybrid genres of internet-communication, which are close to political folklore. Runet is a playing field for aggressive criticism of the ROC's claims on ideological and financial monopoly, while the subject matter of many anti-Orthodox demotivators is close to the atheist propaganda of the Soviet period (ridicule of clergy, criticism of money-grabbing, etc.). However, it is affirmative that the huge intellectual and visual heritage of Soviet scientific atheism is hardly used by the new digital atheists. References to the articles from atheist journals or quotations from Soviet anti-Church comic strips, which in themselves are close to demotivators, are practically absent. It seems that the old atheist discourse that rather aggressively demonstrates the scientific inadequacy of beliefs of Christianity alone lays claims on supremacy. In a post-secular state, such scientific criticism typical of the modernist epoch seems dated. For that very reason, atheist sites, which carry on traditions of Soviet atheism ('The Council of Runet Atheists') or those that duplicate the old Soviet institutions ('The Russian Federation Union of Militant Godless Men') are in ill odour, are rarely kept up to date, and quite rapidly cease to exist. Our analysis of digital anti-clericalism shows that Runet attacks not so much articles of Orthodox faith or Christianity in principle (which was the goal of anti-Church propaganda in Soviet times), but rather various social aspects of the post-Soviet Orthodoxy; first and foremost, the unconstitutional breaching of borders between the secular and church spheres.

It is also important to draw a distinction between the anti-clerical resources that came into being during the initial spread of new technologies (1990s and up to mid-00s) and the anti-clericalism 2.0 (the past decade: the epoch of the social networks starting in the mid-00s). The sites of the first group, for instance, 'Merchants of God's Word Association', are closely tied to the language culture and the word cult typical of the first period of the Russian digital communication development. It is here that we find complex mock players and other types of travesty texts, which require significant linguistic and cultural background knowledge. Communities existing on social networks represent the second group. They are rather primitive, short-spoken with emphasis on the visual. However, these two types of post-Soviet anti-clericalism have something in common, as both of them create and distribute memes and demotivators. The most insular group are 'archaic' atheist sites, which publish atheist materials from the Soviet times; namely, 'The Council of Runet Atheists' and 'The Russian Federation Union of Militant Godless Men'. Here, one would not find links to the newer genres of digital anti-clericalism and atheism, and they totally lack *stiob*. This fact supports our primary argument that digital anti-clericalism on Runet is closer to the 'irony tower' of the late-Soviet underground rather than to the stylistics of Soviet anti-religious propaganda.

The analysis also shows that the new media failed to create a conceptually new type of anti-religious/anti-Orthodox propaganda, as all devices actively employed by the newer genres of anti-clerical internet-communication and political folklore (memes, photoshopped images, demotivators) can be traced back to late-Soviet and post-Soviet literature and culture of the 1970s–1990s. Imitations of church genres and parodies of Church Slavonic texts have even deeper historical roots; namely, mock prayers of Peter the Great's All-Jestering Assembly, anti-clerical poetry of the Age of Enlightenment, traditional popular print, and the Proletkult anti-church poems. However, the new viral genres on Runet allow for rapid mass circulation of critical comments on the specifics of post-Soviet Orthodoxy and its growing influence on public and political life in present-day Russia.

References

Anderson, John (2007). 'Putin and the Russian Orthodox Church: Asymmetric Symphonia?' *Journal of International Affairs* 61, no. 1 http://www.ukrainianstudies.uottawa.ca/pdf/Anderson%202007.pdf (Accessed 15.04.2015).

Baslina, E., Uhova, L. (2014). 'Demotivatsionnyi poster kak rechevoi zhanr setevogo iumora', Iaroslavskii pedagogicheskii vestnik 1, no. 1 (Gumanitarnye nauki): 135–140. http://vestnik.yspu.org/releases/2014_1g/23.pdf (Accessed 15.04.2015).

Berger, Peter (1999). 'The Desecularization of the World: A Global Overview', in P. L. Berger (ed.), *The Desecularization of the world: Resurgent Religion and World Politics*. Washington, D.C.: The Ethics and Public Policy Centre, Wm. B. Eerdmans Publishing Co.

Bikbov, Alexander (2012). 'The Methodology of Studying "Spontaneous" Street Activism (Russian Protests and Street Camps, December 2011—July 2012),' *Laboratorium* 2, http://www.soclabo.org/index.php/laboratorium/article/view/41/114 (Accessed 15.04.2015).

Bodin, Per-Arne (2009). *Language, Canonization and Holy Foolishness*, Stockholm: Acta Universitatis Stockholmiensis.

Boiko, Andrei (2012). 'Pravoslavnye demotivatory, motivatory, plakaty'. http://prihozhane.ru/forums/topic/13142?mobile=1 (Accessed 15.04.2015).

Bomshtein, G. (1958). 'Antiklerikal'naia poeziia Lomonosova i russkie narodnye poslovitsy', in *XVIII vek* 3: 65–90.

Bragina, Natal'ia (2014). '"Demotivatory so smyslom" i naivnye tolkovaniia: o sootnoshenii verbal'nogo i vizual'nogo', *Antropologicheskii forum* 21: 49–65. http://anthropologie.kunstkamera.ru/files/pdf/021/bragina.pdf (Accessed 15.04.2015).

Bugaeva, Irina (2011). 'Demotivatory kak novyi zhanr v Internet-kommunikatsii: zhanrovye priznaki, funktsii, struktura, stilistika'. http://rastko.org.rs/filologija/stil/2011/10Bugaeva.pdf (Accessed 15.04.2015).

Chumakova, Tat'iana (2011). 'Antiklerikalizm v Zhivom Zhurnale' in M. Shahnovich, T. Chumakova et al. (eds.) *Antiklerikalizm kak kul'tumo-istoricheskii fenomen*. Sankt-Peterburg: Izd-vo Sankt-Peterburgskogo gosudarstvennogo universiteta: 121–129.

Cowan, D. (2005). *Cyberhenge: Modern Pagans on the Internet*. New York, Routledge.

Dubin, Boris (2001). 'Kruzhkovyi steb i massovye kommunikatsii: K sotsiologii kul'turnogo perekhoda'. In *Slovo – pis'mo – literatura: Ocherki po sotsiologii sovremennoi kul'tury*. Moscow: NLO: 163–174.

Engström, Maria (2014). 'Ikonens metamorfoser i det postsovjetiska Ryssland', in Per Ambrosiani, Elisabeth Löfstrand, Ewa Teodorowicz-Hellman (red.), *Med blicken österut: Hyllningsskrift till Per-Arne Bodin*, Stockholm Slavic Papers, 23, Artos & Norma bokförlag, 67–78.

Engström, Maria (2015). '"Orthodoxy or death!" Political Orthodoxy in Russia,' in Simons, Greg & Westerlund, David (eds.). *Religion, Politics and Nation-Building in Post-Communist Countries*, Routledge, 65–73.

Erpyleva, Svetlana, Magun, Artemii (2014). *Politika apolitichnykh: Grazhdanskie dvizheniia v Rossii 2011—2013 godov*. Moscow: NLO.

Fagan, Geraldine (2013). *Believing in Russia—Religious Policy after Communism*, Routledge.

Golynko-Vol'fson, Dmitrii (2012). 'Demotivatory'. *Iskusstvo kino* 5. http://kinoart.ru/archive/2012/05/demotivatory (Accessed 15.04.2015).

Ionin, Leonid (2005). 'Novaia magicheskaia epokha'. *Logos* 5, no. 50: 23–40.

Iurchak, Aleksei (2008). 'Mimeticheskaia kritika ideologii. Laibakh i AVIA', *Chto delat'* 19.

Iurchak, Aleksei (2014). *Eto bylo navsegda, poka ne konchilos'. Poslednee sovetskoe pokolenie*. Moscow: NLO.

Iurkov, Sergei (2003). 'Ot lubka k "Bubnovomu valetu": grotesk i antipovedenie v kul'ture "primitiva"', in *Pod znakom groteska: antipovedenie v russkoi kul'ture (XI-nachalo XX vv.)*. Sankt-Peterburg: 177–187.

Jonson, Lena (2015). *Art and Protest in Putin's Russia*, Routledge.

Korablev, Anton (2015). 'Dmitrii Uzlaner: "Novye ateisty – eto fundamentalisty"'. *Metropol'*, 13 April 2015. http://mtrpl.ru/uzlaner (Accessed 15.04.2015).

Kyrlezhev, Aleksandr (2004). 'Postsekuliarnaia epokha', *Kontinent*, no. 120. http://magazines.russ.ru/continent/2004/120/kyr16.html (Accessed 15.04.2015).

Kyrlezhev, Aleksandr (2013). 'Sekuliarizm i postsekuliarizm v Rossii i v mire', *Otechestvennye zapiski* 1, no. 52. http://www.strana-oz.ru/2013/1/sekulyarizm-i-postsekulyarizm-v-rossii-i-v-mire (Accessed 15.04.2015).

Lentz, Robert and Gately, Edwina (2003). *Christ in the Margins*, Orbis books.

Maksutova, Al'fiia (2015). '"Lurkomor'e" kak iskusstvo', *Russkii reporter*, 9 July 2015. http://rusrep.ru/article/2015/07/09/lurkomore-kak-iskusstvo (Accessed 04. 09.2015).

Mitrofanova, Anastasia (2005). *The Politicization of Russian Orthodoxy: Actors and Ideas* (Soviet and Post-Soviet Politics and Society 13), Ibidem-Verlag.

Nevzorov, Aleksandr (2011). 'Pravoslavie golovnogo mozga', *Minaev Live.* https://www.youtube.com/watch?v=GDIZT0qcWKU (Accessed 15.04.2015).

Papkova, Irina (2011). *The Orthodox Church and Russian Politics*, Oxford University Press.

Prozorov, Sergei (2013). "Pussy Riot and the Politics of Profanation: Parody, Performativity, Veridiction". *Political Studies*, http://onlinelibrary.wi ley.com/doi/10.1111/1467-9248.12047/abstract (Accessed 15.04.2015).

Rabkina, Nadezhda, Kameneva, Veronika (2013). 'Funktsional'nyi i pragmaticheskii potentsial demotivatorov kak vizual'no-verbal'noi formy sovremennoi internet-kommunikatsii', *Politicheskaia lingvistika* 1, no. 43: 144-151, http://cyberleninka.ru/article/n/funktsionalnyy-i-pragmaticheskiy-potentsial-demotivatorov-kak-vizualno-verbalnoy-formy-sovremennoy-internet-kommunikatsii (Accessed 15.04.2015).

Richters, Katja (2013). *The Post-Soviet Russian Orthodox Church: Politics, Culture and Greater Russia.* Routledge.

Rutland, Peter (2014). "The Pussy Riot affair: gender and national identity in Putin's Russia." *Nationalities Papers. The Journal of Nationalism and Ethnicity*, 4: 575–582.

Savitskaia, Tat'iana (2013). 'Internet-memy kak fenomen massovoi kul'tury', *Kul'tura v sovremennom mire* 3, http://infoculture.rsl.ru/NIKLib /althome/news/KVM_archive/2013/r_arch-kvm_2013-03.htm (Accessed 15.04.2015).

Schmidt, Henrike (2014). "Russian literature on the internet: from hypertext to fairy tale." Michael S. Gorham, Ingunn Lunde, Martin Paulsen (eds.), *Digital Russia: The Language, Culture and Politics of New Media Communication* (Routledge Contemporary Russia and Eastern Europe Series), Routledge.

Shchurina, Iuliia (2012). 'Internet-memy kak fenomen internet-kommunikatsii', *Filologiia* 3: 160–172.

Simons, Greg (2009). *The Role of the Russian Orthodox Church in Russia Since 1990: Changing Dynamics of Politics and Religion.* Edwin Mellen Press.

Sokolov-Mitrich, Dmitrii (2011). 'Ochen' malen'kaia vera', *Russkii reporter* 13, no. 191. http://rusrep.ru/article/2011/04/05/vera/ (Accessed 15.04.2015).

Sorokin, Vladimir (2013). *Telluriia.* Moscow: ACT: Corpus.

Strukov, Vlad (2007). 'Video Anekdot: Auteurs and Voyeurs of Russian Flash Animation.' *Animation*, 2: 129–151.

Strukov, Vlad (2011). 'Russian Internet Stars: Gizmos, Geeks, and Glory,' in Helena Goscilo, Vlad Strukov (eds.), *Celebrity and Glamour in Contemporary Russia: Shocking Chic*, Routledge, 144–169.

Trakhtenberg, Lev (2005). 'Sumasbrodneishii, Vseshuteishii i Vsep'ianeishii sobor', in *Odissei: Chelovek v istorii*. Moscow: Nauka: 89–118.

Trakhtenberg, Lev (2008). *Problemy poetiki russkoi parodii XVII-pervoi poloviny XVIII vv*. Nauchnaia biblioteka dissertatsii i avtoreferatov, http://www.dissercat.com/content/problemy-poetiki-russkoi-parodii-xvii-pe rvoi-poloviny-xviii-vv#ixzz3J2mOz8S9 (Accessed 15.04.2015).

Turkova, Kseniia (2012). 'Dukhovnye skrepy', *Moskovskie novosti*, 14 December 2014. http://www.mn.ru/opinions/20121214/333069641.html (Accessed 15.04.2015).

Uspenskii, Boris (2002). 'Tsar' i samozvanets. Samozvanchestvo v Rossii kak kul'turno-istoricheskii fenomen', in *Etiudy po russkoi istorii*. Sankt-Peterburg: Azbuka: 149–196.

Vil'chinskii, V. (1961). *Russkoe narodno-poeticheskoe tvorchestvo protiv tserkvi i religii*. Leningrad: AN SSSR.

Zaitsev, Andrei (2014). '"Solidnyi Gospod' dlia solidnykh gospod", ili 6 massovykh psevdosviatyn", *Pravoslavie i mir*. http://www.pravmir.ru /solidnyiy-gospod-dlya-solidnyih-gospod-ili-hit-parad-psevdosvyatyin/ (Accessed 15.04.2015).

Zhuravskii, Aleksandr (2001). 'Genezis i formy postsovetskogo ateizma'. *Russkii arhipelag*. http://www.archipelag.ru/ru_mir/religio/novie-identichnosti/atheism/postsovetsky-ateism/ (Accessed 15.04.2015).

Zitser, Ernest A. (2004). *The Transfigured Kingdom. Sacred Parody and Charismatic Authority at the Court of Peter the Great*, Cornell Univeristy Press, Ithaca, USA.

List of the quoted Runet anti-clerical and atheist sources (accessed on 15.04.2015).

AntiReligion http://ru_antireligion.livejournal.com/
Merchants of God's Word Association http://realigion.me/
Moscow Atheist Society ATOM http://www.ateizm.ru/
Zdravomyslie ('Common sense') http://zdravomyslie.info/
Sciemtific Atheism http://atheism.ru/
Orthodox Kingpins http://orthodoxlaw.info/
Rascerkovlenie ('Leaving Church') http://rascerkovlenie.ru/
Russia for All http://russiaforall.ru/
Alexander Nevzorov's site http://www.hauteecole.ru/ru/news/
Artemii Lebedev's site http://www.tema.ru/
The Council of Runet Atheists http://sovet.ateist.ru/
The Russian Federation Union of Militant Godless Men http://svb.net.ru/

Chapter 8.
Ortho-Media for Ortho-Women:
In Search of Patterns of Piety

Anastasia Mitrofanova
Russian Orthodox University of St John the Divine

'Ortho-media' (*ortosmi*) is a widely used intra-Church slang word, which indicates mass media specially designed for the Orthodox believers—more specifically though, for people who attend churches not to just observe traditions blindly and who take the communion more or less regularly ('enchurched' people). The word has become so common that it can nowadays be found even in the official Church publications (see, for example: 'Nuzhdaiutsia li tserkovnye SMI', 2012). The chapter is focused on women-oriented Orthodox web resources; it aims at finding out how digital media helps people estranged from the living traditions of piety to produce collective vision of a modus operandi appropriate for an Orthodox woman. To answer this question I will (1) make a brief sketch of the parochial subculture of the pre-digital era; (2) summarize why women prefer to discuss things digitally, what they discuss and how; and (3) evaluate successes and failures of web-discussions with regard to finding the lost tradition of piety. Research methods include discourse analysis, participant observation of parish subculture and interviewing.

Web resources for Orthodox women have different forms: forums, digital journals, and some groups in the social media (mostly in the most popular Russian network *Vkontakte*). I have chosen four women-oriented web-resources in the Russian language for intensive study:

Matrony.ru (Matrons)—a 'conservative women's magazine'—is a unique web-resource launched in 2006, but known since 2011, when it became part of a family of portals controlled by an Orthodox web publisher Pravmir.ru—'*Pravoslavie i mir*' (Orthodoxy and the World). It is the largest and the most diverse website for Orthodox women. The Editor-in-chief is Lidiia (Lika) Sideliova. Prior to Matrony.ru, women's topics were discussed at Pravmir.ru by Polina (Pelageia) Tiurenkova, Ol'ga Kurova (now Gumanova), Anna Danilina (the Editor-in-chief of Pravmir.ru) and others. Slavianka.com ('Slavic Woman') is a digital version of a glossy Orthodox periodical for women. The printed version has existed since 2006; the Editor-in-chief is Sergei Timchenko. It is the only women's resource whose printed version has been, in 2011, officially approved by the Synodal Information Department of the Russian Orthodox Church (*SINFO*). Prihozhanka.ru (Woman Parishioner) is a moderated web-forum for female parishioners. To register one must indicate gender and religion with only two available options: female and Orthodox. Matushki.ru (Mothers) is a moderated web-forum initially designed for presbyters' wives (Russian: sing.: *matushka*, pl.: *matushki*), but in fact there is active participation by laywomen too. To register one must indicate religion, but Orthodoxy is the only available option. There is no question about gender, but one must indicate if she is *matushka* or non-*matushka*, thus assuming that all participants are women.

Both forums are designed for 'enchurched' people. Discussions confirm that participants live parish lives on a more or less regular basis, continuously attend specific churches, regularly confess and communicate with priests, and so on. It is important to see that the internet for them does not replace normal liturgical life but performs other important functions. Having analyzed all discussions on selected issues (listed below), I have chosen the most illustrative of them for citation[1].

Since there are not many publications available on the founding principles of the Orthodox media, I have held two unstructured research interviews with the following discourse-makers, whom have contrasting opinions on the Orthodox media-content for women:

---

1   Discussions were selected on the basis of the following qualitative characteristics: (1) one of the many discussions on a popular and recurrent topic; (2) lasts from several months to several years and is participated by many people; (3) included various opinions, both conflicting and congruent; (4) opinions are mostly clear, concise, relevant to the current discussion.

Ol'ga Gumanova was one of the founders and first editor-in-chief of Matrony.ru; now she is a privately consulting psychologist and author. The interview was taken in Moscow, on 10 June 2014.

Polina (for Orthodox web-sites: Pelageia) Tiurenkova is an opponent of Matrony.ru, an author of many renowned articles on women's issues and editor-in-chief of a digital magazine Tat'ianin Den' (Tatiana's Day)—Taday.ru (2011–2013, then 2014). Before the emergence of Matrony.ru, Tiurenkova created a closed *LiveJournal* community for female churchgoers called 'Ortho-women' (now non-existent). The interview was taken in Moscow, on 3 July 2014.

Parish subculture before the advent of the internet

The reason behind the emergence of the Orthodox segment of the internet was the fact that Orthodox Christianity in the post-Soviet Russia transcended the border of a closed parochial subculture (see: Tarabukina 2000; Agadjanian and Rousselet 2006; Naletova 2006; Zigon 2008; Agadjanian 2009; Mitrokhin 2009; Hann and Goltz 2010; Agadjanian and Rousselet 2011; Akhmetova 2011; Beglov 2014). Ol'ga Gumanova provides an extensive description of that subculture and of its *raison d'être*:

> I am a neophyte of the end of the 80s—the beginning of the 90s. In that time it was considered cool to wear something ragged, pilgrim-like, semi-monastic. Some ugly gray skirt, from your grannie's chest. At *'Pravoslavnoe Slovo'* store in Piatntitskaia Street they used to sell such special black ugly scarves. They used to say: these are popular; they make one look like a nun. It was fashionable to have worn shoes; people intentionally put on worn shoes to show how ascetic one is [...]
> It seems, it [the subculture] was widespread in the 90s: this special style of clothing, special words. Someone has even prepared a dissertation about it[2]. About this Orthodox parochial subculture, a culture of monastery hostels, of pilgrims travelling around monasteries, that specific philosophy of life, all those 'forgive-me-bless-me'. Now, when so many other people have come, who were not part of it, many things most likely descended to the sphere of anecdotes. May be, this subculture was justified in that time. For the Church was persecuted, and if they saw a new person, it was important to check if he was one of us, or a stranger. One of us is the one who knows all these passwords,

---

2 She, most likely, means Arina Tarabukina's dissertation.

code words, 'forgive-me-bless-me', the one who knows how to tie a scarf—it means, she is one of us, we can trust her. Now it is generally not so important —if the person is one of us, or a stranger. If one has come to the church, it means he is one of us. Something has brought him here, what makes him one of us.

Everything changed in the early 1990s, when people, having no intention to join the subculture and planning to succeed in mainstream society, started to become open churchgoers (they can be designated as 'the new Orthodox' or, better, 'the new parishioners'—to stress that they not just believed in their souls, but were enchurched). Their vision of the subculture was mostly negative. Gumanova explains:

> And, I believe, the less of it [the subculture]—the better, because apart from being a criterion for insiders, it can also dissocialize. It can be that someone is accustomed to working in this environment. For example, he works many years in an ecclesiastical publishing house... and then something happens: the publishing house is closed, this man has no job, and also family and children. This man is socially completely disadaptated. He has, in principle, some editing skills, but to go to a secular publishing house he should communicate with people differently, and he does not know how. And he can stay without any job at all, outside the society, justifying it by not going against his consciousness. The point is not that he goes against consciousness and commits mortal sins. The point is that he is able to communicate only in the language of that environment.

Polina (Pelageia) Tiurenkova is evidently glad that nowadays an Orthodox parishioner cannot be detected in a crowd:

> It [the subculture] was manifested even outwardly. Now it is even strange to recall, because I remember well that it existed, that it was everywhere, and now it is not. You think that you may have dreamed about it, but it existed. Some sort of dirty backpacks... those skirts, of velvet.... What else was there? Books of prayers, with greasy pages; now the majority has prayers downloaded to iPhones. Could we imagine it even five years ago? We could not... I mean, we, the Orthodox.... they became absolutely equal to the others.

In her widely cited web-article Tiurenkova provided a satirical description of a subculturated woman parishioner: 'There is a scarf of unidentifiable colour on her head. Her skirt is trailing on the asphalt. It is black. Formless. Often of velvet; one can see it because of attrition typical for this textile. Worn out shoes' (Tiurenkova 2006).

Unwilling to tolerate such image of a female churchgoer, Tiurenkova put forward a plan of constructing a media-image of 'Ortho-woman' (below italics indicate words originally written in English):

> It is not so easy to become an Orthodox woman, and hence it is an honor. Being enchurched, having patriarchal family and children (not one and not even two), observing traditions and fasts does not prevent her from having good education, excellent job and well-groomed appearance. She is happy [...] Having formed an adequate image of an Orthodox woman, we must set a global goal to compete such popular female media-images as *'Cosmo-girl'* and *'Vogue*-woman'. An image of *'ortho-woman'* should enter the arena of media market, which, to be honest, already educates and will educate our daughters: an image of a conservative girl (woman), who perfectly fits the contemporary reality, but leans upon eternal values, professed by Orthodoxy (Tiurenkova 2009).

The same striving for another image of a female parishioner can be detected in Gumanova's interview:

> Now this correct feeling has emerged [in Russia], which all the peoples have whose Orthodox tradition was not broken—that Sunday Liturgy is a feast. And one should better look festive during it [...] I see variety of scarves; it means scarves are paid attention to. Before, it happened that they nearly put handkerchiefs on heads. Now one can notice that scarf is part of the outlook, that it was chosen, that they [scarves] can be sort of interesting, hand-painted by designers, and often it turns out to be the most expensive, the most chic, the most interesting detail of an outlook.

The idea of 'Ortho-woman' and this terminology as such were not accepted by everyone. Nevertheless, women who came to parishes in the post-Soviet time and had no interest in joining the subculture were indeed in need of some common understanding of what it means to be an Orthodox woman today.

Step by step, the new parishioners started seeking contacts with people like them. Unlike the previous generation, they did not use direct communication, because the prevalent subculture provided them with no opportunity for mixing. In the early-1990s very few parishes had spaces (literally and metaphorically) for non-liturgical communication of the flock. Even Sunday schools were rare; there was little work done with the youth, with families; no special work with women existed at all. All informal communications took place within the subculture. That is why the internet has become the main space for the new parishioners to exchange their visions and life patterns. I should again emphasize that their liturgical life remains normal and not 'digitalized'; they do not form 'web-parishes', although apparently prefer digital to firsthand extra-liturgical communication.

Ortho-women's talks

For women as a group—not for women with special needs, like mothers with many children, or wives of priests—the internet became the only place to meet. Even now in Russia there are no ecclesiastically-oriented women's organizations, which are abundant in the Catholic and Protestant worlds. Formally the Union of Orthodox Women exists but this organization does not function at the grassroots level and does not affect the lives of average female parishioners.

My essay does not deal with all aspects of web communication between the Orthodox women, but only with topics commonly seen as being restricted to women's issues (more on polyphony in Orthodox publications for women may be found at: Kizenko 2013). The most popular such topics—as well as at the secular recourses for women, such as a huge forum Woman.ru—are:

- Culinary and Lenten food.
- Clothing, inside and outside the church.
- Relations with men (including sex).

Interestingly enough, the globally hot issue of 'women in the Church' seems unimportant for Russia. An American scholar Nadiezda Kizenko writes:

> What seems strikingly absent is any concern in Russia regarding women in the liturgical life of the church. By contrast, at a recent Orthodox women's conference in the United States, participants described examples of growing female liturgical participation: parishes in Beirut, Damascus, England, and Michigan where girls serve with boys in the altar; parishes where girls hold com-

munion cloths; parishes where women are permitted to read the epistle... The situation in Russia is different (Kizenko 2013: 613–14).

The above-listed topics can rarely be found on gender-neutral Orthodox web-resources (there are no purely men's resources, apart from those for the clergy). Thus, they are seen as women-oriented ones, although men can participate in discussing them. Web-discussions represent a collective attempt to find out proper patterns of piety for an Orthodox woman wishing to live a truly Orthodox life in the contemporary libertarian, 'permissive' society.

In the course of discussions women raise questions they find important and bothering yet unsuitable for discussing with a priest because of a topic being 'minor' (e.g., culinary) or too sensitive[3]. Below there are some examples of how they explain their motives themselves.

Prikhozhanka.ru ('Neskol'ko let khozhu' 2014; 'Spiral' dlia lecheniia' 2012): 'suddenly I became fond of a reader... Feelings are pure and good. No lust. There is no opportunity to be introduced to him. I don't want the third parties to interfere. I am ashamed to discuss this topic with a priest' (*Eva* 10.05.2014); 'Advise, please, if an Orthodox woman may use a gynecological hormonal spiral to treat a phybromioma? Of course, it would be better to ask the father, but my acquaintance cannot do it. May some matushki respond—help is much needed!!!' (*Olionushka-Ol'ga*, 26.03.2012). Matushki.ru ('Obychnoe zhenskoe', 2008): 'I am very interested in the issue, what is allowed and what is not allowed on "these" days. I am ashamed to ask the father at the church. Matushki, enlighten me, please' (*Anastasiia T.* 21.03.2008).

But being ashamed is not the only reason not to discuss things with the fathers. In many cases priests have no tailored answers, because contemporary life too openly contradicts the demands of faith. Individual clergymen often have different and even opposing positions on issues like pre-matrimonial sex, divorce or even wearing trousers; the Church hierarchy is simply silent. Fasting rules for lay-

---

3 From here on Cyrillic usernames will be written in italics.

people are even assumed to become part of the agenda of the coming 2016 All-Orthodox Council—it turned out that for two thousand years the Orthodox Church had no firm fasting rules for the non-monastic. Besides, faith and culture are, as usual, tightly interwoven; it is always impossible to sort them apart and patterns of piety can vary significantly between different Orthodoxy-based cultures.

It is not surprising that there are no shared positions on so many issues, and that no one is happy to take responsibility for answering the sore questions. Alternative sources of information about proper Orthodox patterns of piety are not available. Printed literature mainly talks about pious life in general, or provides long lists of rules and recipes (literally) which a woman must navigate without assistance. The parish subculture is able to provide all answers, but the new parishioners do not want to listen. The internet provides the answers many Orthodox women cannot receive offline due to the absence of real-life parochial communities beyond the subculture. There are people, attending this or that church, but they rarely communicate with each other and form no off-liturgical community. The issue of parishes not always being consolidated communities has been many times addressed by His Holiness Patriarch Kirill (for example, here: 'Sviateichii Patriarkh Kirill', 2015). Web-resources, thus, are not just platforms for exchanging ready-made recipes (both literally and figuratively), but places where the patterns of piety may be collectively tested.

Below there are excerpts from some forum discussions (actual posts being much longer) dedicated to the most overtly female topics: making food, proper clothing and family relations. These discussions are the most exemplary and expressing spirit and letter of the forums in the most concentrated form.

A culinary topic discussed at Matushki.ru ('O postnom maioneze', 2010):

> Are you eating Lenten mayonnaise during the fast, including the Lent, is it appropriate? (*Galina* 15.02.2010)
>
> Formally may be yes, but in such case I don't fully understand the meaning of the fast. Fasting is temperance (abstinence of everything unnecessary, includ-

ing delighting your palate), it is not rejection of some specific foods. Let is hypothetically suggest that soon exact imitations of eggs and sausage are produced, but with 'Lenten' ingredients; what would be the meaning of the fast? Just a formality. [...] I think that such mayonnaise is appropriate for some holydays, but as for average fasting days, it seems, it is sort of trick—both to regale yourself and to observe the fast formally. (*Penelopa* 15.02.2010)

Yes, we eat Lenten mayonnaise. For my husband needs calories. (*AleksandraP* 15.02.2010)

We ate mayonnaise during the fast for ages, any mayonnaise; 100% there are no natural eggs there. And we eat 'Rama' [margarine]. As for harm, life is harmful in general. (*IrinaSh* 17.02.2010)

Clothing discussion at Prihozhanka.ru ('Pro pokrov golovy', 2014):

Apostle [Paul] says that women should cover heads while praying. And, according to him, we should be always praying. Logically speaking, we must be always covered to show the angels we are not rebels. Why, then, we have no such tradition? Or am I getting something wrong? (*Gorlitsa* 17.08.2014)

I wear scarf only in the church. In the Sunday school, which is in the church court, all girls are without scarves. (*Marusiok* 17.08.2014)

I have been in so many churches in our oblast; everywhere scarves are at the church and on the territory. At work always in a scarf, and on the parish territory, and the church goes without saying. [...] But generally I rarely wear scarf; I do not cover my head in the street and at home. Due to migraines sometimes I take it off even at work [she works at the church—A.M.] and no one has ever commented on this, not even our father... (*Murlyka* 17.08.2014)

Divorce discussion at Prihozhanka.ru ('Dopustim li razvod', 2010):

What do you think, if in a family, where husband and wife were married in church, love has disappeared... Is it worth to preserve this family? Infidelity, for example, is not confirmed, but there are indirect signs... (...) There are practically no conjugal relations... And relations are fully alienated... :(I just want to know: is divorce justified from the Orthodox viewpoint in such a case? Or should I stand and wait for everything to change? (KoffeMokko 23.08.2010)

Ask him (if possible, in maximally calm tone, without tears or accusations) — how he himself evaluates the family situation. Is he satisfied with everything? Does he want to change anything? When both spouses are enchurched, it would be ideal to ask for assistance of their common spiritual father, or a priest authoritative for both people. But if the worst has happened, then I don't know... I would not stand. Moreover, children would suffer the most. As for

> cases when the Church allows a divorce, we can appeal to the Social Concept of the ROC. (Never Over 23.08.2010)
>
> Does your husband go to church? If yes, come to the priest, may be he is able to get him talking and to help in resolving some problems. (*Murashka* 24.08.2010)
>
> You'd better morally separate yourself from him now. I mean living for yourself and for the kids. And arranging somehow autonomous life for yourself. And warn him in which case you apply for divorce. He must also know that you are not going to stand some things. Anyhow, it is impossible to preserve the family alone. (*Riv'era* 27.08.2010)

Web-forums, in spite of heavy moderation, are characterized by an egalitarian atmosphere. All types of arguments are accepted: from theoretical ruminations to personal habits and experiences. Web-magazines, of course, present information in a more authoritarian manner, resembling glossy style magazines. They are not so much interested in collective discussions, as to providing a ready-made image of a contemporary Orthodox woman. Ideological positions of authors are different, but all of them tend to present their understanding of what a proper Orthodox woman should do as the ultimate truth beyond discussion.

The edifying style of Matrony.ru is reflected in this excerpt from a publication by Gumanova: 'A mature woman has her own opinion and is firm about it. She trusts her feelings, her intuition, and her perception of reality and life experience. She does not need to ask the others for advice at each smallest pretext; she is self-sufficient' (Gumanova 2014).

Similar didactic tone (in spite of completely different ideological underpinning) may be traced in a Slavianka.com publication authored by Sr. Nina (Krygina), a professional psychologist:

> Most men paying a lot of attention to fashion are, as a rule, spiritually bankrupt. They compensate the inner world at the expense of the outer world. And this deficiency will soon become apparent in family life. Young girls, who marry early, should be particularly aware of this. You ask her 'What is he like?' and she answers with aspiration 'He is so handsome!' A mature woman would never answer like this. For her, physical beauty is of secondary significance (Sister Nina 2013).

Pelageia Tiurenkova's recommendations with regard to dress-code for an 'Ortho-woman' also sounded more like orders (italics indicate original Latin):

> One feels uneasy when looking at orange letters on a blue scarf: '*FENDI. Made in China*'. Rough, low quality *fake* ('feik' means cheap imitations of the most expensive brands) is condemned by the whole world for many reasons. But we are interested only in one of them—you look silly and ridiculous with a '*Louis Vuitton*' bag for 500 roubles and in a '*Chanel*' scarf for one hundred (Tiurenkova 2006).

Reading forum discussions, one may notice that digital magazines, indeed, are authoritative in the eyes of participants; they often share links to web-publications to support their individual viewpoints. But both forums and magazines seem incapable of finding patterns of female Orthodox piety in real life; of identifying a 'model Orthodox woman' recognized by everyone.

Figure 8.1. Slavianka.com, the archive of covers.
Source: http://www.slavianka.com/archive/list/. Accessed 25 October 2015.

Even the easy-looking task of creating an ideal external image—a 'style icon'—has proven to be difficult to fulfill. Tiurenkova says that she has some images of *matushki* in her head, but they are not "spun up". The printed version of *'Slavianka'* magazine publishes a glossy photo of a beautiful young woman on every cover (covers are also available in the web-archive), but most of these cover girls are anonymous models. Forum participants tend to publish their own—not someone else's—photos to illustrate, for example, a preferred skirt length. Tiurenkova shared in the interview her own sad experience of publishing in the 'Ortho-women' community a wedding photo of a concrete priest's daughter:

> Women have shown that they are ordinary women. In spite of being Orthodox, they started to discuss her appearance, started to discuss her dress; and, unfortunately, most of the commentaries were negatively tinctured. And somehow, although it was all closed, the young bride, the young wife was informed about this all; it was all printed out. And then her sister came and wrote that the girl, the woman, had cried a lot, that she had really had a small woe in her life.

Tiurenkova has drawn my attention to the fact that the Orthodox milieu seems to be unwilling to perceive a concrete woman, for example a priest's wife, as an ideal to comply with:

> None of our *matushki*, unfortunately, has been able or willing to become sort of icon whom the others would want to imitate. For example, *Matushka* Olesia Nikolaeva could have done it, because she is married to a well-known archpriest [Vladimir Vigilianskii], and is a very famous novelist herself. She has beautiful appearance, has her own style, but for unclear reasons... Normally in subcultures they follow someone. I don't see in the Moscow parish life anyone imitating anyone else.

It is even more difficult to find living women demonstrating not just 'ideal' appearances, but exemplary life styles. Digital periodicals publish interviews with Orthodox women celebrities, but with a limited range of professions: singers and actresses, writers, painters; there are also interviews with *matushki*, independently on their professions. There are no (or very few) interviews with Orthodox female politicians, industrialists, scholars (especially scholars of exact and natural sciences), or women working in the offices of the Patriarchy or the bishoprics. At the same time, Orthodox digital magazines demonstrate a complete lack of interest in 'wives'—they do not interview or promote Orthodox women married to famous men. What strikes more is the lack of interest in families, except priests' families or families with many children—both can hardly be seen as patterns to be imitated by an ordinary parishioner. This focus on a woman per se, not on a woman in a family, seems strange considering that conservative values assume high appreciation of family life. Both Gumanova and Tiurenkova define a conservative woman exclusively via family: '[Conservative] means a web site for women with conservative, traditional vision of the family, wishing to find like-minded women with the same views. They want to get an advice from people who respect such views' (Gumanova); 'What do we mean under conservatism, for women? It means, that family and children are in the first place for you' (Tiurenkova).

In my opinion, the above-mentioned trends in portraying women in ortho-media result from two conflicting influences: of the Soviet women's magazines ('*Rabotnitsa*' and '*Krest'ianka*') and of the Western glossy magazines ('Cosmo', 'Lady's Home Journal', etc.). On the one hand, a woman is portrayed as a socially independent person, a professional in her own right. 'Just a housewife' (if she is not a minister's wife) is not worthy of their attention. This approach is definitely inspired by the Soviet way of doing journalism. '*Rabotnitsa*' (Worker Woman) and '*Krest'ianka*' (Peasant Woman) used to acquaint their readers with important women representing professions and positions untypical for their gender: factory directors, skippers, surgeons, etc. All these professionals were photographed as being good-looking but definitely without 'glamour'; their family life was often shadowed. Housewives could appear in these magazines only in extraordinary situations, such as having many children. On the other hand, women's professional self-realization, according to the ortho-media, is limited by the 'feminine' sphere of liberal arts—here the influence of Western patterns may be detected. This dual influence, unrecognized and not reflected upon, significantly distorts and impoverishes the public image of an Ortho-woman, preventing, at the same time, ordinary women from imitating life patterns they see in the media.

Looking for the lost tradition

In the absence of recognized 'style icons', the web-community of female parishioners needs some external authority to lean upon. They cannot trust their own collective experiences because of being relatively new to the Orthodox way of life and having no tradition behind them (except for the parish subculture of the Soviet past). This need of a living tradition was expressed by Tiurenkova, ruminating on contemporary Orthodox women: 'A broken, unhappy generation of women. Their parents did not baptize them at forty days age in little white chemises; their grandmothers did not teach them to go to church in white, beadworked scarves; their husbands did not marry them in white dresses' (Tiurenkova 2006).

Generally, for the Orthodox, the Holy Scripture and the Tradition of the Church are equally authoritative. But both sources are of little help for women in need not of abstract written regulations, but of real and practicable lifestyles. It seems that forum participants, more than magazines, are prone to relying on their own life experiences—this makes the forums analogous to the parish subculture. Nevertheless, external traditions are also often brought to support the author's viewpoint, especially when it openly contradicts the regulations of the parish subculture (for example, with regard to head coverings).

The most important external source of the living tradition is represented by contemporary Orthodox peoples, such as Greeks, Serbs, Romanians, etc., or even Muslim peoples. Greeks became especially popular role models because Greece is a frequent destination for tourists and pilgrims from Russia.

Ol'ga Gumanova speaks Greek and has published several web-articles on the Greek traditions of celebrating Orthodox feasts (sometimes with attached recipes). Greece attracts her as a country where the Orthodox tradition has never been broken:

> Enchurched Greeks have slightly different vision of the measure of fasting. Many pious parishioners, not mentioning the monastic, strictly observe not using vegetable oil on weekdays of the Lent—they thoroughly follow this requirement of the Typikon. At the same time, on a Lenten weekday in a house of deeply religious people or in a monastery you can be given calamari rings, crab cakes and pilaf with mussels—seafood in Greece is considered very inexpensive, light and unpretentious food (Gumanova 2013).

Sometimes, Greek patterns of piety are used to justify completely opposite clothing styles (because forum participants had different experiences). A participant at Prihozhanka.ru ('Pro pokrov golovy', 2014) holds this opinion: 'As we were on the Crete and walked into Greek Orthodox churches, all women were without headwear. Basing on my scarf, we were immediately classified as the Russians' (*Marusiok* 17.08.2014). A participant at Matushki.ru ('Platok i vsio o nem' 2010) seems to disagree:

> In the Greek churches it is allowed to cover your head with scarf only. All the other things they make put off. Some years ago the Greek 'fathers' once again raised the question of uncovered women's heads. And still they did not dare to ban women in such a condition to enter churches, because for 300 years of forced Catholiciziation women became unaccustomed to the normal Orthodox look. So, in Greece it was not the common sense that won, but feminism. By the way, old Greek ladies wear scarves in churches (*Oblachko* 24.08.2010).

Another important source of the lost tradition is Russian folk culture (partly preserved by the Old Believers of today) and (much rarer) the everyday culture of the prerevolutionary Russia (mostly the 19th century). This appeal to the Russian traditions of the past is another version of looking for traditions of the other peoples; ancestors are seen as 'another nation', which did not lose the genuine Orthodox patterns of piety. Gumanova says:

> It is fine with me that people recall their national roots. It is accepted by many peoples, say, Greeks, Serbs—to put on some national costumes during feasts, to dance national dances. If in our country it only takes place at churches, I think this can only be welcomed. For example, when on Trinity Sunday children in Russian national costumes dance in a ring after the Liturgy, in garlands. What is bad about it? People recall that they are Russians. It is better that they recall about it at the church, than at some hangout, having some other philosophy, incompatible with Christianity. It is better if the Church than someone else revives Russianness.

Polina Tiurenkova links the contemporary parochial practice of wearing lace caps instead of scarves directly to the Russian folk headwear:

> Cap, as I see it, is a simplified *povoinik*. Well, an Orthodox woman should be dressed like this: there must be a *povoinik* and a scarf above, because *povoinik* was always a Russian tradition. If someone fancies you, he should not hesitate, if you are married or not; if you wear *povoinik*, you are married. And if you are not married, you just wear a scarf. But we have lost it, fully lost, everything is turned upside down. But there is some genetic memory, and—comfortable and beautiful—these caps emerged.

Below I am quoting a discussion at Matushki.ru ('Platok i vsio o nem' 2008), where participants appeal nearly to all possible sources of unbroken tradition—or, what the authors consider unbroken tradition (Muslim Tatars, Imperial Russia, folk headwear):

> And, also, I like very much how Muslim women look here (we live in Tatarstan and I see them every day). They can; and we cannot, the Orthodox? There are even special shops now. Where they teach Muslim women to tie and to wear hijabs (scarves), it is very modern and beautiful; I wish the Orthodox could do the same. And women become milder in scarves, more feminine and beautiful. Here there are interesting variants, although they are Muslim: http://www.thehijabshop.com/information/how_to_wear.php. But we can figure out something for ourselves, if we really want (*Irina* 03.03.2008).

> I have a question: can we wear hats instead of scarves? Why is one attacked in the church when they see a non-scarf headwear? The head is covered, anyhow. I watched a documentary about the Holy Royal Family of the Romanovs. And Czarina Alexandra was in the church in a broad-rimmed hat. And many women from the rich estates were wearing hats (*Unesionnaia vetrom* 03.03.2008).

> And peasant women wore *soroki*, brocade *kichki* and other caps. Scarves were to cover this all above for warmth. But if you look at the pictures by Kramskoi and the others of the past century—at haymaking or somewhere else, women wear everyday *soroki*, no scarves (*Verba* 03.03.2008).

Reading digital magazines and forum discussions shows that looking for traditions is relatively easy in the spheres of clothing and culinary. Relations with men and sexual behavior are another story. Here, forum participants turn to their private experiences, while web-magazines have to rely on professional psychologists, or again on personal experiences, even when they are expressed in an authoritative tone. For example, Gumanova started to publish her psychological recommendations before getting professional education in psychology. Authors of psychological recommendations at Matrony.ru may have a variety of professions; the resource even translates texts about men-women 'relations' from popular Western psychology sources.

This is how two major magazines treat the sensitive issue of virginity. Both publications are headlined 'On virginity':

> Matrony.ru, author: Liliia Malakhova, a novelist:
> In the ancient times, the Old Testament paid no such attention to virginity. All the 'uneasy' issues were being resolved calmly: a bride demonstrating no virginity, returned to her parents' home. [...] The Orthodox culture pays too large attention to female virginity, unjustifiably large... [...] To have or not to have sexual life outside [not 'before'—A.M.] marriage is an individual decision of concrete people, and the others have no right to know why they made it; and, of course, we have no right to judge them and to stick labels on them... (Malakhova, 2014).

> Slavianka.com, author: archpriest Sergii Zaozerskii:
> In the Israeli society, according to the Mosaic Law, if no proof of the young woman's virginity could be found, she was supposed to be stoned to death (Deuteronomy: 22, 20). [...] When someone starts marital life being a virgin, marriage and intimate relations are united in one's consciousness. In the opposite case, these concepts will be separated. And since, to stand firm in temptation, many of which may be found in the life of any married person, will be more difficult. Virginity, preserved before marriage, although is terminated by being married, does not fully disappear. In the future, so to say, it safeguards the borders of marriage (Zaozerskii 2013).

Texts from different resources, thus, often contradict each other, including—in this particular case—antagonistic visions of what happened to non-virgins in the Old Testament society. It seems that Malakhova simply made up ancient 'tolerance' to the loss of virginity to justify her own liberal position. The position of archpriest Sergii, although historically correct, is hardly of help to contemporary Russian women, because they live in a society where non-virgins are no more stoned to death. It is worth mentioning that neither forum participants, nor web-magazines, appeal in such slippery issues to the behavioral patterns of Greeks, Serbs, Old Believers, or noble women of the imperial period. It seems that here (unlike in culinary) the search for tradition is doomed from the start. To discuss foreign or long-forgotten traditions in this sensitive sphere one needs much deeper knowledge than that of the current authors. Besides, behavioral patterns loaned from the past or from other cultures would simply not work in contemporary Russia and informing about them would not help a Russian Orthodox woman of today reconcile her faith with the living patterns of the late modern 'permissive' society.

Conclusion

Digital communication between Orthodox women is a supplement to, not a substitute for, the normal liturgical life of the practicing Christians. They constitute no 'digital Church' or 'network parishes'. At the same time, at least some of them apparently prefer on-line to off-life non-liturgical contacts to work out patterns of Orthodox piety collectively. Explaining why they do it is beyond the scope of this essay; however, I suggest that the new parishioners—successful female professionals and other educated women—can find no place and no roles for themselves in the existing parochial subculture[4]. Thus, studying Orthodox parishes remains incomplete without paying attention to the digital spaces where women from different parishes communicate extra-liturgically.

Digital media for Orthodox women perform two basic functions. Forums and similar resources (social networking groups), characterized by an egalitarian atmosphere, are oriented to collective gathering, testing and selecting the best practices of pious life for Orthodox women. The parish subculture performed the same function for the previous generation of parishioners. Digital magazines, on the contrary, are looking for a normative image of an 'ideal' Orthodox woman, a model for the others to imitate.

Both types of media experience difficulties and need to lean upon some external authority presented by life patterns of the Ortho-

---

[4] Most likely—this issue also exceeds the themes of the essay—members of more consolidated, community-style, parishes do not turn to digital media.

dox people with unbroken tradition, or of the Russians of the past (from the pre-Petrine times to the 19th century), and sometimes also of the Old Believers and Muslims. However, this strategy works well only with regard to external manifestations of piety: clothing and food habits. It is of little use when discussing painful issues of human relations, especially when socially acceptable behavior openly contradicts the demands of religious morality (divorce, virginity, abortion, etc.). Right now I see no other strategy the ortho-media could use, taking into consideration that they lack theological resources for working out Orthodox approaches to the contemporary issues on their own.

References

Agadjanian, Alexander (2009). 'Izuchenie pravoslavnykh prikhodov: nekotorye predvaritel'nye idei', *Religion in Contemporary Society*. Moscow: ATISO, 180–188.

Agadjanian, Alexander and Kathy Rousselet; eds (2006). *Religioznye praktiki v sovremennoi Rossii*. Moscow: Novoe izdaetl'stvo.

Agadjanian, Alexander and Kathy Rousselet; eds (2011). *Prikhod i obshchina v sovremennom pravoslavii: kornevaia sistema rossiiskoi religioznosti*. Moscow: Ves' Mir.

Akhmetova, Mariia (2011). *Konets sveta v odnoi otdel'no vziatoi strane. Religioznye soobshchestva sovremennoi Rossii i ikh eskhatologicheskii mif*. Moscow: O.G.I.

Beglov, Aleksei (2014). 'Eschatological Expectations in Post-Soviet Russia: Historical Context and Modes of Interpretation' in *Orthodox Paradoxes: Heterogeneities and Complexities in Contemporary Russian Orthodoxy*, edited by Katya Tolstaya. Leiden, Boston: Brill, 106–133.

'Dopustim li razvod esli poteriana liubov'?' (2010). http://prihozhanka.ru/view topic.php?f=5&t=8 (accessed 20 May 2015).

Gumanova, Ol'ga (2014, 9 July). '7 priznakov zreloi zhenshchiny', *Matrony.ru*. http://www.matrony.ru/7-priznakov-zreloy-zhenshhinyi/ (accessed 20 May 2015).

Gumanova, Ol'ga (2014, 10 June). Interview by Anastasia Mitrofanova.

Gumanova, Ol'ga (2013, 18 March). 'Nachalo posta kak prazdnik', *Prikhody*. http://prichod.ru/aktualniye-voprosy/4113/ (accessed 20 May 2015).

Hann, Chris and Hermann Goltz; eds (2010). *Eastern Christians in Anthropological Perspective.* Berkeley: University of California Press.

Kizenko, Nadieszda (2013). 'Feminized Patriarchy? Orthodoxy and Gender in Post-Soviet Russia'. *Signs*, 38 (3): 595–621.

Malakhova, Liliia (2014, 7 July). 'O devstvennosti', *Matrony.ru.* http://www.matrony.ru/o-devstvennosti/ (accessed 20 May 2015).

Mitrokhin, Nikolai; ed. (2009). *Orthodox Culture in Russia. The Difficulties of Connecting with a Lost Tradition. A special issue of: Kultura. Russian cultural review published by the Research Centre for East European Studies at Bremen University.* April.

Naletova, Inna (2006). *Orthodoxy Beyond the Walls of the Church: A Sociological Inquiry into Orthodox Religious Experience in Contemporary Russian Society.* PhD dissertation. Boston University.

'Neskol'ko let khozhu v odin khram. No vot' (2014). http://prihozhanka.ru/viewtopic.php?f=3&t=2325 (accessed 20 May 2015).

'Nuzhdaiutsia li tserkovnye SMI v polozhitel'noi povestke dnia? Panel'naia diskussiia na festivale "Vera i slovo"' (2012). *Official website of the Synodal Information Department of the Russian Orthodox Church.* http://sinfo-mp.ru/nuzhdayutsya-li-czerkovnyie-smi-v-polozhitelnoj-povestke-dny.html (accessed 20 May 2015).

'Obychnoe zhenskoe???' (2008). http://matushki.ru/viewtopic.php?f=51&t=487 (accessed 20 May 2015).

'O postnom maioneze' (2010)/ http://matushki.ru/viewtopic.php?f=51&t=4638&start=20 (accessed 20 May 2015).

'Platok i vsio o niom' (2008). http://matushki.ru/viewtopic.php?f=51&t=414 (accessed 20 May 2015).

'Platok i vsio o niom' (2010). http://matushki.ru/viewtopic.php?f=51&t=414 (accessed 20 May 2015).

'Pro pokrov golovy' (2014). http://prihozhanka.ru/viewtopic.php?f=19&t=2464 (accessed 20 May 2015).

Sister Nina, Krygina (2013, 23 September). 'Oshibki dobrachnykh otnoshenii', *Slavianka.com.* http://www.slavianka.com/read/brak-i-semya/Oshibki-dobrachnyh-otnoshenij/ (accessed 20 May 2015).

'Spiral' dlia lechniia – da ili net?' (2012). http://prihozhanka.ru/viewtopic.php?f=19&t=1198 (accessed 20 May 2015).

'Sviateichii Patriarkh Kirill: razvitie obshchinnoi zhizni i aktivnoe vovlechenie v nee veruiushchikh – vazhneishaia zadacha dlia Tserkvi' (2015). *Official website of the Moscow Patriarchate.* http://www.patriarchia.ru/db/text/3977067.html (accessed 20 May 2015).

Tarabukina, Arina (2000). *Fol'klor i kul'tura pritserkovnogo kruga.* Candidate of Philological Sciences Dissertation. St.Petersburg, 2000.

Tiurenkova, Polina (2014, 3 July). Interview by Anastasia Mitrofanova.

Tiurenkova, Pelageia (2009, 4 December). 'Obraz sovremennoi pravoslavnoi zhenshchiny', *Pravoslavie i mir.* http://www.pravmir.ru/obraz-sovremennoj-pravoslavnoj-zhenshhiny/ (accessed 20 May 2015).

Tiurenkova, Pelageia (2006, 26 October). 'Ty – zhenshchina, ili vstrechaiut po odiozhke', *Pravoslavie i mir.* http://www.pravmir.ru/ty-zhenshhina-ili-vstrechayut-po-odezhke (accessed 20 May 2015).

Zaozerskii, Sergii, archpriest (2013, 17 June). 'O devstvennosti', *Slavianka.com.* http://www.slavianka.com/read/Brak-i-semya/O-devstvennosti/ (accessed 20 May 2015).

Zigon, Jarrett (2008). 'Aleksandra Vladimirovna: Moral Narratives of a Russian Orthodox Woman' in *Religion, Morality and Community in Post-Soviet Societies,* edited by Mark D. Steinberg and Catherine Wanner. Bloomington and Indiannopolis: University of Indiana Press, 85–114.

_# Chapter 9.
Holy Pixels: The Transformation of Eastern Orthodox Icons Through Digital Technology[1]

Sarah A. Riccardi-Swartz
New York University

Introduction

Philosopher and aesthetics critic Walter Benjamin, in a 1931 essay on the relationship between technology and photography, wrote against what he called a philistine notion that: 'Man is made in the image of God, and God's image can not be captured by an machine of human devising' (1999: 508). While Benjamin's main goal was to highlight the complexities and metaphysical quandaries surrounding the rise in new technological advancements in photography at the time, his essay also serves as a clarion call about the relationship between people and the divine, and the role of new technologies and materialities in the capturing of divine essence or imagery through photographic, and now, digital means. This chapter wrestles with the complex problem of 'the digital' through an examination of how Eastern Orthodox practitioners in the Missouri Ozarks use telematic means to purchase and create icons and relics, highlighting how the internet and digitality is transforming the way holy materiality is circulated and employed in everyday religious practices. In this chapter I explore how the digital, in various manifestations, shapes the materi-

---

[1] I extend my hearty thanks to the members of Unexpected Joy for letting me work on this project in the community for three years. This chapter stems from my Masters thesis and a seminar paper I wrote in the fall of 2013. I'm grateful to faculty members at Missouri State University, my previous institution, for helping me envision and revise this project. Over the past few years, I have presented various versions of this material at the national American Academy of Religion conference and received excellent feedback from my peers. All omissions and errors are my own entirely. With much gratitude, I say thank you to my husband Jeremy and my mother Susan, who spent many hours watching my newborn daughter Clementine Emilia as I worked on drafts of this article.

al culture(s) of American Eastern Orthodoxy, namely icons (and relics), helping contest notions of canonical materiality, while calling attention to how practitioners use the internet marketplace to purchase so-called traditional icons, and how they create photographic representations of the material holy, reproducing images of miraculous icons and incorruptible bodies of saints, thereby displacing the homogeneity of institutional iconography and producing artifacts that function concomitantly as both icon and relic.[2] In order to explore how Orthodox laity use the digital, I draw upon data from my own IRB-approved ethnographic research in an American Orthodox parish.

Deep in the Missouri Ozarks, in the town of Ash Grove, is Theotokos Unexpected Joy Orthodox Church. Part of the Orthodox Church in America diocese, the parish is home to approximately (at the time of my fieldwork), forty-five members from varying socio-economic and educational backgrounds, with the majority considered converts to Orthodoxy. The parish is representative of an American form of Orthodoxy, one that embraces ethnic traditions (primarily Russian, although most members are not of Russian descent), while also being influenced by social and political ideas and practices found in the American religious landscape, such as the addition of coffee hour after liturgy on Sundays, where members of the parish discuss fundraising ideas for the women's league and debate political issues. I conducted fieldwork in this community between 2011–2014, using audio-recorded interviews as my primary methodology; in total, I interviewed eighteen parishioners over three years as part of my Master thesis research on the sensory cultures of home icon corner. All of the ethnographic data found in this chapter is taken from those interviews.[3]

---

2   See Sarah A. Riccardi, 'Praying through Windows and Peering through Wood: Examining Vernacular Devotions in American Eastern Orthodoxy Through a Materialist Lens' (MA Thesis, Missouri State University, 2014).

3   Following in the methodological footsteps of Robert Orsi, I employ a form of reflexive ethnography in this thesis. Scholars, especially ethnographers, often become emotionally and spiritually entangled with the subjects they are investigating. As Orsi notes in *Between Heaven and Earth*, 'Once religion is understood as

The ethos of Unexpected Joy is often described by parishioners as Russian in nature, despite the fact that the church is under the auspices of the ethnically and nationally inclusive Orthodox Church in America and most parishioners are converts with little or no Russian heritage or background. Michele, a convert from Southern Baptism and long-time parishioner at Unexpected Joy, once described the parish as similar to 'a Russian country church,' referring not only to its architecture and rural location, but also to its ethos (interview with author 2011). As sociologist Roger Friedland notes about relationship between religious nationalism, collective identity, and ontologies of power: 'Religious nationalism can be understood as a heterologous project to promote a particular logic of collective representation' (2001: 142). By promoting Russian Orthodoxy through architecture, iconography, music (liturgics), and religious materiality, my interlocutors express both personal and collective identities. This predilection towards Russian Orthodox material culture often appears in the personal icon corners of practitioners. For my interlocutors, the draw towards Russian Orthodox culture and materiality stems from experiences of religious formation in Russia, ideologies about the correctness of Russian Orthodox spirituality, and, often, a feeling of spiritual kinship with the Russian people and saints. In her work on ethnic identity in middle class, suburban communities, sociologist Mary C. Waters suggests that Americans often exercise an 'ethnic

---

a web not of meanings but of relationships between heaven and earth, then scholars of religion take their places as participants in these networks too, together with the saints and in the company of practitioners. We get caught up in these bonds, whether we want to or not' (5). By choosing to interview members of my own parish, I became enmeshed within the complex relationships some of my interlocutors have with God and the saints. Orsi sees this type of self-reflection as anthropological in nature, suggesting that since 'anthropologists no longer occlude themselves from the field' neither should scholars of American religion (14). Quoting Sartre, Orsi stresses the relational aspects of research, urging scholars to situate themselves within their fieldwork and then include themselves in the written outcome (174–75). Furthermore, by acknowledging their own religious background, Orsi concludes that scholars can help participate in the 'deepening historical self-consciousness of religious studies today' (14). See Robert Orsi, *Between Heaven and Earth: The Religious Worlds People Make and the Scholars Who Study Them* (Princeton, NJ: Princeton University Press, 2005).

option' that allows them to enjoy specific actions of an ethnic group, despite having no genealogical link to that community (Waters 1990: 160). This seems to be the case at Unexpected Joy, where practitioners purchase Russian items in order to perpetuate a Russified ethos because they favor this national form of the Church.

The globalization and digitization of Orthodoxy in contemporary culture brings with it hybridity, assimilation, and solidarity, for 'as social networks expand, contract, and interconnect according to historical events, people are thus likely to accumulate a wide range of dispositions, including knowledge, skills, tastes, and habits, pertaining to different facets of their identity' (Gosselain 2000: 209). Purchasing and creating material religious goods becomes a form of symbolic belonging to a group, in this case Russian Orthodoxy. In this way, icons are more than conveyors of the holy; they are markers for socio-religious identity—'ethnic banners' that proclaim a practitioner's affiliation with a preferred national form of the Church (Gosselain 2000: 209). This 'elective affinity' is further commodifed and mediated by the use of new digital technologies as a means through which practitioners obtain icons and holy images that help reinforce their constructions of the self, taking into consideration their spiritual aesthetics, religious loyalties, and economic constrictions (Agadjanian 2001: 484).

Defining 'the digital'

The various registers of the digital in the lifeworlds of parishioners at Unexpected Joy require a brief interrogation, in order to better understand how they permeate the everyday piety of the faithful. *What is the digital?* I use the term *digital* within the scope of this chapter informed by the works of Heidi Campbell and Jóse Bragança de Miranda. In recent years, there has been a rise in research on the effects of the internet on spirituality and nexus of religion and digital technologies. Campbell explains how digital religion gives us 'a new frame for articulating the evolution of religious practices' both online and offline (2013: 1). For Campbell, 'digital religion' is 'religion that is constituted in new ways through digital media and cultures' (2013: 3). Furthermore, Campbell suggests that 'digital cultures negotiate our understandings of religious practices in ways that can lead to new experiences, authenticity, and spiritual reflexivity' (2013: 3). While Campbell is more focused on religious practices found online, such as cyber churches, she does provide space for the impact of the digital on offline activities.

In conjunction with Campbell, I look to Bragança de Miranda's work on digital technology as an example of how religion and the digital come into conversation with each other. My conception of digital and telematic cultures in this chapter is reliant on Bragança de Miranda's critique of distance and transmission, in which he suggests that technology affects the metaphysics of theology, diminishing the amount of separation—spatially and temporally—between divinity and humanity, and that new technologies change the way holiness is transmitted. From my vantage point, this theoretical concept is best exemplified in the purchasing and creation of icons in Eastern Orthodoxy, which is a post-modern technological invention that has become more popular in the last decade, particularly in the United States. Bragança de Miranda argues through a critique of Walter Benjamin, that scholars are not fully cognizant of the effects technologies have on images:

> 'The analysis of teletechnologies would, however, be of little avail, if we were to fail to detect the way they are inscribed not only in our experience, presiding over the transmission of innumerable 'traces' (images, objects, desires, bodies), but also on the very real. Such traces constitute a kind of screen of the real, which receives all that have been filtered by the necessities of a general economy that develops within telematic systems' (2008: 149–174).

In order to understand how these digital innovations are transforming the way in which iconography is produced and disseminated, it is imperative to briefly look at the tradition and theology of iconography in Eastern Orthodoxy.

Theology of iconography

In Eastern Orthodox theology, icons are understood as 'theology in color'; therefore practitioners often view artistic renderings of the saints or Christ as secondary to the icon's deeper theological meaning and function as a connective tool for communication and interaction with the celestial realm.[4] The theological importance of icons is grounded in their materiality, with each element that composes an icon symbolizing a theological or spiritual concept. The layers of paint, glue, and fabric work together to build the story of Christian life, death, and salvation (Ouspensky and Lossky 1978: 53–55).[5] As the icon of a saint or Christ begins to take shape, specific details of composition are added to ensure the revelation of theology, specifically the transfigurement of the flesh in resurrection through the personification of the figure. Certain physical characteristics of the saints are drawn in such a way that the 'sensory aspect of the corruptible flesh' is lost and the figure becomes deified and spiritualized, symbolically conveying the transfiguration of the saint (1978: 38). Therefore Orthodox Christians place icons in their churches, homes, places of employment, and even their automobiles as a way to express the eventual sanctification and transfiguration of the earth through

---

4   The phrase 'theology in color' is often employed by Orthodox theologians to describe the religious significance of iconography. See Eugene N. Trubetskoi, *Icons: Theology in Color* (Crestwood, NY: St. Vladimir's Seminary Press, 1973). One of the theological understandings of icons expressed in this study comes from the work of Léonide Ouspensky, who wrote extensively about the theological significance of iconography. For further reading see Léonide Ouspensky, *Theology of the Icon* (Crestwood, NY: St. Vladimir's Press, 1978).

5   Ouspensky, an iconographer, and Lossky, a theologian, provide a detailed examination of the technique of iconography, beginning with the panel of non-resinous wood that is chosen by the iconographer, to the laborious process of applying layer upon layer of chalk, egg-yolk tempera, oil paints, water, and other pigments (53–55). The material nature of an icon represents 'the fullest participation of the visible world,' which 'includes representatives, so to speak, of the vegetable, mineral and animal worlds' (55). Once finished, hand-painted icons are covered in olipha—'boiled linseed oil'—which 'connects all the layers of colour and penetrates through to the ground, fixes them and with time transforms them into a uniform solid mass' (55). Essentially, the material elements of a hand-painted icon are constantly transforming, despite the fact that they appear, on the surface, to be completed and fixed.

the use of holy objects. While an icon may be considered two-dimensional in terms of Western art, Orthodox iconographers and theologians declare that icons are three-dimensional, although the 'the plane of the panel' is never violated. The three-dimensional nature of icons is exhibited in the 'inverse perspective, the point of departure of which lies not in the depth of the image, but in front of the image' (Ouspensky and Lossky 1978: 35–41).

While icons are only two-dimensional in materiality, practitioners see them as beyond dimensional, for they possess a perspective that pushes the images depicted towards the eyes of the beholder. Because of this visual dynamic, the viewer's attention is directed entirely to the image in front of him or her, which is an important element of the focusing prayer that occurs in icon corners, enabling practitioners to perceive that they peer through time and space into the spiritual realm. Essentially, icons 'act as a meeting point between the living members of the Church [Militant] on earth and the Saints who have passed on to the Church [Triumphant] in Heaven' (A Monk of St. Tikhon's Monastery 1968: 271).[6]

Keeping the theology of iconography in mind, the following questions must be asked: How are icons transformed by digital and telematic cultures? How do practitioners feel about icons purchased or created through digital means? It is these questions I address in this chapter, using the words of my interlocutors. I look first at the commodification of icons through an examination of where and how my interlocutors purchase traditional icons (generally reproduced, mounted icons) in the internet marketplace, before turning to the production of digital icons—images found online and printed onto paper. Through an exploration of how the internet and digital technologies are used by the laity, we can gain a better understanding of vernacular Orthodoxy and the pietistic practices of the faithful (Primiano 1995).

---

6   Cf. Chapter 3 in this volume.

Commodification of holy materiality

The purchasing and fabrication of traditional icons using digital technologies has become an almost ubiquitous part of Eastern Orthodox culture in the United States and abroad. Indeed, the internet has opened up the wide world of Orthodoxy, allowing practitioners to select icons from countries that identify as historically (and often ethnically) Orthodoxy. From websites run by individual iconographers, to monasteries selling reproductions of ancient icons, to images of icons found via a Google search or shared on social media sites such as *Facebook*, Instagram, and Pinterest, the material holy now has a digital interface. This new way of sharing and finding icons is part of the commodification of iconography, and is key in the economic selection of icons. Cost and personal taste are both aided and complicated by the internet, for the rise in digital and 'telematic culture'—electronic equipment ranging from iPads to computers to inkjet printers—alters the transmission of the holy, affecting the 'modes of mutation,' or how informational flows shift via new technologies (Bragança de Miranda 2008: 149).

The economics of iconography is transformed by the mediation of digital technology, which creates a complex dynamic in which practitioners must take into consideration the authenticity and reliability of vendors and the wide range of options available when purchasing religious items. Parishioners at Unexpected Joy purchase icons from a select handful of vendors that they deem authentic purveyors of Orthodox iconography. Cheryl pointed to both the non-canonical St. Isaac Skete and the canonical Holy Transfiguration Monastery in Ellwood, Pennsylvania, as the two main vendors through which she purchases icons online. Donna noted that she uses All Merciful Saviour, a women's monastery 'that has a lot of good icons,' Archangels Bookstore (a St. Louis-based Orthodox bookstore run by Donna's brother-in-law), and Holy Trinity Monastery bookstore's online marketplace, although she noted that the Holy Trinity's website 'has changed: it looked more difficult to order from' (interview with author 2013). This would cause her to purchase from a different online purveyor, since ease of use is important for her.

Other interlocutors also mentioned Archangels; thus the physical and online bookstore seemed quite popular among the parishioners at Unexpected Joy. This popularity may be due to the connection the bookstore has to Donna and John, who are long-time members of the parish.

Parishioners also select icons from reputable eBay sellers. Roger, a convert from Catholicism and elderly widower, explained that he acquired most of the icons in his sizeable cache through bidding on eBay:

> I bought numerous icons, and I was really into it, and I bought most of them from eBay, actually. I would pay an amount [submit a bid] to see if I could get the icon, and I was very good at doing that. I was very good with eBay and manipulating [the bid] . . . and I was able to get some very beautiful icons. . . . I put in my subject of interest and wow, page after page of icons—and from Russia usually. And some of them were very, very reasonable—a dollar and a half, two dollars as a starting bid. I would say thirty to forty percent of the time I would get that icon for just four or five dollars. There was an icon from a convent—a Catholic convent—but it was a true Orthodox icon and the icon had been at the convent for about thirty years, but they were renovating and getting rid of a lot of things. This icon, which I still have, of the Theotokos of the Sign, I bid on that and I won it—it was thirty dollars. It was actually more than I wanted to pay, but it was a large icon. Another one—the Mystical Supper of Christ—and I got that icon for a dollar! So, I really got addicted, so to speak. I bought about seventy-five percent of my icons from eBay. (interview with author 2013)

Roger's bidding and buying highlights the impact of digital commerce on the purchasing of the material holy, while also denoting the economic limitations that practitioners face as they search for material religious goods for their spiritual lives.

One of the first things Donna, a convert, long-time parishioner, and local therapist, mentioned when we discussed purchasing icons was the cost associated with acquiring hand-painted and even reproduction icons, 'They're more expensive, that's why I don't get mounted ones. You can get some very expensive ones, especially the screen silk mounted ones—they're quite a bit. They're beautiful, but with our budget we just go with what we can' (interview with author 2013). For Donna, even the mounted icons are too expensive; thus she selects paper icons. Indeed, as one looks around Donna's home and icon corner, the majority of her icons are prints that are either framed or laminated. This speaks to some of the facets of Orthodox consumption, namely the incorporation of digital technologies, buying icons via the Internet marketplace, and producing them on digital printers, are important aspects of Orthodox spirituality that are endebted to economic factors. The blending of religion and economics creates what Colleen McDannell terms 'the economy of the holy,' an economic venture that takes place 'between those on earth and those in heaven' using materiality as a means to enhance spirituality (1995: 133). If the printed-paper images of the saints that abound in the homes of my interlocutors are any indication, this new form of religious commerce is a widely accepted and practiced aspect of the faith, suggesting that practitioners view digitally acquired religious paper goods as appropriate forms of the material holy.

Most of my interlocutors use the internet to purchase icons and other religious items, but they also acquire religious stuff through more traditional means, often opting to pick up a catalogue, phone in an order to a monastery or church, or walk into the bookstore at Unexpected Joy after Divine Liturgy on any given Sunday.[7] Practitioners select these tactile options because they provide a greater sense of tangibility. The various forms of telematic culture—digital websites, phone sales, and print catalogues—provide commodifed access to religious goods, offering practitioners flexible and wide-ranging options in terms of economy and aesthetics. No longer are parishioners limited to buying icons at their church bookstore; instead, they are able with the click of a mouse to order icons from around the world. In this way, practitioners are able to choose their preferred forms of religious goods, thereby crafting a personalized form of spirituality, one that takes into account authenticity and aesthetics.

---

7   In late 2013, the bookstore at Unexpected Joy shut down in order to use the room for a pastoral office. However, the contents of the bookstore were transferred to a local antique mall.

Aesthetics and the art of authenticity

Members of Unexpected Joy have specific aesthetic preferences that are comprised of both personal taste and the desire for authenticity. Through iconography, practitioners are able to express their spiritual and personal beliefs and desires. Icons are more than windows to heaven; they are socio-religious markers of identification that have become consumer products with wide-ranging implications for better understanding the role of ethnic and religious identity, transnational movements of art and materiality within religious and public cartographies and cybergeographies, the relationships between intersensory materiality, built and digital spaces, and cultural authenticity. The commodification of iconography via the internet means that practitioners have more icon styles from which to select, allowing them to express their personal aesthetics more readily, and to distinguish themselves as Orthodox. Choosing icons becomes a personal experience that encompasses a wide variety of opinions, wants, needs, and desires, helping practitioners craft their religious selves.

Brigid, a convert from Roman Catholicism and budding iconographer, explained how she selected an icon of her patron saint:

> First, I researched Brigid, of course, and learned everything I could about her, and then I wanted to find an icon that was already written where it showed the things of her history. . . and I couldn't find anything except for her holding the reed cross. And came across this one and it had the monastery in the background, it had her holding a scroll that explained how she gave things away and how she prayed for people and it also had the cross. It had a lot of deep meaning in relationship to her life, even after her death when she became a saint. So that really touched my heart when I saw it. I actually found it at Archangels [bookstore] online. And I went ahead and ordered it online and it was way over my budget, but I wanted it anyway, because it meant that much to me. . . It's very dear to me and [the] one that I copied for my first attempt at iconography. (interview with author 2013)

Brigid, cognizant of the aesthetics of the icon, was also focused on the history of her patron and how it was manifested in the interface of the icon, which depicts scenes from the life of the saint, and, thus, offers a more complete visual hagiography. Brigid also notes how she struggled with the cost of the icon. For Brigid, the digital world opened up aesthetic options, while pinching her economically. Yet, she chose to purchase the icon because of its aesthetics, and because it was painted in Ireland, the homeland of St. Brigid of Kildare. Therefore, Bridge saw the icon as an authentic rending of her patron.

Authenticity is a key word that came up quite frequently in discussions with my interlocutors, for it is an important part of both the selection process and the veneration of an icon. In her article on Haitian Vodou, e-commerce, and identity, Alexandra Boutros explains that authenticity and legitimacy are key elements in a practitioner's selection of an online vendor and merchandise (2012). The online presence of Vodou practitioners and shops brings with it opportunity for global commerce and accessibility to a variety of material religious goods, providing a multitude of choices for consumers. Similarly, Eastern Orthodox practitioners are confronted with a wide range of vendors who sell icons for use in home icon corners. Faced with these choices, practitioners often favor economy over their preferred sellers, keeping in mind that the icon can be raised to a higher spiritual standard through a priest's blessing (Boutros 2012: 254–59). However, my interlocutors are also highly selective, choosing icons that seem to be authentic representations of the saints. While personal aesthetics play a pivotal role in the purchasing process, it appears that legitimacy is the key element in the selection process. Practitioners select icons that conform to the teachings of the Church, even if they often stretch the boundaries of aesthetic acceptability, especially when creating their own icons from digital files.

In the Orthodox theology of icons, authenticity can only exist in the image if it maintains a direct connection to the original and does not stray too far from the prototype it depicts. Margaret Kenna explains, 'As with Christ, so with the saints—copies cannot stray far from the original without breaking the link with the prototype and thus losing their authenticity. In other words, an icon is not just a picture, not simply a copy or a reminder of an original' (1985: 348). According to official doctrinal teachings, iconicity—the similarity between the sign and the meaning or the prototype—can become degraded if the image depicted is artistically distorted, veering away from an orthodox rendering of the figure (Davis 2007: 201). This is particularly important for understanding the aesthetics of icon selection because the majority of the interlocutors from Unexpected Joy cling to Russian iconography as orthodox in its rendering of celestial beings, which suggests that vernacular practices decide what is authentic and what is not. In his work on country music, sociologist Richard Peterson argues, through the use of Halbwachsian theory, that collective memory aids the fabrication of authenticity within a social group (1997). Peterson also suggested that this fabrication process is furthered by industrialization. In the Unexpected Joy community, the internet, a digital form of industrialization, does aid the quest for authenticity, although it appears as if authentic forms of iconography are both found and created by practitioners, which indicates that my interlocutors see themselves as authenticators of the faith (1997: 5–6).

Iconographic transformation

As noted earlier, icons are a fundamental aspect of Eastern Orthodox Christianity, the basis upon which the rest of Orthodox sensory culture is built, and digital technology, in the form of cameras, scanners, computers, and the internet, among many things, has changed the interface between these holy things and the practitioners who employ them in their devotional lives (Hodder 2012: 89).[8] I suggest that practices employed by adherents—the digital reproduction of religious materiality—create iconographic relics, reimagining the imaged holy. Icons serve as windows to the spiritual realm, channels of connectivity, providing practitioners with haptic and ocular access to celestial figures. So, too, do photographs of icons and relics serve as vernacular forms of intersensory iconography (Connolly 2010: 182). In traditional iconography, the grace of the saint is transmitted

---

8 Ian Hodder contends that things and humans have a tenuous relationship in which both objects and humans affect each other and themselves. Moving away from an anthropocentric understanding of materiality, Hodder shifts his focus to the world of things, in which objects 'have lives, vibrant lives and temporalities, and they depend on each other and humans' (89).

through the elemental components of the icon—wood, paint, and image—infusing the object with holiness, rendering it a connective religious artifact to the celestial figure depicted (Ware 1993: 33; Kenna 1985: 345–368).[9] Building upon this theological idea, practitioners validate their digital reproductions, and their actions call into question canonical authority and the agency of the laity.

The members of Unexpected Joy acquire photographs of icons (and relics) through a variety of ways, from gifts, to photographs taken during pilgrimages, to printing out images off the internet via digital printers. These reproduced images often become part of practitioners' home icon corners, which are typically small devotional altars located in a central area of the home, such as the living room or dining room, that house icons, relics, holy oils and water, and liturgical texts for prayers and home services (**figure 9.1**). Much like the Polaroids taken at sites of Marian devotion in Roman Catholicism, photographs of icons and relics in Eastern Orthodoxy become, in the words of folklorist Daniel Wojcik, 'accessories to personal devotion and the recollection of past religious experience' (1996: 142).

---

9   Kallistos Ware writes, 'God has 'deified' matter, making it 'spirit-bearing'; and if flesh has become a vehicle of the Spirit, so then—though in a different way—can wood and paint' (33).

HOLY PIXELS 275

Figure 9.1.

Paper icons and photographic relics

Michele, a convert from Protestantism and long-time parishioner at Unexpected Joy, possesses hand-painted, mounted, and photographic icons, all of which she believes hold the same spiritual weight: 'A hand-painted icon is blessed as well as the paper ones, and the image they depict [is also blessed], so to me they are the same as far as being a prayer aid' (interview with author 2013). Sitting in front of her home icon corner located in her dining room, Cheryl, a convert and local novelist, explained her understanding of photographic icons: 'I see the photograph as an icon. I don't really make a distinction—they're all icons to me' (interview with author 2013). Cheryl's statement is salient because it suggests that, for her, photographs are icons, with no spiritual variance between mounted icons and photographs. As Donna, a local therapist and convert, and I had coffee at her kitchen table in the late summer of 2013, she picked up a large, glossy paper icon and proclaimed, 'I venerate it as an icon, but it's just a photo from a calendar. This is a photo of an icon I love and I will treat it as an icon' (interview with author 2013). Donna acknowledges both the iconicity of the photograph and the thingness of the holy object. The photograph captures the image of the icon, but it is Donna who transforms that image into an icon through her prayers, devotion, and belief. However, she is mindful of thingness of the icon as photo from a calendar, which highlights the complex negotiations practitioners undertake as they become manufacturers of icons. Although, Donna does not express concerns over the spiritual quality or iconicity of the photo, choosing instead to deem the photo an icon through her own authority.

Michele, along with many other members of Unexpected Joy, possesses a paper copy of the Kursk Root icon, a thirteenth-century wonder-working icon from Russia that is in the care of the Russian Orthodox Church outside of Russia (ROCOR) and 'tours' North America frequently (interview with author 2013). Michelle's paper icon was pressed to the original Kursk icon, a fact that caused her to exclaim, 'It's a relic, too!' (interview with author 2013). At Unexpected Joy, photographic icons often function concomitantly as relics, a fact that brings with it a great number of complications and questions; namely, how does an icon become a relic? John, husband to Donna, a small-business owner, convert from Catholicism, and acolyte, seemed to answer this question with his comments about a photograph of St. John Maximovitch, a Russian-American saint whose remains are enshrined at the Holy Virgin Cathedral in San Francisco, California:

> A picture, an actual picture—reposed—of St. John Maximovitch. We got it at his canonization and they [the photographs distributed] were either blessed or touched on his casket. I treat it [the photograph] as an icon-slash-relic or relic-slash-icon. (interview with author 2013)

Thus, icons become relics through physical encounters with other relics, but also through the authoritative belief of the practitioner.

Relics and icons often become enmeshed within the ink and fibers of photographic paper. Donna described an iconographic relic photograph of Christ that current resides in her home icon corner as 'a copy of a copy' (interview with author 2013). The original icon, which was from Mt. Athos, was gifted to a parish in Atlanta, Georgia. After the icon began weeping myrrh tears, the priest in charge of the parish took photographs of the relic/icon and distributed them to Orthodox Christians around the United States. Donna sees this reproduced image, which is a copy of a photograph she borrowed from Fr. Moses, her parish priest, as a relic: 'Because [the photograph is] a representation of the relic. I would consider the tears to be relics. I guess if you could take a copy, and the original was copied, then somehow it had to be touched to the copy. I've just considered it to be a relic. I just know that the prints have wept themselves' (interview with author 2013). The materiality of the photograph transmits, even after duplication at a local Kinko's, the nature of the original relic icon.

In a recent series of articles published through the *Orthodox Arts Journal*, an online publication dedicated to examining Orthodoxy and art, Fr. Silouan Justiniano, a monk with a background in art history, raises theological concerns about the degraded iconicity of an icon when it is mechanically reproduced. Using Walter Benjamin's work on materiality and symbols, Justiniano argues that reproduced icons—photographs of hand-painted icons—'are cheap solutions that seek to satiate consumer demand for holy images' (Justiniano 2013).

Justiniano continues, offering an institutional view of iconographic reproduction: 'The image is there, but something essential seems to be lacking. It is an icon and yet somehow not *fully* an icon' (Ibid). Here the traditional theology of iconography is expressed, while also suggesting that consumers—Orthodox practitioners—are responsible for corrupting the sanctity of holy images through digital means. The creation of digitized icons by my interlocutors would be an error on their part, according to Justiniano's theology of iconicity, for they would be creating 'unconvincing shadows of the original' (Ibid). Justiniano's sentiment, however, is not shared by the members of Unexpected Joy who readily create and employ reproductions of icons in their icon corners.

Using the teachings of St. John Maximovitch, Cheryl explains why she feels that paper icons are tantamount to those that are mounted or hand painted:

> Somebody asked St. John Maximovitch about icons and which styles you should have and which icons were good to have. He said that even paper icons have worked miracles, and he said that you can pray in front of one kind of icon, or you can pray in front of another kind of icon, but the important thing is that you are praying. I kind of work on that assumption—if I am praying in front of these icons then the saints are still hearing my prayers, whether it is a paper icon of St. Macrina or a beautiful hand-painted one, I feel that it is the same saint that I am praying to. (interview with author 2013)

Cheryl points out critical elements in the formation of digital icons—the agency and belief of the devotee. All icons are equal because practitioners exert their agency to legitimize all forms of iconography—from hand-painted antique icons, to Googled and Xeroxed copies of icons. Because icons are images of their heavenly prototypes, the principle of iconicity can be applied to all digital reproductions of icons, even those printed from a practitioner's home office laser printer (Herzfeld 1990: 110).

Through the lens of the camera, practitioners not only capture images of the holy, they also reframe institutional conceptions of what are appropriate and legitimate forms of iconography and relics. No longer pieces of chemically sensitized paper on which images are produced, photographs take on a life of their own, becoming carriers of divine energy and grace, providing devotees with artifacts of religious devotion. Just as silver halide is suspended in the colloid materials of the photographic paper, so, too, is the essence of the saint transfixed within the composite materials of the image (Tadaaki 1995). With the advent of digital photographic production, images of the saints are now readily accessible to any practitioner who owns a computer and a desktop printer. With the click of a computer mouse, devotees become digital iconographers, reproducing holy images composed of pixels rather than brush strokes, laser ink rather than egg-based tempura paints. By infusing these photographs with their own agency, belief, and emotion, the members of Unexpected Joy displace the homogeneity of institutional iconography and produce artifacts that function concomitantly as both icon and relic (Belting 2005). Viewing photography through the lens of Eastern Orthodoxy offers new ways to think about the connective aspects of holy objects and the intersubjective nature of domestic piety, while raising more questions about the importance of agency, transformation of holy images, and the impact of materiality on formations of the self. One noticeable aspect of my interlocutors' photographic creations is the fact that they primarily depict images of Russian Orthodox saints. Furthermore, the means by which parishioners assert their iconographic license is supported by the teachings of Russian-American saints. With the wide world of Orthodoxy virtually at their fingertips, the parishioners of Unexpected Joy navigate towards a Russian form of the faith, guided by hierarchs and images that are geographically connected to former Soviet Union.

Conclusion

The rich and dynamic sensory cultures of American Eastern Orthodoxy in the Missouri Ozarks are more than just the focus of this study. Indeed, an investigation of the dynamic practices of my interlocutors conveys salient insights into the nature of vernacular religion, the formation of group and individual identities, the commodification of ancient Christian practices via new technologies, and the relationships among humans, divine figures, and holy things. Viewing vernacular domestic devotional activities through the lens of Eastern Orthodoxy offers new ways to think about the connective aspects of holy things and the intersubjective nature of domestic piety, while raising more questions about agency and transformation.[10] Through engagement with Orthodox devotional items, practitioners are continually transformed in the process of *theosis*, with the eventual hope of becoming like their spiritual counterparts represented in icons. This process is aided by implementation of digital technologies and e-commerce, which opens up manifold opportunities for practitioners to craft not only personalized icon corners, but also identities of the individual self and the corporate group. These practices offer future opportunities for exploring adopted religious identities, especially among converts.

Investigating the place of the internet and the use of telematic culture is vital to understanding the practices of the laity—at least at Unexpected Joy. Digital technology is an actor in the lives of my interlocutors, entangled in the canonical and vernacular understandings of authenticity and authority. The digital, then, is an agentive thing that is enmeshed in the socio-religious networks of these Orthodox Christians. As archeologist Ian Hodder explains in regards to the relationship among things:

> Things flow through us. The nutrients from food flow through our body and are excreted. The warmth from the fire heated in a blanket flows through and revives our senses. The light from the sun streams through our eyes and awakes our vision. The smells and sounds from animals alert our fear and protective impulses. We hold and handle objects and become aware of perspective. Spiritual energies flow through icons and relics and awake our devo-

---

10 In an essay posted to the *Reverberations* website, Robert Orsi suggests that Catholic devotional praxes can help scholars better understand the intersubjective nature of prayer. While using Catholic prayer practices as a lens through which to explore how prayer connects the celestial and temporal realms is helpful, using Eastern Orthodox practices to further question the connective implications of prayer practices allows for a more complex understanding of holy images, items, and the agency of the laity in creating and maintaining bonds between themselves and the saints. See Robert A. Orsi, 'Real Presences: A Curatorial Introduction,' Reverberations http://forums.ssrc.org/ndsp/2013/03/18/real-presences-catholic-prayer-as-intersubjectivity/ (accessed October 10, 2013).

tion. Familiar things are absorbed into our sense of identity; they become recognized and owned. Things provide psychological comfort after tragedy and loss. Things stimulate our cognitive capacities, flowing through our neural processes, leading to reflection upon reflection, creating pathways that stay with us. There is a dependence of human on things. (Hodder 2012: 38)

Hodder sees humans and things as entangled, always affecting each other in an exchange that is fluid and dynamic. This idea is seen in the follow statement by Cheryl: 'Iconography, icons as a part of my prayer life, and just my life: I mean we have icons in every room of our house, except the bathroom. So, no matter which room I am in, there's an icon reminding me of who I am and what I am about. So [they are] very much a part of how I see myself as Orthodox' (interview with author 2013). Icons, much like other forms of art, 'imply a whole system of beliefs about the world,' providing material networks of 'interrelated beliefs' that are expressed in the visual elements of icons, with each brush stroke and pixel helping practitioners live out their theologies, identities, and transtemporal social interactions (Van Laar and Diepeveen 1998: 33). As my interlocutors use icons and other forms of materiality in their icons corners, they acknowledge through their actions the whole of Orthodox theology, for the materialities they engage with—even digital materiality—are tangible expressions of their beliefs and their communal bonds, however entangled and otherworldly they may be.

References

Agadjanian, Alexander. 2001. Revising Pandora's Gifts: Religious and National Identity in the Post-Soviet Societal Fabric. *Europe-Asia Studies* 53, no. 3 (May): 473–488.

Alvares, Claudia, ed. 2008. *Representing Culture: Essays on Identity, Visuality, and Technology*. Newcastle, UK: Cambridge Scholars Publishing.

Ammerman, Nancy. 2003. Religious Identities and Religious Institutions.In *Handbook of the Sociology of Religion*, ed. Michele Dillon, 207–224. New York: Cambridge University Press.

Ardévol, Elisenda. 2012. Virtural/Visual Ethnography: Methodological Crossroads at the Intersection of Visual and Internet Research. In

Advances in Visual Methodology, ed. Sarah Pink, 74–94. Los Angeles: Sage.

Belting, Hans. 2005. Image, Medium, Body: A New Approach to Iconology. *Critical Inquiry* 31, no. 2 (Winter): 302–319.

Benjamin, Walter. 1999. Little History of Photography. In *Walter Benjamin: Selected Writings Volume 2, Part 2 (1931–1934)*. Ed. Michael W. Jennings, Howard Eiland, and Gary Smith. Cambridge: Harvard University Press.

Boutros, Alexandra. Virtual Vodou, Actual Practice: Transfiguring the Technological. In *Deus in Machina: Religion, Technology, and the Things in Between*, ed. Jeremy Stolow, 239–260. New York: Fordham University Press, 2012.

Brigid. 2013. Interview with author. Ash Grove, MO, August 4.

Campbell, Heidi. 2013. *Digital Religion: Understanding Religious Practice in New Media Worlds*. Ed. Heidi A. Campbell. London: Routledge.

Charmé, Stuart Zane. 1991. *Vulgarity and Authenticity: Dimensions of Otherness in the World of Jean-Paul Sartre*. Amherst: University of Massachusetts Press.

Cheryl. 2013. Interview with author. Springfield, Missouri, August 13.

Connolly, William E. 2010. Materialities of Experience. In *New Materialities: Ontology, Agency, and Politics*, ed Diana Coole and Samantha Frost, 178–200. Durham, NC: Duke University Press.

Davis, Thomas C. 1999. Revisiting Group Attachment: Ethnic and National Identity. *Political Psychology* 20, no. 1 (March): 25–47.

Davis, Whitney. 2007. Abducting the Agency of Art. In *Art's Agency and Art History*, ed. by Robin Osborne and Jeremy Tanner, 199–219. Malden, MA: Blackwell.

Donna. 2013. Interview with author. Springfield, MO, August 10.

Friedland, Roger. 2001. Religious Nationalism and the Problem of Collective Representation. *Annual Review of Sociology* 27: 125–152.

Gosselain, Oliver P. 2000. Materializing Identities: An African Perspective. *Journal of Archaeological Method and Theory* 7, no. 3 [Ethnoarchaeology] (September): 187–217.

Harrison, Nonna Verna. 2010. *God's Many-Splendored Image: Theological Anthropology for Christian Formation*. Grand Rapids, MI: Baker Academic.

Herzfeld, Michael. 1990. Icons and Identity: Religious Orthodoxy and Social Practice in Rural Crete. *Anthropological Quarterly* 69, no. 3 (July): 109–121.

Hodder, Ian. 2012. *Entangled: An Archaeology of the Relationships between Humans and Things*. West Sussex, UK: Wiley-Blackwell.

John. 2013.Interview with author, Springfield, Missouri, September.

Justiniano, Fr. Silouan. 2013. Degraded Iconicity III: Mysteriological Matter; As Above, So Below.*Orthodox Arts Journal* (April 2). http://www.ortho doxartsjournal.org/degraded-iconicity-iii-mysteriological-matter-as-above-so-below/ (accessed October 31, 2013).

_____. 2013. Degraded Iconicity VI: Towards Fullness of Iconicity. *Orthodox Arts Journal* (July 18). http://www.orthodoxartsjournal.org/degraded-iconicity-vi-towards-fullness-of-iconicity/ (accessed October 31, 2013).

_____. 2013. The Degraded Iconicity of the Icon: The Icon's Materiality and Mechanical Reproduction. *Orthodox Arts Journal* (March 6). http://www.orthodoxartsjournal.org/the-degraded-iconicity-of-the-icon-the-icons-materiality-and-mechanical-reproduction/ (accessed March 7, 2013).

Kenna, Margaret E. 1985. Icons in Theory and Practice: An Orthodox Christian Example. *History of Religions* 24, no. 4 (May): 345–368.

McDannell, Colleen. 1995. *Material Christianity*. New Haven: Yale University Press.

McGuckin, John Anthony. 2008. *The Orthodox Church: An Introduction to its History, Doctrine, and Spiritual Culture*. Malden, MA: Blackwell Publishing.

Michele. 2011. Interview with author. Ash Grove, MO. December 4.

Michele. 2013. Interview with author. Willard, MO, August 15.

de Miranda, José Bragança. 2008. The End of Distance: The Emergence of Telematic Culture. In *Representing Culture: Essays on Identity, Visuality, and Technology*, ed. Claudia Alvares, 149–179. Newcastle: Cambridge Scholars Publishing.

Morgan, David. 2005. *The Sacred Gaze: Religious Visual Culture in Theory and Practice*. Berkeley: University of California Press.

Orsi, Robert A. 2006. *Between Heaven and Earth: The Religious Worlds People Make and the Scholars Who Study Them*. Princeton, NJ: Princeton University Press.

_____. 'Real Presences: A Curatorial Introduction.' Reverberations. http://forums.ssrc.org/ndsp/2013/03/18/real-presences-catholic-prayer-as -intersubjectivity/ (accessed October 10, 2013).

Park, Jerry Z., and Joseph Baker. 2007. What Would Jesus Buy: American Consumption of Religious and Spiritual Material Goods. *Journal for the Scientific Study of Religion* 46, no. 4 (December): 501–517.

Peterson, Richard A. 1997. *Creating Country Music: Fabricating Authenticity*. Chicago: University of Chicago Press.

Primiano, Lenard Norman. 1993. Intrinsically Catholic: Vernacular Religion and Philadelphia's 'Dignity.' PhD diss., University of Pennsylvania.

_____. 1995. 'Vernacular Religion and the Search for Method in Religious Folklife.' In 'Reflexivity and the Study of Belief.' *Western Folklore* 54, no. 1 (January). http://www.jstor.org/stable/1499910 (accessed April 24, 2013).

Sökefeld, Martin. 2001. Reconsidering Identity. *Anthropos* 96, no. 2: 527–544.

Song, Miri. 2003. *Choosing Ethnic Identity*. Cambridge, UK: Polity Press.

Stolow, Jeremy, ed. 2012. *Deus in Machina: Religion, Technology, and the Things in Between*. New York: Fordham University Press.

Tadaaki, Tani. 1995. *Photographic Sensitivity Theory and Mechanisms*. New York: Oxford University Press.

Tweed, Thomas A. 1997.*Our Lady of the Exile: Diasporic Religion at a Cuban Catholic Shrine in Miami*. New York: Oxford University Press.

Waters, Mary C. 1990. *Ethnic Options: Choosing Identities in America*. Berkeley: University of California Press.

Ware, Timothy Kallistos. 1964. *The Orthodox Church*. London: Penguin Books.

Wojcik, Daniel. 1996. 'Polaroids from Heaven': Photography, Folk Religion, and the Miraculous Image Tradition at a Marian Apparition Site. *The Journal of American Folklore* 109, no. 432 (Spring): 129–148.

Van Laar, Timothy, and Leonard Diepeveen. 1998. *Active Sights: Art as Social Interaction*. Mountain View, CA: Mayfield Publishing Company.

Chapter 10.
'Ortho-Blogging' from Inside: A Virtual Roundtable

Irina Kotkina*, Mikhail Suslov**
*Södertörn University
** Uppsala University

Introduction

The idea of this publication came in August 2014 when Mikhail Suslov was collecting materials for his article on how the Russian Orthodox Church is 'colonizing' the internet. Using the snowball method, he chose 38 blogs for in-depth research. Most of them were opened around the year 2007 (the oldest blog started in 2003); 20 of them continued well into 2014 whereas others had been terminated before the beginning of the study. A typical social portrait of an 'Ortho-blogger' is a young man (average age 30 years), who graduated from an institution of higher Orthodox education in Moscow or St Petersburg (among the most common choices are Moscow Spiritual Academy, and Orthodox University of St Tikhon), and received a position of a priest in a parish, usually in the province.

The Orthodox bloggers constitute a fairly tight group of *svoi*, 'ours' who share the same assumptions and values (Yurchak 2013: 108–109). This 'interpretive community' (Dorfman 1996) has a core of some five hundred blogs on the platform of *LiveJournal*, which constitute a net of interconnected 'friendships', and established traditions of commenting on each other's posts. All in all, 'Ortho-blogosphere' took shape as a relatively closed safe niche, to which heated debates and unwelcomed intruders are not welcome. Thus, 'Ortho-blogosphere' reproduced the offline exclusion of the (sub-)culture of regular Church goers ('churchized', *votserkovlennye*) from the broader community.[1]

---
1 On the *LiveJournal* community of 'Ortho-bloggers' see Chapter 5 by Ekaterina Grishaeva 'Heretical Virtual Movement in Russian *LiveJournal* Blogs: Between

By contrast, the Church's officials consider social networks as first and foremost venues for the Christian mission. Thus, Patriarch Kirill's report to the Bishops' Council of 2013 emphasized the importance of the ROC's presence on the internet and especially in social media, which 'provide new possibilities for a Christian Testimony' (Kirill 2013). Likewise, hegumen Agafangel Belykh avers that a contemporary Orthodox preacher has to have a blog of no less than two or three thousand readers (Agafangel 2007). In this way, blogging priests could bridge the offline gap between the subculture of the 'churchized' [*votserkovlennyi*], i.e. of regular Church-goers, and the rest of Russian society. The widespread justification among Orthodox priests of their online presence focuses on the fact that the non-'churchized' population, which nevertheless feels its attachment to religion and builds its identity on the Russian Church, experience difficulties with church customs. People often do not know how to behave themselves in the church, or how to approach a priest and ask him a question. Blogs of the priests could effectively solve this problem, providing those 'drop-iners' [*zakhozhanin,* a derogative name for those who occasionally drop in the church] with a medium, in which they feel more 'at home' and do not hesitate to speak about their religious needs. In this sense, the 'Ortho-blogs' provides a new social infrastructure for practicing religion and recruiting co-believers, thereby collapsing the divide between the online and the offline religious life (Lövheim 2013: 52).

However, priests logging online do not explicitly speak about the task of the Orthodox mission as such, and usually share online their views about faith, politics, or just everyday impressions. In the international context, blogging has recently become central for religious traditions, aiming at 'cultivation of the self' (Bakardjieva & Gaden 2012; Lee 2009). Likewise, the leader of 'Ortho-bloggers' deacon Andrei Kuraev shared his vision of blogging as his '[spiritual] quest, his perception of this world', not an ambo for preaching (Krug 2006). Often, blogging priests self-reflexively take issue with the

---

Religion and Politics' and Chapter 8 by Anastasia Mitrofanova 'Ortho-Media for Ortho-Women: In Search of Patterns of Piety' in this volume.

notion of their missionary responsibility and defend complete freedom from professional obligations in their web logging. For example, fatherpenguin (anonymous) playfully entreats his readers not to look for lofty truths in his blog: '[if you are searching for spiritual food] you have to go to the church. I've been there today, ministered and even preached... But only thoughtless people can detect anything spiritual in my diary [filled with] idle talks' (fatherpenguin@lj, 31.07.2011). Blogging priests admit, that this activity is a foible for a priest, a distraction from ministering and family commitments, which is not to be taken seriously.

Trying to conceptualize the difference between what the Church wants its clerics to do online and what they are actually doing there, we came an idea to ask 'real' bloggers what they think about this, and whether they perceive any challenge which new communicative technologies cast to the Church as a traditional 'communicative mechanism'. Having this in mind, Mikhail Suslov designed a questionnaire and distributed it among 28 'Ortho-bloggers' by email; eleven of them responded and eight finally filed their answers. For Orthodox priests and activists, this response rate is extremely high, to be accounted for the interest in the topic as well as respondents' specific profiles. One can surmise that more often than not they view themselves as public figures whose opinions are consequential, experience is more extensive than that of an average 'Ortho-blogger', and the degree of independence from the Church hierarchy is relatively greater in comparison with their fellows who chose not to answer the questionnaire. From these eight responses Irina Kotkina cherry-picked four most detailed answers and arranged them as a 'virtual roundtable'. Its 'virtual participants' represent different ideological strands, different Church's constituencies (clerics and laypeople), and even different ecclesiastical bodies (canonical and non-canonical Churches), but all of them are well-educated and highly intellectual religious thinkers, as well as very active Orthodox bloggers. Naturally, all respondents were informed about the ongoing research in which they had been invited to take part.

One of the participants, hieromonk Makarios (Markish), did the translation of the text himself, whereas others were translated by Irina Kotkina. Father Makarios was born in Moscow and graduated from the Moscow Institute of Transport Engineers. In the mid-1980s he emigrated to the U.S. with his family and worked there as a programmer. He baptized on the eve of the Epiphany in 1987 in the Church of the Epiphany in Boston, and in 1999 he graduated from Holy Trinity Orthodox Seminary in New York. After the U.S. bombing of Serbia he returned to Russia for good (2000) and settled down in Ivanovo, where he was tonsured (2002) and ordained a priest (2003). Father Makarios is the author of numerous books and publications, one of the developers of 'Bases of the Russian Orthodox Church on Human Dignity, Freedom and Rights', adopted by the Council of Bishops of the Russian Orthodox Church in 2008. He is active on radio, television and internet (aka p_m_makarios), ideologically close to ruskline.ru news agency, notorious for cultural fundamentalism and Russian 'great power' nationalism.

The second is priest Sergii (Kruglov) of the Russian Orthodox Church (of Moscow Patriarchate) from Krasnoyarsk. He is a professional poet, essayist and journalist in the local newspaper. In 1996 he baptized and in 1999 was ordained a priest. In 2008 he won the Andrei Belyi prize with the book *Zerkal'tse [The Mirror]* (2007) and *Perepischik [Scribe]* (2008). Father Sergii is a prolific blogger known as kruglov_s_g.

The third participant is Dmitrii Vaisburd, a layman born in Moscow and the graduate of the Moscow State Academy of Fine Chemical Technology. He came to the faith in the mid-1990s and enrolled to the St. Filaret Orthodox Christian Institute (1995), where he obtained a bachelor's degree in theology. From 1995 to 2011 he was a member of the Brotherhood of the Transfiguration, headed by a well known father confessor Georgii Kochetkov, popular among liberal intelligentsia. He is an active internet blogger (aka vaysburd), writing mostly on religious topics. He stipulates that this is being done without a blessing, as a completely private endevour. Dmitrii Vaisburd writes for a number of online projects for civic journalism such as *Ezhednevnyi Zhurnal* (ej.ru), kasparov.ru, and grani.ru; two last websites are now being blocked by the Russian government because of their oppositional stance.

The fourth participant is from a non-canonical Orthodox Church who had experienced persecutions and physical attacks due to his dissenting views. After perusing the English manuscript, he asked not to publicize his answers, so we decided to anonymize his replies.

Questions and Answers

Why and how have you decided to start a blog?

Dmitrii Vaisburd: In fact, I started it by blessing of [my] spiritual father, [who asked] to publish one document online. I had no idea how to do this, and [in order to accomplish this task] I started a blog. And I came to enjoy it [*vtianulsia*]. It is hard to overestimate [the internet's] importance. This is especially true for our gangster [*banditskii*] state, where people even stopped to pay visits to each other.

Father Makarios (Markish): Why am I maintaining a blog? [...] Because of the direct call from the [Church] hierarchy.

Is the internet, for you, a merely technological achievement? Or do you see the internet as something capable of changing our perception of the faith, of Orthodox theology?

Father Sergii (Kruglov): The internet is a space which connects all people, including Christians. Virtual life only mirrors real life with its passions, thoughts and projects. The internet can challenge the prejudice that Christianity is something that belongs to the Middle Ages and cannot be adapted to modernity. A person who reads a parchment or a text on a computer screen remains basically the same in nature, and the Gospel of Christ is relevant at all times.

Father P.: Being a new technical achievement, internet is a means of conversation, education and reading. To sum it up, the internet is just words addressed to me and words that I address to others.

Father Makarios (Markish): To suggest that technological development can affect the faith or theology is sheer nonsense. Technological developments are quite diverse in nature, from the toothpick to genetic engineering, from the slingshot to the ballistic missile. Depending on their nature, they might affect the way people live to their faith—rather than the faith itself.

Dmitrii Vaisburd: The internet is just a means of communication and mass information. It is unable to impact my faith.

Is it possible, then, that the internet changes ecclesiology, e.g. introduces democracy into Church life, reduces the Church's hierarchical authority, and takes it back to the practices of the Early Church?

Father Sergii (Kruglov): It is certainly possible and it is happening today. For Christians, the internet opens a horizon beyond the narrow circle of their remote parish, shows them the life of other parishes, acquaints them with the priests and parishioners who have experience of church life other than their own, and gives them the opportunity to read books by classic and contemporary ecclesiastical writers, which reflect theological and canonical opinions that are different from the usual views of a parish priest or a diocesan bishop. To give just one example: dramatic changes of consciousness that can cause a new internet experience still depend first and foremost on whether a Christian is able to accept new ideas or is just looking for confirmation of his already entrenched beliefs. The internet provides a Christian with both opportunities.

Father Makarios (Markish): "I believe in One Holy Catholic and Apostolic Church", —states the Creed. Thus, Church reality, with its principal tenets as well as its practices developing in time and space, is inseparable from the reality of the Christian faith, and no more subject to change by external means than any other element thereof.

However, as I said, the way people live is always subject to change; and some people, driven by the phantoms they get from the internet and elsewhere, might indeed drop out of the Church and consequently join the synagogue of Satan (Rev. 2:9). That occurred in the past more than once by the agency of the whip, guillotine and barbed wire; nowadays the same thing might occur in the field of information.

Father P.: Internet itself is unable to change anything, but people are able. Internet can be of use as a source of information, which is easier to find there than in books. As for belittling the authority of the hierarchy, I do not think that this in itself could become an aim of Christians. The problem is not the authority, but in the absence of conciliarism in the Church. If each of us suddenly becomes aware of its necessity and indispensability for the church, the question of authoritarianism will disappear by itself. In this sense, the internet, of course, may be useful.

Dmitrii Vaisburd: The internet is certainly not able to change the perception of Church reality. But it allows spiritual bonds to be created through virtual communication (which is extremely important for the Church), which was not possible before. Thanks to the internet I have brothers and sisters in Christ in various parts of the world.

Is it possible to achieve a genuine religious experience with the assistance of digital technologies?—There are "virtual chapels" on the Net wherein one is invited to light a "virtual candle", listen to a sermon by a priest, utter a prayer, request an intercession service etc. Are these activities truly religious?

Father Sergii (Kruglov): I think it is still not occasionally that the Liturgy—in the form of prayer, chanting, venerating icons, entering into living contact with the priest, not to mention participating in the Communion—is focused on personal presence. The experience of modern Orthodoxy in Russia shows that even if a believer has the opportunity to listen to the recorded or broadcast service from home, to light candles in a virtual chapel (these virtual chapels, by the way, are still perceived by the mass of Orthodox believers as an electronic toy), or to communicate with the confessor in absentia by e-mail or online chat, it is not felt as genuine participation.

However, being in touch with the world of faith through digital technology can give a person a certain feeling of the authenticity of the religious action. This is particularly the case for people with disa-disabilities who are unable to go to the temple and who spend days in bed with a laptop. In short, everything is determined by the words of Christ, given by the Evangelist and Apostle John, that genuine religious action is the worship of God in spirit and truth, and whether this is achieved in a, so to speak, digital format or in the real world, depends on personal circumstances.

Father Makarios (Markish): No other assistance but the personal assistance of Christ is necessary for a believer; material factors, however, including those of a technical nature, can certainly facilitate (or hinder) any spiritual efforts.

Thus it should be clear that the category of *"digital technologies"* in this case is fruitless: "virtual chapels and candles" are a silly fake, while e-mail, on the other hand, is a most convenient means of communication, and the capability to find and retrieve from the internet liturgical, historical and theological texts, icons, music and much more is a huge advantage of our age.

Father P.: No, nothing virtual can be real. The internet as a huge library may be of some value, but to the very religious experience the internet has no relations. I do not even want to talk about virtual chapels, candles, notes, etc. In my opinion, it is an opiate on sale. I believe traders will be punished for their poison when their time comes.

Dmitrii Vaisburd: If you are interested in gaining religious experience and emotions, then you can get them in any way that suits you personally, including the internet. But the Church is not a producer of spiritual services, but a community of believers. It is not religious emotions, but deep interpersonal communication that is of prime importance. And of course it is much easier to communicate looking into each other's eyes. Although, when this is not possible, the internet can help a lot.

What do you think of virtual (digital) icons? Is it possible to pray before an icon downloaded from the internet, displayed on the computer screen?

Father Sergii (Kruglov): It does not matter if the icon is painted or highlighted on the screen. I believe that the controversy about colours, boards, and materials was overcome in the iconoclastic era.

Father P.: I do not see any difference between an icon on the wall or on the screen. Aesthetically, of course, the traditional icon is preferable. After all, the paint and modern screens—all consist of the same chemical elements.

Father Makarios (Markish): It is possible and incumbent upon a Christian to pray in any circumstances (1Thess. 5:17), even before such unappealing objects as a pine stump or the muzzle of a rifle— like the New Martyrs of Russia did. Keeping that in mind, we nonetheless prefer iconographic images of a better quality; it should be noted that technological developments in recent years have brought computer images quite close to the original.

Dmitrii Vaisburd: An icon is an image, but not only the board and paint. An image can be produced by any means, traditional or hi-tech. It is valid as long as it fulfills its purpose—to help us to pray.

Jesus said: "Where two or three are gathered together in My name, there am I in the midst of them". What if these two or three are gathered in a virtual internet community?

Father Sergii (Kruglov): Jesus will be in the midst of them. Everywhere. God loves us so much that for our sake Jesus went to the cross—I do not think that He ceases to love us because we invented the internet ... For our sake He had been in places much more terrible than the internet.

Father P.: I do not know. Rather Jesus could have been asked if He had in mind such unity. I think as long as there are no visible obstacles to real Christian unity in the Church, all virtual 'substitutes' are out of the question. Holy Communion Bowl has always been the center of the Church union. What could be the 'virtual' center? The screen? Even if we assume the open persecution of Christians, virtual unity cannot meet spiritual needs of true believer.

Father Makarios (Markish): Virtual gathering in order to pray is better than no gathering at all, but is worse than a personal gathering.—Precisely the same ought to be said about a phone con-conversation.

Dmitrii Vaisburd: There were precedents in the twentieth century when people who were hundreds of miles away from each other agreed in advance on a joint prayer at a certain time every day and kept this agreement for many years. Judging by the results, it is possible to say that the unity in Christ between them existed even without the internet. But communication via the internet can create this unity easily. One important condition should be observed— people should not communicate via the internet because they do not want to see each other in real life.

In your opinion, are digital technologies a threat to personal faith and Orthodoxy in Russia, or vice versa—are they opening up new opportunities?

Father Sergii (Kruglov): I see mostly new possibilities that are opening up. What kind of a 'threat' could it be? For example, all correspondence in the dioceses of the Russian Orthodox Church of Moscow Patriarchate has long been conducted by e-mail. There are many Orthodox internet resources, and a large number of bishops, priests and laity have websites and blogs in social networks.

Father P.: Digital technology by itself does not constitute a threat or benefit. It's like a knife that can cut a piece of bread to the hungry, or can kill. Digital technologies offer great possibilities of both evil and good, and every person determines what is closer to him.

Father Makarios (Markish): The internet is a tool in the hands of man. It helps the free person to be free, but to the slave owner it helps him to retain voluntary slaves. Everybody creates rules and spheres of social communication in the internet based on personal discretion.

Dmitrii Vaisburd: The internet is a tool, and a very effective one. When used properly, it can bring much good. For example, one can preach the word of Christ. But of course abuses are possible.

Another problem that may be noticeable is the alleged deterioration of cultural identity resulting from global phenomena on the internet, which are perceived as a menace to Russian Orthodox Christianity.

Father Makarios (Markish): There is no menace to Christianity. There is a menace to some Christians, especially young ones who, of course, need protection from it.

The menace, indeed, has something to do with cultural identity—but very little, if at all, with Russian identity. Pornography, gambling, violence, promiscuity, perversions of any sort, obscenity, totalitarian cults and sects, stupidity ("dumbing-down") and a score of other champions of subhumanity are as hostile to Russia as to any other nation (if it is a nation rather than a herd of cattle), and as adverse to Christians as to followers of any other religion (if it is a religion rather than a sham). And the internet could either promote the above-mentioned "global phenomena", or defend us from them—depending on how we use it.

It is believed that the internet contributes to the development of a rational discussion on blocking the acquisition of mystical experience. Is this a threat to Orthodoxy?

Father P.: I think that this comment is worth of attention. This is a threat only when your Christianity it just a 'discussion'. In fact, Christianity can be a place for discussions, but does not consist only of discussions. St. Gregory the Theologian said: 'Be tied to God more than defend the doctrine of God.' These ties are always a mystical experience.

Father Sergii (Kruglov): Sometimes there are so many sinful passions and so much vanity in the comments on *Facebook* and *LiveJournal* that I question whether the internet can really facilitate 'the development of rational discussion'! ... I do not agree that the internet is somehow blocking the acquisition of mystical experience. The internet is just a part of life. Yes, life is full of noise, silencing the voice of Heaven—but this Voice is heard nevertheless through any obstacles if your heart is set to hear.

Commentary

It should be born in mind that our interlocutors do not represent the whole of the Orthodox segment of the Runet, because with the exception of *Father P.* they are *professional* bloggers, writers and publicists. Being most thoughtful and reflexing Church intellectuals, they express concerns and ideas, central to the Orthodox sensibility towards the internet. Importantly, participants of this 'virtual roundtable' rarely refer to blogging as a missionary activity, framing it mostly as an element of the lifestyle of a present day believer, who sees the internet as a handy tool for personal development. Respondents resist the idea of the internet as a theological problem, interpreting the digital technologies as ethically neutral. Likewise, the question of digital icons does not seem to be interesting for them, because, as *Father Sergii* pointed out, the controversy of iconic visuality had been solved already in the era of iconoclasm.[2]

At the same time, they explicitly manifest discomfort about disembodiment of the religious communication in the virtual world. Regardless of their ideological disposition, they discard such novelties as a virtual chapel, regarding it as a 'toy', or 'fake', or 'opiate'. From their viewpoint, Orthodox faith requires corporeal contacts in order to perform sacraments, or just to talk to a priest privately, and whatever perfect technical devices could never mediate these contacts. In this sense, the advent of the internet sensitized the Church intellectuals about the challenges to biopolitical governmentality (Foucault 2003), associated with virtualization of human life.

Digital possibilities of slipping from the 'pastoral power' reactivated old debates, traditional for Russian Orthodoxy, between conservative supporters of the authority of clerics and reformist advocates of laypeople's participation in Church's life (Shevzov 2004). Thus, *Father P.* observes the reformatory perspective in the use of the internet for promoting greater conciliarity in Orthodox

---

2 See Chapter 3 'Wi-Fi in Plato's CaveThe Digital Icon and the Phenomenology of Surveillance' by Fabian Heffermehl in this volume, which, in spite of this view, problematizes the take of the Orthodoxy on icons and virtual reality.

ecclesiology.[3] In particular, as has been approvingly mentioned by *Father Sergii*, the internet gives people an access to the literature, previously monopolized by clerics. In principle, this could support the development of lay theology and culture of religious debates, thereby rectifying one of the mostly oft-noted deficiencies of Russian Orthodoxy—the accent on ritualism (*obriadoverie*). Probably, some of the respondents recollected their formative years as Orthodox believers and marked off the role of freely downloadable reading materials in this process. By contrast, *Father Makarios* raises his voice to warn against joining 'the synagogue of Satan' as a possible outcome of reconsideration of the role of the church in people's life. All in all, the 'virtual roundtable' corroborates the conclusion that Orthodox intellectuals do not sufficiently theorize the theological dimensions of the digital environment, which hinders thematization of the 'digital anxiety' when it comes to the processes of virtualization of 'real' bodies.[4]

References

Agafangel (Belykh) (2007). 'Sovremennyi propovednik dolzhen imet' blog v internete'. Accessed 6 September 2015: http://gazetakifa.ru/content/view/1112/13/.

Bakardjieva, Maria, & Gaden, Georgia (2012). 'Web 2.0 Technologies of the Self.' *Philosophy & Technology,* 25: 399–413.

Dorfman, Marcy (1996). 'Evaluating the Interpretive Community: Evidence from Expert and Novice Readers.' *Poetics,* 23: 453–470.

fatherpenguin@lj. (31.07.2011). 'Kholostiatskii kulesh' / 'A Bachelor's Soup.' *LiveJournal.* http://fatherpenguin.livejournal.com/2011/07/31/ (accessed 6 September 2015).

Foucault, Michel (2003). 'The Subject and Power.' In *The Essential Foucault,* edited by P. Rabinow and N. Rose (New York: New Press): 126–144.

---

3 See Chapter 4 'The Body of Christ Online: The Russian Orthodox Church and (Non)Liturgical Interactivity on the Internet' by Alexander Ponomariov in this volume.
4 See Chapter 1 by Mikhail Suslov 'The Medium for Demonic Energies: 'Digital Anxiety' in the Russian Orthodox Church' in this volume.

Kirill (Gundiaev) (2013). 'Missiia v virtual'nom prostranstve ne mozhet podmeniat' soboi prikhodskuiu rabotu' / 'A [Church] Mission in the Virtual Environemnt Should Not Substitute [Missionary] Work in Parishes'. Accessed 6 September 2015: http://www.patriarchia.ru/db/text/2770747.html.

Krug, Pavel (2006). 'Pravoslavie: Elektronnaia versiia.' / 'Orthodoxy: Electronic Version.' *NG-Religii,* 186(14).

Lee, Joonseong (2009). 'Cultivating the Self in Cyberspace: The Use of Personal Blogs among Buddhist Priests.' *Journal of Media and Religion,* 8: 97–114.

Lövheim, Mia (2013). 'Identity.' In *Digital Religion: Understanding Religious Practice in New Media Worlds,* edited by Heidi Campbell. (New York: Routledge).

Shevzov, Vera (2004). *Russian Orthodoxy on the Eve of Revolution.* (Oxford: Oxford University Press).

Yurchak, Alexey (2013). *Everything Was Forever, Until It Was No More: The Last Soviet Generation.* (Princeton: Princeton University Press).

Chapter 11.
The Religious Identity of Russian Internet Users: Attitudes Towards God and Russian Orthodox Church

Viktor Khroul
Moscow State University

Introduction

Religious identity studies are being conducted in the context of the broader academic and public debate on secularism. The classical theory of secularization has been criticized by many well-known scholars in the late twentieth and early twenty-first century under the evident influence of increasing the role of religion and religious institutions in many countries. In particular, Peter Berger considers the assumption that we live in a secularized world to be a mistake, as well as the idea that modernization inevitably leads to the decline of religion. Modernization has also a powerful effect of counter-secularization (Berger 1999).

Based on religious identity the influence of religion on society during the last decade has attracted the reflection of prominent philosophers. The book *The Power of Religion in the Public Sphere,* published in 2011 in New York, brought together the reflections of Jurgen Habermas, Charles Taylor, Judith Butler, and Cornel West resulting in a dialogue on a vibrant subject (Butler, Habermas, Taylor and West 2011). Rethinking traditional approaches, these scholars evidently show that many ideas about religion and public life are myths still rooted in mass consciousness. The book reminds readers that religion is neither totally private nor totally irrational, and that the public sphere is not necessarily the place for radical deliberation on religion if the analysis is to be deep and objective.

The approach to the attribution of religious identity has always been a challenge for researchers—both in Russia and abroad. Scholars suggested many criteria to classify subjects to a particular religious group for certain empirically observable indicators (Taylor 1989; Sinelina 2001; Filatov and Lunkin 2005; Luchenko 2008; Kloch 2011; Campbell 2013). Formal belonging to a particular religion, even in cultures and countries with fixed membership in religious communities (Germany, Italy, Sweden) in the context of the dynamic processes of secularization and counter-secularization sociologically and psychologically does not guarantee the same religious identity. In modern Russian Orthodoxy this problem becomes even more complicated.

Different approaches often give contradictory results. The most natural approach is based on *self-identification* data. Approximately from 60 to 80 % of Russian population claim themselves to be Orthodox Christians. Radically different results are obtained by estimating the number of *observant followers* of every religion, the reason being that members of many ethnic groups often choose to self-identify as adherents to a certain religion for cultural reasons, although they would not fit any traditional religiousness criteria (church attendance, familiarity with basic dogmas of their faith). For example, even though 80% of ethnic Russians self-identify as Russian Orthodox, less than 10% of them attend church services more than once a month and only 2–4% are considered to be integrated into church life. This corresponds with the concept of the 'vicarious religion'.

According to three sociological indicators of religiosity, analyzed by Levada center—the level of practicing (participation in liturgical life), observing of God's commandments (do not kill) and Church commandments (to observe Lent), Russian population is far from keeping Orthodox Christian identity. According to Levada center data, 73% of respondents painted eggs but just—6% attended Easter liturgy—what is a must for Orthodox believers. Only 3% of respondents observed Lent, 51% does not consider abortion to be a killing—what again is not in line with Orthodox teaching (Levada 2013; 2014).

Religious identity for Russians is still much less significant in comparison to ethnic identity. Responses to the question 'Who do you perceive yourself with pride that in the first place add your self-respect?' show that during the period from 1989 to 2008 the share of respondents that chose 'I am Russian' rose from 43% to 50%, while those who chose option 'I am a believer'—from 4% to 15%. Independent research organization 'Sreda' in early 2012 conducted nationwide representative survey (field work: FOM-Penta, sampling size: 1,500) showing that People rarely confess (2%—'once a month or more often') and rarely observe Lent (5%).

Conducting critical analysis of public opinion polls on religious self-identification and their methodology, Russia sociologist Iulia Sinelina raised the problematic question of the 'identification of respondents who identify themselves as Orthodox Christians, but poorly know dogmatic and rarely attend church worships' (Sinelina 2001). Sociologist T. Varzanova found out in 1990s that 'respondents were ready to justify from personal experience their beliefs in witchcraft, horoscopes, communication with spirits much better than Christian faith'. At the same time, according to Varzanova Orthodox faith 'proved to be very far from ideal prescribed 'Orthodox Creed' (Varzanova 1997). Describing in his research the increase the ideological uncertainty and eclecticism with beliefs in reincarnation and astrology, ufology, energy vampires, witches, shamans and so on, sociologist Dmitrii Furman suggested, than religion is not winning vs atheism in Russia, rather atheism wins vs religion (Furman and Kaariajnen 2006).

Additional difficulties in defining religious identity appear in studies of internet communications. Expanding research methods to the internet and on-line practices faces a number of advantages over traditional methods of gathering information (Boyd and Heer 2006), but as well raises the problem of interpretation in the reconstruction of the religious identity of users of their profiles, because rather often users—for different reasons—falsify their personal information. We consider not user profiles but their texts to be a more valid empirical field for discovering their religious identity from a methodological point of view.

In sociological perspective texts of web discussions may be considered as 'spontaneous responses to a big open-ended question' and therefore allow to explore a more subtle and detailed picture of Russian mentality and spirituality than can be obtained by representative public opinion polls (Anikina and Khroul 2011). German scholar Oliver Krüger underlines the promising perspectives of internet based research: 'Immanent Internet research offers many new perspectives for religious studies. While traditional media like books, magazines, and television enable us to see only the supplier and the supplies on the *religious market*, the Internet—as an *interactive* medium—now makes it possible to be aware of the consumer's perspective as well'. (Krüger 2005: 1). Krüger suggests that although the internet enables us to trace many instances of 'invisible religion,' the empirical field of research causes some new methodological challenges that must not be ignored.

Russian internet users' attitudes towards God and their religious identity

The traditional, proved and dominant methods of acquiring knowledge on religious identity are sociological studies which use the methods of mass survey, expert survey, content analysis, focus groups etc. Popular attitudes towards God and beliefs since the times of George Gallup have been traditionally studied with public opinion polls methodology and techniques.

'Mass self-communication' (Castells 2007) is becoming more and more promising subject of popular culture studies in general and religious identity research in particular. But by the moment the booming of 'big data' research methodologies and techniques still has not provided the academia with a valid methods of representative public opinion surveys based on the self-expression texts analysis. Another promising approach to mass consciousness studies proposed in 1980-s by Soviet and Russian sociologist professor Grushin: 'Text analysis will help answer the question of mass consciousness far more completely and reliably that this can

THE RELIGIOUS IDENTITY OF RUSSIAN INTERNET USERS 303

be done using the traditional public opinion polls'—this is the es-essence of 'Grushin hypothesis' (Grushin 2010: 75). The idea is that the same subject could be reflected and explicitly fixed not only in responses to the sociological questionnaire but also in spontaneous texts.

In order to receive a more detailed description of the religious beliefs and identity of Russian Internet users we analyzed texts of visitors of the lovehate.ru website, which is one of the most known places for spontaneous self-expression and discussions. We coded and rubricated it taking into consideration the attitude towards God and arguments used. As of 10 August 2014, the site had 249,812 registered users (125,556 men and 124,256 women) who expressed their attitude to 76482 subjects and the total number of messages exceeded one million (1,000,352).

Figure 10.1. Screenshot from the lovehate.ru website.
Source: http://lovehate.ru/God/54. Accessed 2 September 2015.

The discussion topic 'I love / I hate God'—is one of the largest on lovehate.ru. We conducted semantical and structural analysis of all 1,715 posts on that topic ('I love' = 1039, 'I hate' = 676). The procedural 'framework' of statements about God, which is set by the administrator for all themes, is sharply polarized: I love / I hate. This opposition led some people to certain confusion: 'I write this column, not because I hate God, but because there is no neutral option'; 'In my opinion, you can not just say I like God or not.' 250 thousand users is a relatively small number comparing with tens of millions of users of vk.com and other site, but the most valuable is the a structure of the texts which presumes arguments what is not necessary in vk.com.

Another problematic area—the question if the users' statements reflect their real attitudes towards God and religious identity. Some reports clearly show that there may be significant 'gaps' between the text and the real authors' position. The problem of the interpretation was mentioned by Mia Lövheim from Sweden during the analysis of her research results: 'The experiences of the informants show how it rather leads to a reaffirmation than a reconstruction of stereotypes about religious identities, and to a construction of boundaries in order to separate authentic or 'serious' religious identities from 'fake' versions. These findings show that we need a more critical and nuanced discussion of the anticipation that online interaction, due to its differences in cues for presenting and interpreting identity' (Lövheim 2005: 17). For example, the 'positive' column 'I love God' one of the users published the following messages: 'I do not believe in God do not believe in the devil.... I am my own god and the devil'; 'I think so: one day you will understand that it is absolutely not necessary to believe in God'.

Several specific features of Russian internet users' relationship to God have been found after processing the data.

1. Relationship with God is described mostly in personal and group (family) context, not the context of public sphere.
The space of the user-God relations is characterized by an evident shift towards personal space (698 of total 40,7%) and small groups (family and friends—27,8%), while the entire society as a context is mentioned in 13.8% and global—in 23.4% of the users' messages (total sum exceeds 100% because there are several levels in some posts). Many submissions emphasized the personal aspect of a relationship with God, and for some authors religious dogmas are

secondary in relation to the inner feeling 'Religion—this is what a person feels within himself'; 'God is yourself, you can manage own destiny by yourself'; 'God is not necessary to impose, God is personal to everyone'; 'He is always with me, with my friends and relatives!'

In principle, it can be assumed that the proportion of private / public and individual / global, found in the texts in the target site, it reflects the proportion of the mass consciousness of Russians, but this assertion needs further verification using other tools (for example, opinion polls).

2. Spontaneous texts describing the relation to God, internet users mostly refer to their own experience (59.5%) and the experience of other people (16.4%), not on faith (10,6%), authority (6.1%) or tradition (3.1%).
Generalized theoretical understanding of personal experience: 'Just cannot live without faith, I cannot believe in nothing'; 'I communicate with God without intermediaries'; 'I believe in God. Only a few in his own way, no incense and candles. Just he and I are good friends.' Concrete evidence of site visitors on the intervention of God in their personal experience: 'I am not religious, and not from such a family. Just noticed a strange phenomenon—I feel bad and want help. And then I come to the old icon and pray. And intervene unearthly powers! Helps for 6 day of my period is no easy exams!';

As a working hypothesis, we assumed that faith and tradition ('the holy Orthodox Russia—*Sviataia Rus"*) will be the dominant way to justify the relationship to God. However, the hypothesis has not been confirmed—by faith referred only 10% Orthodox Christianity is mentioned very rarely and mostly in a neutral and negative way: 'I'm not sentenced to Christianity. I just believe.'

3. The arguments in the text are based mainly on emotions and feelings (61.6%), much less—on logical arguments (34.1%).
Sometimes feelings are not specified, but simply described as feelings ('God is. 'Cause I can feel his presence'), sometimes referred to as feelings, and they do not need to reconstruct ('I do not

love God, I'm afraid of him'). Some users try to equate God with the mind ('This is the highest cosmic intelligence of the universe, without which there would be no life on Earth'), or to perceive its presence in all the surrounding world ('If he—all, how can you not love him and ignore'—*him is written with small letters in original*), as well as to emphasize the rational principle in God ('The proof of the existence of God can be built on an empirical basis', 'There's pure logic. And it's pretty logically painted '). The opposite side is a uniquely configured and expresses itself less nuanced way ('Reason is the greatest enemy of faith', 'Any religion restricts the bounds of reason and imagination').

Generally speaking, the text analysis of the self-expressions and discussions on lovehate.ru website shows that young Russians in matters of belief/disbelief rely mainly on their own experience and the experience of other people (family, friends, acquaintances), and not on faith, authority or tradition, as would be expected initially. The most convincing is the socio-historical explanation for this phenomenon: in the Russian tradition of faith and consistently eradicated over a fairly long period of time. Minimizing appeals to faith, tradition and authority—a 'birthmark' of Russian history, which is found in the minds of users.

Another notable 'birthmark'—the exclusion of religion from the public sphere in the minds of the Russians and the displacement of it ad marginem and into the inner circle of communication (family, relatives, friends). In western societies, this process is related to the general secularization, whereas in Russia a more active influence of religion in the public space was probably to be expected after Perestroika, which also implied some political manifestations of religiosity, including the creation of the Christian or Islamic parties. However, this has not happened. And, in addition to the external factors of a social nature, during the investigation found one of the internal reasons—visitors rarely even think about the possibility of a public-level consideration of the relation to God. Global level is manifested in the form of a stereotype ('all have to believe in God' / 'everyone understands that there is no God').

Self-identity towards Orthodox Christianity and the Russian Orthodox Church

The situation with the traditional media formats within the Russian Orthodox Church (ROC) is far from being advanced: ROC is not controlling any big media project. First reason is financial but also there is lack of professional media managers. ROC has neither a newspaper with a wide circulation, nor a 24-hours FM radio station, nor a competitive television channel except a rather unprofessional cable one. Occasionally some priests take part in some talk shows, there even once was several Orthodox ones. Currently the most widely used media tool is the internet—there are more than a thousand sites on any topic, including official webpages, online magazines, special interest pages, calendars, possibility to ask a priest online etc. These groups recruit Orthodox or pro-Orthodox members and therefore can not represent average users in comparison to lovehate.ru and other neutral, not religiously marked websites.

In contrary to the topic of self-expression towards God, that demonstrated mostly positive attitudes ('I love' = 1039, 'I hate' = 676), the analysis of lovehate.ru discussion topics on Orthodox Christianity and Russian Orthodox Church (ROC) evidently shows rather negative attitudes and opinions. Our observation is proved by the numbers of pro/contra messages 'ROC' (46/151), 'The idea of studying in secondary schools Orthodoxy' (227/507). Interestingly, the general evaluation of Orthodoxy is more balanced and less negative: 'Orthodox Christianity' (191/195).

Social and political activity of ROC face more criticism than Orthodox Christianity as religion: 'ROC proposal to impose a dress code for the people of Russia' (8/18), 'ROC proposes to create a criminal penalty for heresy' (36/50), 'when Orthodoxy is called the only true religion' (27/42). This suggestion may be proves not only statistically, quantitatively, but also qualitatively, with the rhetoric of users' voices: 'ROC is a bunch of scams, to brainwash people. Their desire is just power'; 'What is the ROC? Ordinary sect, pumping money from gullible citizens and providing a corrosive effect on the moral and cultural foundations of the nation'; 'ROC is a business project'; 'ROC, in most cases do not care about people, but about the godless government'.

The difference of the attitude towards Orthodox Christianity and the ROC is evident in the following suggestion: 'I love the Orthodox religion and Orthodox culture, myself; I am an Orthodox man, but terribly hate the ROC...'; 'Orthodox faith, in my humble opinion, the only leads to salvation of the human soul ... But there is a wish to the ROC. I would not like to see our church was transformed into a house of merchants'. The arguments of those who are in favor of ROC and defend it, are mostly rooted in ethnical and geopolitical discourse: 'I am Russian and therefore I am an Orthodox. It is natural'; 'ROC is an integral part of the thousand-year history of Russia, she has always supported our morals and I will always be with her, as the rest of the true believers'; 'It is the link between Russia and Ukraine and other fraternal Orthodox peoples' (written in 2013, far before the war in Eastern Ukraine).

Conclusion: the failure of public dialogue in religious identity perspective

Public dialogue management is an essential part of mediatization culture. The role of contemporary mediatization of religion in religious identity formation in Russia may be illustrated by the coverage of one case. On the 25th of January 2011, the Russian Orthodox Church presented for public discussion a list of so-called 'eternal Russian values'. According to one of the co-authors of the text, archpriest Vsevolod Chaplin, the project entitled 'The National System of Values' had been elaborated in order to 'fill in the vacuum of values in society.' The list of values included eight public virtues ranked according to their importance—justice, freedom, solidarity, unity, self-restraint and sacrifice, patriotism, welfare and love. Each point was accompanied by a commentary: freedom presumes personal freedom, freedom of expression and freedom of conscience and sovereignty and independence of the Russian people. According to

Chaplin, these virtues have remained invariable in Russia 'despite all the conservation and modernization processes' (Russian Church Calls 2011).

The Russian Orthodox Church called for the public debate of the document, saying the list was not fixed and could be amended. 'There were many interesting comments, and some of them are included in the document. It will be further updated and modified in line with the debates involving various non-government organizations,' Chaplin said.

But this call was almost ignored by the Russian media and was almost invisible in the Russian public sphere—the dialogue on values failed because of the journalists' ignorance. On the very first day the document was widely and fairly acidly commented on the internet, but the big media were almost silent about the initiative, and the discussion died from the very beginning. The Church officials were portrayed as a very aggressive people, imposing their values towards entire society (see **figure 10.2**).

Figure 8.2. Screenshot from www.lenta.ru webpage.
Source: http://lenta.ru/news/2011/01/25/values/. Accessed 2 September 2015.

The question is who is passive—journalists, the audience or both? The question is always urgent in societies where the rules of the game and the framework of interaction have been determined from above. The case described above explicitly shows a lack of comprehending the necessity of public dialogue and the accountability in the professional culture of Russian journalists. Another question is whether this 'dialogue manager' is free enough in Russia to be an independent and influential actor?

The phenomenon of 'monologization' of the dialogue with the public sphere has been analyzed by Swedish Kristoffer Holt: 'When Benedict appeared officially on *Facebook* in May 2009, as a 'famous' person that *Facebook* users could become a fan of, there was a section for free discussion among the fans. During the first year, there were many lively discussions in this discussion group, ranging from spiritual questions to criticism of various positions of the church... But, after a while, this feature disappeared from Pope Benedict's *Facebook* page. Now, the *Facebook* page mainly channels content from *Radio Vaticana* and the Vatican's *YouTube* channel. The interaction allowed is restricted to 'liking' content or writing short comments on it'... This is not intended as a criticism of the lack of interactivity, merely pointing out that for the Church, these new participatory media soon turned into new channels of one-way communication' (Holt 2011: 60).

The logical and processing sequence *'pluralism—dialogue— consensus'* in the context of religious identity in contemporary Russia has problematic fields located in the *dialogue* area. Some of our observations of recent years, based on interviews with journalists and data analysis, lead to the conclusions of: 1) *narrowing the debate* on the religious identity in mainstream media; 2) *reducing the possibility* for journalists to articulate the Christian values and their identity (for example, some journalists fired for expressing their anti-homosexual views); 3) *removing of the dialogue* on religious values and identity *into uncensored and free area* of internet resources, mostly—to blogs or forums of similar value orientations users.

The public dialogue on values in Russia has evident difficulties rooted in the religious identity focused on private sphere and distrust to ROC in public sphere. The set of objections and protests against the politically marked activity of ROC, expressed by lovehate.ru users, generated the set of arguments against the 'establishment of moral censorship' in Russian media within the frames of public debates over the idea for Public Council for Morality on TV (2008– 2011). Finally the idea has been rejected both by public opinion and State Duma (see Khroul 2010; 2011; 2012).

Examined in the paper user-God relations in Russia still do not presume the expansion from private into public sphere therefore the attempts to mobilize wider circles of people support Orthodox Church actions (new churches construction in Moscow, protests against profanation of religious symbols etc) normally faces ignorance and even intolerance.

The domination of private over public and personal experience over authority and tradition ('I'm not sentenced to Christianity. I just believe.') in religious identity respective do not give much space for religion as a mobilization factor in Russia. Ethnical issues are still much more influent, therefore the slogan *'Russkii mir'* [Russian world] is much more popular in Russia than *'Pravoslavnyi mir'* [Orthodox world].

References

Anikina, Maria and Viktor Khroul (2011). 'Memories about the Brezhnev Era in Public Opinion Polls and Mass Consciousness Texts: a Comparative Study' in *World of Media 2011. Yearbook of Russian Media and Journalism Studies,* edited by Elena Vartanova. Moscow: Moscow State University, 50–70.

Boyd Danah and J. Heer (2006). 'Profiles as Conversation: Networked Identity Performance on Friendster'. *Proceedings of the Hawai'i International Conference on System Sciences* (January 4–7, 2006). www.danah.org/papers/HICSS2006.pdf (accessed 01 September 2014).

Butler, Judith, Jürgen Habermas, Charles Taylor and Cornel West (2011). *The Power of Religion in the Public Sphere.* New York: Columbia University Press.

Campbell, Heidi (2010). *When Religion Meets New Media.* London: Routledge.

Campbell, Heidi; ed. (2013) *Digital Religion: Understanding Religious Practice in New Media Worlds.* New York: Routledge.

Castells, Manuel (2007). 'Communication, Power and Counter-Power in the Network Society'. *International Journal of Communication,* 1: 238–266.

Russian Church Calls for Relying on Faith, Motherland and Freedom Virtues in 21st Century (2011). Interfax, March 11, 2011. - http://www.interfax-religion.com/?act=news&div=8271 (accessed 01 September 2014).

Filatov, Sergei and Roman Lunkin (2005). 'Statistika rossiiskoi religioznosti: magiia tsifr i neodnoznachnaia real'nost''. *Sotsiologicheskie issledovaniia,* 4: 35–45.

Furman, Dmitrii and Kimmo Kaariajnen (2006). *Religioznost' v Rossii v 90-e gody XX - nachala XXI veka.* Moscow: OGNI TD.

Anikina, Maria; ed. (2010). *Otkryvaia Grushina.* Moscow: MGU.

Holt, Kristoffer (2011). 'Participatory Culture and the Church. Contrasting Communicative Ideals?' Viktor Khroul; ed. *Religion and New Media in the Age of Convergence.* Moscow: MGU: 57–64.

Khroul, Viktor (2010). 'Initiatives of TV Ethics Control by Religions in Russia: Challenges for the Implementation'. *Religion in Eastern Europe,* 30 (1).

Khroul, Viktor; ed. (2011). *Religion and New Media in the Age of Convergence.* Moscow: MGU.

Khroul, Viktor (2012). *Religion and Media in Russia: Functional and Ethical Perspectives.* Saarbrueken: LAP Lambert Academic Publishing.

Kloch, Józéf. (ed.) (2011). *Internet i Kościół.* Warsaw: Elipsa.

Krüger, Oliver. (2005). 'Methods and Theory for Studying Religion on the Internet. Introduction to the Special Issue on Theory and Methodology'. *Online–Heidelberg Journal of Religions on the Internet,* 1(1). http://journals.ub.uni-heidelberg.de/index.php/religions/article/view/379. Accessed 01 September 2014.

Levada (2013). 'Obshchestvennoe mnenie o kontratseptsii, abortakh i 'surrogatnom materinstve'. http://www.levada.ru/02-12-2013/obshchestv ennoe-mnenie-o-kontratseptsii-abortakh-i-surrogatnom-materinstve. Accessed 01 September 2014.

Levada (2014). Prazdnovanie Paskhi. http://www.levada.ru/05-05-2014/praz dnovanie-paskhi. Accessed 01 September 2014.

Lövheim, Mia. (2005). 'Young People and the Use of the Internet as Transitional Space'. Online–Heidelberg Journal of Religions on the Internet, 1(1). http://journals.ub.uni-heidelberg.de/index.php/religions/article/view/383. Accessed 01 September 2014.

Luchenko, Ksenia (2008). 'Internet i religioznye kommunikatsii v Rossii. Mediaskop, 1. http://mediascope.ru/node/32/. Accessed 01 September 2014.

Berger, Peter; ed. (1999). *The Desecularization of the World: Resurgent Religion and World Politics*. Grand Rapids: Eerdmans.

Sinelina, Iuliia (2001). 'O kriteriiah opredeleniia religioznosti naseleniia'. *Sotsiologicheskie issledovaniia*, 7: 89–96.

Taylor, Charles (1989). *Sources of the Self: The Making of the Modern Identity*. Cambridge, MA: Harvard University Press.

Varzanova, Tat'iana (1997). 'Vo chto veriat rossiiane'. *NG-Religii*, 2 (27.02.1997); 4 (24.04.1997).

List of Contributors

Magda Dolińska-Rydzek is a Ph.D. Candidate at the Graduate Centre for the Study of Culture, Justus Liebig University in Giessen (Germany), where she is working on a dissertation about the idea of the Antichrist in post-Soviet Russia. She holds a bachelor's degree in Eastern European Studies at the Adam Mickiewicz University in Poznan and a master's degree in European Studies at the University of Lodz. Her P.hD project examines in which ways and why the Antichrist legend is being employed and appropriated in various post-Soviet contexts, both religious and secular. magda.dolinska@rydzek.pl.

Maria Engström (Associate Professor of Russian, School of Humanities and Media Studies, Dalarna University, Sweden) focuses on the role of Orthodox Church in Russian politics, contemporary Russian utopian imagination, and imperial aesthetics in Russian literature and art. Her current research examines the Post-Soviet right-wing intellectual milieu and explores cultural manifestation of identity in contemporary Russia. Her most recent publications include the following articles and book chapters: 'Orthodoxy or death!' Political Orthodoxy in Russia' (*Religion, Politics and Nation-Building in Post-Communist Countries*, 2015); 'Contemporary Russian Messianism and New Russian Foreign Policy' (*Contemporary Security Policy*, 2014); and 'Forbidden Dandyism: Imperial Aesthetics in Contemporary Russia' (*Nordic Fashion Studies*, 2012). She co-edited 'Digital Orthodoxy: Mediating Post-Secularity in Russia and Ukraine', a special issue of *Digital Icons: Studies in Russian, Eurasian and Central European New Media* (2015). mae@du.se

Ekaterina Grishaeva is a candidate of science in philosophy, obtained at the Ural Federal University, Yekaterinburg, Russia; as a doctoral student she specialized in orthodox theology, mainly in neopatristic synthesis. Since 2011 she is a lecturer at the Department of Philosophy at Ural Federal University. In 2014 she was a junior fellow in the Institute for Human Science, Vienna; the title of the research project is *Orthodox Christianity and Politics in Post-Soviet Culture as Depicted in Russian Blogs*. She works as a postdoc fellow at the Jagiellonian University at the project *The criticism of European model of development in Russian neoconservative discourse of traditional values* which is aimed to compare how the criticism of the European modernity is constructed in official documents issued by the ROC and Russian government, and how it is changed in social networks. katherina.grishaeva@gmail.com

Fabian Heffermehl (http://fabianheffermehl.wordpress.com), PhD, postdoctoral researcher at the University of Oslo (Department of Literature, Area Studies and European Languages), is a scholar of Russian literature, specializing in media theories of the humanities. Heffermehl has published several articles in Russian, German and Norwegian about Pavel Florenskii and Fedor Dostoevsky. In Heffermehl's monograph 'The Image Seen from the Inside' (in Norwegian, forthcoming in an English translation) he analyzes the interaction between mathematical concepts in the 20th century and theories of the Orthodox icon. Fabian.heffermehl@ilos.uio.no.

Fr. Cyril Hovorun is a priest of the Russian Orthodox Church (Moscow Patriarchate); currently a senior lecturer at Stockholm School of Theology / Sankt Ignatios Academy in Sweden and a researcher at Columbia University. From 2007 to 2009 he was Chairman of the Department of External Church Relations of the Ukrainian Orthodox Church. From 2009 to 2012, he was the first deputy chairman of the Educational Committee of the Russian Orthodox Church. He was also a research fellow at Yale University. He is the author of *Will, Action, and Freedom: Christological Controversies in the Seventh Century* (Brill, 2008) and *Meta-Ecclesiology: The Chronicle of Church Awareness* (Palgrave Macmillan, 2015).

Victor Khroul, Ph.D., holds a Diploma of St. Thomas Aquinas Catholic Theology College, Moscow, Russia (1995) and a Master's (1986) and a Ph.D. (1993) degree in Journalism from Moscow State University, Russia. He is currently an Associate Professor at Moscow State University, Journalism Faculty, with the following teaching responsibilities and research areas: religion and media, ethics of journalism, audience studies. In 2010 Victor Khroul received an International award 'Excellence in Journalism'. He was a visiting professor at Central European University (Budapest, 2011) and Rooney International Scholar at Robert Morris University (Pittsburgh, 2014). Author of 'Media and Religion in Russia' and over 70 publications in Russian and English. amen@mail.ru

Irina Kotkina holds a Ph.D. from European University Institute (Florence) in History and also Candidate of Cultural Studies degree (Ph.D. equivalent) from Russian State University for Humanities in Moscow. She is employed as project researcher at Sodertorn University in Sweden. Her current project is called 'The Vision of Eurasia: Eurasianist Influences on Politics, Culture and Ideology in Russia Today'. Dr. Kotkina is studying cultural politics and all aspects of Russian culture. She publishes broadly on Russia's cultural policy, opera and theatre. She is particularly interested in the Bolshoi Theater opera history in the XX century and among her recent peer-reviewed publications are articles on Medvedev's modernization and the Bolshoi Theater, Stalinist Bolshoi Theater and the search for the model Soviet opera, and building of national operatic traditions in the Soviet republics under Stalin. irina.kotkina@sh.se

Anastasia Mitrofanova is the Chair of Political Science, Church-State Relations and the Sociology of Religion at the Russian Orthodox University of St John the Divine, Professor at the Financial University at the Government of the Russian Federation. She received her M.A. (1994) and Ph.D. (1998) in Political Science from the Moscow State University, her Dr. habilitat degree—from the Diplomatic Academy of the Foreign Affairs Ministry of the Russian Federation (2005). In 1998–2012 she was Director of the Center for Euroatlantic Studies at the Diplomatic Academy. Anastasia Mitrofanova's research interests include: religious politicization, fundamentalism, Orthodox Christianity and politics, nationalism in post-Soviet states, religiopolitical movements. Main publications: *Politizatsiia 'pravoslavnogo mira'* (Moskva: Nauka, 2004); *The Politicization of Russian Orthodoxy: Actors and Ideas* (Stuttgart: ibidem-Verlag, 2005). anastasia-mit@mail.ru.

Alexander Ponomariov wrote his Ph.D. dissertation on the Russian Orthodox Church and modernity at the University of Passau, Germany. His research interests include Orthodox Christianity, theology, history, Bible criticism, and ancient languages. Inter alia, he is the author of *The Pussy Riot Case in Russia: Orthodox Canon Law and the Sentence of the Secular Court* article (Ab Imperio, 4/2013), of *The Lord's Prayer in a Wider Setting: A New Hebrew Reconstruction* article (Journal of Northwest Semitic Languages 41–1/2015), and of some book reviews. aponmaster@gmail.com.

Sarah A. Riccardi-Swartz is a Ph.D. student in Sociocultural Anthropology at New York University. She is the author and co-author of print and digital articles about the material and visual cultures of Eastern Orthodoxy, and has presented widely on the same topic. riccardi@nyu.edu.

Hanna Stähle is a Ph.D. candidate in Slavic Cultural Studies at the University of Passau and currently a research fellow at the Higher School of Economics, Moscow. She obtained her Master's degree in Russian and East Central European Studies from the University of Passau in 2011. In 2008, she graduated from Minsk State Linguistic University with a degree in German language and literature. Her Ph.D. thesis examines digitally mediated image of the Russian Orthodox Church in post-Soviet Russia from the perspective of Church critics. hanna.staehle@gmail.com

Mikhail Suslov is a Marie Curie researcher at the Uppsala Center for Russian and Eurasian Studies, Uppsala University. He obtained his Ph.D. in history from the European University Institute in Florence in 2009. His research interests include Russian, and post-Soviet intellectual history, conservative and right-wing political ideology, critical geopolitics, conceptual history of the Russian Orthodox Church. His current study deals with the post-Soviet geopolitical ideas and new media. Mikhail.suslov@ucrs.uu.se.

Index

A

Adagamov, Rustem 210, 211
Alberti, Leon Battista 87, 96, 97, 100, 102
Aleksii II (Ridiger), Patriarch 31, 61
Alipii (Svetlichnyi), archimandrite 39, 69
Anonymity 88, 198, 199
  and Pseudonymity 38, 41, 42
  'name-worshipping' 29, 30
  re-naming 39
Antichrist 9, 53–75, 148
  Immoral Other 9, 53, 55–59, 71–74
  Apostasy 62
  Devil 8, 24, 28, 31, 32, 34, 57, 64, 71, 73, 304
  Satan 64, 65, 106, 222, 231, 290, 297
  'seal of the Antichrist' 64, 66, 67
  Demonization 36,
  Apocalypse 53, 54, 56, 63, 64, 66, 69, 74
    eschatological myth 54
Anti-clericalism
  Digital anti-clericalism 11, 195–200, 205, 220, 221, 231–233
    Memes 10, 12, 179, 197–200, 202, 204, 207, 212, 213, 217, 224, 232, 233
    Demotivators 12, 197–200, 204–212, 223, 224, 229–233
    Pastafarian Church 198
    'Orthodoxy of the Human Brain' (also PGM) 200–201, 207
    fotozhaby 212,

Arshakian, Lev 65,
Atheism 224, 231, 233, 301
  Soviet atheism 199, 232
  Scientific atheism 223, 225, 232
  Neo-atheism 196, 227
Authenticity
  Faith online 8, 32, 33
  and Orthodox iconography 265, 268, 270–273, 280, 291
Avdiugin, Aleksandr 42

B

Balandin, Spiridon 39,
'Bases of the Orthodox Culture' 3
Bednii, Demian 219
Belovolov, Gennadii 25, 30
Belykh, Agafangel 286
Benjamin, Walter 261, 265, 277
Berdiaev, Nikolai 55
Berestov, Anatolii 32, 36, 66
Blogosphere 25
  Russian blogosphere 141, 175
  Post-denominational bloggers 141, 142, 146, 147, 155, 157, 158
  'Ortho-bloggers' 24–27, 32, 285–287
Bragança de Miranda, José 265, 268
Buddhism 199
  Zen Buddhism 149, 152, 158
Bulgakov, Mikhail 221
Bulgakov, Sergei 39
Butler, Judith 299

C

Cathedral of Christ the Savior 161, 184
Chaplin, Vsevolod 35, 42, 167, 209, 212, 224, 308, 309
Chapnin, Sergei 27–29
Cheremnykh, Mikhail 206
Church mission 4, 43
Church-Slavonic language 113, 118, 127, 130
  Church-Slavonic fonts 130, 131
Conciliarity (and *sobornost'*) 10, 112, 121, 126, 132, 133, 296
Conservatism 2
  Conservatives XI
  Traditionalists 35
  Anti-Western sentiments 169, 210
  Nationalism (and nationalistic rhetoric) 3, 165, 263, 288
Converts 262, 263, 280
Counter-culture
  Late-Soviet counter-culture 12, 223
'cultivation of the self' 286
cultural imaginary 54, 55, 65, 73

D

Da Vinci, Leonardo 97
Darth Vader 84, 85, 107
Degas, Edgar 94
Deineka, Alexander 206
De-sacralization 31, 33, 43
Digital technologies of communication
  Digital religion 3, 6, 20, 111, 112, 264
    Religion online (also Online religion) 5, 7, 113–115, 153
    Online church (also Cyberchurch) 113, 131

Virtual chapel X, 32, 33, 291, 292, 296
Virtual reality 29, 31, 32, 38, 83, 85, 92, 96, 97, 104, 106, 107, 296
Internet IX, X, 1, 4–13, 19–42, 53, 60–62, 83–89, 95, 104–109, 111–118, 120, 121, 124, 131, 132, 143, 154, 157, 158, 162, 174, 181, 195, 197, 198, 204, 215, 226, 229, 232, 233, 240, 241, 244, 246, 261, 264, 268, 271, 273, 280, 285, 286, 289–297, 301, 307, 309
Virtual (and real) identity 155–157
Disembodiment 296
Internet-addiction 35, 36, 84, 85
De-virtualization 40
Discourse theory 56
Dostoevsky, Fedor 30, 54, 72

E

Eastern Christianity (Orthodoxy) IX, 158
  Orthodox Church in America 12, 42, 262, 263, 279
  Old Believers 9, 253, 255, 257
  Russian Orthodox Church Outside of Russia (ROCOR) 276
Ebay 269
Ecclesiology 10, 112, 122, 132, 290, 297
Ecumenism 69, 74
Efanov, Andrei 70
Enteo (Tsoreonov), Dmitrii 226, 228
Erofeev, Venedikt 218

F

Florensky, Pavel X, 84, 96, 98, 102–107
Frolov, Kirill 181, 226
Fundamentalism (also fundamentalist religions and fundamentalist worldview) 4, 21, 43, 227, 288
  Orthodox fundamentalists 21, 146
  Taliban 5, 228

G

Gel'man, Marat 226, 227
Geopolitics
  Geopolitical threat (also geopolitical discourse) 308
  Geopolitical metaphor 23, 24
  Geopolitical weapon 28
  Dugin, Aleksandr 71, 72
  'Russian World' (*Russkii mir*) 311
Golyshev, Vladimir 11, 142–145, 147–155, 157, 158

H

Habermas, Jürgen 20, 299
Hegemony 56, 57, 59, 225
  ROC's cultural hegemony 22, 43
heresy (and heterodoxy) 10, 11, 141, 142, 144–147, 150, 152–155, 158, 307
  heretical community 141, 155, 157, 158
  heresy and theologumen 145
  heresy and theological dogma 150
Hesychasm
  'kenosis' 34, 93, 95
  Hesychastic tradition 149

Hilarion (Alfeev), Metropolitan 34, 144, 228
Hinduism 4, 111
Holbein, Hans 98, 99
homosexuality (also LGBT) 1, 11, 163–169, 171–173, 176, 178–181, 185–189
  homophobia 163, 165, 173, 189
  gay lobby 11, 162, 171, 172, 174–181, 187, 190
  ban of homosexual propaganda 165
  traditional values 75, 148
  Western influences 72, 74, 163, 165
  sodomy 164, 169, 173, 176, 185–187
  paedophilia 186, 189, 215, 225
  and moral panic 9, 21, 22, 37, 43, 53, 55–59, 63, 66–69, 71–75
Human rights 20, 34
Human dignity 34, 288

I

Ignatii (Pologrudov), Metropolitan 25
Il'iashenko, Aleksandr 69
interactive sobornost' 133
Interactivity
  Liturgical (and non-liturgical) interactivity 111, 113–115, 121, 131, 310
'interpretive community' 285
Iona, Metropolitan of Moscow 202
Irony (also stiob) 22, 60, 200, 201, 205, 207, 212, 215–218, 220–225, 230, 231, 233
Islam 111, 199, 306
Ivan the Terrible (*Grozny*) 54, 55

J

John Maximovitch, St. 277, 278
John of Damascus 92, 93, 105, 106, 221
Judaism 4, 111, 124, 199
Justiniano, Silouan 277, 278

K

Kandinsky, Wassily 99–101, 103
Karpenko, Dimitrii 40, 41
Khodorkovskii, Mikhail 172
Kholmogorov, Egor 32, 41
Kirill (Gundiaev), Patriarch 2, 3, 5, 23, 24, 26, 35, 38, 41, 42, 61, 63, 65, 69, 119, 132, 141, 144, 146–148, 158, 166, 181, 202, 208, 209, 212, 216, 228, 246, 286
Kirill (Iliukhin), hegumen 170
Kliment (Kapalin), Metropolitan 28
Kochetkov, Georgii 288
Kononenko, Maksim 218
Kosach, Aleksandr 39
Kovalenko, Georgii 38
Kozlov, Maksim, priest 31, 126, 169
Krotov, Iakov 26, 29
Kruglov, Sergii 29, 288–291, 293–295
Kupriianov, Nikolai 206
Kuraev, Andrei 5, 6, 11, 40, 61, 145, 170–172, 176, 178–185, 188, 189
Kukryniksy 206

L

Lacan, Jacques 96, 98, 99, 103
League for Safe Internet 1, 38
Malofeev, Konstantin 38

Lebedev, Artemii 6, 207, 212, 214, 225–227
Lenin, Vladimir 55, 216
Leon'tev, Konstantin 55
Lepin, Sergii 24
Lomonosov, Mikhail 219
Longin (Korchagin), Bishop 28
loss of agency 35
Lurkmore 201
Luther, Martin 182

M

Mao Zedong 218
Markish, Makarii 26, 32, 39, 288–295
Marxism-Leninism 161
Matvienko, Valentina 203, 204
McLuhan, Marshall 108, 118
Medinskii, Vladimir 122
Medvedev, Dmitry 215
Merezhkovskii, Dmitrii 55
Messianism
   Katechon 54, 66
   Holy Russia (*Sviataia Rus'*) 305
   'Moscow the Third Rome', doctrine 54, 66
Mileant, Aleksandr 63
Milonov, Vitaly 215, 224
Mizulina, Elena 215
Moiseenkov, Aleksandr 64
'monstrous double' 27
Moor, Dmitrii 206
Moral panic 9, 21, 22, 37, 43, 53, 55–59, 63, 66–69, 71–75
Moral threat 57
Moscow Theological Academy 68, 171, 188, 189
Mozgov, Kirill 128, 129

N
Neo-Paganism 195
  Wicca rituals 5
Nevzorov, Alexander 200, 224–227
New Age 4, 69, 199

O
Okhlobystin, Ivan 5
Orthodox iconography 12, 182, 262, 263, 265, 268, 273
  Iconoclasm X, 107, 296
  Icon and picture 27, 85, 97, 101, 105, 272, 277
  Illusion 97, 107
  Byzantine icon 97, 101
  Reverse perspective 96, 101–104
  Acheiropoiesis 87, 89, 90, 93
    Shadow 89, 90, 95, 108
    Mirror 89, 91, 93, 95, 106, 108
  Theology of icons 10, 84, 104, 105, 108, 266, 267, 272, 278
  Digital icon 103, 105, 106, 267, 278, 296
  Buying icons online 269, 270
  Materiality of icons 266–268, 273, 277, 281
  Aesthetics of icons 270–273, 293
  Iconicity 272, 276–278
  Hand-painted icons 266, 269, 275, 276–278
  Printed (also Xeroxed, photographed) icons 267, 268, 270, 274, 277, 278, 279
  Icon corner 263, 267, 270, 272, 274, 276, 277, 278, 280
  False icon 84, 104, 106
Orthodox University of St Tikhon 285

Orthodoxy in the United States 265, 268
Orwell, George 88
Osipov, Aleksei 56, 68

P
Paper icons 105, 269, 275, 278
Parfenov, Filip 26
Parish sub-culture 239, 241, 246, 252, 256
  Orthodox parish 122, 243–247, 256, 262, 263, 269, 277, 285, 290
  Matushki 240, 245, 246, 250, 253
  Model Orthodox woman 249, 256
  Lenten food 244, 246, 247
  Headscarf 242, 243, 247, 249, 253, 254
  Virginity 255, 257
  Divorce 245, 247, 248, 257
  Abortion 257, 300
Paul, apostle 113, 247
Pelevin, Viktor 218
Peter the Great 55, 164, 233
Photography 261, 279
Platonov, Andrei 219
Pope Benedict 310
Prayer
  Concerted prayer 115–118, 294
  Digital prayer 32–34, 113–115, 219, 221, 222, 242, 291
Prekup, Igor 40
Protestantism 152, 275
  Protestant Reformation 182
  Baptism 252, 288
Pseudo-Dionysius Areopagita 92
'Pussy Riot' 2, 69–71, 141, 172, 183, 184, 196, 197

319

Putin, Vladimir 1, 3, 69, 70, 144, 161, 165, 169, 183, 190, 197, 199, 201, 202, 204, 208, 213, 228

R

Rafail (Karelin), archimandrite 128, 129, 132
Rasputin, Grigorii 216
Religiosity 43, 71, 141, 150, 152, 153, 300, 306
 Mixed religiosity 152–154
 Religious pluralism 12, 153
 Asceticism 154
 'do-it-yourself' religion 142, 155
Religious identity 11, 13, 19–22, 24, 53, 60, 131, 157, 264, 271, 299–304, 310, 311
 Russian-Orthodox self-identity 307
 Private and public religiosity 145, 305, 311
 Securitization of religious identity 21, 37
Religious sects 295
 Khlyst sect 195
Roman-Catholicism 4, 112, 116, 126, 271, 274
Rublev, Andrei 102, 105
Russian language internet (Runet) 1, 5, 6, 10, 12, 28, 59, 60, 112, 121, 197, 199, 200, 202, 204–207, 210, 212, 213, 215, 217, 220–225, 227, 228–233, 296
 Orthodox Runet (also 'Orthonet') 5, 6, 26, 37, 195
Russian Orthodox Church (ROC) 1, 41, 53, 54, 58, 60–62, 64–68, 70–72, 75, 113, 118, 121, 123, 127, 130, 161, 163, 166–171, 178–180, 183–185, 187, 190, 198, 220, 288, 307–309
 Internet policy 10, 113, 121
 Moscow Patriarchate 5, 22, 27, 31, 38, 41, 42, 119, 228, 288, 294
 Synod Informational Department (SINFO) 119, 130, 240
 Church-state relations 170, 190
 Political Orthodoxy 2, 11, 61, 63, 141–143, 147, 150, 152, 158, 195, 198, 201, 205, 307, 311
  'symphony' between the church and the state 3, 196, 201, 205
 and media (also Ortho-media) 5, 239, 251, 257
Russian Orthodox Church Outside of Russia (ROCOR) 63, 276

S

Sacraments 31, 33, 113, 117, 118, 122, 125, 167, 296
 Communion (Eucharist) 1, 113, 116, 118, 122–126, 291, 293
  Hybrid Communion 117
  Female impurity 123, 124
 Confession X, 10, 113, 117, 122, 125, 126, 132
  Common Confession 117, 118
 Liturgy 20, 116, 117, 127, 128, 243, 262, 270, 291, 300
  Translation of liturgical texts 20, 128, 129
 Mobile gadgets 131
Saint Brigid 271
Savel'ev, Dimitrii 31,
Secularism

Post-secularism (also neo-secularism and counter-secularization) 6, 7, 11, 19, 20, 22, 43, 166, 195, 299, 300
Securitization
and Religious identity 21
securitization of human biology 37
Shargunov, Aleksandr 65
Shpolianskii, Mikhail 36
Slavophilism
Khomiakov, Aleksei 10, 126, 132
Smirnov, Dmitrii 70, 209, 216
Sobchak, Ksenia 210
'Social Concept of the Russian Orthodox Church' 166, 168
Social shaping of technology, theory 7, 8, 118
Religious-social shaping of technology, theory 118
Solov'ev, Vladimir 54, 65
Solzhenitsyn, Alexander 26
Sorokin, Vladimir 218, 221
spacetime bridge 116
'spiritual bonds' 202, 203, 207, 225, 291
Stalin, Iosif 180, 216, 218
Struev, Dimitrii 25, 33
Struggle for recognition 23, 43

T

Taylor, Charles 299,
Technophobia 84, 85
'digital anxiety' 9, 23, 42, 43, 297
surveillance 84, 87–89, 95, 97, 98, 104, 109
dystopia 88, 112
Television 115, 132, 288, 302, 307

Theology 8, 26, 89, 122, 142, 147, 150, 151, 265, 290, 297
Orthodox theology 8, 19, 113, 131, 145, 145, 149–152, 154, 266, 272, 281, 289
Tikhon (Shevkunov), bishop 121
Tolstaya, Tatiana 212

U

Uminskii, Aleksii 31
Union of Orthodox Women 244
Utkin, Vitalii 26

V

Velikanov, Pavel 62
Vialov, Konstantin 206
Vicarious religion 2, 300

W

'web-wars' 10, 162
West, Cornel 299
Wurst, Conchita 210, 225

Z

Zhukov, Georgii 216
Zizioulas, Ioannis 19
Zosima (Sokur), archimandrite 68

SOVIET AND POST-SOVIET POLITICS AND SOCIETY

Edited by Dr. Andreas Umland

ISSN 1614-3515

1 Андреас Умланд (ред.)
Воплощение Европейской
конвенции по правам человека в
России
Философские, юридические и
эмпирические исследования
ISBN 3-89821-387-0

2 Christian Wipperfürth
Russland – ein vertrauenswürdiger
Partner?
Grundlagen, Hintergründe und Praxis
gegenwärtiger russischer Außenpolitik
Mit einem Vorwort von Heinz Timmermann
ISBN 3-89821-401-X

3 Manja Hussner
Die Übernahme internationalen Rechts
in die russische und deutsche
Rechtsordnung
Eine vergleichende Analyse zur
Völkerrechtsfreundlichkeit der Verfassungen
der Russländischen Föderation und der
Bundesrepublik Deutschland
Mit einem Vorwort von Rainer Arnold
ISBN 3-89821-438-9

4 Matthew Tejada
Bulgaria's Democratic Consolidation
and the Kozloduy Nuclear Power Plant
(KNPP)
The Unattainability of Closure
With a foreword by Richard J. Crampton
ISBN 3-89821-439-7

5 Марк Григорьевич Меерович
Квадратные метры, определяющие
сознание
Государственная жилищная политика в
СССР. 1921 – 1941 гг
ISBN 3-89821-474-5

6 Andrei P. Tsygankov, Pavel
A.Tsygankov (Eds.)
New Directions in Russian
International Studies
ISBN 3-89821-422-2

7 Марк Григорьевич Меерович
Как власть народ к труду приучала
Жилище в СССР – средство управления
людьми. 1917 – 1941 гг.
С предисловием Елены Осокиной
ISBN 3-89821-495-8

8 David J. Galbreath
Nation-Building and Minority Politics
in Post-Socialist States
Interests, Influence and Identities in Estonia
and Latvia
With a foreword by David J. Smith
ISBN 3-89821-467-2

9 Алексей Юрьевич Безугольный
Народы Кавказа в Вооруженных
силах СССР в годы Великой
Отечественной войны 1941-1945 гг.
С предисловием Николая Бугая
ISBN 3-89821-475-3

10 Вячеслав Лихачев и Владимир
Прибыловский (ред.)
Русское Национальное Единство,
1990-2000. В 2-х томах
ISBN 3-89821-523-7

11 Николай Бугай (ред.)
Народы стран Балтии в условиях
сталинизма (1940-е – 1950-е годы)
Документированная история
ISBN 3-89821-525-3

12 Ingmar Bredies (Hrsg.)
Zur Anatomie der Orange Revolution
in der Ukraine
Wechsel des Elitenregimes oder Triumph des
Parlamentarismus?
ISBN 3-89821-524-5

13 Anastasia V. Mitrofanova
The Politicization of Russian
Orthodoxy
Actors and Ideas
With a foreword by William C. Gay
ISBN 3-89821-481-8

14 Nathan D. Larson
    Alexander Solzhenitsyn and the
    Russo-Jewish Question
    ISBN 3-89821-483-4

15 Guido Houben
    Kulturpolitik und Ethnizität
    Staatliche Kunstförderung im Russland der
    neunziger Jahre
    Mit einem Vorwort von Gert Weisskirchen
    ISBN 3-89821-542-3

16 Leonid Luks
    Der russische „Sonderweg"?
    Aufsätze zur neuesten Geschichte Russlands
    im europäischen Kontext
    ISBN 3-89821-496-6

17 Евгений Мороз
    История «Мёртвой воды» – от
    страшной сказки к большой
    политике
    Политическое неоязычество в
    постсоветской России
    ISBN 3-89821-551-2

18 Александр Верховский и Галина
    Кожевникова (ред.)
    Этническая и религиозная
    интолерантность в российских СМИ
    Результаты мониторинга 2001-2004 гг.
    ISBN 3-89821-569-5

19 Christian Ganzer
    Sowjetisches Erbe und ukrainische
    Nation
    Das Museum der Geschichte des Zaporoger
    Kosakentums auf der Insel Chortycja
    Mit einem Vorwort von Frank Golczewski
    ISBN 3-89821-504-0

20 Эльза-Баир Гучинова
    Помнить нельзя забыть
    Антропология депортационной травмы
    калмыков
    С предисловием Кэролайн Хамфри
    ISBN 3-89821-506-7

21 Юлия Лидерман
    Мотивы «проверки» и «испытания»
    в постсоветской культуре
    Советское прошлое в российском
    кинематографе 1990-х годов
    С предисловием Евгения Марголита
    ISBN 3-89821-511-3

22 Tanya Lokshina, Ray Thomas, Mary
    Mayer (Eds.)
    The Imposition of a Fake Political
    Settlement in the Northern Caucasus
    The 2003 Chechen Presidential Election
    ISBN 3-89821-436-2

23 Timothy McCajor Hall, Rosie Read
    (Eds.)
    Changes in the Heart of Europe
    Recent Ethnographies of Czechs, Slovaks,
    Roma, and Sorbs
    With an afterword by Zdeněk Salzmann
    ISBN 3-89821-606-3

24 Christian Autengruber
    Die politischen Parteien in Bulgarien
    und Rumänien
    Eine vergleichende Analyse seit Beginn der
    90er Jahre
    Mit einem Vorwort von Dorothée de Nève
    ISBN 3-89821-476-1

25 Annette Freyberg-Inan with Radu
    Cristescu
    The Ghosts in Our Classrooms, or:
    John Dewey Meets Ceauşescu
    The Promise and the Failures of Civic
    Education in Romania
    ISBN 3-89821-416-8

26 John B. Dunlop
    The 2002 Dubrovka and 2004 Beslan
    Hostage Crises
    A Critique of Russian Counter-Terrorism
    With a foreword by Donald N. Jensen
    ISBN 3-89821-608-X

27 Peter Koller
    Das touristische Potenzial von
    Kam''janec'–Podil's'kyj
    Eine fremdenverkehrsgeographische
    Untersuchung der Zukunftsperspektiven und
    Maßnahmenplanung zur
    Destinationsentwicklung des „ukrainischen
    Rothenburg"
    Mit einem Vorwort von Kristiane Klemm
    ISBN 3-89821-640-3

28 Françoise Daucé, Elisabeth Sieca-
    Kozlowski (Eds.)
    Dedovshchina in the Post-Soviet
    Military
    Hazing of Russian Army Conscripts in a
    Comparative Perspective
    With a foreword by Dale Herspring
    ISBN 3-89821-616-0

29 Florian Strasser
    Zivilgesellschaftliche Einflüsse auf die
    Orange Revolution
    Die gewaltlose Massenbewegung und die
    ukrainische Wahlkrise 2004
    Mit einem Vorwort von Egbert Jahn
    ISBN 3-89821-648-9

30 Rebecca S. Katz
    The Georgian Regime Crisis of 2003-
    2004
    A Case Study in Post-Soviet Media
    Representation of Politics, Crime and
    Corruption
    ISBN 3-89821-413-3

31 Vladimir Kantor
    Willkür oder Freiheit
    Beiträge zur russischen Geschichtsphilosophie
    Ediert von Dagmar Herrmann sowie mit
    einem Vorwort versehen von Leonid Luks
    ISBN 3-89821-589-X

32 Laura A. Victoir
    The Russian Land Estate Today
    A Case Study of Cultural Politics in Post-
    Soviet Russia
    With a foreword by Priscilla Roosevelt
    ISBN 3-89821-426-5

33 Ivan Katchanovski
    Cleft Countries
    Regional Political Divisions and Cultures in
    Post-Soviet Ukraine and Moldova
    With a foreword by Francis Fukuyama
    ISBN 3-89821-558-X

34 Florian Mühlfried
    Postsowjetische Feiern
    Das Georgische Bankett im Wandel
    Mit einem Vorwort von Kevin Tuite
    ISBN 3-89821-601-2

35 Roger Griffin, Werner Loh, Andreas
    Umland (Eds.)
    Fascism Past and Present, West and
    East
    An International Debate on Concepts and
    Cases in the Comparative Study of the
    Extreme Right
    With an afterword by Walter Laqueur
    ISBN 3-89821-674-8

36 Sebastian Schlegel
    Der „Weiße Archipel"
    Sowjetische Atomstädte 1945-1991
    Mit einem Geleitwort von Thomas Bohn
    ISBN 3-89821-679-9

37 Vyacheslav Likhachev
    Political Anti-Semitism in Post-Soviet
    Russia
    Actors and Ideas in 1991-2003
    Edited and translated from Russian by Eugene
    Veklerov
    ISBN 3-89821-529-6

38 Josette Baer (Ed.)
    Preparing Liberty in Central Europe
    Political Texts from the Spring of Nations
    1848 to the Spring of Prague 1968
    With a foreword by Zdeněk V. David
    ISBN 3-89821-546-6

39 Михаил Лукьянов
    Российский консерватизм и
    реформа, 1907-1914
    С предисловием Марка Д. Стейнберга
    ISBN 3-89821-503-2

40 Nicola Melloni
    Market Without Economy
    The 1998 Russian Financial Crisis
    With a foreword by Eiji Furukawa
    ISBN 3-89821-407-9

41 Dmitrij Chmelnizki
    Die Architektur Stalins
    Bd. 1: Studien zu Ideologie und Stil
    Bd. 2: Bilddokumentation
    Mit einem Vorwort von Bruno Flierl
    ISBN 3-89821-515-6

42 Katja Yafimava
    Post-Soviet Russian-Belarussian
    Relationships
    The Role of Gas Transit Pipelines
    With a foreword by Jonathan P. Stern
    ISBN 3-89821-655-1

43 Boris Chavkin
    Verflechtungen der deutschen und
    russischen Zeitgeschichte
    Aufsätze und Archivfunde zu den
    Beziehungen Deutschlands und der
    Sowjetunion von 1917 bis 1991
    Ediert von Markus Edlinger sowie mit einem
    Vorwort versehen von Leonid Luks
    ISBN 3-89821-756-6

44 *Anastasija Grynenko in Zusammenarbeit mit Claudia Dathe*
Die Terminologie des Gerichtswesens der Ukraine und Deutschlands im Vergleich
Eine übersetzungswissenschaftliche Analyse juristischer Fachbegriffe im Deutschen, Ukrainischen und Russischen
Mit einem Vorwort von Ulrich Hartmann
ISBN 3-89821-691-8

45 *Anton Burkov*
The Impact of the European Convention on Human Rights on Russian Law
Legislation and Application in 1996-2006
With a foreword by Françoise Hampson
ISBN 978-3-89821-639-5

46 *Stina Torjesen, Indra Overland (Eds.)*
International Election Observers in Post-Soviet Azerbaijan
Geopolitical Pawns or Agents of Change?
ISBN 978-3-89821-743-9

47 *Taras Kuzio*
Ukraine – Crimea – Russia
Triangle of Conflict
ISBN 978-3-89821-761-3

48 *Claudia Šabić*
"Ich erinnere mich nicht, aber L'viv!"
Zur Funktion kultureller Faktoren für die Institutionalisierung und Entwicklung einer ukrainischen Region
Mit einem Vorwort von Melanie Tatur
ISBN 978-3-89821-752-1

49 *Marlies Bilz*
Tatarstan in der Transformation
Nationaler Diskurs und Politische Praxis 1988-1994
Mit einem Vorwort von Frank Golczewski
ISBN 978-3-89821-722-4

50 *Марлен Ларюэль (ред.)*
Современные интерпретации русского национализма
ISBN 978-3-89821-795-8

51 *Sonja Schüler*
Die ethnische Dimension der Armut
Roma im postsozialistischen Rumänien
Mit einem Vorwort von Anton Sterbling
ISBN 978-3-89821-776-7

52 *Галина Кожевникова*
Радикальный национализм в России и противодействие ему
Сборник докладов Центра «Сова» за 2004-2007 гг.
С предисловием Александра Верховского
ISBN 978-3-89821-721-7

53 *Галина Кожевникова и Владимир Прибыловский*
Российская власть в биографиях I
Высшие должностные лица РФ в 2004 г.
ISBN 978-3-89821-796-5

54 *Галина Кожевникова и Владимир Прибыловский*
Российская власть в биографиях II
Члены Правительства РФ в 2004 г.
ISBN 978-3-89821-797-2

55 *Галина Кожевникова и Владимир Прибыловский*
Российская власть в биографиях III
Руководители федеральных служб и агентств РФ в 2004 г.
ISBN 978-3-89821-798-9

56 *Ileana Petroniu*
Privatisierung in Transformationsökonomien
Determinanten der Restrukturierungs-Bereitschaft am Beispiel Polens, Rumäniens und der Ukraine
Mit einem Vorwort von Rainer W. Schäfer
ISBN 978-3-89821-790-3

57 *Christian Wipperfürth*
Russland und seine GUS-Nachbarn
Hintergründe, aktuelle Entwicklungen und Konflikte in einer ressourcenreichen Region
ISBN 978-3-89821-801-6

58 *Togzhan Kassenova*
From Antagonism to Partnership
The Uneasy Path of the U.S.-Russian Cooperative Threat Reduction
With a foreword by Christoph Bluth
ISBN 978-3-89821-707-1

59 *Alexander Höllwerth*
Das sakrale eurasische Imperium des Aleksandr Dugin
Eine Diskursanalyse zum postsowjetischen russischen Rechtsextremismus
Mit einem Vorwort von Dirk Uffelmann
ISBN 978-3-89821-813-9

60 Олег Рябов
    «Россия-Матушка»
    Национализм, гендер и война в России XX века
    С предисловием Елены Гощило
    ISBN 978-3-89821-487-2

61 Ivan Maistrenko
    Borot'bism
    A Chapter in the History of the Ukrainian Revolution
    With a new introduction by Chris Ford
    Translated by George S. N. Luckyj with the assistance of Ivan L. Rudnytsky
    ISBN 978-3-89821-697-5

62 Maryna Romanets
    Anamorphosic Texts and Reconfigured Visions
    Improvised Traditions in Contemporary Ukrainian and Irish Literature
    ISBN 978-3-89821-576-3

63 Paul D'Anieri and Taras Kuzio (Eds.)
    Aspects of the Orange Revolution I
    Democratization and Elections in Post-Communist Ukraine
    ISBN 978-3-89821-698-2

64 Bohdan Harasymiw in collaboration with Oleh S. Ilnytzkyj (Eds.)
    Aspects of the Orange Revolution II
    Information and Manipulation Strategies in the 2004 Ukrainian Presidential Elections
    ISBN 978-3-89821-699-9

65 Ingmar Bredies, Andreas Umland and Valentin Yakushik (Eds.)
    Aspects of the Orange Revolution III
    The Context and Dynamics of the 2004 Ukrainian Presidential Elections
    ISBN 978-3-89821-803-0

66 Ingmar Bredies, Andreas Umland and Valentin Yakushik (Eds.)
    Aspects of the Orange Revolution IV
    Foreign Assistance and Civic Action in the 2004 Ukrainian Presidential Elections
    ISBN 978-3-89821-808-5

67 Ingmar Bredies, Andreas Umland and Valentin Yakushik (Eds.)
    Aspects of the Orange Revolution V
    Institutional Observation Reports on the 2004 Ukrainian Presidential Elections
    ISBN 978-3-89821-809-2

68 Taras Kuzio (Ed.)
    Aspects of the Orange Revolution VI
    Post-Communist Democratic Revolutions in Comparative Perspective
    ISBN 978-3-89821-820-7

69 Tim Bohse
    Autoritarismus statt Selbstverwaltung
    Die Transformation der kommunalen Politik in der Stadt Kaliningrad 1990-2005
    Mit einem Geleitwort von Stefan Troebst
    ISBN 978-3-89821-782-8

70 David Rupp
    Die Rußländische Föderation und die russischsprachige Minderheit in Lettland
    Eine Fallstudie zur Anwaltspolitik Moskaus gegenüber den russophonen Minderheiten im „Nahen Ausland" von 1991 bis 2002
    Mit einem Vorwort von Helmut Wagner
    ISBN 978-3-89821-778-1

71 Taras Kuzio
    Theoretical and Comparative Perspectives on Nationalism
    New Directions in Cross-Cultural and Post-Communist Studies
    With a foreword by Paul Robert Magocsi
    ISBN 978-3-89821-815-3

72 Christine Teichmann
    Die Hochschultransformation im heutigen Osteuropa
    Kontinuität und Wandel bei der Entwicklung des postkommunistischen Universitätswesens
    Mit einem Vorwort von Oskar Anweiler
    ISBN 978-3-89821-842-9

73 Julia Kusznir
    Der politische Einfluss von Wirtschaftseliten in russischen Regionen
    Eine Analyse am Beispiel der Erdöl- und Erdgasindustrie, 1992-2005
    Mit einem Vorwort von Wolfgang Eichwede
    ISBN 978-3-89821-821-4

74 Alena Vysotskaya
    Russland, Belarus und die EU-Osterweiterung
    Zur Minderheitenfrage und zum Problem der Freizügigkeit des Personenverkehrs
    Mit einem Vorwort von Katlijn Malfliet
    ISBN 978-3-89821-822-1

75 Heiko Pleines (Hrsg.)
    Corporate Governance in post-
    sozialistischen Volkswirtschaften
    ISBN 978-3-89821-766-8

76 Stefan Ihrig
    Wer sind die Moldawier?
    Rumänismus versus Moldowanismus in
    Historiographie und Schulbüchern der
    Republik Moldova, 1991-2006
    Mit einem Vorwort von Holm Sundhaussen
    ISBN 978-3-89821-466-7

77 Galina Kozhevnikova in collaboration
    with Alexander Verkhovsky and
    Eugene Veklerov
    Ultra-Nationalism and Hate Crimes in
    Contemporary Russia
    The 2004-2006 Annual Reports of Moscow's
    SOVA Center
    With a foreword by Stephen D. Shenfield
    ISBN 978-3-89821-868-9

78 Florian Küchler
    The Role of the European Union in
    Moldova's Transnistria Conflict
    With a foreword by Christopher Hill
    ISBN 978-3-89821-850-4

79 Bernd Rechel
    The Long Way Back to Europe
    Minority Protection in Bulgaria
    With a foreword by Richard Crampton
    ISBN 978-3-89821-863-4

80 Peter W. Rodgers
    Nation, Region and History in Post-
    Communist Transitions
    Identity Politics in Ukraine, 1991-2006
    With a foreword by Vera Tolz
    ISBN 978-3-89821-903-7

81 Stephanie Solywoda
    The Life and Work of
    Semen L. Frank
    A Study of Russian Religious Philosophy
    With a foreword by Philip Walters
    ISBN 978-3-89821-457-5

82 Vera Sokolova
    Cultural Politics of Ethnicity
    Discourses on Roma in Communist
    Czechoslovakia
    ISBN 978-3-89821-864-1

83 Natalya Shevchik Ketenci
    Kazakhstani Enterprises in Transition
    The Role of Historical Regional Development
    in Kazakhstan's Post-Soviet Economic
    Transformation
    ISBN 978-3-89821-831-3

84 Martin Malek, Anna Schor-
    Tschudnowskaja (Hrsg.)
    Europa im Tschetschenienkrieg
    Zwischen politischer Ohnmacht und
    Gleichgültigkeit
    Mit einem Vorwort von Lipchan Basajewa
    ISBN 978-3-89821-676-0

85 Stefan Meister
    Das postsowjetische Universitätswesen
    zwischen nationalem und
    internationalem Wandel
    Die Entwicklung der regionalen Hochschule
    in Russland als Gradmesser der
    Systemtransformation
    Mit einem Vorwort von Joan DeBardeleben
    ISBN 978-3-89821-891-7

86 Konstantin Sheiko in collaboration
    with Stephen Brown
    Nationalist Imaginings of the
    Russian Past
    Anatolii Fomenko and the Rise of Alternative
    History in Post-Communist Russia
    With a foreword by Donald Ostrowski
    ISBN 978-3-89821-915-0

87 Sabine Jenni
    Wie stark ist das „Einige Russland"?
    Zur Parteibindung der Eliten und zum
    Wahlerfolg der Machtpartei
    im Dezember 2007
    Mit einem Vorwort von Klaus Armingeon
    ISBN 978-3-89821-961-7

88 Thomas Borén
    Meeting-Places of Transformation
    Urban Identity, Spatial Representations and
    Local Politics in Post-Soviet St Petersburg
    ISBN 978-3-89821-739-2

89 Aygul Ashirova
    Stalinismus und Stalin-Kult in
    Zentralasien
    Turkmenistan 1924-1953
    Mit einem Vorwort von Leonid Luks
    ISBN 978-3-89821-987-7

90 Leonid Luks
    Freiheit oder imperiale Größe?
    Essays zu einem russischen Dilemma
    ISBN 978-3-8382-0011-8

91 Christopher Gilley
    The 'Change of Signposts' in the
    Ukrainian Emigration
    A Contribution to the History of
    Sovietophilism in the 1920s
    With a foreword by Frank Golczewski
    ISBN 978-3-89821-965-5

92 Philipp Casula, Jeronim Perovic
    (Eds.)
    Identities and Politics
    During the Putin Presidency
    The Discursive Foundations of Russia's
    Stability
    With a foreword by Heiko Haumann
    ISBN 978-3-8382-0015-6

93 Marcel Viëtor
    Europa und die Frage
    nach seinen Grenzen im Osten
    Zur Konstruktion ‚europäischer Identität' in
    Geschichte und Gegenwart
    Mit einem Vorwort von Albrecht Lehmann
    ISBN 978-3-8382-0045-3

94 Ben Hellman, Andrei Rogachevskii
    Filming the Unfilmable
    Casper Wrede's 'One Day in the Life
    of Ivan Denisovich'
    Second, Revised and Expanded Edition
    ISBN 978-3-8382-0044-6

95 Eva Fuchslocher
    Vaterland, Sprache, Glaube
    Orthodoxie und Nationenbildung
    am Beispiel Georgiens
    Mit einem Vorwort von Christina von Braun
    ISBN 978-3-89821-884-9

96 Vladimir Kantor
    Das Westlertum und der Weg
    Russlands
    Zur Entwicklung der russischen Literatur und
    Philosophie
    Ediert von Dagmar Herrmann
    Mit einem Beitrag von Nikolaus Lobkowicz
    ISBN 978-3-8382-0102-3

97 Kamran Musayev
    Die postsowjetische Transformation
    im Baltikum und Südkaukasus
    Eine vergleichende Untersuchung der
    politischen Entwicklung Lettlands und
    Aserbaidschans 1985-2009
    Mit einem Vorwort von Leonid Luks
    Ediert von Sandro Henschel
    ISBN 978-3-8382-0103-0

98 Tatiana Zhurzhenko
    Borderlands into Bordered Lands
    Geopolitics of Identity in Post-Soviet Ukraine
    With a foreword by Dieter Segert
    ISBN 978-3-8382-0042-2

99 Кирилл Галушко, Лидия Смола
    (ред.)
    Пределы падения – варианты
    украинского будущего
    Аналитико-прогностические исследования
    ISBN 978-3-8382-0148-1

100 Michael Minkenberg (ed.)
    Historical Legacies and the Radical
    Right in Post-Cold War Central and
    Eastern Europe
    With an afterword by Sabrina P. Ramet
    ISBN 978-3-8382-0124-5

101 David-Emil Wickström
    Rocking St. Petersburg
    Transcultural Flows and Identity Politics in
    the St. Petersburg Popular Music Scene
    With a foreword by Yngvar B. Steinholt
    Second, Revised and Expanded Edition
    ISBN 978-3-8382-0100-9

102 Eva Zabka
    Eine neue „Zeit der Wirren"?
    Der spät- und postsowjetische Systemwandel
    1985-2000 im Spiegel russischer
    gesellschaftspolitischer Diskurse
    Mit einem Vorwort von Margareta Mommsen
    ISBN 978-3-8382-0161-0

103 Ulrike Ziemer
    Ethnic Belonging, Gender and
    Cultural Practices
    Youth Identitites in Contemporary Russia
    With a foreword by Anoop Nayak
    ISBN 978-3-8382-0152-8

104   Ksenia Chepikova
      ‚Einiges Russland' - eine zweite
      KPdSU?
      Aspekte der Identitätskonstruktion einer
      postsowjetischen „Partei der Macht"
      Mit einem Vorwort von Torsten Oppelland
      ISBN 978-3-8382-0311-9

105   Леонид Люкс
      Западничество или евразийство?
      Демократия или идеократия?
      Сборник статей об исторических дилеммах
      России
      С предисловием Владимира Кантора
      ISBN 978-3-8382-0211-2

106   Anna Dost
      Das russische Verfassungsrecht auf dem
      Weg zum Föderalismus und zurück
      Zum Konflikt von Rechtsnormen und
      -wirklichkeit in der Russländischen
      Föderation von 1991 bis 2009
      Mit einem Vorwort von Alexander Blankenagel
      ISBN 978-3-8382-0292-1

107   Philipp Herzog
      Sozialistische Völkerfreundschaft,
      nationaler Widerstand oder harmloser
      Zeitvertreib?
      Zur politischen Funktion der Volkskunst
      im sowjetischen Estland
      Mit einem Vorwort von Andreas Kappeler
      ISBN 978-3-8382-0216-7

108   Marlène Laruelle (ed.)
      Russian Nationalism, Foreign Policy,
      and Identity Debates in Putin's Russia
      New Ideological Patterns after the Orange
      Revolution
      ISBN 978-3-8382-0325-6

109   Michail Logvinov
      Russlands Kampf gegen den
      internationalen Terrorismus
      Eine kritische Bestandsaufnahme des
      Bekämpfungsansatzes
      Mit einem Geleitwort von
      Hans-Henning Schröder
      und einem Vorwort von Eckhard Jesse
      ISBN 978-3-8382-0329-4

110   John B. Dunlop
      The Moscow Bombings
      of September 1999
      Examinations of Russian Terrorist Attacks
      at the Onset of Vladimir Putin's Rule
      Second, Revised and Expanded Edition
      ISBN 978-3-8382-0388-1

111   Андрей А. Ковалёв
      Свидетельство из-за кулис
      российской политики I
      Можно ли делать добро из зла?
      (Воспоминания и размышления о
      последних советских и первых
      послесоветских годах)
      With a foreword by Peter Reddaway
      ISBN 978-3-8382-0302-7

112   Андрей А. Ковалёв
      Свидетельство из-за кулис
      российской политики II
      Угроза для себя и окружающих
      (Наблюдения и предостережения
      относительно происходящего после 2000 г.)
      ISBN 978-3-8382-0303-4

113   Bernd Kappenberg
      Zeichen setzen für Europa
      Der Gebrauch europäischer lateinischer
      Sonderzeichen in der deutschen Öffentlichkeit
      Mit einem Vorwort von Peter Schlobinski
      ISBN 978-3-89821-749-1

114   Ivo Mijnssen
      The Quest for an Ideal Youth in
      Putin's Russia I
      Back to Our Future! History, Modernity, and
      Patriotism according to Nashi, 2005-2013
      With a foreword by Jeronim Perović
      Second, Revised and Expanded Edition
      ISBN 978-3-8382-0368-3

115   Jussi Lassila
      The Quest for an Ideal Youth in
      Putin's Russia II
      The Search for Distinctive Conformism in the
      Political Communication of Nashi, 2005-2009
      With a foreword by Kirill Postoutenko
      Second, Revised and Expanded Edition
      ISBN 978-3-8382-0415-4

116   Valerio Trabandt
      Neue Nachbarn, gute Nachbarschaft?
      Die EU als internationaler Akteur am Beispiel
      ihrer Demokratieförderung in Belarus und der
      Ukraine 2004-2009
      Mit einem Vorwort von Jutta Joachim
      ISBN 978-3-8382-0437-6

117 Fabian Pfeiffer
     Estlands Außen- und Sicherheitspolitik I
     Der estnische Atlantizismus nach der
     wiedererlangten Unabhängigkeit 1991-2004
     Mit einem Vorwort von Helmut Hubel
     ISBN 978-3-8382-0127-6

118 Jana Podßuweit
     Estlands Außen- und Sicherheitspolitik II
     Handlungsoptionen eines Kleinstaates im
     Rahmen seiner EU-Mitgliedschaft (2004-2008)
     Mit einem Vorwort von Helmut Hubel
     ISBN 978-3-8382-0440-6

119 Karin Pointner
     Estlands Außen- und Sicherheitspolitik III
     Eine gedächtnispolitische Analyse estnischer
     Entwicklungskooperation 2006-2010
     Mit einem Vorwort von Karin Liebhart
     ISBN 978-3-8382-0435-2

120 Ruslana Vovk
     Die Offenheit der ukrainischen
     Verfassung für das Völkerrecht und
     die europäische Integration
     Mit einem Vorwort von Alexander
     Blankenagel
     ISBN 978-3-8382-0481-9

121 Mykhaylo Banakh
     Die Relevanz der Zivilgesellschaft
     bei den postkommunistischen
     Transformationsprozessen in mittel-
     und osteuropäischen Ländern
     Das Beispiel der spät- und postsowjetischen
     Ukraine 1986-2009
     Mit einem Vorwort von Gerhard Simon
     ISBN 978-3-8382-0499-4

122 Michael Moser
     Language Policy and the Discourse on
     Languages in Ukraine under President
     Viktor Yanukovych (25 February
     2010–28 October 2012)
     ISBN 978-3-8382-0497-0 (Paperback edition)
     ISBN 978-3-8382-0507-6 (Hardcover edition)

123 Nicole Krome
     Russischer Netzwerkkapitalismus
     Restrukturierungsprozesse in der
     Russischen Föderation am Beispiel des
     Luftfahrtunternehmens "Aviastar"
     Mit einem Vorwort von Petra Stykow
     ISBN 978-3-8382-0534-2

124 David R. Marples
     'Our Glorious Past'
     Lukashenka's Belarus and
     the Great Patriotic War
     ISBN 978-3-8382-0574-8 (Paperback edition)
     ISBN 978-3-8382-0675-2 (Hardcover edition)

125 Ulf Walther
     Russlands "neuer Adel"
     Die Macht des Geheimdienstes von
     Gorbatschow bis Putin
     Mit einem Vorwort von Hans-Georg Wieck
     ISBN 978-3-8382-0584-7

126 Simon Geissbühler (Hrsg.)
     Kiew – Revolution 3.0
     Der Euromaidan 2013/14 und die
     Zukunftsperspektiven der Ukraine
     ISBN 978-3-8382-0581-6 (Paperback edition)
     ISBN 978-3-8382-0681-3 (Hardcover edition)

127 Andrey Makarychev
     Russia and the EU
     in a Multipolar World
     Discourses, Identities, Norms
     With a foreword by Klaus Segbers
     ISBN 978-3-8382-0629-5

128 Roland Scharff
     Kasachstan als postsowjetischer
     Wohlfahrtsstaat
     Die Transformation des sozialen
     Schutzsystems
     Mit einem Vorwort von Joachim Ahrens
     ISBN 978-3-8382-0622-6

129 Katja Grupp
     Bild Lücke Deutschland
     Kaliningrader Studierende sprechen über
     Deutschland
     Mit einem Vorwort von Martin Schulz
     ISBN 978-3-8382-0552-6

130 Konstantin Sheiko, Stephen Brown
     History as Therapy
     Alternative History and Nationalist
     Imaginings in Russia, 1991-2014
     ISBN 978-3-8382-0665-3

131 Elisa Kriza
    Alexander Solzhenitsyn: Cold War
    Icon, Gulag Author, Russian
    Nationalist?
    A Study of the Western Reception of his
    Literary Writings, Historical Interpretations,
    and Political Ideas
    With a foreword by Andrei Rogatchevski
    ISBN 978-3-8382-0589-2 (Paperback edition)
    ISBN 978-3-8382-0690-5 (Hardcover edition)

132 Serghei Golunov
    The Elephant in the Room
    Corruption and Cheating in Russian
    Universities
    ISBN 978-3-8382-0570-0

133 Manja Hussner, Rainer Arnold (Hgg.)
    Verfassungsgerichtsbarkeit in
    Zentralasien I
    Sammlung von Verfassungstexten
    ISBN 978-3-8382-0595-3

134 Nikolay Mitrokhin
    Die "Russische Partei"
    Die Bewegung der russischen Nationalisten in
    der UdSSR 1953-1985
    Aus dem Russischen übertragen von einem
    Übersetzerteam unter der Leitung von Larisa Schippel
    ISBN 978-3-8382-0024-8

135 Manja Hussner, Rainer Arnold (Hgg.)
    Verfassungsgerichtsbarkeit in
    Zentralasien II
    Sammlung von Verfassungstexten
    ISBN 978-3-8382-0597-7

136 Manfred Zeller
    Das sowjetische Fieber
    Fußballfans im poststalinistischen
    Vielvölkerreich
    Mit einem Vorwort von Nikolaus Katzer
    ISBN 978-3-8382-0757-5

137 Kristin Schreiter
    Stellung und Entwicklungspotential
    zivilgesellschaftlicher Gruppen in
    Russland
    Menschenrechtsorganisationen im Vergleich
    ISBN 978-3-8382-0673-8

138 David R. Marples, Frederick V. Mills
    (eds.)
    Ukraine's Euromaidan
    Analyses of a Civil Revolution
    ISBN 978-3-8382-0660-8

139 Bernd Kappenberg
    Setting Signs for Europe
    Why Diacritics Matter for
    European Integration
    With a foreword by Peter Schlobinski
    ISBN 978-3-8382-0663-9

140 René Lenz
    Internationalisierung, Kooperation
    und Transfer
    Externe bildungspolitische Akteure in der
    Russischen Föderation
    Mit einem Vorwort von Frank Ettrich
    ISBN 978-3-8382-0751-3

141 Juri Plusnin, Yana Zausaeva, Natalia
    Zhidkevich, Artemy Pozanenko
    Wandering Workers
    Mores, Behavior, Way of Life, and Political
    Status of Domestic Russian Labor Migrants
    Translated by Julia Kazantseva
    ISBN 978-3-8382-0653-0

142 Matthew Kott, David J. Smith (eds.)
    Latvia – A Work in Progress?
    100 Years of State- and Nation-building
    ISBN 978-3-8382-0648-6

143 Инна Чувычкина (ред.)
    Экспортные нефте- и газопроводы
    на постсоветском пространстве
    Анализ трубопроводной политики в свете
    теории международных отношений
    ISBN 978-3-8382-0822-0

144 Johann Zajaczkowski
    Russland – eine pragmatische
    Großmacht?
    Eine rollentheoretische Untersuchung
    russischer Außenpolitik am Beispiel der
    Zusammenarbeit mit den USA nach 9/11 und
    des Georgienkrieges von 2008
    Mit einem Vorwort von Siegfried Schieder
    ISBN 978-3-8382-0837-4

145 Boris Popivanov
    Changing Images of the Left in
    Bulgaria
    The Challenge of Post-Communism in the
    Early 21st Century
    ISBN 978-3-8382-0667-7

146 Lenka Krátká
A History of the Czechoslovak Ocean Shipping Company 1948-1989
How a Small, Landlocked Country Ran Maritime Business During the Cold War
ISBN 978-3-8382-0666-0

147 Alexander Sergunin
Explaining Russian Foreign Policy Behavior
Theory and Practice
ISBN 978-3-8382-0752-0

148 Darya Malyutina
Migrant Friendships in a Super-Diverse City
Russian-Speakers and their Social Relationships in London in the 21st Century
With a foreword by Claire Dwyer
ISBN 978-3-8382-0652-3

149 Alexander Sergunin, Valery Konyshev
Russia in the Arctic
Hard or Soft Power?
ISBN 978-3-8382-0753-7

150 John J. Maresca
Helsinki Revisited
A Key U.S. Negotiator's Memoirs on the Development of the CSCE into the OSCE
With a foreword by Hafiz Pashayev
ISBN 978-3-8382-0852-7

151 Jardar Østbø
The New Third Rome
Readings of a Russian Nationalist Myth
With a foreword by Pål Kolstø
ISBN 978-3-8382-0870-1

152 Simon Kordonsky
Socio-Economic Foundations of the Russian Post-Soviet Regime
The Resource-Based Economy and Estate-Based Social Structure of Contemporary Russia
With a foreword by Svetlana Barsukova
ISBN 978-3-8382-0775-9

153 Duncan Leitch
Assisting Reform in Post-Communist Ukraine 2000–2012
The Illusions of Donors and the Disillusion of Beneficiaries
With a foreword by Kataryna Wolczuk
ISBN 978-3-8382-0844-2

154 Abel Polese
Limits of a Post-Soviet State
How Informality Replaces, Renegotiates, and Reshapes Governance in Contemporary Ukraine
With a foreword by Colin Williams
ISBN 978-3-8382-0845-9

155 Mikhail Suslov (ed.)
Digital Orthodoxy in the Post-Soviet World
The Russian Orthodox Church and Web 2.0
With a foreword by Father Cyril Hovorum
ISBN 978-3-8382-0871-8

156 Leonid Luks
Zwei „Sonderwege"? Russisch-deutsche Parallelen und Kontraste (1917-2014)
Vergleichende Essays
ISBN 978-3-8382-0823-7

157 Vladimir V. Karacharovskiy, Ovsey I. Shkaratan, Gordey A. Yastrebov
Towards a New Russian Work Culture
Can Western Companies and Expatriates Change Russian Society?
With a foreword by Elena N. Danilova
Translated by Julia Kazantseva
ISBN 978-3-8382-0902-9

ibidem-Verlag
Melchiorstr. 15
D-70439 Stuttgart
info@ibidem-verlag.de

www.ibidem-verlag.de
www.ibidem.eu
www.edition-noema.de
www.autorenbetreuung.de